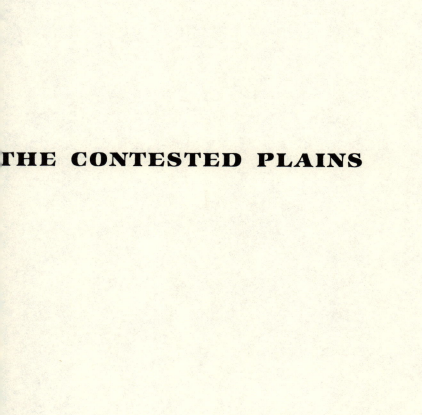

THE CONTESTED PLAINS

Elliott West

THE CONTESTED PLAINS

Indians,

Goldseekers,

& the Rush

to Colorado

University Press of Kansas

Published by the University Press of Kansas (Lawrence,
Kansas 66049), which was organized by the Kansas Board
of Regents and is operated and funded by Emporia State
University, Fort Hays State University, Kansas State University,
Pittsburg State University, the University of Kansas, and
Wichita State University

Library of Congress Cataloging-in-Publication Data

West, Elliott, 1945–
   The contested plains : Indians, goldseekers, and the rush to
Colorado / Elliott West.
       p.   cm.
   Includes bibliographical references and index.
   ISBN 0-7006-0891-5 (alk. paper)
   1. Great Plains—History.   2. Colorado—Gold discoveries.
3. Indians of North America—Great Plains—History.   4. Human
ecology—Great Plains.   I. Title.
F591.W4527   1998
978—dc21   97-36478

British Library Cataloguing in Publication Data is available.

Printed in the United States of America

10 9 8 7 6 5 4 3 2 1

FOR SUZANNE

good wife, best friend

You turn us back to dust and say,

"Go back, O child of earth."

For a thousand years in your sight are like

   yesterday when it is past

and like a watch in the night.

You sweep us away like a dream;

we fade away suddenly like the grass.

In the morning it is green and flourishes;

In the evening it is dried up and withered.

       . . . .

So teach us to number our days

that we may apply our hearts to wisdom.

                — Psalm 90:3–6, 12

Life is messy.

     — Mary Steenburgen to Steve Martin, in *Parenthood*

Contents

Illustrations

Acknowledgments

During the ten years of researching and writing this book, I have been graced with support, favors, and kindnesses that have added up to an obligation as unpayable as the national debt. All I can do is offer my gratitude, which begins with my thanks to the Fulbright College of Arts and Sciences of the University of Arkansas and its dean, Bernard L. Madison, a most excellent and supportive boss. I also thank the National Endowment for the Humanities and the Newberry Library of Chicago, Illinois. Both provided fellowships that allowed me to study at the Newberry for ten wonderful months. I give special thanks to the superb staff and research fellows at the Newberry, especially Fred Hoxie, Jim Grossman, Dick Sattler, John Aubry, Helen Tanner, and Dick Brown. Much of my tentative work on Native American and environmental history was presented as part of the Calvin P. Horn Lectures in Western History and Culture at the University of New Mexico. I give great thanks to sponsors of that series and to Richard Etulain of the university's Center for the American West.

The staffs of several other archives provided guidance and help. I owe a particularly large debt to those at three libraries where much of this research was done: the Colorado State Historical Society, the Western History Collections of the Denver Public Library, and the Beinecke Library at Yale University. I also spent hundreds of hours being helped by those at the Nebraska State Historical Society, Missouri Historical Society, Missouri State Historical Society, and the Henry E. Huntington Library. In every place and in every case, I was treated with exceptional courtesy and given invaluable advice in finding my way through the archival thickets.

Friends and colleagues in the guild have also given generously in criticism, suggestions, and encouragement. I am particularly grateful to Richard White, Robert Utley, Charles Rankin, Patricia Nelson Limerick, Jim Sherow, Dan Flores, John Mack Faragher, Budd Saunders, Tom Noel, John Guice, and Bill Cronon. Special thanks go also to three summers' worth of wonderful teachers at institutes at the University of Colorado; they goaded me along with their questions and infectious enthusiasm. I am especially appreciative of the institutes' staff and faculty—Jim Giese, Patty Limerick, Gary Holthaus, Barbara Miller, and Lori Eastman. My research assistants— Brian Miller, Michael Nelson, Julie Smith, and Jeff Littlejohn—did valiant duty in the trenches. In stumbling through the enormous literature in the archaeology and anthropology of the plains and Rocky Mountains, I was lucky to have near me several excellent specialists, including George and Deb Sabo, Fred Limp, Tom Green, and Marvin Kay. Anne Gisiger applied her many skills to testing some of my ideas through new and imaginative computer methodologies. Many friends along the corridors of Old Main have helped me along the way with their great humor and many ideas: Tom Kennedy, Jeannie Whayne, Randall Woods, David Sloan, Elizabeth Payne, Robert Finlay, David Edwards, David Chappell, and others. Several have done the academic equivalent of holding my elbow as I crossed treacherous streets and patting my hand and saying, "There, there." Our departmental office staff, headed by Suzanne Smith, has been unfailingly helpful in every tedious chore. William Nelson provided four excellent maps. The splendid folks at the University Press of Kansas, especially Fred Woodward, Nancy Scott, and Susan Schott, have been patient far beyond what anyone could expect. I am thankful for that and for their superb skills.

Closer to home, I offer my thanks as usual for the support and love of my family—my mother, Betsy West, and my brothers, Richard and George. I am grateful as always for the patience and presence of my five wonderful children—Elizabeth, Bill, Richard, Garth, and Anne. It is with special pleasure and thankfulness that I can add to that list my daughter-in-law Stacy, my grandson Jacob, and, as of ten days before this writing, another grandson, Noah, the latest West to endure my strange preoccupations.

I dedicate this book to my wife, Suzanne Stoner, with deepest thanks for her intelligence, good sense, patience, and humor. This book is about people trying to conceive a better world for themselves. In my own life, where Suzanne is concerned, I happily admit failure. I cannot imagine a more generous spirit or finer companion.

Introduction

In Thomas Berger's novel *Little Big Man,* the ancient narrator Jack Crabb recalls a barroom conversation when he was a dissipated sixteen-year-old in Santa Fe. Crazy Charley, a whiskey-sodden prospector in his seventies, was full of tales of Apache torture, desert wanderings, and fortunes that always slipped away. On this particular day Charley told of making a fabulous gold strike in the Front Range of the Rocky Mountains, somewhere between the Arkansas and South Platte Rivers, only to be robbed by Utes and forced to walk barefoot back to Taos. He was too old to return, he said; then he swirled his liquor in a toothless mouth, swallowed, and said that a young fellow like Jack, flush with money from pimping for his girlfriend, Estrellita, ought to follow up: "'If I had your pecuniary endowments, sonny, I'd buy a set of possibles and rambunctulate northwards, coming back within six months as a man of means beyond the dreams of algebra.'"[1]

Crazy Charley's unlikely story, of course, turns out to be true, more or less. In 1858 gold was discovered along streams flowing out of the Rockies, and the next year more than 100,000 persons flooded across the plains to the new diggings. The Colorado gold rush attracted more than twice the number of persons who crossed to California in 1849. The scale of the event was impressive, the results profound, the details colorful.

In graduate school at the University of Colorado it was difficult not to be caught up in the story of the great rush. The archives were fat with sheaves of letters, diaries, and other documents. Local lore dwelt on the events, real and imagined, sometimes to a distressing degree. Some faculty and many fellow students were caught in the gravity field of this episode. My interest was mainly elsewhere, but I was not immune. I read up on it, listened to discussions and overripe opinions, and kept an eye out for interesting tidbits. I started taking notes.

Over time I accumulated a lot of material on the rush, and several years ago I decided to fit it together into a book about the thousands who tramped over the plains with plans to sweep the wondrous money-dust into large pouches before heading home to lives of ease. I planned a short, light, "Ho,

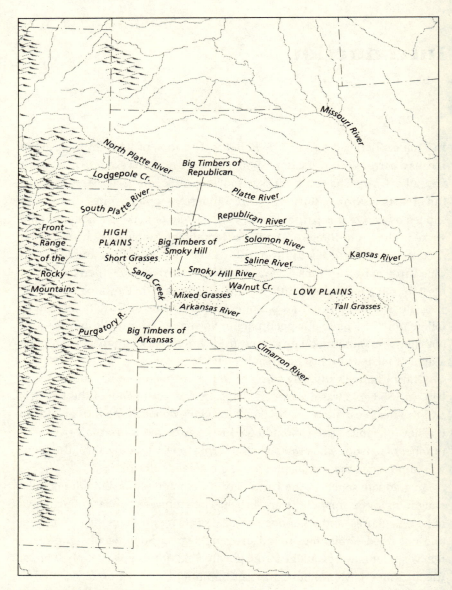

The Central Great Plains

for the Gold Fields!" sort of book. Before proceeding, however, I needed to push a little harder into the story, filling gaps and pinning down details.

That's when the trouble started. As I began to pose what I figured would be a few relatively simple questions, the perspective began to refocus. I found, for instance, that historians had devoted most of their attention to the effects of the rush in the Rockies and on Denver and other towns along the mountain base—an understandable and proper interest, but one that neglected what I decided was an equally interesting angle. The great stampede changed the plains at least as much as the mountains, and yet we have kept our gaze on what was rushed *to* rather than what was rushed *over*.

Once that insight became clearer, I began to think that the stories of the mountains and plains were not only connected but that the connection and the dynamic play among the mountain settlements, the enterprises on the plains, and the Missouri valley towns to the east were also basic to understanding the region's history from that point on. This part of the story was not merely significant. It was absolutely crucial.

Part of my opinion came from seeing what should have been obvious all along. Native Americans played critical roles that went far beyond the pitifully small parts usually assigned to them. Historians have generally given most of their attention to the bloody confrontation between whites and Indians, especially the appalling hours along Sand Creek and the ugliest encounters over the next five years. The disturbing consequences of the rush for the Indians are certainly mentioned, but usually in brief and stereotypical ways. As I looked a little further into the meaning of the gold rush for the plains tribes, I felt there were compelling and disturbing lessons there.

Understanding those lessons was quite a challenge, because I soon realized that the Indians' disaster could not possibly be explained simply by the sudden invasion of goldseekers and townmakers. Indians were partly responsible for their own difficulties. Unraveling that part of the story required, first, a close look at the environmental history of the plains during the century and a half before the gold rush and, second, an acquaintance with the social, political, economic, and cultural histories of several tribes of the central plains.

That was a tall order, but it revealed a remarkable chapter in North American history. The tribes, their move to the plains, their emerging view of themselves as new peoples, their astonishing adaptations, their trials and conflicts, their wrestling with unanticipated implications of their choices—I found all this an engaging and neglected part of our common past. Certainly it was essential to any appreciation of the larger story of the rush to the Rockies.

I used a year's sabbatical to learn something about the environmental history of the plains, the fascinating and ambiguous story of Native Americans and their pursuit of a new life there, and the complications that followed. One result of that was a book of four essays, *The Way to the West,* which grew from lectures given at the University of New Mexico.[2] It was a useful side trip on the way to the present book, but I apologize to any readers who might notice that some material inevitably has overlapped.

Things got still more involved as I appreciated that the Comanches, Kiowas, Cheyennes, Lakotas, and Arapahoes did not move into a place empty of history, just as the white pioneers did not march into a storyless land. The plains have some of the oldest, richest history in North America. That past, furthermore, is one of great diversity within enduring themes—patterns that can help illuminate the course of events that is the core of this book. I came to believe that the dramatic, amusing, appalling, wondrous, despicable, and heroic years of the mid-nineteenth century have to be seen to some degree in the context of the 120 centuries before them.

A FRUSTRATED FRIEND once told me that I couldn't comment on a new traffic light at Maple and Arkansas without starting with the Magna Carta. Explanations do indeed seem to seep backward in all directions. The hard part is keeping them under control and giving them some focus. A few themes run clearly through this story: the ancient past of the plains and mountains, the dense connections between Indian and white histories, and the continuous conversation between human action and its wondrously varied environment.

I've chosen to pay special attention to one aspect of that last theme. For nearly twenty years a superb body of work in environmental studies has attacked the ridiculous conceit that people can act—and can understand past human acts—apart from the environment in which those actions are taken. Like every good lesson, however, this one can lead in its own dangerous direction. In particular, the idea that humans are inextricably enmeshed with everything around them—that we are bound in the same world with hedgehogs, elms, topsoil, junebugs, and the rest of creation—might subtly suggest that the human role is also equal with that of everything else.

But of course it is not. We *are* different, and not simply because we walk upright, use opposable thumbs, and tend to go bald. Humans are set apart in their environmental exchanges because they consider and think about their environment as nothing else apparently can. This part of our condition has inspired some of the most important—and the vaguest—terms in the humanities. We debate and study the meanings of consciousness, for instance, including our ability to ponder how we fit within the world around us. Another notoriously elusive term, culture, is a product partly of our contemplation of ourselves and our surroundings. A basic human difference, that is, lies in the realm of perception.

I have focused on an aspect of perception especially important to environmental studies. Biologists distinguish between "perceived" and "effective" environments. The first includes everything an animal is aware of in its surroundings. The second is composed of everything that actually influences that animal and everything that the animal in turn affects. A lot in these two environments overlap. Animals correctly perceive plenty of what is in their effective world. A prairie dog notices rain and coyotes; vultures know about carrion; farmers worry about the seasons. But a lot in each environment is not in the other. Much that affects us goes unperceived. Pronghorns and hawks are probably unaware, at least in the usual meaning of the word, of the nitrogen cycle, and yet the conversion of that element from its pure form into something digestible is absolutely essential to antelopes and birds of prey. And people certainly remain ignorant about their full effect on their surroundings and about their environment's impact on them.

Similarly, part of the perceived environment does not exist in fact. Animals can observe relations of cause and effect that are not there. Our dog once spent ten minutes barking at his own echo, apparently deep in conversation with a perceived canine neighbor that was, in fact, the far side of a gully. People are especially given to misperception. My friend's great grandmother thought that keeping scissors under her bed would prevent conception. He is descended from one of her nine children. In short, there is always a dissonance between how animals view the world and how they actually fit into it. That disparity sometimes gets them into deep trouble.

These generalizations apply to human and nonhuman animals alike, but people are different in one crucial way. Because of their unique minds, humans have by far the most dynamic perceptual environment in the animal kingdom. Compared to those of most species, our senses are ludicrously stunted. A male silk moth can smell a potential mate 500 yards away, and from one mile's distance a barred owl can hear an inch-long mouse burrowing under half a foot of snow. I, on the other hand, cannot do either. The elusive quality of "intelligence," however, has permitted my species to expand its senses well beyond those of other organisms. We can "look" at distant galaxies with telescopes that detect light and other radiation many billions of years old. Other animals are deaf to what we can "hear" in our environment with a Geiger counter. Partly through artificially expanded senses, we can also "see" more clearly our surroundings in a more basic sense; we can discover some of the millions of connections and relationships at work in what we are seeing in that word's usual meaning.

In one other essential way our perceived environments are vastly greater. People use their brains to create mental variations of the places they observe, variations that exist only inside their heads. They imagine changes in the world as it presently exists outside themselves; they visualize new connections and relationships that are not there yet. So besides the perceived environment in the first sense—the outer world as humans encounter it through their senses—there can be many alternate environments existing simultaneously as imagined places. We cannot be sure, of course, that other creatures don't also invent such fancied environments, but one thing can be said for certain: The human animal is the only one with a history of acting out that imagination. Only people have tried on a massive scale to move imagined environments out of their heads and to duplicate them in the world where others live.

This complicates considerably the relation between man's perceived and effective surroundings. Other animals, such as viruses, might have more impact on the world as it is, but imagination gives humans by far the greatest power to alter established arrangements and conditions. A naked man looks at a bear and thinks that he would be warmer if he could grow such hair. Then he wonders what would happen if he simply took the bear's hair for himself. The result—clothing—makes the man more comfortable, increases his ability to move around, lengthens his lifespan, and therefore expands his influence on things around him. The crucial event was not his killing of the bear, or the fashioning of a garment, but the first picturing of himself, bear-robed, inside his own head as he stood shivering and wondering.

Through imagination humans thus gain enormous manipulative influence over their surroundings. They can perceive a new effective environment from the current one. Most dreaming is useless. "If frogs had wings, they wouldn't bump their ass so much," my grandfather, Dirt West, would say when he tired of my "what if" speculations as a six-year-old. We can't put wings on frogs any more than we can cause the skies to rain beer and hail barbecue. Our impact is limited by what we have to work with. Much of what we change, furthermore, is inconsequential. If I imagine the light brown walls of my study are given more to yellow or gray, repainting them will probably not affect my environment even as far as the kitchen. Human events will remain steadily on course. The cumulative results of imagined change, however, are immeasurable. Brown or yellow, my study sits inside a house on a street that runs through a town situated in country that is part of a region. I cannot begin to understand any of them without thinking about several thousand years of human beings trying to improve their condition by redreaming it.

Of the imaginings that *have* made a difference, some of the most consequential have involved power, broadly defined. Part of an effective environment is the energy that moves continuously around us. All organisms draw on that energy, convert it, and use it in order to live. As energy is captured and set to a purpose, it becomes power. The application of energy is power in its widest meaning. Once again, people are different. Through their imagination they have been especially handy at devising new paths to energy and new methods of turning it into something they can use. Because humans can imagine more means of gaining power, their impact on their world is obviously greater as well.[3] Our applied dreaming is doubly influential. Simply rearranging the flow of energy has one set of results. Another set comes from using the power that energy gives. The isolated act of making and controlling fire, for instance, has changed the relationship among people, wood, and the many creatures involved with both. Applying fire has produced changes beyond calculation.

The problem is, just as we cannot truly perceive all of our effective environment at any moment, so we cannot imagine anything close to the full consequences of changing things. Some repercussions are simply beyond our ability to see or understand. We also tend to think only about the best results of what we might do, neglecting anything else. Killing a lot of bears for their skins might keep people warmer, but it also touches everything directly and indirectly involved with a bear's living. Many of the effects inevitably fall outside the realm the hunters have considered, and some of those changes will probably cause them problems.

It is the downside of the human advantage. We are vastly superior to any other species in stretching our world into the shape we want; that also makes us infinitely more capable of creating unforeseen difficulties. As a general rule, the greater the changes we think into being, the more problems we have to face. Environmental history is, among other things, a lengthy account of human beings over and over imagining their way into a serious pickle.

SENSIBLE READERS are asking what this has to do with a book about the plains, the Indians living there, and the Colorado gold rush. I think there is a connection. These generalizations apply anywhere on earth at any time that people have lived there, but the pace and scale of change has varied. Some conditions more than others encourage people to rethink their surroundings, and once in a long while events line up to produce explosions of imagination. Of the latter, some of the most spectacular have come when previously separate cultures suddenly find one another. Besides killing each other, these people exchange material goods, animals, diseases, plants. They also swap environments as perceived in their heads. As those imagined worlds meet and resonate, new possibilities are spun out. It is fertile ground for change.

At some point in chasing the story of Indians and the gold rush, I decided—in fact, offered serious wagers to friends and colleagues—that the Great Plains offered North America's most revealing examples of this process. Nowhere else on the continent can we see more dramatically the human envisioning of new lifeways and routes to power, the effects of that search on physical and social environments, and the dilemmas and disasters that so often follow. It began earlier than almost anywhere else on the continent. For many thousands of years people saw their way into varied connections among the scattered and diverse resources in that demanding country with its erratic climate. They juggled energy and power in combinations of dazzling variety.

Then came the Europeans. Frontiers, waves of new experience, rolled from three directions into the continental center, and as they did they set loose changes that surpassed in speed and scope anything the region had known. First Native Americans and then Euro-Americans fashioned new material and social lives on this old stage of human action. Above all the merging of worlds was a revelation of routes to power in its largest sense. People suddenly saw how they might expand their command by pulling more from their surroundings. The essential changes, however, came not so much from people using new tools for new advantages, or from older residents and newcomers pushing their surroundings into new shapes. The basic force was imaginative, the perceiving of the country as a fundamentally different realm of human use. Nowhere else in America was this historical universal acted out so nakedly and with such stark results.

Imagining such new arrangements becomes a kind of storytelling. People are inspired to compose a fresh account of themselves that explains, literally, who in the world they are. These overarching stories describe how a people fit into their surroundings and what their purposes have become. They argue that certain beliefs and values are natural, self-evident expressions of a people being exactly where they are and nowhere else. Such stories become guides and encouragements for living out a newly dreamed existence. Almost invariably they justify possession. When people look back, the stories become proof to them that they have been summoned by fate or history or God into their rightful homes.

There is no obvious word or phrase for these radical reconceptions. They might be called "living myths" or "stories lived forward." I've used the term "visions." After at least 12,000 years of many visions informing many people's use of the plains and mountains, the coming of frontiers brought a terrific unsettling. The effects were at once horrifying and magnificently creative. Changes came so rapidly and with such wrenching effects partly because of the roll of the historical dice. The place, its resources, its alignment of peoples, and especially the timing of the frontiers' arrival made for a volatile combination.

But there was more than that. Across the planet and through many millennia of history, two objects, one alive and the other inert, have inspired in humans an unmatched passion for new visions. Both of these were newly discovered with the arrival of frontiers in mid-America. Indian peoples discovered the horse, which first stepped into this country in its modern form with the earliest European contact. A bit later Euro-Americans found gold in the Rocky Mountains. As they had for thousands of years, horses and gold triggered fresh imaginings and set loose quests for power. People heard a summons to new lives. They were called out to greatness.

They found it, but the stories that inspired them also carried them into conflict, suffering, bloodshed, and disaster. Exactly because the visions born of horses and gold were so seductive, they drew their followers into treacherous miscalculations. In a continent full of long and confident reaches toward power over the natural world, these were some of the grandest, and they led to some of the bleakest calamities. The new plainsmen, both Indian and white, finally had to face the truth of what Francis Bacon had written two-and-a-half centuries earlier: "We cannot command nature except by obeying her."

The two visions of horses and gold were also irreconcilable. When moved out of human heads and set to life in the effective world, they could not exist in the same place. The reason was simple. They conceived of and used power in conflicting ways, yet each drew its power from the same sources. Two peoples cannot pull on the same limited energy for contrary uses, just as the same dollar cannot be legally spent at the same time for both bread and cheese. Something has to give. What in fact *would* give was the basic question behind the famous conflicts between Indians and whites in the 1860s and their appalling consequences.

So what started as a brief look at argonauts "rambunctulating" to the Rocky Mountains became an expanding pursuit that worked me hard but taught me a lot. It helped me appreciate better the value of reconstructing as full a historical portrait as possible. Drawing lines is dangerous. The remarkable events in mid-America in the mid-nineteenth century are seen most clearly when we take into account the deep and the recent past, the interwoven choices of Indians and whites, and the inseparability of the environment from human society and action. And just as important, we need to recognize the play between the "natural" world and human minds. If the environment is always helping shape and limit human understanding, people (and only people) are forever imagining new environments and trying to muscle them into being.

Nowhere is the uselessness of lines more obvious than in the history of peoples called out to the plains. The rise of the plains nomads and the Colorado gold rush were at the center of what I came to believe is one of the great American stories. I can only hope that some readers will agree.

1

PROLOGUE: A SCRAP AND A PANIC

Two events in summer 1857 turned the course of western history sharply in a new direction. The first was a military campaign against some plains Indians, the second a ruinous contraction among eastern financial houses. One touched mainly a few hundred cavalrymen and an equal number of warriors and their families. The other affected millions of stockholders, merchants, speculators, laborers, and farmers. If people of that time ever thought of the two events together, they would have seen no more in common than between oatmeal and the Prince of Wales. But they would have been wrong.

EARLY IN JUNE 1857 Col. Edwin Vose Sumner led two companies of the U.S. First Cavalry over a rise of sandhills and looked down into the Platte River valley. Not far up the shallow, turgid river was Fort Kearny, where he would rest his troops and horses before picking up others and continuing west. Directly below him the Platte was full from spring runoff, more than a mile across and flowing in several channels among sandy bars. To the east and north Sumner could see the tops of the valley's only trees, cottonwoods that grew thickly on parts of Grand Island, which began just downstream and divided the Platte for seventy-five miles.[1]

Sumner may have looked at the trees more thoughtfully than usual, because a bloody moment at Grand Island had brought him to his present task. On August 24 of the previous year a pair of young Cheyenne men had hailed a mail coach near where Sumner now rode. They were from a party, led by Little Spotted Crow and Little Gray Hair, who had come east from the high plains to fight Pawnees. They had found none. In camp near Grand Island the group saw the stage approaching and sent the two men—one was a mixed-blood who spoke English—to ask the driver for tobacco. When the rattled driver saw them gesturing, however, he lashed his mules, pulled his pistol, and started firing. The Cheyennes sent back a volley of arrows that wounded the driver slightly in the arm. The ruckus brought Little Gray Hair and Little Spotted Crow at a run, and when told the details they lashed the two men furiously with their quirts and bows for their impetuosity. The Cheyennes then retired to their camp.

The next day soldiers from Fort Kearny attacked the lounging Indians in retaliation. They killed several and pursued others through the thick trees for a few miles. About fifteen escaped, including the party's two leaders. The soldiers took the Cheyennes' horses, destroyed all lodges and supplies at the Grand Island camp, and returned to the fort.[2]

When the surviving warriors told their story, the outraged Cheyennes struck back along the Platte road in their home territory farther west. At least a dozen travelers were killed during September, including the secretary of Utah Territory, before the Cheyennes pulled back to wintering grounds on streams south of the Platte. In October 1856 a large number of their leaders met with the agent of the upper Platte, Thomas Twiss. Both sides gave assurances that there would be no more attacks.[3]

Those promises would be hard to keep, however. Emerging younger leaders among the Cheyennes called for further retaliation. They were angered by several episodes over the past few years—the nasty bloodletting among Lakotas and soldiers in the Grattan massacre and in Col. William Harney's subsequent attack on a Lakota village, and more recently by the death of two of their own warriors in a squabble over horses at the Platte River bridge. Over an especially cold winter of 1856–1857 and into a summer that was hotter and drier than usual, their anger grew. Meanwhile, back in November, Secretary of War Jefferson Davis had tentatively ordered a chastising expedition against the Cheyennes. As the Kansas Free-Soil conflict cooled, soldiers were available for campaigning, and in April 1857 Sumner was told to prepare the First Cavalry for the field.

His command, stationed at Fort Leavenworth on the Missouri River, would first be divided. Three companies under Maj. John Sedgwick were to march up the Arkansas River to the Rocky Mountains, turn north, ride to the South Platte River, and wait for their commander. Sumner was to lead his two companies to the Platte, take on a squadron of dragoons at Fort Kearny, proceed to Fort Laramie on the North Platte and add another three infantry companies, then finally rendezvous with Sedgwick. On May 18 Sedgwick left Fort Leavenworth for the Arkansas, and two days later Sumner's column departed, its band playing the traditional "The Girl I Left Behind Me." A march of twelve days brought Sumner to Grand Island and the Platte, roughly at the spot where the two warriors and the stage driver had set things in motion eight months before.

On Independence Day the two commands completed their grand circuit and met on the South Platte. Helped by Delaware scouts, especially their feisty leader Fall Leaf, the cavalry and infantry proceeded to the southeast, directly into the watersheds between the Platte and Arkansas, country favored by the Cheyennes during high summer. On Beaver Creek, a tributary of the Republican River, they found a great lodge built by the Cheyennes a few weeks earlier for their sun dance of annual renewal. They followed the lines of dragging lodgepoles southward, and in the closing days of July they approached the south fork of the Solomon River.[4]

In the Cheyenne camps feeling was running high. Two young men, Ice and Dark, twenty-two and twenty-seven, had been assuring warriors that Maheo, the All Being, was pleased with them and their courage. Because they had lived faithfully they would be rewarded. The cavalry's great advantage in battle was their carbines and horse pistols, against which the Cheyennes could offer only their lances, bows and arrows, and a few outmoded firearms. Ice and Dark said that Maheo had given them medicine that offered full protection from enemy bullets and gave absolute accuracy to the Cheyennes' own weapons.[5] The two men made their case with confidence and conviction, and as scouts reported daily on the cavalry's approach, support grew for a confrontation. Warriors made extra preparation for battle, shaping and feathering arrows, cleaning their few firearms and loading them with powder blessed by the two young men, preparing their feather-rimmed shields. On July 29 the warriors stripped to breachclouts, painted themselves, prayed, and by instruction washed in a small blue lake that Ice and Dark called sacred. Afterward more than 300 men rode to a place along the Solomon they had chosen for battle. Early in the afternoon their scouts appeared at a distance and rode their horses rapidly in small circles, the signal that bison (or in this case the enemy) were approaching.[6]

The Cheyennes were mounted and in a long line across the valley between the river's north bank and some bluffs when Sumner and six companies rode into view from around a rocky point. "Gentlemen," the commander had told his officers shortly before, "you will probably soon have something to do."[7] When he saw the warriors at the other end of the valley, Sumner ordered his men to form their own battle line and to move forward at a trot. The Delaware scout Fall Leaf dashed into the open ground while firing his rifle and shouting a challenge across the gap, a bit of bravado that amused Sumner.

The Cheyennes also advanced, beginning their battle and death songs. They expected the soldiers to come close enough to fire a rifle volley before drawing their pistols and moving in for the kill, although this time, of course, the warriors' powerful medicine would send the bullets rolling harmlessly to their horses' hooves. They in turn would charge the baffled soldiers and take their victory. As the two sides closed, groups of warriors on each end of their line rode outward and forward in a try at turning the cavalry's flanks. Sumner ordered two of his own companies to do the same. Horse soldiers and Cheyennes rode steadily at one another, both massed at the center and with flanking arms ahead: two lobsters reaching for supper.

Then, just as the two lines were in rifle range, Sumner ordered two bugled commands that surprised his own men and left the Cheyennes stunned: "Draw sabres" and "charge." As his men pulled the steel weapons from their scabbards and leveled them at the enemy, they spurred their horses into a full run. To the Cheyennes, this was not so much an unexpected maneuver as a terrifying portent. They had been assured of safety from the usual threat, a rain of bullets, not against the slash of sabres. The charging soldiers could have only a few meanings, all bad. Ice and Dark might have misunderstood Maheo, or might have deceived the people, or might have been tricked by malevolent spirits. At worst, the All Being might have withdrawn his favor because of some unintended sacrilege. Whatever the explanation, the basic assumption of their being there evaporated. The equivalent for the First Cavalry would have been an angry Christ appearing to shake his finger from the clouds. As the spiritual ground fell from under the Cheyennes, they fired one great cloud of arrows at the charging cavalry, then wheeled and ran.[8]

The battle became a chaotic chase. Most soldiers broke off in pairs and pursued the main body of Cheyennes who fled southward toward their camps. In close skirmishing just beyond the Solomon a warrior was surrounded and killed after wounding Lt. James E. B. (Jeb) Stuart with a pistol shot to the breastbone. A private pinned another Cheyenne to the ground with his sabre after the two had fought with a variety of weapons, at one point throwing an empty carbine back and forth at each other. In the end two privates had died and nine cavalry were wounded. Sumner estimated nine of his enemies killed, although Cheyennes later reported four dead. A fortified sod-walled field hospital, grandly named Fort Floyd, was built to nurse the wounded soldiers. The dead were laid in graves topped with prickly pear to discourage wolves.[9]

Sumner found a large village abandoned fifteen miles to the south. Many tipis had been carried off but nearly 200 remained standing, and in the panicked flight many more had been struck but abandoned. Soldiers took some dried bison meat and burned the rest—lodges, lodgepoles, robes and other animal skins, utensils, clothing, and children's toys. The command proceeded to the Arkansas in hopes of another engagement. When Sumner heard that the agent to the Cheyennes, Robert Miller, held annuity goods at a nearby central trading site, Bent's Fort, the colonel confiscated the flour, rice, sugar, hard bread, and other food for his men and ordered the gunpowder, flints, and shot flung into the river. Late in August he led his men downriver to Walnut Creek, a large tributary of the Arkansas with excellent stands of trees and good forage.[10]

There he received orders to send most of his men under Sedgwick back to Fort Laramie on the North Platte, possibly to join an expedition being sent to Utah in a confrontation with Mormon authorities. Sumner and two companies were told to come home. They broke camp shortly afterward and began their eastward march along the Santa Fe road. On September 16 they arrived at Fort Leavenworth, four days shy of four months in the field.

Most Cheyennes meantime had fled south of the Arkansas, close to the Hairy Nostrilled White People (Mexicans/New Mexicans). They lived and hunted among the Kiowas and Comanches until spring, then returned to their home territory. Several leaders, all with reputations for promoting peace, met with the venerable trader William Bent to complain of actions they saw as unprovoked hostilities. They would do what they could to keep matters under control, they said, but they were having increasing difficulty controlling their younger men, who chafed at the treatment and humiliations.[11]

That restiveness was clear to others along the valley. In August, two weeks after the fight, an express rider had met a party of young Cheyennes who had been on the Solomon. They told of dead friends and the loss of 150 horses. They would shun Bent's Fort, they said angrily, unless it was to fight. They wanted no presents, no dealings with whites, and no peace.[12]

THE EASTERN KANSAS that Sumner found on his return was not the one he had left. During the Cheyenne campaign American financial centers were swept by one of the most severe business panics of the century.[13] The trouble started in midsummer with a calamitous decline of gold reserves in English banks, a hemorrhaging of specie that drove up London discount rates to such delicious levels that investors began shedding American securities and buying short-term English bonds. That drove down the prices of U.S. stocks, especially those in railroads. These investments represented many of the assets beneath most major banks and financial houses, and as the market nosed steadily downward, directors of these institutions grew increasingly nervous.

The crash came on August 24. On that Monday, as the First Cavalry rode seventeen miles along the north bank of the Arkansas, the New York branch of the Ohio Life Insurance and Trust Company of Cincinnati closed its doors, the victim of embezzlement as well as shrinking assets. The news was ominous, since this firm had connections to many others across the country and obligations to prominent eastern financial houses; and when a second business house collapsed, New York bankers panicked, suspended specie payments, and called in millions of dollars in loans.[14] A financial shock wave spread outward from the epicenter. The stock market plunged. Banks from New England to California failed, and survivors faced mobs of depositors clamoring to pull out their savings. A Missourian hoping to wire money to his brother held back, unsure of what it would be worth on arrival: "Times are squally. The express was broke. . . . We must be cautious in these times of doubt."[15] In state after state desperate officials refused to release further specie, and by October 14, specie payments had virtually ceased throughout the nation. The American monetary system, wrote a financial editor, "now lies before us a magnificent and melancholy ruin."

By the end of the year, the nation was in a full-blown depression. The panic alone was not to blame. The economy was badly overextended. The enormous output of California gold had doubled the amount of money in circulation and pushed prices steeply upward. The lusty growth of the 1850s had produced more goods than the public could buy, while the orgy of railroad construction far surpassed the needs of the day, and people invested merely on an imagined future. The panic of 1857 simply made the collapse more rapid and dramatic.

The devastation was much worse in some areas than in others. The South, protected by healthy prices for cotton on the Continent, suffered the least; secessionists soon would point to their immunity as proof that Dixie could go its own way. The middle Atlantic states and the Northeast were hit much harder, especially major financial centers. In New York City 40,000 jobless workers marched through the streets with banners reading "We Want Work" and "Hunger Is a Sharp Thorn." In November the U.S. district attorney called in troops to protect government property.[16]

The full cuff of the depression was felt in the Midwest and the middle border. Indiana, Illinois, Michigan, and Wisconsin were hit hard, and Iowa, Missouri, and the new state of Kansas even harder. By a rough justice, these states suffered most because they had prospered most during the past several years. If the United States grew prodigiously during the 1850s, far and away its lustiest expansion came in the lower Ohio valley and especially on the middle border.

This was a transition region. It received the push of westward expansion and helped pass it on. From the 1820s to the 1850s, the Anglo-American frontier pressed out of the trans-Appalachian country and poured its families into the lower Ohio valley, western Great Lakes, the Mississippi valley, and the first tier of states beyond it. Simultaneously the lower and middle Missouri River, from St. Louis to Iowa, emerged as a zone of departure for points farther west. In the 1820s freighters began an increasingly vigorous trade along the Santa Fe Trail, out of Westport, Missouri, to the Arkansas River and across the Cimarron River basin to New Mexico. Beginning tentatively in the early 1840s, then surging in 1849, emigrants to the Pacific Coast and Utah traveled up the Platte River on the great overland trail, also called the California and Oregon Trail. River ports on the Missouri saw themselves as launching places for traders and travelers.

In 1854 this region felt a new surge of growth when Kansas and Nebraska were organized as territories. During the next three years tens of thousands of persons were drawn to Kansas by ideological and material passions. Advocates on both sides of the slavery issue wrestled for control in country that was the stuff of agrarian dreams—a vast, well-watered bluestem prairie where oak and hickory trees grew thickly along the rivers and in clusters on higher ground. The great majority of settlers stayed within 100 miles of the Missouri line. A few score towns appeared, the most important along the largest watercourses. Lawrence, Lecompton, and Topeka sprang to life along the Kansas River and Leavenworth and Atchison on the 125-mile stretch of the Missouri River that formed the territory's crumpled northeastern corner. Because these towns were linked by water to Kansas City, Westport, Independence, and St. Louis, they stood also to profit from Pacific-bound emigrants. The fiercely competitive urban centers grappled for political leadership— there were eight capitals of Kansas during the first seven years—and for the trade of the expanding economy.

The region immediately to the east was growing almost as rapidly. Imagine a line 300 miles long, anchored at Kansas City and sweeping in a great arc, like a clock's hand, starting straight up at due north and moving clockwise to the east and around to due south. The four states within this half-circle—Iowa, Illinois, Missouri, and Arkansas—grew in population by nearly 1.7 million persons during the 1850s, an increase equal to about 20 percent of the growth of the entire nation. Minnesota, Wisconsin, and Indiana grew by another million. Encouraging this headlong rush was the rising price of farm products, which were higher between 1854 and 1857 than they had been since 1818 and would be until the middle of the Civil War. By the late 1850s each of these seven states was at least twice as crowded as ten years earlier. In Iowa the density of persons per acre increased nearly four times over. With that, naturally, land prices began to rise precipitously. So did the frustrations of those people looking for the better chance.

These years also saw an extraordinary expansion of the nation's railroad system, and again the most frenzied growth was in the Midwest and the middle border. Indiana and Illinois together added more miles of track than the five mid-Atlantic states; Missouri and Iowa laid more than New England. Virtually all this construction ran generally to the west, linking the well-established systems of New York and Pennsylvania with cities of the Ohio valley and beyond. By the late 1850s, eight railroads offered passage to the Mississippi River. Travelers moved over this iron web by various routes. Some funneled through Chicago and headed southwest to St. Louis or west to Rock Island, Dubuque, and Burlington. Others rolled through central and southern Ohio, Indiana, and Illinois to St. Louis or veered northwest to the Iowa border. Construction in the South, though less vigorous, had a similar effect. A new line out of Chattanooga linked systems of Virginia, the Carolinas, and

Georgia with Memphis, and the Illinois Central connected New Orleans and Mississippi with Memphis and St. Louis.

The great thrust of this transportation revolution, that is, came east to west and, as with the rivers, made the border towns natural destinations and transition points for farmers and Pacific emigrants. Crossing the Mississippi by ferry or by the Rock Island bridge, passengers could continue westward along several lines. Four Iowa roads had begun construction toward Nebraska by 1857. In Missouri workers were laying track to connect Hannibal with St. Joseph, with a spur to St. Louis. Another line ran from St. Louis halfway across the state toward Kansas City. Emigrants looked forward shortly to moving easily by rail from several points along the Mississippi to Council Bluffs, St. Jo, and Kansas City.

Truly the West had become "the great theatre of railroading," as the editor of the *American Railroad Journal* wrote. Farmers in the borderlands could send their products eastward over these tracks to feed the growing cities. Ambitious and curious easterners could follow the same rails westward to chase whatever dreams arose. The very names of the companies suggested the grand visions of rail executives and their customers: the Toledo, Wabash, and Western, the Pacific Railroad of Missouri, the Great Western.

Unfortunately, this feverish development came with a cost. Like all rapidly growing regions, the middle border lived by credit. Farmers were "buying more land, buying machinery, carriages, sewing machines, melodeons, and fine furniture and generally running into debt," an Illinois businessman remembered; "merchants gave credit to any one who would buy."[17] Farms were heavily mortgaged, businesses financed by loans, and keeping up with this debt demanded a brisk exchange of goods. Much of that business, furthermore, was done with notes issued by western banks, and the commercial flow relied partly on faith that those banknotes were worth what they said they were. Ultimately, everything was buoyed by a general optimism; things kept going because people believed they would keep going.

Soon after the panic began in New York, the region's mood turned cautious. "Promises are a drug," Horace Greeley wrote from Wisconsin, "and faith in human solvence sadly alloyed with skepticism." There was money on hand, he added, but those who needed it most didn't have it, and those who had it were holding tight. Creditors now squinted hard at western banknotes. Most of this paper was heavily discounted and a lot of it refused entirely. That retarded all commerce, which in turn made it harder for debtors to keep up with their payments. In short, the same elements that had allowed the economic advance of the last ten years—credit and paper wealth—turned it around with equal vigor once optimism waned. By the end of the year more than 1,000 businesses had failed in Indiana, Illinois, Michigan, Iowa, and Missouri. A Minnesotan wrote that the panic had become "a perfect whirlwind destroying and breaking our ablest men."[18]

Trade moved slower than cold syrup. Stores looked lonely, with only a few customers buying necessities. Most building stopped, and workers of all sorts saw their jobs vanish. The chug of steamboats was heard less often up and down the region's waterways, and the recently booming midwestern towns had a stagnant look. Greeley found "railroads partly constructed and then stopped for want of means; blocks of buildings ditto; counties and cities . . . practically insolvent; individuals trying to stave off the satisfaction of debts, obligations, judgments, executions." A Kansas editor poetized:

> There's not a day but some one fails
> Some house that goes to smash;
> And names that once stood high on Change
> Are out for want of cash
> Those whom we thought were millionaires,
> And rich in shares and stocks,
> Their MILLION HEIRS now disappoint,
> They fail and leave no rocks.[19]

An Ohio merchant wired his agent in Independence with the lowest price he would accept for some furniture. If the goods didn't move, he added, give them away to some worthy person, "& if such persons will not have them, then apply a match to them."[20]

The diary of a St. Louis merchant captures the mounting alarm felt by thousands of persons throughout the Mississippi and Missouri valleys. Meriwether Lewis Clark, son of one famous explorer and named for another, wrote throughout spring and summer of his city's economic vigor. Suddenly, in mid-September, he told of a tightening money market and a drastic slackening of trade. By early October, St. Louis was in "an awful state," with banks collapsing and businessmen panicked. The state's massive debt from railroad bonds caused special concern, since sagging revenues might demand a huge increase in property taxes. By month's end the mills and factories were idle, and "nothing doing at the Levee." The price of everything from whiskey to onions slid downward, but that was no consolation as income fell and savings evaporated. Hardest hit were the mechanics and laborers. As the days cooled and the nights lengthened, Clark wrote, there was "great fear entertained of a hard winter for the poor."[21]

His concern was well grounded. Throughout the region shopkeepers stared at full shelves, farmers at unpaid mortgages. A Kansas City newspaper printed a front-page Baptist sermon blaming the troubles on human vanity and speculation: "God governs by His own law of accumulation: By the sweat of our brow shall we eat our bread."[22] It was small consolation to workingmen who knocked on doors and pleaded for a day's labor. In St. Louis workers met en masse to deplore the apathy of the rich and to call for public works to help them through the winter. The same day two men were charged with vagrancy in a local court. They had found a job that paid with food, but with no place to spend the cold nights they had slipped each evening into a doctor's office. They stole nothing and were found with only their own small basket of crackers, bread, and peach jam. The judge dismissed the charges.[23]

Like these men, some were desperate for the means of living. Others were merely frustrated. They had tripped and stumbled along fortune's road, and now they were looking for a way to regain their stride. As the financial pall deepened, so did this vague but general restlessness.

THE CONNECTIONS between these two episodes are not obvious, even in retrospect. The history of mid-nineteenth-century America has usually been read as two nearly independent stories, East and West. Events between the Atlantic Coast and the Mississippi River, like the panic of 1857, appear as their own dynamic swirl. They are tied to developments in Europe and even Asia but seem mostly insulated from what was happening on the plains and in the mountains a short distance to the west, in the country where Sumner's soldiers met their Cheyenne opponents.

The perspective of distinctly separate stories has grown from a tradition rooted deeply in the East and in Europe. By this tradition North America was starkly divided, not just culturally but into spheres of fundamental experience. Europeans and Euro-Americans were dynamic peoples with long histories and cultures evolved over millennia. When they expanded into new regions they supposedly carried this dynamism with them. They initiated vibrant change—some say progressive, others degenerative—in each place they occupied. Beyond their settlements were other peoples who had never known such dynamism. These societies always had been largely static. As the invading European change-bringers moved to the interior, the story goes, indigenous people were conquered and pulled into the land of flux and development, but as long as others were still ahead of the advancing wave, the basic division remained. The line between the two spheres of experience was "the frontier." Crossing the frontier, one found land mostly untouched by history.

In the 1850s the plains Indians supposedly lived in one of the last areas beyond the frontier and outside the full grasp of change. Edwin James wrote that some of the people he met in 1820 apparently had moved around a bit, but they had only the gauziest collective memory and lacked a basic requisite of true culture—a sense of history and destiny. They did not even number years, James added, but measured time by seasons and "changes in vegetables."[24] By prevailing opinion, of course, immunity to historical change meant they were backward as well. "They are in the lowest stage of . . . heathenism," Thomas Twiss wrote of the Cheyennes and Lakotas just before his peace parley in October 1856. Indians felt the dim influence of a few depraved white refugees, but generally they lived frozen in cultural exile: "In the heart and centre of this great and powerful republic, and in the middle of the nineteenth century, there exists a nation of barbarians, living in the hunter state, among whom the use of the plough and hoe is unknown, and to whom the word of God is not preached. Why?"[25]

But the battle on the Solomon and the panic of 1857 are reminders that no clean frontier existed between ways of life, between change and stasis, except in the minds of people like Twiss. When Sumner ascended the Platte he did not ride over the edge of history. The warriors who sang their death songs to the First Cavalry had come to be there out of intricate sequences of change. Their historical roots had grown for centuries before their first meetings with Europeans sent them in new directions. The Indians' old story was increasingly entangled with that of whites, most recently in the vigorous trade in furs and in the passage of .25 million persons over the plains to the Pacific. The Cheyennes along the Solomon could not possibly have explained their dynamic past apart from the history of the whites they fought.

One recent bit of that history, the panic of 1857, was similarly snarled with the Indians' story. The collapsing banks and frantic speculators were just one result of the explosive growth that for generations had unsettled the American interior. That turbulence had brought both crisis and opportunity to the Cheyennes and to other plains tribes and indeed had drawn them into the country they now considered their rightful homes. Various details of the clash along the Solomon—the Cheyennes' horses and weapons and clothing, the cavalry's methods, the presence of Delaware scouts, and even the name they went by—were grown from stories, folded together, that tied bison hunters to bond agents.

If nothing else, then, tracing the threads of these two events ought to convince anyone that Indians lived as much in a world of change as anybody else, and always had. It is just as clear that trying to draw a distinct line between white and Indian worlds is a silly business. From the moment of their first contact the histories of the two peoples have rippled into each other, and nowhere was that entanglement more obvious, vigorous, and fascinating than where those changing, mutually influential cultures rubbed closest against each other. A frontier never separated things. It brought things together.

Sumner's scrap and the panic of 1857, however, had more in common than a general involvement in the shared history of the continent's peoples. They were preludes to a transforming moment in western and American history. Sumner's victory at first hit painfully at the Cheyennes, but its influence, as usual, bled into white society to the east. It persuaded people there that the plains and the mountains beyond were suddenly a much safer and more alluring place to look for the main chance, whatever that might be. Whites thought they could probe western Kansas for possibilities without ending up as a story around a Cheyenne campfire. Simultaneously, the panic and depression gave tens of thousands of persons good reason to chase whatever possibilities came from reaching into this latest frontier.

But one element was obviously missing. People would chase after a chance only if the probing turned something up. In fact that last step was partly taken. At the foot of the Rockies some of Sumner's soldiers had met some Missourians, frightened by Cheyennes and now running home, who said they had found in nearby creeks flecks and nuggets of something with unsurpassed power to set people in motion—gold. A year later, not far from where Sumner's and Sedgwick's columns had had their rendezvous, a party of prospectors, at odds and ends because of the depression, confirmed the claim by finding gold dust on tributaries of the South Platte.

Within months the response was building, pushed hard by rough economic times. A few more years brought changes unprecedented in scale and impact to plains and mountains. One of the continent's most remarkable stories, that of the nomadic plains Indians and their brilliantly imaginative culture, took a cataclysmic turn. In less than a decade the region was reshaped—and more important, re-envisioned. The manic quest for gold and the rapidly spreading consequences gave mid-America a wholly new meaning within the continent and the nation.

The transformation came so quickly that the Colorado gold rush seemed an entirely fresh beginning, especially to those people who believed the moving frontier brought change to a changeless land. But it was far messier than that. As the region's story moved in a startling new direction, it carried forward the design of a very old world.

Part One:

VISIONS

THE OLD WORLD

A cavalryman on the Solomon who drew his sabre and charged the Cheyennes probably had given little if any thought to those Indians' lives and origins. If anything, like most white Americans, he most likely considered his opponents remnants of a timeless past. No idea among Euro-Americans was older than this one—that Indians, wherever found, had lived in a kind of historical limbo while waiting for Europeans to appear. The warriors waiting in the field along the Solomon obviously had known whites before this, but the impression persisted of a boundary of experience between the two sides. Whites met Indians by crossing a line from their own world of dynamic change to one where others lived in the perpetual present.

Or so they thought. In reality the Cheyennes had come to their battlefield through a history as richly convoluted as that of any people. The country they called home had taken its shape partly from them and from others who had played out their own stories for thousands of years, through long swings of climate and countless twists of human choice. Places are defined in part when people infuse them with imagination. They are what they are because of the visions lived out over the years. By those terms the central plains were a very old place indeed.

In fact, this country might have been among the first American land to feel human feet. The most common theory of early migration holds that nomadic hunters crossed the land bridge of Beringia from Asia into Alaska, then moved southward along an open corridor between towering blue walls of Pleistocene ice. That route funneled them onto the northern Great Plains. From there they most likely drifted southward along the face of the Rockies, taking advantage, as people have ever since, of the more moderate weather close to the mountain base. In the waning millennia of the last ice age, at least 15,000 and maybe 25,000 years ago, the first Americans might have camped along creeks and in clusters of timber where Denver and Colorado Springs later appeared. They may have stayed for decades or for centuries.[1]

Whether or not the earliest immigrants passed that way, the central plains have been layered more deeply in human experience than almost any other part of North America. If I extend my right arm and look down it to my pointing index finger, I can picture that distance as the full stretch of plains history. At my shoulder is the first certain presence of people in the midcontinent; the fleshy end of my fingertip is today. On this timeline the first Europeans show up on my second knuckle. The rush for gold in the Rockies began at about the quick of my fingernail. A lot happened before knuckle and nail—before the time we insist on calling the "historic" period. Trying to understand the most recent fifteen generations apart from the 400 before them makes no more sense than hoping to understand the physiology of my arm and fingers while ignoring the first three feet of flesh, sinew, bicep, tricep, wrist, humerus, and the rest.

Europeans entered country that had seen the rise and collapse of dozens of cultures. They set loose sweeping influences—changes that eventually brought (among others) the Cheyenne people as the latest in a long lineage of immigrants—but their impact still built on what came before it. The clash on the Solomon was part of the most recent chapter of an ancient history of dizzying successes and dreadful calamities, of transformation, crisis, and adaptation.

No HARD-AND-FAST EVIDENCE has been found for human presence on the central plains before about 9500 to 10,000 B.C., near the end of the last ice age. The plains were wetter and cooler then. They had a mottled look, a mix of tallgrasses and hardwood groves punctuated with lakes and rain-fed ponds. The lush diversity supported a wide and profuse community of wildlife.[2] The peoples who lived there were part of the Clovis complex, a widespread culture eventually found in many other parts of North America. Presumably they were descendants of the first arrivals.

The Clovis peoples were among the most accomplished hunters in human history.[3] They preyed on an extraordinary abundance of game, collectively called the Pleistocene megafauna. There were wild horses, camels, prong-horns, deer, peccarries, bison of an earlier, larger type, and Columbian mammoths that weighed up to eight tons. Probably these people hunted smaller game as well, from rabbits and ground squirrels to prairie dogs and turkeys, but they were primarily hunters of the great game animals that proliferated in the continental interior.[4] Clovis hunters relied on a tool kit, including thrusting spears and projectile points, that had evolved from a col-lection developed by Asian ancestors. The most distinctive of the Americans' tools were elegant, beautifully crafted points that were fluted, graced with smoothly knapped grooves running from tip to base.

Few hints of material life have survived. The hunters most likely lived in temporary camps suited to the great chase, and except for the points, scrap-ers, and other stone tools, they left little to tell about themselves. No one really knows what they looked like. Human remains from the Clovis period are extremely rare throughout the range of those remarkable people, and not a single skeletal fragment has ever been found on the central plains. Enough evidence of their kills have surfaced, however, to suggest that they lived what was, for that time, a good life.

By the time they first arrived on the plains, however, things were chang-ing. The climate warmed. By about 9000 B.C. the pattern of vegetation was shifting. The old diverse and mottled landscape was becoming more con-sistent. Kansas and Nebraska by then featured great sweeps of unbroken grasslands bordered by thick stands of timber. Plaids gave way to stripes, as one writer has put it. Within those savannas, especially to the west in Colorado, tallgrasses gave way to shorter. These changes in flora and in the weather almost certainly were linked in some way to another stunning change—the disappearance of dozens of species on the plains and in North America at large. It was one of the most dramatic extinctions in the history of life on the continent. Particularly vulnerable were some of the prey most favored by the Clovis hunters—mammoths, sloths, horses, camels, and others.

According to some recent opinion the Clovis hunters were partly—some scholars would say mainly—responsible for the great dying. Clovis people after all stepped very late into a finely tuned balance of life, a web delicately spun among many species. They arrived with the skills and technology to have quite an impact quickly. Human predators may have been in such command, and their prey so unaccustomed to the threat, that the new hunters pushed over the edge of extinction some species already under extraordinary stress from other changes in climate and plant life.[5] If there is anything to this explanation, the collapse of the Pleistocene megafauna is the earliest and one of the most dramatic cases of human hands helping to bring on an environmental crisis. It was not the last.

With many of their favored prey gone, Clovis and later (after about 8500 B.C.) the Folsom peoples responded by concentrating their hunt on certain species, one in particular. Some animals weathered well the climatic shift. Cervids, elk, and deer prospered in the open grasslands. Hunters focused on them and especially on another animal that took advantage of the new landscape—the huge *Bison antiquus,* which proliferated and swarmed over the highlands and river valleys in fantastic numbers, filling the ecological space opened by the calamitous die-off of other animals.[6] The next era was a dual adaptation of people and beasts. The ungulates exploited newly emptied niches; people concentrated on the survivors' booming populations.

For the next few thousand years, until about 5000 B.C., this bison-hunting culture flourished on the central plains. *Bison antiquus* was far larger than the modern version. Its horns were up to six feet tip to tip, and five of the animals together weighed as much as a mammoth. Hunters probably used a range of methods to bring them down—springing from blinds at water holes, creeping close disguised in animal skins, stampeding herds into man-made corrals or into snow-choked gullies. Whatever they did, it could be quite successful. One site on the Arikara fork of the Republican River in Yuma County, Colorado, contains the remains of more than 300 bison slain, skinned, and butchered and their bones pulled apart. It was quite an operation—each animal yielded up to 500 pounds of meat—that probably represented several mass kills.[7]

As with the Clovis before them, little can be said about the lifeways of these great bison-killers. Butchering sites contain many varieties of tools but no evidence of long-term residence. Hunters also gathered to quarry stone, especially jasper, and shape it into lance points, scrapers, hammerstones, knives, and choppers. The residue is filled with a variety of bones besides the bison's—wolves, beavers, rabbits, antelopes, rats, voles, prairie dogs, and others. At another site the remains of a firepit contain dozens of shattered mud dauber nests.[8] Were the firebuilders also wasp-hunters, harvesting the protein-rich larvae? Were they just ridding themselves of bothersome pests? However they fed themselves, these plainsmen probably shifted with season and opportunity among temporary camps, adapting to evolving circumstances and living by what the country offered.

For 5,000 years, nearly half its human story, the central plains were home to a series of societies of master hunters. Preying first on the Pleistocene herds, then concentrating on one of that era's survivors, they established a remarkably successful, sustaining way of life. Several millennia before the birth of Christ, the plains already lay deep in a history of movement and adjustment, crisis and resolution.

ABOUT 5000 B.C. this long first stage of plains history ended. The climate changed, although there is even more argument than usual about what happened. Some scholars believe that during the Altithermal (or Atlantic) period from about 5000 B.C. to 2500 B.C. the plains were stricken by a prolonged drought.[9] The high and middle plains, country that had been graced with a profusion of grasses and considerable rainfall, became much more arid. What is now eastern Colorado and western Kansas and Nebraska took on a look somewhat like today, except that the precipitation was even lighter and this dry spell was much, much longer than anything in the recent record. The *Bison antiquus* disappeared and was replaced by the smaller modern plains bison (*Bison bison*), another hint, perhaps, of terrible aridity. This drought lasted not for years (as in the 1930s) or decades (as in the 1200s) but for centuries—if, that is, it happened at all. Other authorities argue that the evidence for such a drastic deviation is too sketchy to say for sure.[10]

Speculation over the megadrought is bound up with another puzzling fact. Archaeologists have found very few remains of human presence on the plains during the Altithermal period. After fifty centuries of vigorous activity, the record for the next twenty-five is nearly empty. Possibly people abandoned the plains during those millennia. More likely the inhabitants shifted to patterns of living that left little behind, at least where archaeologists have looked so far.

If a deep, long-lasting drought did settle onto this region, plainsmen probably had to turn to lifestyles even more nomadic than before. They might have lived like recent peoples in extreme arid climates, such as the Great Basin. If so, they ranged over large territories and maximized their options by hunting whatever animals they could, working the precious streams and searching out valuable wild plants. A rare site from this era, about 3250 B.C., seems to have been a camping spot beside a small lake just north of Manhattan, Kansas. Among the remains are some bones of the plains bison, but more significant is the scarcity of such large animals. Instead there is a mix of small animal remnants—rabbits, catfish, gar, and mussels—as well as the blackened seeds of bullrushes, grapes, goosefoot, and smartweed. Perhaps the people around these cooking pits visited here periodically to fish from a valued water source and to take in plants along its shore.[11]

The vegetal cover would have changed considerably as the rains slowed, which in turn must have altered the mix of animals, particularly the herds of grazers. The wherewithal of life became scarcer. Within this general decline, however, conditions may have varied considerably from one place to another. Plains peoples may have withdrawn toward the east, where rainfall was greater, and then ranged periodically westward on hunting forays. Whether traveling onto the plains occasionally or living there year-round, people would have had to cover more ground to find what they needed, so there were few or no long-term habitation sites with enduring cultural residue to leave behind. These plainsmen would have left few tracks.

A dramatic exception to this lack of remains is on the far side of the plains from the Missouri River, along and immediately into the Front Range. Recent investigations have shown that this area, where some of the continent's first humans might have passed on their journey through the hemisphere, contains one of the oldest confirmed stories of continuous human use anywhere in the West.[12]

The key to this area's enduring appeal is a unique feature of the westernmost high plains. Although the central plains rise steadily in altitude from east to west, they suddenly dip as they approach the Rocky Mountains. Eighty miles out from the Rockies the land is nearly 6,500 feet above sea level, but at the base of the foothills the altitude is slightly over 5,000 feet. As human living space, this erosional trough offers several advantages. Rivers and creeks flow into it both from the mountains and the plains—quite a commendation in country given to drought. The double drainage supports lush pasture that in turn lures whatever grazers the plains are allowing at the time. Nice stands of timber also grow along the streams, and those groves, plus the lower altitude and the looming hills immediately to the west, provide superb shelter and resources for people and animals during the plains' bitter winters. Temperatures are consistently warmer in winter than on the plains. For these reasons people have always pressed up against the mountains during the coldest months, like pups cuddling their mother.

From the first human habitation to the present, this coincidence of traits has made the foot of the Front Range some of the most appealing terrain in an often demanding region. During the Altithermal it offered a hospitable setting at an apparently difficult time. The most distinctive evidence left by these people is in the mountains—elaborate rock structures used for hunting elk, mountain sheep, deer, and others mammals. Such structures have been used from the Arctic to the Great Basin, but in most regions they disappeared long ago; usually they were made of perishable wood and brush or were dismantled by later inhabitants. High in the Front Range, however, 10,000 feet or more above sea level and well above timberline, builders had to use stone, and few people came later to change the land. The stone construction survived, in some cases for several millennia.

Stone walls, many more than 100 meters long, were built in funnel- or V-shaped alignments, and along them were stone cairns and other small shelters. The wide mouth of each pair of narrowing walls always opened on terrain favored by grazing animals, and typically the narrow end emptied at a saddle formation or at some other site capable of hiding a lot of people. The funnels pointed in the direction taken by prevailing winds. The small dwellings probably were blinds. Herds of game were spooked and driven into the broad maw of these systems. People most likely stood on the cairns spaced along the walls, yelling and gesturing to keep the terrified animals within the tapering stone channel. Funneled downwind, the elk, sheep, deer, and other prey were compressed to a point where hunters sprang on them with spears, darts, and stones. Some of these systems, in use at least by 4175 B.C. and maybe as early as 7400 B.C., were remarkably elaborate. One high in today's Rocky Mountain National Park had three walls, one nearly 160 meters long, and several blinds made from granite and gneiss. Dozens of projectile points and handstones have been found there. A much larger system on nearby Flattop Mountain has 14 stone walls, nearly 850 cairns, and 90 blinds. Sites are littered with projectile points and handstones, and nearby are butchering stations and camping spots.

The builders of these systems apparently lived by a finely choreographed annual cycle. They spent their winters close along the Front Range, protected by mountains from heavy snow and warmed occasionally by chinooks, with plenty of wood and some game close at hand. In early spring they moved in small bands northward into southern Wyoming, then westward over a low pass into North Park, a protected valley full of animals and quartz outcroppings they quarried to make tools. Summer was spent in the high country. They moved gradually southward into Middle Park and neighboring areas. Early each autumn the bands converged to conduct cooperative hunts with the help of the stone game-drive systems. Bighorn sheep, elk, and deer were butchered on the spot and the meat carried to lower camps, where it was dried and smoked during those weeks of shortening days and cooling nights. As autumn snows began to accumulate, the hunters broke again into small bands and drifted down to their protected winter camps at the foot of the mountains.

That rotorlike migration proved extraordinarily enduring. The long swings in climate and shorter fluctuations of drier and wetter years apparently had little influence on what must have been a highly reliable means of providing peoples' basic needs. On this grand circuit hundreds of generations played out their lives within evolving societies. At one point on the counterclockwise round, just outside the present-day tourist town of Estes Park, a tall conical hill of granite apparently became a sacred site of religious rituals and vision quests. Old Man Mountain, as it is known today, was first used at least 3,000 years ago, not long after Moses was on Sinai; as late as the 1840s Arapahoes and Utes still fasted and prayed there in search of the divine.[13]

The weathered stone cairns and shard-littered holy sites are reminders of an ancient and remarkably resilient way of life that emerged with a change in climate 7,000 years ago. As the great bison herds shrank and the possibilities of life on the plains narrowed, native bands responded by developing a cycle of movement that united the seasonal offerings of plains, hills, and high mountain terrain. This arrangement proved flexible and sustaining for more than sixty centuries, from the time when Sumerians were founding Babylon until the eve of the present.

To the east, on the other side of the plains, other peoples apparently found their own answer to the climatic crisis, keeping on the move to find what they needed or withdrawing to the wetter east and venturing periodically onto the drier, more open country. In any case the higher plains between, in western Kansas and eastern Colorado, thinned in human numbers and apparently stayed that way for a very long time.

For 2,000 YEARS before the birth of Christ the plains remained fairly dry, although somewhat wetter than the few millennia before them, and the human record for this period is also sketchy. Then, about the beginning of the Christian era, a dramatic new feature appeared. On the eastern plains, and reaching west to the lower Republican River valley, people began building mounds. Usually they were situated high on bluffs or headlands overlooking a river valley, as if chosen for a commanding view. They ranged from twenty to fifty feet in diameter and from a few inches to six feet in height. Some were solid dirt and some were laced and scrambled with stone. Some were burial places with remains of twenty or more persons.[14]

The significance of these mounds, and the identity of their builders, as usual are open to speculation. They surely were related in some way to the Woodland tradition that had emerged east of the Mississippi about 1500 B.C. As part of this tradition mounds had been built in the Ohio valley and eventually throughout the Mississippi valley and Gulf Coast. Another Woodland characteristic, ceramic production, also appeared in the plains mounds in the form of long, baglike clay pots similar to others found to the east. The plainsmen, like the hunters of the Mississippi valley, by then had acquired bows and arrows; smaller serrated points are found among the spearheads. Woodland peoples were horticulturists, particularly tillers of maize—and there is some evidence of cultivation among these plains moundbuilders.[15]

The most obvious explanation, then, might seem to be an expansion westward of Woodland peoples. On the other hand, the mounds might have been built by groups whose ancestors had been living for centuries in central Kansas and southern Nebraska. They might have borrowed from the lifeways and material culture—and presumably from some of the social traits and religious life as well—of those living in what must have seemed an impressive collection of communities only a short journey to the east. The mounds, that is, might be the most noticeable evidence that longtime plains residents were blending their own lifeways with cultural projections from Woodland villages, with the result a mix of traits unique to the place. Early gardeners, for instance, apparently developed cultigens best suited to where they were. The primary crop to the east was maize, but around these plains mounds other plants better suited to that region, especially marshelder and sunflowers, predominated. Even farther west on the higher plains the more scattered remains of human life suggest nomadic peoples were relying mostly on hunting and gathering—a means of subsistence, that is, similar to those still farther west who moved by the grand circuit along and through the Front Range but who also had their own variations, including annual hunts on traditional sites with the help of stone game runs.

The emerging picture of the period from about 500 B.C. to A.D. 1000, then, is of a spectrum of lifeways. Archaeologists have spread over this time and place a broad term that sounds oxymoronic—the Plains Woodland. As the term implies, plains people were certainly influenced by dramatic changes among Woodland peoples of the Mississippi and Ohio valleys, but their cultural patterns also were well adapted to and reflecting the varied needs and possibilities of their own diverse region. It was a cultural patchwork that suggested dynamic evolution and many influences.

That impression is heightened by intriguing materials found among burial pits. Scattered among the bones, and sometimes wound among them, are thousands of beads, some disk-shaped and made from freshwater mussel shells and others carved into tubes from animal bones and inscribed with graceful scrolls. And more: conch shells and pendants made from marine shells, bits of copper and sheets of mica, belongings that had traveled quite a distance before coming to rest in these Kansas mounds.[16]

Those items were reminders of one of the most remarkable aspects of plains life during these centuries. Long before the mounds were built, this country had been linked to other peoples thousands of miles away through an extraordinary system of trade, part of a vigorous commerce covering most of the United States and well beyond its borders. One southern Nebraska gravesite dates from about 230 B.C. Some of its artifacts are much like those of the Ohio valley. There are also shells that could have come only from the shores of the Gulf of Mexico, others from the upper Atlantic Coast, still others out of the Pacific.[17] The ornaments laid in that grave had moved along a complex nexus of trade that was still an important part of plains life centuries later, when the moundbuilders did their work.

The details of the Plains Woodland trade system are once again a matter of informed guesswork. Some say that priests and chiefs presided over the large Ohio valley villages at the center of the Hopewell culture. These men, whose remains are found in the great Woodland mounds, supposedly oversaw an enormous trade network stretching far into Canada, south to the Gulf, east to the Atlantic and west at least to the Rocky Mountains, a system encompassing many different peoples. At the far-western edge of that system were natives of the mountains and central high plains, perhaps descendants of the transient peoples who had drifted over the region from the time of the great drought, some of them following the great rotor from the mountain base to the Continental Divide.

The people who ranged over the plains and along the rivers flowing from the Front Range probably kept to small groups of a few families. They lived in temporary camps of skin tents, and in colder months they found shelter in such places as a cave at Ash Hollow along the North Platte, later one of the most famous stopping points of white pioneers of the overland trail.[18] In the Rockies and on the plains these nomads gathered items they knew were highly prized in the mound towns in the Missouri, Mississippi, and Ohio valleys—dried bison meat and probably skins, grizzly claws, obsidian, and flint. They swapped these for goods carried hundreds of miles from the east and later unearthed in Kansas mounds, including mica and gorgets of marine shell. Large villages around Kansas City apparently played a key role as a collecting point in this exchange.

If this scenario is close to accurate, the plains mounds marked an economic boundary between the populous centers to the east and the nomadic hunters and traders living on the high plains and in the mountains. The vicinity of Riley and Clay Counties in Kansas, the area around Abilene, Upland, and Elmo would have been a kind of cultural borderland. During the first five centuries of the Christian Era, central Kansas would have been one of the more interesting places in North America to watch the interactions among the continent's peoples and their ways. The first white pioneers would look on these open, rolling grasslands as empty and isolated. But fourteen centuries earlier, and in fact for centuries before that, the central plains sat squarely in the middle of a system of trade reaching from British Columbia to Florida and from New England to Baja California.

THE PLAINS WOODLAND CULTURE prevailed on the central plains for nearly 1,000 years. Then the region witnessed another dramatic change. Once more the climate played a critical role. Around A.D. 700–800 the plains entered into one of the wettest periods of its history. For the next several centuries moist tropical air pressed much farther northward than in the past, and with that the plains became a very different place. Suddenly it was raining as much along the ninety-ninth meridian, in Osborne and Russell Counties, Kansas, as it does today in western Missouri. The prairie moved westward with the rainfall, pushing the shortgrass plains 100 or 200 miles back toward the mountains.

The change in the weather opened the way for an unprecedented development on the central plains.[19] By around A.D. 1000, families were farming along the Republican, Solomon, and Smoky Hill Rivers. Early forms of agriculture had been practiced by Woodland peoples to the east for many centuries, and around A.D. 800 eastern communities began an intense cultivation of maize. Horticulture was much more limited on the central plains, however, and farming had never been possible this far west. Yet in these newly rain-soaked times, farming communities of fifty or seventy-five people each sprang up along the main rivers and their feeder streams.[20]

In this wetter world, manipulated by a new technology, many more people could live than in the past. The result was a long-term land rush. Along virtually every watercourse in the greater Kansas River drainage a little probing today will show evidence from these horticultural settlements; while there are dozens of sites from earlier periods, many hundreds can be found from this era. By A.D. 1200 there were more Native Americans living in west central Kansas and Nebraska than had ever been there before—or have ever lived there since.

Apparently these settlers were newcomers, not descendants of earlier inhabitants. They seem to have moved in from somewhere to the south. They apparently were related, speaking dialects of Caddoan languages. One group concentrated along the lower Smoky Hill River, and another along the middle and lower valley of the Republican River, but farming seems to have been practiced as far west as the high plains of eastern Colorado and the Nebraska panhandle.[21]

These people made their gardens immediately beside the streams, sheltered in low places from the hot, withering winds of late summer. Periodic floods enriched the soil. A single family probably needed about two or three acres to feed itself. They dug in the soft soil of stream banks with sharpened sticks and deer antlers and weeded with hoes fashioned from the shoulder blades of bison. They planted variations of the famous "three sisters" cultivated by native peoples across North America—maize, beans, and squash—as well as marshelder, or sumpweed, and sunflowers. They gathered from a range of wild plants, not only to supplement their meals but also for medicines, decorations, and a variety of domestic needs.

They hunted an array of larger and smaller game. Excavations into river hamlets have uncovered the remains of three dozen species of mammals, including bison, deer, antelopes, bears, woodchucks, cougers, pocket gophers, kangaroo rats, voles, jackrabbits, and skunks. There are also bones of bullheads and channel catfish and the shells of snapping turtles.[22] Besides hunting locally, the farmers ranged westward to draw from wildlife on the higher plains that rolled to the Rockies. Land between the settlements and the mountains became a vast hunting ground used both by older nomadic groups and by the farmers, who probably organized large-scale annual or semi-annual expeditions among the herds of bison and other grazers.

The gardeners were the first high plainsmen ever to stay put. In the preceding millennia, hundreds of generations had kept on the move, living in temporary or seasonal camps. They had traveled light and left little behind. The farmers who took up long-term residence in streamside communities accumulated more and left behind the most valuable resource for future archaeologists—garbage. Consequently more is known about these plains peoples than about any others before the arrival of Europeans.

They lived in squarish houses, most about 700 square feet in size. Each was dug and bermed slightly into the ground with walls made of standing logs sealed and plastered with mud. Four posts held up the roof. A firepit for cooking and warmth was in the middle of the floor. In trash heaps were chipped stone knives and choppers, round-shouldered pots, bone fishhooks, and pendants made from animal teeth. One site held a cup or bowl crudely shaped from the top of a human skull.[23]

Mixed in were conch-shell amulets and other items obviously traded from far to the east and south. Like the Plains Woodland people before them, these farmers were tied into a network of exchange reaching all the way to the Atlantic. Goods moved back and forth through settlements of the Mississippian culture that flourished during these centuries in the Mississippi and Ohio valleys and the Gulf coastal region. Their trade may have been funneled through the great city of Cahokia about 500 miles due east, just outside present-day St. Louis. Cahokia was far and away the continent's largest urban center. As many as 25,000 persons lived there in the thirteenth century, more than could be found in New York City at the time of the American Revolution.

If the communities were even remotely like those of more recent Native American farmers, family labor probably was divided by sex. Women tended the gardens, and perhaps controlled the produce, as well as making the meals and overseeing domestic chores. They may also have had authority over an important family asset—the dogs that sniffed around the camps in great numbers. Men hunted. Everyone must have developed an intricate and detailed knowledge of their homeland and its many parts. Children probably were left to play mostly on their own during their early years, then gradually eased into a practical education in the scores of skills and tasks necessary for collective survival. Whatever the day-by-day arrangements of tasks were, this agrarian society worked well enough. It sustained thousands of people in a fairly affluent and seemingly peaceful way of life for close to 400 years.

A few scholars have tried to penetrate deeper into the lives of these plains peoples, to enter their spiritual world with the help of material remains. On a bluff overlooking the confluence of the Republican and Smoky Hill Rivers, near Junction City, Kansas, archaeologists have excavated a lodge.[24] It was built around 1300, and there is reason to believe it was home to a Native American priest. The lodge sits precisely on an east-to-west axis. Its four support poles are positioned at the semicardinal points of the compass (northwest, northeast, southeast, southwest), directions that descendants of these farmers considered sacred. The structure's orientation is intriguing. One (and only one) morning each year—at the spring equinox—the rising sun would have shone through the doorway and cast its light to the rear of the lodge at a spot that apparently was an altar. A storage pit next to this spot contained the remains of an eagle, a bluejay, a woodpecker, and a long-eared owl, birds that later Indians of this tradition believed were protectors, spiritual guides, and messengers to divine powers in the heavens.

Also in this pit were bones and feathers of four bobwhite quail. According to one speculation, these people may have looked on quail as symbols of their own collective lives, perhaps as their closest kin. Quail nested in the grass in homes closely resembling the farmers' earthlodges dug partly into the ground. The quails' annual cycle ran parallel to what was probably the people's pattern of springtime coalescence, when men stayed close to help prepare the fields, and dispersal in the fall, when men left to hunt and women stayed home. The distinctive scalplock and face decoration of Pawnee men, descendants of these people, closely resembled the features of an aroused male bobwhite, with its upright crest and dark band across the eyes. And quail, as later white pioneers often commented, have plenty of humanlike qualities. They band together in coveys, with chicks following behind the mother while both parents watch over their brood and seem to instruct their young in the intricacies of being bobwhite. A covey of quail must have had a familiar look to a people well nested on the central plains.

Did these farmers think of themsevles as the Quail People? Growing corn and sunflowers on the riverside, did they look on the plains as something like the center of the earth, the locus of a generous life? No one can say. But they did devise a remarkably successful accommodation with a demanding land. These plains farmers maintained a productive, largely self-supportive way of life for twice as long as the history of the American Republic.

But ultimately it was not enough. During the thirteenth century the climate swung back into another of its dramatic changes. Tree-ring analysis from western Nebraska shows that of the ninety-seven years following A.D. 1220, sixty-three were years of drought. One dry spell lasted thirty-eight years. Several other severe droughts hit the region over the next two centuries. As the wet period that had drawn the farmers westward ended, the shortgrasses pushed the prairie back toward the east. The gardeners of western Kansas and Nebraska retreated with it.

Rather than staying on the plains and adapting to a changing environment, the horticulturalists clung to the environment they knew and followed it eastward. Just who went where over the next two-and-a-half centuries is not clear. The best guess is that the people who had farmed along the upper Republican River settled along the Loup River in southeastern Nebraska. Their descendants were the Skidi Pawnees, met by some of the earliest European arrivals in the seventeenth century. Those to the south of the first group, in the basins of the Smoky Hill and the Solomon Rivers, ended up along the Loup and lower Platte Rivers. They were the South Band Pawnees. Distant Caddoan-speaking relatives of these two groups moved up the Missouri to a point near the Nebraska–South Dakota boundary. They became the Arikaras.

During the few hundred years after dry weather returned, new groups emigrated to the region where the gardeners had been. More Caddoans came from the south to raise what food they could along the middle Arkansas, and waves of others came later out of the Rockies to take the more arid high plains. All began their own variations of ancient patterns and scratched their marks into the long history of the place.

WHITE PIONEERS who moved onto the plains east to west believed they were leaving the old country for the new. They had it exactly backward. Before the first human habitation on the eastern seaboard—and

5,000 years before the first Sumerian writing and 7,000 before the Old Kingdom was established in Egypt—plainsmen had fashioned flourishing economies. During the millennia that followed, diverse cultures moved and adapted
within broad turns of climate. Their only point in common was not any particular way of living but their approach to finding one. Different peoples lived
with shifting resources—sometimes abundant, often scarce—that were rarely
close at hand. The one essential was knowing the land very well—its wondrous diversity and its unforgiving limits. Beyond that, the keys were finding
those places that offered what was needed most, making the right connections and linking disparate elements within a huge area, then reaching out
much farther to trade for more. The region's deep history was a continuing,
dazzling improvisation on those few themes.

Then, in the mid-sixteenth century, the plains and Rockies suddenly felt
the effects of forces that were, in their own way, as relentless and powerful
as the weather. In 1541 a column of horsemen under the command of Francisco Vasquez de Coronado rode out of the south, across the Arkansas River,
and onto the plains beyond. Like so many who would follow them, these
soldier-explorers were looking for gold.

3

FRONTIERS AND VISIONS

The changes brought by Europeans were so great that they usually are called the start of history itself, the breaking of a slumbering spell. They were not that, but the consequences of that first contact came so fast and ran so deep that they made for a material and imaginative revolution.

Frontiers eventually unsettled power in its usual historical meaning—the ordering of people into stronger and weaker, winners and losers, rulers and subjects. Almost instantly, however, the European intrusion began to break down and reform power in its more fundamental arrangements. Native peoples, suddenly exposed to new practices and ideas, imagined new ways of meeting old demands. With a single imported life-form Indians broadened enormously their embrace of the energy around them, then used it to shape and manipulate their world. The plains—as a system of users and used and as perceived living space—became a different place.

Spanish envoys came, looked around, left, and stayed away for decades. By simply doing that, and by living just beyond the plains rim, they scrambled relations among plains peoples, their environments, and most of all their understanding of the possible.

WHEN FRANCISCO VASQUEZ DE CORONADO left Tiguex Pueblo on the Rio Grande he led his command south and east, onto the Texas staked plains, and then north across the Texas and Oklahoma panhandles and into Kansas. Coronado hoped to find cities with storehouses bulging with gold and gems and a land densely populated with future converts and workers. He was looking for the Aztecs of Kansas. Instead he found Quivira, a few villages of conical grass huts in present-day Rice and McPherson Counties in Kansas. Several hundred Indians lived there, "a very brutish people," according to an expedition member, "without any decency whatever in their home nor in anything." Besides growing some corn, melons, and beans, they showed little civilized behavior. They kept no chickens and owned no ovens.[1]

The country around these rude villages intimidated and repelled the Spanish. Its numbing sameness and deceptive blend of flatness and roll left them disoriented. On the staked plains a conscript wandered away from a hunting party and within moments was lost. Friends waved flares of dried grass while horsemen searched for hours, blowing trumpets as they rode in widening circles, but he was never found. (In a similar incident more than three centuries later a private in Sumner's command lost his way near the Pawnee Fork of the Arkansas. Although found a week later, he was stark mad and ignored his rescuers while frantically stuffing grasshoppers into his mouth.)[2] As they marched over the plains soldiers raised piles of bones and bison dung as points of reckoning but still were bewildered. They worried too about the scarcity of wood and above all about the lack of water. The whole region seemed a swallowing deprivation. Long-term occupancy was incomprehensible.

Incredibly, however, people lived there. Small bands of hunters drifted over the open country with packs of rangy dogs. The Querechos, as Coronado called them, lived in camps of smallish conical tents easily pitched and stricken. The Spanish found them interesting, as odd wrinkles of the human condition. They were skilled archers who hunted on foot among the herds of bison (called cattle by the conquistadors) and other ungulates. They somehow lived without farming; they painted their bodies; they chipped flint with their teeth. But they scarcely registered as possible imperial subjects. They were gentle and kind but had nothing apparent to offer, and in their habits and level of living they seemed barely above the animals they ate.[3]

The expedition shattered both Coronado's health and the Spanish hopes for a new gilded empire. It was more than forty years before the next foray into the area, and contact with the central plains and its inhabitants remained sporadic until well into the eighteenth century. Parties led by Bonilla and Humana (1586), Saldivar and Onate (1599 and 1601), Archuleta (1664), Ulibarri (1706), Hurtado (1714), and Valverde and Villasur (1719 and 1720) pursued a range of motives. Onate, a conquistador's son and the husband of Cortez's granddaughter and Montezuma's great-granddaughter, clung to the old dream of cities of gold. Once that vision dimmed, the region north and east of the Rio Grande settlements took on an essentially negative meaning. The Spanish hoped its dangers would make it an effective barrier against imperial rivals, especially the ambitious French.

Early accounts elaborated on Coronado's first impressions. Saldivar described nomadic bands that traveled with snarling dogs harnessed to travois. In camp the dog-nomads lived in red and white tents "built as skillfully as those of Italy." Onate met Indians who neither sowed nor reaped but followed "wild cattle" and lived in hide dwellings, and beyond them were the Quiviras with their crude villages and gardens of gourds and maize. Ulibari and those after him found other settlements west of Quivira. Directly east of the Rio Grande Pueblos, in the Texas panhandle and west central Oklahoma, were more villages and other itinerant hunters.[4]

The plains, as imagined inside Spanish heads, quickly devolved, then stayed that way for two centuries. When they looked at the land, the Spanish saw some trouble, but mostly they saw nothing at all. Destinations were few and disappointing; movement through empty distance was at best fruitless and at worst fatal. The people appeared strange and exotic, potentially dangerous and always primitive. This country, in short, lacked almost everything needed to turn neutral space into a human place. It was not imbued with purpose, not perceived through unbloomed potential. There was no story to give it character. It was not enlivened by any vision of what it had been and what it might become. The Spanish descriptions were the earliest expressions of a doggedly persistent image of the plains at the instant of European contact—a static world on the edge of history.

The Spanish were right in one sense. As they drew close to the plains, they were approaching a kind of fringe. But the edge they found was the rim of their own imagination. Leaving the Pueblo settlements and the Rio Grande, they crossed the boundary between an area they could conceive of in terms of human purpose and development, a place with a past that would grow into a future, and they entered a space they experienced as perceptually flat and historically stunted.

The same events, however, look different when seen from the plains outward. This continental center had an ancient history of dynamic adaptation. Its current residents lived as did people anywhere else, by cobbling together resources into a system of intricate use. They were playing out the most recent variations of old patterns evolved through centuries of change. As a place, the plains existed in their heads, woven together through memory and perceived design, and when the Spanish suddenly appeared, queer people astride bizarre creatures, plains natives almost instantly began to reimagine their country into something else again. The Spanish may have pictured themselves as moving into the land of the historically fixed, but in fact they set loose potent changes into the continent's longest story.

Coronado's misapprehension is not so surprising. The country he approached was some of the continent's most deceptive. Like most grasslands, the plains sat between deserts and woodlands, in this case the Chihuahua and Sonora deserts to the southwest and the prairies and forests of the Missouri and Mississippi valleys to the east. They shared traits of both. The average rainfall fell between the two: about twelve inches on the western high plains to twenty inches per year on the eastern fringe. As in deserts, plants had adapted with dense, shallow root systems that took advantage of the scantiest sprinkling, but the range and profusion of plants were far greater than in the arid southwest. Grasses were extraordinarily abundant on much of the western plains, and to the east was a dazzling array of plant life. Most of the profusion was knee-high or lower, however, because relative aridity, and just as important the frequent grass fires, confined the most obvious trait of a woodland, its trees, almost entirely to the streamsides.

Those creeks and rivers, especially on the western plains, were an environment starkly different from the highlands that drained into them. Their shallow water table, protective shoulders, and annual flooding permitted plant life—shrubs, forbs, trees (mostly cotttonwoods but sometimes hardwoods), mid- and tallgrasses—characteristic of the low plains and prairies. If the plains are pictured, moving west to east, as a spectrum from semidesert to quasi woodland, the western streams allowed life from the second to flourish surrounded by terrain much closer to the first. High plains river bottoms were essentially veins of eastern landscape intruding far into the west. They offered a fine opportunity for many life-forms. Moving between highlands and rivers, people and animals could telescope a few hundred miles into twenty or thirty, ecologically speaking, and so they could combine the advantages of two very different sets of resources.

The plains region was a coy deceiver. Newcomers invariably missed two facts of life in particular. The plains, first, offered much more than they seemed to. Openness was easily mistaken for emptiness; in fact, this country was exceptionally rich in resources. After spending some time there, outsiders sometimes came to sense the plains' potential, but that left them open to a second misunderstanding. To use those resources people had to live within wildly undependable conditions. The supply of some vitals might swing around erratically—crazily—within any of the usual units of human time. A normal day could go from cold to hot and dust to deluge; on an extreme, a day's temperature could rise or fall by 50°, 80°, even 100° Fahrenheit. A year typically was spread over 100°; one has been recorded at 180°. During a year rainfall normally rises from an inch or less per month to seven or eight, but some months have received twenty inches (and some days eight or nine); other years get less than four inches, with stretches of eight or ten months getting hardly a drop. Droughts and wet periods can last months, years, decades, or centuries. The plains are a mix of desert and woodland, that is, in a double sense. From the loftiest God's-eye overview, the region blends the traits of desert and forest, with conditions sliding steadily and predictably from one to the other, traveling west to east. Living on the ground, however, one need not move far to feel the range of conditions. Standing in one spot, a plainsman will most likely find a bit of Sahara and of Illinois by waiting long enough. Sometimes it takes only a day.

The people Coronado met had adapted splendidly to the country's peculiarities and had learned to make the best of what was there. The villagers of Quivira were Wichitas, a Caddoan-speaking people related to the Pawnees and to other groups in the region. As farmers they lived a variation of one of the two basic patterns on the central plains, this one derived from the especially wet centuries from about A.D. 800 to 1200. Horticultural villages of square bermed houses and well-tilled fields had appeared in much of western Kansas and eastern Colorado during those years. These gardeners had moved east when the rains slackened after A.D. 1200; they probably became the Pawnees and Arikaras. New migrants meanwhile arrived from the south to settle in the Arkansas basin eastward from the river's great bend.[5]

Some of these were the Wichitas, or Quiviras. The villagers who greeted Coronado were transitional peoples, geographically and economically. They were the westernmost representatives of the Caddoan horticulturalists. Other settlements of related Wichitas were scattered along lower tributaries of the

Arkansas River.[6] Their Caddoan cousins, the Pawnees, lived in large villages of distinctive dirt-walled lodges on the lower Republican, lower Platte, and Loup Rivers in northeast Kansas and southeast Nebraska. These peoples farmed by techniques grown from centuries of trial and error. At Quivira, outside the clusterings of beehive-shaped huts, women bent over gardens of maize, beans, sunflowers, and pumpkins, working the soil with deer antlers and chopping weeds with hoes made from bison scapulas. Strains of maize and other plants had been carefully chosen and subtly manipulated, so particular types changed and shaded from one set of villages to another, each one matching the peculiars of its home.

Villages always were built along watercourses. Besides their good soil enriched by silting floods, stream bottoms offered some timber for fuel and the low-lying terrain shielded the river dwellers from the bitterest winter blasts and their crops from the desiccating summer winds. Streams became progressively more valuable the farther west the gardeners lived. In the drier, more exposed land, like that of Quivira, farmers were tied closely and absolutely to the vital veins of water running through the open country. They were prisoners to rivers.

Gardening was never enough, however. Farmers relied to some extent on the second basic pattern of plains life—hunting. Besides their day-to-day searches for game, they ranged far to the west onto the shortgrass plains to gather meat and hides of elk, deer, and above all bison. Entire villages sometimes packed up and filed away into the great pasture during these forays, especially in the early fall, as all hands worked to harvest as many animals as they could before winter set in. The expeditions were essential to all farmers, but the mix of gardening and hunting ranged along a spectrum between the lusher prairies to the east and the drier plains to the west. The Quivirans, pushing the limits of farming along the great bend of the Arkansas, leaned toward crops needing the least rainfall and hunted more than their eastern relatives among the prolific grazers on the nearby pasturelands.

When Coronado rode with his column into Quivira, then, his perception may have been of stunted possibilities and the lack of seizable wealth, but in truth he was looking at people as they straddled two worlds and blended two traditions. His initial encounter, on July 2, 1541, was with a party of Quivirans hunting bison along the Arkansas close to the present town of Larned, Kansas; four days downstream, at a point roughly aligned with the westernmost reach of the earliest plains horticulturalists, Coronado entered the villages of maize growers.[7] Europe's first human touch on the central plains happened by chance along the seam between the country's two basic meanings, among people living a distillation of fifteen centuries' experience.

The second basic pattern, that of hunting, dominated the plains west of Quivira. This was home to the seminomadic Querechos, whom Coronado first met on the Texas staked plains and in the arid country below the Arkansas. The Querechos were Apaches. Like Wichitas, the term Apaches describes people related by language, Athapascan in this case, but living scattered over a large region. Some were as far north as central Nebraska along the Dismal River, some well to the south along New Mexico's Pecos River. Others ranged between, in far northeastern New Mexico and the Texas panhandle, along the Front Range, and in western Kansas and eastern Colorado. The Apaches were the most recent arrivals on the central plains, having migrated from the west and north sometime during the century before Coronado, perhaps only a generation earlier.[8]

These newest plainsmen, however, lived by the oldest means. "These Indians subsist . . . entirely on cattle [bison], for they neither plant nor harvest maize," Coronado's chronicler wrote.[9] He exaggerated; the Dismal River Apaches certainly did some gardening, and probably those along the Front Range and in northeastern New Mexico.[10] Besides bison, hunters preyed on huge numbers of deer, elk, and pronghorns. The streams, with their clusters of willows and thick growth of wild berries, were home to many thousands of grizzly bears. The weight of the hunters' work, however, was with the pursuit of plains bison. Apaches were the functional descendants of the earliest inhabitants of the central plains, the master predators of the Clovis period, and this hunting tradition, like farming, had evolved with both the slow rolls of climate and the expertise of its people. Stalking afoot, the Querechos used old methods of the surround and, where terrain allowed, the jump. They relied especially on exceptional skill with bows and arrows.

Bison could be found year-round, but hunting was best between June and September when they massed on the highlands for courtship and rut. After skinning, the flesh was cut into long strips and sun-dried, then some of it pounded and ground into a kind of pemmican that was easily carried and that swelled into a meal when tossed into a pot of heated water. The Spanish were quick to see the animals' many uses:

> With the skins [the Indians] build their houses; with the skins they clothe and shoe themselves; from the skins they make ropes and also obtain wool. From the sinews they make thread, with which they sew their clothing and likewise their tents. From the bones they shape awls, and the dung they use for firewood, since

there is no fuel in all that land. The bladders serve as jugs and drinking vessels. They sustain themselves on the flesh of the animals, eating it slightly roasted . . . and sometimes uncooked. Taking it in their teeth, they pull with one hand; with the other they hold a large flint knife and cut off mouthfuls, swallowing it half chewed, like birds. They eat raw fat, without warming it.[11]

The hunters' challenge was not so much in finding prey but in moving around the high plains and living on the animals' terms. Farmers might be confined to the streams, but at least their nourishment stood still. And plants grew best where people did well, too. Hunters had to fashion their living in the great spaces away from dependable rivers. The Spanish despaired at this country that seemed to threaten so much and offer so little. Even so they missed some of the most intimidating parts. Northwest of Quivira and east of the Rockies, in far western Kansas and eastern Colorado, the plains rose to 6,000 feet above sea level. This was the roof of the central plains, and no great rivers ran through the rolling swells of land, nearly treeless and covered with shortgrasses. Outlanders stayed away almost entirely from this region. Much of it was unseen by non-Indians until well into the nineteenth century.

Apaches were there, however. Their lifeways were an adaptive show of methods and knowledge with roots thousands of years deep. Water was available for those who knew where to look. Tributaries of the Platte and Arkansas drained the area's northern and southern edges, and another system, composed of the Smoky Hill, Republican, and Saline Rivers, rose about 100 miles east of the Rockies and converged to form the Kansas River. Small feeder creeks ran intermittently, especially during the spring and summer when nearly three-fourths of the year's rain normally fell.[12]

Water flowed from the ground in hundreds of springs and seeps. High plains soil was made of sand and loose gravels. Rainwater and snowmelt sank easily through it but stopped and collected at a lower level of impenetrable clay and shale. The result was an enormous underground reservoir, the Ogallala aquifer. Where the upper soil was thinnest, usually in the broad drainages of stream systems, this subterranean lake spilled out on the surface, collecting in pools and creating small flows unnoticeable until almost underfoot. Across much of the region springs were no more than twenty-five miles apart on the average; often they were only ten or fifteen miles from one another.

The highest ground had few springs, but these benchlands were flecked by thousands of depressions, some only a foot or so deep and less than ten yards around, some thirty feet in depth and more than a mile in diameter. A basin in far western Kansas covered nineteen square miles and was six miles across at its widest point. The largest indentations were sink holes formed when the surface collapsed into a leached-out cavity. The smaller ones were buffalo wallows. These had begun as salt or alkali licks or shallow collections of rainwater. Bison and other grazers were drawn to these spots. The subtle depressions deepened as the wind blew away soil loosened by the animals' hooves, and bison further crushed and carried away surface dirt by rolling and wallowing in the shallow water holes to rub off their hair in summer, to cool their bodies, and to coat themselves with mud against biting insects. Repeated thousands of times, this sequence provided a system of water collection in terrain otherwise without drinking places.[13] Water birds found the vast dimpling of wallows ideal for resting on their long flights, so the high plains became one of the earth's great migratory routes. Twice a year waterfowl in uncountable millions clouded huge portions of the high ground, offering food that hunters could wash down with the ponds' muddy water.

Some highlands, especially north of the middle Arkansas, lacked even these water sources, but there, and elsewhere when droughts left the high plains waterless, Indians had a short-term solution—the bison. Those animals were great sacks of fluid on the hoof. Nomads would slit the throat of a freshly killed cow or bull and drink the blood, pouring some also into the emptied large intestine for carrying around the neck. Finally, before renewing their march, they would pull out the bison's stomach, open it, press dry the sop of digesting grass and drink the water and juices.[14]

For fuel they used the dried dung of bison—it burned quickly but there was plenty of it—and what wood they could find in pockets of trees. Although dominated by shortgrasses, the highlands supported an immensely varied flora whose leaves, roots, and stems could nourish and heal, and like the river-dwelling gardeners, the hunting bands diversified their diet through an intricate knowledge of the uses and reliable location of dozens of types of wild plants.

The Querechos' greatest challenge came with winter. After October the rains slowed nearly to nothing and the bison dispersed as small groups into lowlands along streams. Sudden storms made the high, open country unlivable. High plainsmen had to find sanctuary somewhere. Some may have withdrawn to permanent villages on the region's edge. Many may have broken into small groups and camped along the timbered watercourses, in effect moving east by occupying low plains environments that intruded westward into the river basins. Almost certainly some stayed along the face of the Rockies, the sheltering terrain where the first plainsmen found sanctuary 12,000 years earlier. It was an appropriate response in this oldest American homeland.

The high plains, in short, were much more hospitable than outlanders thought. Querechos ranged over the country with reasonable confidence; they made opportunistic connections among useful but scattered elements. There were rigid rules, to be sure. For part of the year they had to be free to move, and for part they needed sure access to safe, confining havens. Within those limits they found room to maneuver and to give their own twists to some of the continent's oldest patterns of survival.

As with the farmers, however, their best was not enough. If river gardeners needed meat from the hunt, hunters had to have something from the soil. Their diet was especially starved of carbohydrates, and except for some gathered from wild plants, the most concentrated source was America's earliest cultivated plant, maize. Limited gardening was possible in parts of Apacheria, and the nomads could trade with and raid the villages from Quivira eastward, but the richest supply of corn and other crops was elsewhere. The Pueblo villages on the upper Rio Grande and Pecos Rivers produced substantial harvests in good years. These villagers had their own problem, a shortage of something equally indispensable for humans—proteins. They produced some in their gardens, in several types of beans, but they ran chronically short of the most concentrated source, animal flesh. Their healthy, irrigated fields supported dense populations that consistently overhunted the game in their neighborhoods. But help was nearby. On the plains huge chunks of proteins were running around in colossal numbers, grazing and reproducing, waiting to be taken in.[15]

The plains grasslands and the Pueblo villages can be pictured as deep reservoirs of two vital, complementary life elements—proteins and carbohydrates, bison and corn. It was a perfect fit that brought a vigorous trade between the regions. Here was yet another variation on an ancient theme. For more than 2,000 years goods had flowed in and out of the central plains along routes that eventually connected the Gulf of Cortez, the north Atlantic Coast, Florida, and Mexico. The oldest axis was the well-worn corridor running north and south off the high plains down the Rockies' face into New Mexico. That route still fed people who rigged together the country's needs and offerings.

The Apache caravans must have been an arresting sight. Men and women hefted dried meat and hides to their shoulders and wrestled fifty-pound packs onto their largest dogs. Other animals were harnessed to travois. Teams of dogs staggered forward with their loads of jerky and hams, howling from the oozing sores rubbed into their backs. Weeks later caravans returned loaded with corn, other garden foods, and crucial items they could not make for themselves, especially pots and other ceramics. When relations turned balky, plainsmen presumably raided villagers for what they needed.[16] Wichitas had their own arrangements. From their place on the cusp between hunting and farming lands, they exchanged their relative abundance of meat for surpluses from the larger gardens in the rainier east.

Some goods went farther afield. Hundreds of miles to the southeast, on the lower Arkansas and Mississippi Rivers, other dense concentrations of farmers lived around fortified towns that held up to 20,000 persons. They had the same advantages and the same crying needs as the Pueblos, and they reached for the same solution. Villages in eastern Oklahoma became transition points of a trade where meat and corn were funneled back and forth between the plains and the lush drainage of the Mississippi.[17] These trading entrepots featured mounds reminiscent of the Plains Woodland era. Later probing would yield magnificent "prestige goods" from the east—copper headdresses in the shape of falcons and long-nosed gods, cloaks intricately embroidered with bird feathers, and splendid pipes of red stone quarried in Alabama and carved into birdmen, sinuous dancers, and a warrior holding his victim by the neck as he smashes his face with a club.

The world Coronado entered was far wider, more tangled and confounded than he suspected. It had varied parts that people meshed together and connected to places far away, even to the swamps and palisaded towns that his archrival, Hernando de Soto, was trying to plunder at the hour Coronado crossed the Arkansas and rode into Quivira. His blindness and irritation were understandable. Naked men and women drinking animal blood and living in dusty, chickenless villages are easy to underestimate. And it's always disappointing to ask for gold and be handed melons.

But the central plains were not an empty space without a story, and Querechos and Quiviras were not fringe dwellers and cultural simpletons. In their heads the region was an enormously complex map of mixed terrain, diverse resources, and changing options. They lived by finely fashioned strategies that reached widely across space and drew deeply from the past. They accepted three unbendable requirements. They had to be able to move easily over great distances. They had to control a few vital places, the river sites of the farmers and the hunters' winter sanctuaries. And they had to reach out through trade for what was not found at home. Within those rules they struck a shrewd balance. They understood how power is found by squeezing the most from within enduring, unchangeable limits.

Then those possibilities suddenly expanded. In a final blindness, Coronado took an unwitting role in one of America's oldest narratives. He thought he was seeing people beyond change, but in fact he stepped into an ancient human sequence and pushed it vigorously onto a new course.

THE FIRST EFFECTS came slowly during the next 200 years of limited contact. Once the Spanish were firmly established in New Mexico, some discontented Pueblos fled up the old routes to the plains and took up residence among the Apaches. They brought new skills that Querechos used to widen the options of high plains life. With techniques borrowed from the Pueblos, Apaches could garden with greater confidence; they could shift along the spectrum of plains subsistence from the nomadic toward the horticultural. Those closest to the new influence changed the most. By the early eighteenth century the Querechos near modern Cimarron, New Mexico, were tilling irrigated fields and living in flat-topped adobe houses.

Most striking was a somewhat mysterious settlement in far western Kansas, El Cuartelejo.[18] The setting was a geographic anomaly, a protected valley fed by generous springs. It was a kind of island, not of land amid water but of water surrounded by the typically semiarid high plains terrain. By the late seventeenth century the valley was the site of a fully settled village with adobe dwellings of obvious Pueblo influence. With the Pueblo revolt of 1680 and the turmoil that followed, El Cuartelejo took in a fair number of New Mexican exiles. Their position there was a mix of refugee, slave, and instructor, and the cross-fertilization of cultures continued. Juan de Ulibarri visited there in 1706 to retrieve Pueblos who had fled earlier and was greeted by crowds of friendly Apaches who "brought us much buffalo meat, roasting ears of Indian corn, tamales, plums, and other things to eat."[19] El Cuartelejo maintained an ambiguous relationship with New Mexico. For decades it offered refuge for Pueblos restive under Spanish rule as well as an amicable resting place for the Spanish on their forays toward the northeastern rim. In a broader context it spoke of the Apaches' adaptive skills, the vital connections between the central plains and the Rio Grande valley, and the ongoing change brought by the Spanish.

This earliest frontier also aggravated old conflicts. Raiding and warfare almost surely had been part of plains life from the start. The basic division at Coronado's arrival was between the mostly nomadic Apaches on the western high plains and the more settled Wichitas and Pawnees to the east. Apaches needed maize, beans, and other crops found in the river gardens of their enemies; the farmers depended on bison taken in annual expeditions into the Querechos' domain. Both sides had another reason to fight—slaves. Apaches relied on human captives as a valuable commodity to supplement their trade in bison meat and skins. On their pilgrimages to New Mexico they carried large numbers of people taken in raids against eastern villages. Coronado's guide, the man who fed him gilded tales of Quivira, was a slave in Tiguex Pueblo known as the Turk (because he looked like one). He apparently was a Pawnee who tried to lie his way back home. The Pueblos were a hungry market for slaves like the Turk because they needed vassals to work their fields; so did the Wichitas and Pawnees, who took workers from among the same Querechos who raided their villages for human goods to sell into New Mexican bondage.

With the coming of the Spanish the demand for slaves increased considerably, and during the seventeenth and eighteenth century thousands were brought in from the plains and the Rocky Mountains. Apaches responded with intensified raiding against the eastern villagers. By the early 1700s the Pawnees and Wichitas in turn were being encouraged westward by a second European frontier, French traders and emissaries reaching into the region for barter and native allies. The Spanish, always alert to a challenge, felt northward for trouble. In 1720 Don Pedro de Villasur led a column of forty-two experienced soldiers, three settlers, sixty Indian allies, and a priest onto the central plains to reassert the Spanish dominance. It was a disaster. Villasur found a large village of Pawnees and Otoes near the junction of the North and South Plattes. After some diplomatic groping by both sides, the Pawnees and Otoes, apparently bouyed by recent support from the French, swarmed the Spanish camp one morning and killed all but a dozen men, who stumbled back to El Cuartelejo and then to Santa Fe.[20] European frontiers were unsettling the balance of plains power and shifting the boundary between the Apache and the Pawnee-Wichita spheres. Encouraged by the French, the Pawnees pushed hard to the west, expanding their reach into the herds of bison. In 1719, by one account, they were dominant all the way to the South Platte (Rio Jesus Maria).

By then the pace of change was quickening. In the year of Villasur's disaster Etienne de Veniard, Sieur de Bourgmont led a French delegation up the Missouri and west into Kansas. He visited several tribes close to the Missouri and went as far as some Wichita towns in central Kansas, not too distant from the point reached by Coronado from the south 180 years earlier.[21] After presenting gifts and promising future support, Bourgmont returned eastward and invited three tribes to send leading men with him to France, on "the other side of the sun." Nine men and a woman accepted. It was a fantastic odyssey. The plainsmen went first to New Orleans, then across the Atlantic to France. One died on the way and five stayed on the coast while three men and the woman took a coach to Paris. They were wooed and toasted by the fifteen-year-old Louis XV and his court at the Chateau de Fontainebleau and were cheered at the Paris opera. At the royal woods they stripped to breachclouts and took up bows and arrows to demonstrate their hunting skills, bagging large numbers of the king's peacocks. The delegation was escorted home to Kansas after their two-year tour in what must have seemed another dimension.[22]

When Indian men could pass their hours recalling the sensual details of Parisian evenings—the women at court, they said, smelled like alligators— the plains were becoming quite a different place. But the changes since Coronado were feeble compared to what was about to happen. The children of the Indians who toured France would see their homeland swept by furious forces unimaginable a few decades earlier. Their grandchildren would live in a world transformed.

The years between 1700 to 1850 might be called the unsettling of mid-America. During those years the central plains and neighboring regions experienced transformations more rapid and sweeping than any since the arrival of the first humans. These tumultuous events were set in motion by the arrival of three frontiers. The first was the Spanish intrusion begun by Coronado in 1541. It pushed from southwest to northeast, out of New Mexico into Kansas and eastern Colorado. The second came from the opposite direction, from east and northeast to southwest. First the French and after 1763 the British reached onto the plains from connections in the middle and upper Missouri valley.

The third frontier, the one that usually dominates regional histories, pressed more directly east to west. It began well after the others. Born with the United States, it spilled over the Appalachians in the 1780s and rolled into the Ohio River valley and the Gulf coastal south. Although it started late,

its momentum was by far the greatest. It carried tens of thousands of restless, aggressive farming families. These pioneers (a word derived appropriately from the Old French term for foot soldiers) brought new technologies
that transformed the land and undermined native economies. They repro-
duced like brewer's yeast. Their influence rolled ahead of them as they displaced indigenous societies and set in motion complex patterns of migration
and flight. By 1800 this arc of disruption had reached the Missouri valley
and was edging onto the plains.

If these three frontiers are imagined as arrows thrusting into the continent's interior, their points came together in Kansas, Nebraska, and eastern
Colorado. For a century and a half after 1700 the central plains was a focal
point of forces spanning more than 100 meridians. This country, the home
of some of the oldest continuing human history in the Western Hemisphere,
felt a new storm of change.

One of the most powerful agents of change was also the grimmest—disease. Most contact diseases evolved in the Eastern Hemisphere during the
past 5,000 to 10,000 years. Indians had none of the immunities that Europeans had developed over time, and the sudden arrival of these scourges had
a dreadful impact. Tribes of the plains and Missouri valley were caught in a
crossfire of epidemics. Smallpox seeped in from each source of Euro-American
contact. This, the most contagious human disease known, ravaged the region from the northern plains to the Red River in the late 1770s. It came
again in 1801 to the Red River, apparently brought by Pawnees returning
from a raid into New Mexico. Fifteen years later as many as 4,000 persons
died in another ravaging on the southern plains. Measles and cholera brought
their own devastations, and malaria, venereal diseases, and other endemic
afflictions chewed away at populations. Like the invading pioneers, diseases
unsettled relations among tribes. An epidemic might hit one group and spare
its neighbor, might encourage a tribe to migrate or cause two or more related
groups to coalesce into one. Microbial expansion affected native politics and
diplomacy.[23]

A second transforming force was trade. Europeans brought hundreds of
new articles, from fishhooks to waistcoats, that effected extraordinary changes
among plains peoples. Many items had been manufactured in distant shops
and forges. Others were organic—new plants, foodstuffs, and especially animals that Europeans had domesticated and used for thousands of years.

Indian peoples welcomed this change. Cheyennes called white persons
the *veho;* Arapahoes called them *niatha.* Both words meant spider. Although

veho connoted some trickery, the terms had none of the negative tone of English, and in fact both also meant clever or skillful.[24] Spiders and whites both created astonishing things. Some goods—metal awls and iron pots, for instance—made traditional tasks much easier. A metal scraper allowed a woman to process an animal hide more quickly. Muslin or bed ticking made a durable and lightweight inner lining for a traditional tipi. An iron vessel, unlike the ceramic ones used for centuries, was virtually indestructible, and so it eased the ancient jobs of cooking and potmaking. Other items tickled the human vanity, or fed people's playfulness, or tasted good. Indian peoples found European crafts powerfully seductive, and no plainsmen were unaffected, not even those most hostile to the invading whites. The Kiowa leader Satanta, or White Bear, an outspoken resister of white encroachment, lived in a carpeted tipi and ate from small wooden tables that were brightly painted and studded with shiny brass tacks. To call guests to dinner he stood at his lodge entrance and blew lustily on a French horn.[25]

Most trade goods allowed plainsmen to change their surface existence and to do more efficiently what they had done for centuries. A few new items, however, altered their life at a much deeper level. These goods redrew relationships between people and their surroundings and established new connections between humans and other forms of life. They restructured the environment in its broadest definition. Although coffee, needles, and blankets gave a gloss and an ease to a familiar life, these other goods opened for their owners new sources of fundamental power. Through these goods the frontiers of trade altered reality. They transformed the world as people saw it inside their heads. Of these introductions, two stood above everything else in significance—firearms and horses.

GUNS, SHOT, AND POWDER in some ways had less impact on the plains than in the eastern woodlands where Indians had first acquired them. A man hunting deer, bear, turkeys, and squirrels in a forest could kill his prey from a considerable distance while concealed among trees and undergrowth. On the open plains, however, where bison and other large prey lived in widely scattered groups that bolted cross-country if alarmed, it was more difficult to draw within range of wary animals. Bison were best hunted from horseback and on the run. Short, powerful bows were far more effective than clumsy guns that could be reloaded only slowly and with great difficulty while the hunter was galloping over open terrain.

In a fight, on the other hand, the ability to kill and wound from farther away was an unalloyed blessing, particularly if the enemy was outgunned or ungunned. Raiders with firearms attacking a village could remain at a distance and do their worst, out of danger's range. If attacked by warriors with bows and arrows, defenders with firearms, even if badly outnumbered, could keep their foes backed away and relatively harmless while taking their own long-distance toll. Gunshots often did greater damage and left wounds that native healers were less accustomed to treat. The disadvantages in hunting did not apply to battle. If gunshots frightened away bison, it was a disappointing loss; when enemies ran away, it was a victory.

Behind these advantages was a change more fundamental. A firearm, as a new technology of metalwork and chemistry, was more than a stretch of old killing tools. A gun gave its owner access to energy otherwise denied him. The user of a stone ax or a lance played with physical laws to increase his own capacity, in this case to shape or harm something or somebody. The ultimate source of his greater power, however, remained the same: his own energy. But a gun's energy was recruited elsewhere—from natural materials that were found far away, processed into a powerful combustible, then stored and carried long distances. A loaded gun or rifle was an addition to the basic source of a person's power. Gunpowder was immigrated energy patiently waiting for someone to set it loose. Trading for guns did have one important disadvantage. Because firearms and gunpowder were produced far away by a technology unknown to Indians, this new power source depended on others—white traders. That made gun owners vulnerable, but it also gave them a potential edge. Not only could they kill and maim more effectively; they also possessed technology and imported energy their enemies could not duplicate, short of finding a similar trade connection.

Horses offered benefits at once greater and more subtle.[26] They were beautifully suited for life on the plains. Ten thousand years earlier their smaller ancestral cousins had lived here in vast numbers. They had disappeared in the great extinction at the close of the Pleistocene, but now their evolutionary descendants—swifter, more powerful, and bred to be congenial with human masters—returned to an environment that had become one of the earth's great pastures. The first horses had appeared with Coronado's expedition, but their spread to the plains came much later. Although it probably began with a thin leakage from Spain's Rio Grande settlements, the great occupation did not start before the Pueblo revolt of 1680. Within a few decades significant numbers could be seen on the plains, and in less than a century the horse—and its integration into human culture—had become an essential fact of life.

Horses appealed to plainsmen, most obviously, because they helped them do traditional work more efficiently, just as a pot made cooking easier. For the first time in the region's long history men and women were not limited by their own speed and endurance. Hunters on horseback could range more widely for game and could kill it more often; they could cover more ground in search of water and useful plants. The Indians' reach of trade was greatly expanded, and with horses they could also carry around more possessions, including larger lodges to contain them. Horses revolutionized warfare, as they had from their first domestication. Mounted warriors not only dominated those on foot, but far-ranging horsemen also could raid villages almost at will while remaining out of retaliation's reach. The overall effect was to increase a plainsman's realm of control over both his material world and other humans with less access to horseflesh.

A horse was unlike other new trade goods in one fundamental way. It was a living creature. But for this, too, there was a precedent among Indians. For centuries plainsmen had controlled another life-form—dogs. Unlike knives or atlatls, domesticated dogs were *living* tools that contributed independently to people's effective strength. Someone might "use" both a knife and a dog, but the first was an extension of his personal effort; the second was power that he captured and applied to his own purposes. When survival depended on maximum control of limited resources, this difference was more than abstract. A knife subtracted from a person's energy; a dog added to it.

Strictly as hidebound bags of potential power, horses again were simply an improvement on something Indians already had. They were larger living tools that permitted their owners to move farther and faster, carry larger burdens, and hunt and fight more effectively. In this sense Indians would have been similarly helped if they had suddenly caught and tamed a lot of very large, strong, swift, odd-looking, long-legged canines.

But this misses the point. The crucial gift of the horse concerned not power itself but where that power came from. Like all of us, Indians lived surrounded by potential they could tap in only a few limited ways. The horse rearranged the basic alignment among people and the possibilities that flowed through the plains. The result was a revolution both of material life and of vision.

Every living tool, like its owner, must take energy from something else in order to do its work. People tame and direct an animal's power, but they are really using the animal's ability to acquire energy. It follows that an owner must pay at least as much attention to that energy source—to the animal's food—as he does to the creature itself. The crucial relationship, in short, is not so much between people and their animals. It is between people and the things their animals eat.[27]

With horses, people suddenly gained access to an enormous storage of energy—the grasses that had waited uselessly around humans and dogs for 12,000 years. When a man swung onto a horse's back, he was commanding power that arose from the prolific plant life that grew beneath him, and to the horizon, and much beyond that. It was a fabulous shortcut. And that vast expansion of available energy was translated and focused, not in a twenty-pound animal that woofed and padded at a person's feet, but into a magnificent creature of breathtaking strength, speed, and grace. It was a leap of power far greater than any before it in plains history.

Horses had another practical advantage. Dogs are carnivores; they get their energy from eating flesh. A lot of flesh-fuel was running around on the plains, but it was not always easily found and gathered in. Especially troubling were winters, when game was most difficult to find and when moving around was most dangerous and most costly in energy. People faced a similar problem. As omnivores, humans pursued both plants and meat, but although Indians gathered and consumed many types of plains plants, they could not digest the most prolific forms, the grasses. Gathered foods, furthermore, were especially scarce during the coldest months. In fact, plains residents faced a continuing shortage in edible flora. Valuable foods, most notably maize, had to be imported, usually by an exchange of meat and animal products.

Plains Indians consequently were often situational carnivores. Keeping dogs was an advantage in one sense. Since most nomads ate their canines, dogs became storage containers. Dogs ate scraps tossed to them and held that protein in their bodies until their masters called on them to give it up. One moment a dog was a tool; in the next it might be supper. But this arrangement had a built-in conflict as well. At the most difficult time of year people relied mostly on meat—the same nourishment sniffed out by their hungry, whining dogs. Dogs could hunt on their own, of course, but that risked losing them to packs of feral canines, wolves, and coyotes, so owners were obliged to provide most of their animals' food. This made people and dogs commensals—organisms that lived together and ate the same foods from the same natural table. Unfortunately, that table was sometimes nearly empty, especially during the cold months from November to April. It built up to a dilemma. Dogs existed only to serve their masters, yet always, and particularly at the most difficult time of year, those masters had to surrender precious resources that they themselves needed to stay alive.

But horses were herbivores. They ate what people and dogs could not—grasses and, in the deepest winter difficulties, the soft green shoots of cottonwood trees. These animal servants did not compete directly with people for food; the two species lived together but ate at separate tables. By acquiring horses, then, Indians were spreading out their society's effects over a wider range of resources. It was a far more efficient arrangement of consumers.

The benefits went still deeper. Every expression of plains power drew originally from the sun. Combined with soil and water, solar energy produced plants. Grazers ate those plants and turned them into flesh and bone and the energy to move about. This twice-changed energy then was taken by carnivores and ominvores and reshaped to their own forms and set to work for their own needs.

The farther an organism lived along this chain of changing energy—the more removed it was from the sun's gift—the more vulnerable it was. For one thing, energy dissipates drastically as it moves through this system. Plants use just a tiny fraction of the sun's energy. A grazer captures only about one-tenth of the energy in the plants it eats, and a meateater takes only about one-tenth of the grazer's smaller portion. The farther along the flow, obviously, the less life that can be supported. That is why there was so much more grass than bison and so many more bison than wolves. For the same reason horses were better suited to the plains than dogs. They drew more directly on the sun's offerings. In a sense a horse was ten times closer than a dog to the ultimate source of life.

Meateaters, such as wolves, dogs, and people, furthermore, had to wait until solar power had passed through two steps, from sun to plants and from plants to grazers. And for every step there could be a stumble. This was a special concern here, in one of world's most erratic and unstable environments. In a normal year (if that term had any meaning at all) rainfall might vary by half from the year before or after, and in a full drought the amount could drop nearly to nothing. This slowed or stopped the conversion of the sun's energy to forage. Some grass died and the part that survived concentrated on nurturing its roots and sent virtually no new growth to the surface. Less grass meant fewer grazers; that in turn threatened the carnivores. And by a terrible math of starvation, the dissipation of energy meant that the harm from reduced forage compounded as it moved from step to step and struck each stage of consumption. Overhunting, diseases, and other disruptions could have similar effects. Horses, living one step closer to the sun, had a valuable edge over dogs in this erratic, undependable environment. As animal servants, that made them even more appealing to humans.

Unfortunately, a horse also had disadvantages. Compared to the care of inanimate tools, an animal's upkeep was far more complicated. Every living tool had its own needs as a separate organism, its own natural cycles and patterns of behavior, and it could surrender its power to others only as long as those needs were met and that behavior respected. On this point a horse's appeal became a hindrance; its hugely increased power came from a vastly greater hunger for energy, a craving Indians had to meet if they hoped to reap the benefits. A horse was well designed for life on the sun-bathed grasslands, but it was no more exempt than any other creature to the pressures of living on the plains. The wrong coincidence of circumstances could leave it as vulnerable as anything else. An owner had to learn, understand, and respect an animal's complicated needs if his breathing, eating tools were to do what he asked of them. A dog's or horse's master, in other words, was also a servant to his animal's requirements.[28]

This is not to say, of course, that horses could survive only with people's help. They were inherently suited to the high plains country. The millions of acres of shortgrasses offered feed year-round, curing naturally into a kind of living hay and, unlike the taller grasses to the east, keeping much of their nourishment during the winters. Horses could survive perfectly well on their own; in fact, large herds of wild horses lived on the high plains, especially south of the Arkansas.[29] The difficulties arose when people and horses lived together. When Indians chose to capture and use the horse's power, they inherited the need to keep the animal in large numbers close at hand. That meant concentrating the demands of both master and horse in ways that horses would not otherwise have done. And that could cause problems, especially in a country where essentials were often in desperately short supply.

The danger, that is, lay in the Indians' envisioning a life of expanded power. Seeing that lifting possibility, they made choices that also brought greater and more complicated responsibilities. As it turned out, meeting the complex needs of both themselves and their horses was much more of a challenge than they could have realized.

Nonetheless, the advantages were irresistible. An Indian on a horse was literally harnessing, more directly and reliably, the energy poured out by the sun in unimaginable generosity. A horse's appetites complemented, rather than conflicted with, its rider's needs. And finally, in the worst times horses were a superior source of energy in another way. People could eat them, and there was much more of them to eat than dogs.

These were great practical advantages, but no one should look on them too cold-bloodedly. A horse was a liberation. Native Americans on the plains took to the horse with a heady feeling of suddenly widening potential, and that must have brought a sense of grand destiny. N. Scott Momaday tells of his Kiowa ancestors emigrating from the northern to the southern plains around 1800, acquiring horses along the way. Riding freely over those open grasslands, the Kiowas must have felt they had "reached the time and place of their fulfillment." He writes, "They had become centaurs in their spirit."[30]

MOMADAY'S REMARK suggests how horses and firearms brought a more profound change. A centaur is a fusion of human will and animal strength into something wholly new, a fundamentally different creature that cannot be understood as just an aggregate of man and beast. Similarly, when a man rode a horse over the plains or pointed a gun at an enemy, the results went beyond a new combination of person, tool, energy, and setting. The first and most important consequence was invisible. It happened inside people's heads.

This change involved the meanings of the land—what people saw when they looked at the country and imagined its future. Guns and horses were part of a far larger transformation in North America after about 1700. This force arose both from the movement of frontiers and from extraordinary technological innovations. A place, as an area of human use, is created not just by the arrangements people forge between themselves and resources, the day-to-day working connections between humans and things. It is partly the possibilities that people envision, the linkage between what they see and what they dream. Throughout the continent during these years, new technologies were both redefining how people lived within their surroundings and reshaping the land as people imagined it into the decades ahead.

In the Gulf coastal south, for instance, the cotton gin brought such a change after 1800, about the time the horse culture was firmly established on the plains. Invented by a New England Yankee visiting a Georgia plantation, the cotton gin suddenly made the inland South the largest continuous area on earth capable of growing marketable short-staple cotton. When Eli

Whitney first turned the crank to demonstrate his simple prototype, the meaning of the South, as perceived promise, changed instantly. Overnight the mental shape of the region's future shifted and grew. In a fundamental sense the South became a different place, before a single new cotton seed was planted.

A bit farther west at about the same time, steamboats had a similar effect on America's inland waterways. Powerful steam-driven shallow-draft crafts, first developed in the Northeast, quickly made it possible to carry large cargoes of goods and people upstream. The combustible energy of wood and other fuels could be captured and used to push against what had been almost irresistible—the downhill flow of water. The Mississippi and Ohio Rivers, as fancied environments in daily relationships with humans, suddenly were different. Without changing physically in the slightest way, a great river became something else, not a muscular rush of energy to be temporarily ridden but a two-way avenue of commerce, a broad path of free movement.

Guns and horses in this sense were the cotton gins and steamboats of the high plains. Once people understood what these things could do, those people looked at the country and thought it into another shape. Grass, dirt, bison, water, distance, and cottonwoods took on new meanings as humans drew new mental pictures that realigned themselves and the components of their world. As the eighteenth century turned into the nineteenth, frontiers of material and perceptual change were rolling over America, and as they swept into the continental center, the plains quickly became a different realm of imagined possibility.

In one final way, however, horses and guns had a creative power beyond that of the grandest technological wonders of the age. A firearm was not just a more effective killing tool and giver of energy; it seemed closer to a Promethean force, an elemental source of power that raised whoever held it to what seemed another human category. No wonder the earliest European emissaries bestowed guns on favored indigenous leaders. A flintlock was as much talisman as weapon, an outward sign of the mystery offered when two creative universes suddenly touch.

Horses carried a much older load of meaning. Every culture that has adopted the horse shows signs of spiritual transformation. Riding such animal power awakens a belief that the horseman's genius has been altered and ancient limits transcended. Old World myths were filled with dreamlike images of liberation—princes soaring on winged steeds over the swipe of monsters' claws, warriors galloping with the divine. The images are of a fusion of theological, sexual, and physical power. In the Hindu final age Vishnu, the Preserver, will appear on a white horse; the Christ of judgment is predicted to arrive on a mare; horses are "the supreme blessing" in the Koran, and one of them, Bukraq, carried Mohammed to heaven. The variations seem endless. In a twelfth-century coronation ritual, an Irish king-to-be would copulate with a newly slain mare, then bathe in and drink a thick soup made from the carcass.[31]

Of all creatures with special symbolic gravity—bears, wolves, cats, snakes, cranes, and dogs—only the horse has held out the possibility of a full union between the human and nonhuman, not as a fantastic individual aberration, but as the basis for a new society. Once on horseback, whole peoples see entirely new potential both in the land they ride above and within themselves. They recast their meaning and change their story to explain their new social shape. They literally re-member themselves.

If this has been true of all cultures that acquire horses, the transformations have been deepest among people living in the world's most open spaces, especially grasslands. On the savannas and steppes horses can find their widest spread of nourishment, and there the freedom of movement and the bodily union of power is felt most fully. Horses were first domesticated at least 5,000 years ago in the grasslands of central Asia. They created their greatest equestrian empires there and in other open landscapes, northern China and the deserts of the Near East and northern Africa. In 1492, however, vast open patches of the planet were still without horses. The imagined marriage of species was not possible—until Europeans rode into those regions and the gap was suddenly bridged.

In an odd reverse way, the effect was similar to the cataclysmic arrival of Old World contact diseases. Measles, whooping cough, smallpox, and other maladies ravaged Indians so viciously because those diseases had been circulating in the Eastern Hemisphere for five to seven millennia, about as long as horses had been domesticated, long enough for humans and diseases to negotiate rough biological arrangements with one another. This evolutionary armistice made Europeans highly efficient carriers of illnesses, and when they suddenly met peoples unexposed to those diseases, the result was spectacular and horrifying. In a similar sequence, Europeans rode into America displaying the trappings and skills perfected by horsemen over 5,000 years. They presented Indians with the distilled result of 20,000 generations of exploring the implications of horses. The imaginative impact must have been magical.

In the long history of horses and people, no place and time were better primed for transformation than the Great Plains in the eighteenth century, when the irresistible vision of what Scott Momaday calls the centaurs of the spirit appeared in one of the earth's largest and lushest horseless pastures. One bit of archaeological evidence suggests just how seductive the new dream was. Since at least 4200 B.C., and perhaps 3,000 years before that, native peoples had lived by the great rotor, wintering along the base of the Rockies and moving into the high country in summer to harvest animals with elaborate stone game-drive structures before returning in autumn to the shelter of the Front Range. This cycle and system were so dependable that people kept at it through 6,000 years of climatic and cultural changes. Then the rotor abruptly ended. The last evidence for the use of the game drives is a charcoal fire built beside one of the stone blinds. Its date was about 1740— precisely the period when horses were spreading onto the plains from the southwest.[32] The dream of a life on horseback was seductive enough to break a pattern 25,000 generations old.

The horse was transforming the human experience on the plains at the time when life was being scrambled by other forces carried into mid-America by successive waves of new peoples. The changes brought disaster, but also previously unimagined possibilities for country that people had used variously and well for a long time.

ENERGY LOOSED, connections broken and realigned, ideas ebullient, biota merged, death invigorated, imaginations freed, the world remade: frontiers were a bewildering, calamitous, glorious mess. Despite their grim consequences, they were also full of creative energy born of people's ability to dream something new from the land and themselves. Frontiers converging on mid-America set loose that power with a vigor rarely matched in modern history.

In July 1541 Coronado crossed the Arkansas River, entered the central plains, and perceived a land with little past and no potential. His impression of an empty, largely unchanging country stayed in the heads of outsiders for the next 300 years. But what about the people who stood on the plains that July day and looked at Coronado? Almost instantly they saw new ways to find power in a place that people had used imaginatively for thousands of years. For lovers of irony, it was a delectable moment. A man was perpetuating a vision of static wilderness in the same place he inspired a perceptual revolution.

The consequences came slowly at first, then accelerated, then shot forward. New technologies and ideas threatened old relationships and opened fresh opportunities. Plains people acquired new objects, rethought their surroundings, and found new ways to die. One organism, the horse, alone let loose changes broader and more vigorous than any in the region's history. It all began with a Spaniard's first misapprehending touch.

This extraordinary dynamic, however, was not unprecedented. Elsewhere in the world another combination of image and circumstance had set people in motion with even greater passion. The inspiration was not an animal but one of the earth's elements. Its mythic allure, however, was as ancient and potent as the horse—gold.

Marker of an Old World. Rising beside the modern tourist town of Estes Park, Colorado, this granite formation, known locally as Old Man Mountain, is a reminder of the region's ancient history. It was used by native peoples for rituals and spirit quests from at least 2000 B.C. until the 1840s. (Courtesy of James B. Benedict)

When the Rains Came. The unusually wet centuries between A.D. 800 and 1200 fostered a great surge in plains population. Small streamside settlements like this one appeared on the western plains, country previously dominated by nomadic hunters. (Original painting by Linda Meigs)

An Echo of Quivira. This beehive-shaped house is much like those of the Witchita farmers near the great bend of the Arkansas River when Coronado arrived in search of golden cities. The disappointed Spanish explorers described a backward and unchanging people. (Courtesy of the Kansas State Historical Society)

Lords of the Horse. In 1836 George Catlin visited Comanches in camp and while practicing the skills that made them masters of the southern high plains. Seeing the practical as well as spiritual possibilities of horses, they built a new life around these animals in only a few generations. (Courtesy of the Gilcrease Museum)

Hunkering Down. What seemed a free-roaming life on the high plains depended absolutely on finding sanctuary during winter in a few locations that had the precious combination of water, forage for horses, and the fuel and shelter offered by cottonwoods and willows. (Courtesy of the Denver Public Library)

THE CALLED OUT PEOPLE

Once the plains were freshly imagined, outward forms of power began to shift as well. The most obvious result was a wave of new emigration. Native Americans of varied backgrounds and lifeways, the latest of scores of peoples who had come and gone over the millennia, arrived from several directions. They moved in crooked, deflected routes as they met, fought, and allied with each other and with people already there. Each group in its own way was inspired by a new understanding of the country's meaning, a waking dream taking shape from the frontier's unsettling force. Each found its own accommodations with the place. Some of those people would sit on their horses to face the First Cavalry along the Solomon River.

This invasion was an audacious performance with momentous consequences—zoological, political, botanical, economic, military, diplomatic, and spiritual. Newcomers tapped more directly into the land's inherent energy; they upended old alignments of power; they took command of entrenched economic arrangements and set them to new purposes. They also got more than they bargained for. Although some transformations were conscious efforts to fashion a better life, others were unintended and far beyond their control. By the 1850s, as another set of invaders stood ready to carry their own shaping vision into mid-America, plains Indians were facing the full implications of their work.

THE EMIGRATION'S FIRST WAVE began in southwestern Wyoming and northwestern Colorado. Late in the seventeenth century Shoshonean-speaking people began moving southward from there through the Rocky Mountains. Within a few decades they had filtered to the Spanish settlements in the upper Rio Grande valley and had descended the Front Range eastward onto the central plains. Along the way they formed a military partnership with the Utes, who gave these emigrants the name most widely used during the next 300 years: the Comanches (from *Komantcia*). The Comanches called themselves *Numinu* ("the people").

The Spanish first noted their arrival in 1706. Significantly, the occasion was a call of alarm from the Taos Pueblo and a report from Apaches that Comanches and Utes had been lashing their villages with bloody assaults. Soon the Apaches were also pressed hard from the opposite direction by Pawnees encouraged by the French. Although the details are sketchy, Apaches were routed within a couple of generations. Pressed from east and west, they were driven southward off the central plains. They took up residence among relatives in settled communities closer to the New Mexican Pueblos.[1]

At some point in these years the Comanches also acquired horses, although once more the timing is unclear. As late as 1726, by one report, dogs still carried their belongings, but within another decade or so Comanches were traveling with great herds of horses stolen and traded from New Mexico. They quickly learned the advantages of their mounts in their furious campaigns against Apaches and other plains tribes. By midcentury the Comanches had laid the basis for their legendary status as the plains' most adept and feared horseback warriors. "[They are] a very barbarous people, heathen," wrote a visitor to a village of 400 lodges on the Arkansas River. The camp bristled with bows and arrows, lances, hatchets, swords, and a few muskets. Grazing nearby were large numbers of horses, asses, and mules.[2]

Such villages were now the region's new centers of power. From them the Comanches alternately attacked and bartered in New Mexican settlements. A Spanish governor reported that they had killed at least 150 villagers in only five years, even as they crowded into frequent trade fairs in Taos and other towns. They arrived at these fairs with hundreds of horses laden with bison- and deerskins and dried meat as well as with dozens of children taken in their many raids against plains enemies. In return they received maize, sugar, horses, mules, and other fruits of European trade. "Here is collected all the ironware possible," a priest reported: "axes, hoes, wedges, picks, bridles, machetes, *belduques* [broad-bladed iron "trading" knives], knives [of other styles] . . . , everything possible for trade and barter." They also reached eastward to trade with French delegations that traveled far up the Arkansas. Comanches exchanged horses, slaves, skins, robes, and meat for large stores of hatchets, knives, tobacco, brandy, and muskets. Similar arrangements were struck with French operatives from Louisiana and their surrogates on the southeastern plains.[3]

These new lords of the region thus assumed the pivotal position in the old exchange between the plains and its fringes. As others had before them, they bartered animal products from the huge herds of plains grazers for foodstuffs grown by villagers, especially maize. This trade was enriched by European goods and invigorated by colonial rivalries. Rough rates were established. A bison hide brought one or two *belduques*. A horse was worth thirteen knives, and a female slave in her teens was swapped for two horses and a short cloak. Comanches worked this lively trade with French emissaries and at Spanish fairs that drew a "multitude . . . so great that it is impossible to enumerate it," all the while raiding tribes to the east and New Mexican settlements. They added steadily to their horse and mule herds and acquired a limited number of firearms from the east; according to one source (probably exaggerated) they stole up to 10,000 horses annually from the Spanish. By the early 1800s they had solidified their command of a huge domain from the upper Arkansas valley to the hill country of the Edwards Plateau in central Texas.[4]

A similar upheaval was taking place a few hundred miles to the north. This time the plains were invaded from the east. Several related but independent groups pushed west and south of the middle Missouri valley between the 1680s and the 1830s. Collectively called the Western or Plains Sioux, they included two broad divisions, the Nakotas and the Lakotas (or Tetons). Each of these was divided into tribes, which in turn were composed of bands. These groups had no unifying political structure or leadership, although they recognized their kinship, cultivated shared traditions, and spoke closely related dialects.

The Western Sioux had first moved out of the Great Lakes woodlands to the Minnesota prairies and then to the Missouri valley. They had felt some pressure from Cree and Ojibway competitors, but they were also attracted by the large populations of beaver and bison on the eastern fringe of the plains. Aggressive and well supplied with firearms traded from the French, they entrenched themselves on the middle Missouri by the late eighteenth century. By then they had acquired horses, which they used in forays onto the plains to hunt bison, mainly for subsistence. At that point the Missouri valley was thrown into tumult by several coincident developments—epidemics, new white traders ascending the river and challenging settled patterns, and a fresh injection of trade goods. The Sioux responded with an expansionist burst. They warred against other riverine tribes and seated themselves as the dominant power upstream to the Yellowstone. Some drove west and south, away from the river and onto the plains. There they grappled with nomadic equestrian groups—Arapahoes, Kiowas, Crows, and Cheyennes, tribes who were also caught up in the region's dynamic changes—in a struggle to dominate the area between the arc of the Missouri and the Black Hills.[5]

As the Comanches tightened their grip on land to the south, many Plains Sioux, especially Lakotas, were casting loose from the Missouri and bidding to control a huge portion of the northern plains. They were aided by a rapid birthrate and a strong grip on trade from the east, including access to the formidable advantage of guns. The shift to the plains required a much closer reliance on horses, and the size of the Lakota herds did indeed increase, in general mimic of the Comanches. The Sioux, however, faced two problems that the southern horsemen avoided. Vicious northern winters bit deeply into the horse populations, leaving their numbers thinned every spring. Besides that, the Sioux were far removed from the best source for replenishing their mounts—the prolific herds and Hispanic villages in the southwest. Too often the Lakotas found themselves poorly mounted. This weakness, close to the heart of their drive for dominance, helped shape their actions during the years ahead.

By the 1830s the Lakotas were the preeminent power of the northern plains. With the Black Hills as their spiritual and geopolitical center, they ranged west to the Continental Divide, east to the Missouri basin, south to the South Platte and Smoky Hill Rivers, and north to the lands of two powerful rivals, the Crows and the Blackfeet. Like the Comanches, they had parlayed the opportunities of converging frontiers into a position of dominance.

Other tribes were caught up in the turbulence, chasing opportunities and pressed by new adversaries. The Kiowas left the Montana mountains near the Missouri headwaters about the same time the Comanches began their move south and the Sioux headed east. They migrated first to the plains around the Black Hills, where they discovered horses and allied with the Crows. Then the expanding Lakotas drove them rapidly southward, beyond the Platte. About 1790 the Kiowas, under the leadership of Hare-Lip and Wolf-Lying-Down, made a lasting peace with the Comanches. They made their homes along and to the south of the upper Arkansas and settled into the economic system developed by their new allies.[6]

Arapahoes had lived as farmers in northwest Minnesota before migrating to the Missouri and beyond. Like the Kiowas, they were caught up in the struggle to control the region around the Black Hills and were shouldered southward by the numerous, well-armed Sioux. They formed a durable alliance with the Cheyennes, and by the 1820s they were living in the watersheds of the Platte and North Platte Rivers. They ranged to the south and east in their hunt. In winter they camped along the South Platte in timbered bends where plainsmen had found wood and shelter for centuries (and where other newcomers soon would be testing for gold). Arapahoes also adopted the horse as the prime element of their new means of living, and like all the others, they began to learn the adaptations essential to equestrian hunting.

The plains had never seen such movement and displacement of people in such a blink of time. The high plains population rose steeply in the late eighteenth century, then climbed more sharply after 1800. The number of persons using the central high plains more than doubled between about 1820 and the mid-1850s.[7] Emigrants brought tens of thousands of other new life-forms and dozens of new types of material goods, all of which carried their own powers of change. The transformational forces set loose seemed nothing less than revolutionary.

People had come and gone for millennia, of course, but in this old, unbroken story most of the slow changes were responses to climate and long-term evolution of skills, as seen in the most recent boom of farmers from the ninth to the thirteenth centuries. The inwashing of frontiers, full of new life-forms and technologies, redefined the plains' potential far faster than anything ever had. In the longest leap, horsemen could exploit the sun and soil, not through maize and sunflowers, but through natural grasses that fueled their power to travel, hunt, carry loads, and fight. Before, the riverlands had provided the prime living places, the rich alluvial soil for gardening. Now the grasslands, as suddenly exploitable sun power, offered the stuff of dominance. The open plains abruptly inflated in value.

As emigrants moved in to control the new potential, there was a shuffling of power in its crudest form—force used by some people to control, exploit, and kill other people. Some Indians had easier access to the possibilities, some were quicker to see them and more aggressive in acting them out. As Old World peoples had known for thousands of years, the new horse nomads learned that sedentary farmers were easy prey for mounted raiders.[8] Villagers on the low plains and in New Mexico were suddenly vulnerable to horsemen applying the energy in grass to warfare. First the Comanches, then the Lakotas, Kiowas, and others started to live by the Bedouin proverb: "Raiding is our agriculture."

Rarely in North American history had native peoples found such an open, inviting road to wealth and power. Horseback emigrants followed that road into a time they later considered the pinnacle of their modern story. This path, however, also took them into deceptive terrain full of unforeseen risks and difficulties.

THE BEST WAY to see the opportunities and dangers of this turbulent time is through the story of the people who became the dominant force on the central plains—the Cheyennes. Around 1680, as the Comanches began their odyssey toward the southern plains, the Cheyennes left their homes on the upper Mississippi River and moved westward to the Minnesota River. Soon they moved to the James River in eastern North Dakota and then, by the 1770s, to the upper Missouri valley in central North Dakota. By then they had abandoned their wigwams for the earthen houses typical of villages along the Missouri, but they continued to live by their traditional economy of horticulture, hunting, and trade.

The Cheyennes settled in three villages near others of the Mandans, Hidatsas, and Chippewas. Their neighbors were not entirely happy with the intrusion, and within a few years tensions were increasing. Two events around 1780 forced the Cheyennes to make a critical decision. The Chippewas struck one of the Cheyenne villages with a devastating raid, and a series of terrible epidemics, probably smallpox and measles, ravaged their whole population. In the wake of these twin disasters, bands of Cheyennes began moving westward again, this time away from the Missouri and toward the plains.[9]

This move was more than a continuation of their century-old westward drift. Emigration to the plains would demand a far greater adjustment in

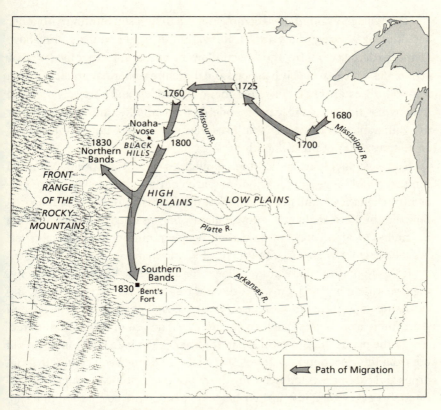

The Migration of the Cheyennes/Tsistsistas

economy and lifestyle than any previous move. Besides that, the Cheyennes were being drawn onto the plains by two new and powerful inducements. Both opportunities offered unprecedented power, but both were very risky.

They were drawn first by an older resident of the plains—the bison. Bison had long been hunted by virtually all Indian peoples living between the 85th and 115th meridians. By 1800 the animal's population was shrinking drastically east of the Mississippi, but bison still lived in astonishing numbers where they were best adapted—on the Great Plains. Tribes living in the Missouri basin, including the Cheyennes during their sojourn there, made long forays onto the plains to harvest from the herds. No animal was more useful and widely revered. It walked prominently through Native American cosmologies. Various parts of the bison were eaten, worn, fought with, slept on, traded, played with, and worshiped.

River villagers nonetheless complemented their bison hunting with other activities—gathering wild plants, trading, hunting other animals, and above all the gardening of maize, squash, sunflowers, beans, and other foods. Their economies were reasonably balanced and therefore somewhat protected from full-scale disaster. Their collective energy was widely and shrewdly invested in activities that were fairly independent of one another and thus were not too vulnerable to each other's failures. Bison were very important in such economies, but not preeminently so.

Horses suddenly expanded the possibilities of hunting bison. Mounted hunters could range much farther in search of their prey, kill far more efficiently when they found it, and transport the results more easily. It appeared now that hunters could concentrate mainly on this one resource and bring in enough to supply most of what their people required, plus a surplus left over to trade for whatever else was needed and more.

It was tempting. Abandoning villages for a nomadic life would mean living year-round on the plains, but the rewards appeared to be worth it. Besides, the opportunity to hunt bison on horseback meshed with the second powerful reason to take that leap of faith into a new homeland—commerce.

On the plains the Cheyennes had the chance to play a vital role in an old but expanding economic system.[10] The plains had long been central to a vigorous and extensive trade spanning the continent. European contact invigorated this old system, just as their horses expanded the power to hunt bison. New products appeared, and new peoples to trade for them. New trading centers sprang up. The changes presented opportunities for peoples willing to take advantage of the rapidly evolving situation.

The main axis of this new trading arrangement ran 800 miles, from the middle Missouri valley in North Dakota to northern New Mexico. Villagers along the middle Missouri had long traded surplus maize, pumpkins, melons, and tobacco to plainsmen, who provided bison meat and robes, pemmican, flour from grinding and pounding prairie turnips, tents, dressed robes and skins, moccasins, and clothing of deer and antelope skin ornamented with beads and quillwork. With the coming of Europeans, villagers now could offer manufactured goods from French and English traders—axes, kettles, awls, mirrors, knives, scrapers, and more—along with the food products. Plains hunters also brought silver, sugar, and other articles from Hispanic settlements in New Mexico and the far southwest.

Two items, firearms and horses, the pair of European imports that inspired the greatest bursts of power, affected trade more than any others.

Firearms came mainly from the east. The Spanish, fearing that Indians might ally with their French and English rivals, always were extremely reluctant to provide weapons to plains natives. English and French traders, by contrast, were happy to offer guns, powder, balls, and bullets at trade fairs and in commercial forays conducted from the middle Missouri valley to central Texas. Horses and mules came from the opposite direction, from their original source in the southwest and from the southern plains. A line running roughly along the 40th parallel separated two climatic zones of relative hospitality for horses. Above the line a fierce attrition of weather took a heavy toll on the animals. The northern herds were especially depleted in the spring, at the end of the murderous cold. Below the parallel, winters were not as vicious; the cured winter shortgrasses were also more accessible, and the midgrasses greened earlier in the spring along the streams to replenish the hungry herds.[11]

This irregularity—guns to the north and east, horses to the south and west—created a forceful dynamic. By a kind of commercial gravity firearms were pulled from the area of their greater concentration toward the lesser— that is, from the east to the south and west. The same was true of other manufactured goods more easily obtained from the English and French. Just as predictably, the trade in horses flowed from the great southwestern herds toward the horse-poor country north of the 40th parallel, out of New Mexico, the staked plains, and the Arkansas valley northward across the Platte and into the Dakotas and to the middle Missouri.

This dynamic imbalance called for someone to play the middleman. Whoever facilitated the movement of goods back and forth might ride the flow to a new level of power and affluence. The Cheyennes answered the call. Doing so, however, required them to move with a full commitment away from the Missouri and into the main channel of trade on the plains. That move, in turn, demanded that they depend far more heavily on horses. Those animals were not merely a key item of commerce; they were the Cheyennes' essential tool in carrying out that trade and in pursuing and defending their new way of life.

Across America, from Philadelphia to Astoria, swiftly changing economies were offering unprecedented chances for the people who could see and act on them. One of the most promising was squarely in the continental center, on the Great Plains. The Cheyennes responded. After taking several steps westward over the previous 100 years, they then took another that was more consequential than any before it.

The next twenty years are among the fuzziest in tribal history, at least to outsiders. The Cheyennes' course ran west and sharply southward through the center of North and South Dakota. They returned often to trade on the Missouri but remained on the plains proper most of the year. They acquired many more horses. To take the crucial step away from villages to a nomadic life, native peoples needed a critical mass of about six horses for every man, woman, and child, with considerably more, as many as a dozen per person, for a secure life.[12] The first credible estimates from a few decades later show the Cheyennes with ten or more horses per person. In the years after 1780 they must have steadily acquired these essential elements of their new existence.[13]

The country's gifts must have seemed irresistible—and nearly limitless. By chance the grasslands of the early nineteenth century were watered by a stretch of unusually high rainfall, so the Cheyennes saw the country much greener and lusher than usual. Grazing there were bison in herds that sometimes covered 200 or 300 square miles during the mating congregations of high summer. They found the profusion of deer, pronghorn antelopes, elk, and grizzlies that had fed the Querechos and Quiviras and so many more before them, only now they had vastly better means of hunting them. Like all jobbers, Cheyenne traders could increase their own share from the marketplace, in this case in both horses and trade goods. They began to flaunt their wealth. An Englishman on the Missouri about 1810 described a Cheyenne man draped in a magnificent robe, acquired from Arapahoes, that was worked with red and yellow split quills and bordered entirely with hooves of young fawns. As the man walked, he whirred like a rattlesnake.[14]

Like the Comanches, Kiowas, Lakotas, and others, the Cheyennes quickly put these resources to the service of their vision. They adopted skin lodges (tipis), much larger variations of those first seen by Coronado, and learned to transport them and other possessions by horse travois. They ferreted out the parts of the high plains that best met their varied needs for water, pasture, shelter, and fuel. They sharpened hunting techniques that later impressed visitors to the plains. Racing after bison on carefully chosen ponies, hunters brought down their galloping quarry with rapid volleys from powerful shortbows that could send arrows entirely through the dense muscle of the mighty animals. They learned the fine distinctions among their main prey. Cheyennes had twenty-seven words for bison in their varieties of age, sex, and condition. A newborn or "yellow" calf was *heovoksa*, a two-year-old heifer, *moncess. Ookoenemehe* referred to a late-bearing cow. *Hotoxpeoeva* was a young, scabby bull.[15]

Other skills were less obvious. Although an elderly informant recalled planting corn as a child in the Black Hills, the Cheyennes gradually abandoned gardening, but they continued to use a remarkable range of native plants.[16] Some of this knowledge they brought with them; some they learned in their new homes. They ate lambsquarters (*Chenopodium berlandieri*) in their eastern homes and throughout their odyssey, but many plants were new to them. The stems of one thistle (*Cirsium edule*) were so sweet they were considered a fruit. The roots of American licorice (*Glycyrrhiza lepidota*) were especially choice in early spring, when the groundplum milkvetch (*Astragalus crassicarpus*) also put out its succulent, sweet fruits that staved off thirst. Chokecherries (*Prunus virginiana*), one of the plains' most ancient food sources, were dried and pounded and added to soups and pemmican; women stuck the stripped stems into roasting meat as a spice and gave the juice as a special treat to a favored child. The greasy-tasting roots of the drought-resistant gayfeather (*Liatris punctata*) were eaten only in emergencies. The prairie turnip (*Psoralea esculenta*), however, was a staple for both meals and trade. Children were taught to find the plants by their hairy stems and yellowish-blue flowers. Mothers then dug the thick roots and stored them for winter meals. Rich in protein, prairie turnips were exchanged for maize from the gardening tribes. The Indians' enthusiasm for this wild plant found its way into their myths. In a Dakota story a pregnant woman dug for turnips with such vigor that she burrowed through the earth and fell into the prairie sky.[17]

Plants also served as medicines. Purple coneflower (*Echinacea angustifolia*) relieved toothaches, sore necks, rheumatism, arthritis, mumps, boils, and sensitive gums. It was also chewed during sun dances to stimulate saliva and reduce thirst, as was wild licorice, which was brewed as well into a tea for diarrhea and nausea. Gayfeather treated gonorrhea; its roots were chewed to form a poultice for open wounds; the juice from mastication soothed swollen testes. The breadth of purposes was impressive. Cheyennes considered aromatic sumac (*Rhus aromatica*) a direct gift from God. When blended with tobacco, red willow dogwood, and bearberry, it was a favorite smoke; brewed into tea, it was used to treat head colds. Chewed roots of a prairie turnip were blown into an infant's rectum to stop gas pains. The ground leaves, roots, and stems of the puccoon (*Lithospermum incisum*) were rubbed on an arm or leg to reduce paralysis.[18]

Uses ranged from the mundane to the metaphysical. Gayfeather was a living calendar. When its spiky flowers turned bright purple, it was time to take prairie turnips, meat, and robes to trade for corn. Parents combed their hair with the bristly seed heads of purple coneflowers while their children turned the stalks into whirling toys. Buffalo gourd (*Curcurbita foetidissima*) was the source of great spiritual power. Improperly cutting its roots could lead to early death; respectful use as medicine promoted a long life. The bush morning glory (*Ipomoea leptophylla*) had a torqued human-size root (white settlers called the bush man-of-the-earth, Pawnees *kahts-tuwiriki*, or "whirlwind medicine"). This root could be eaten in emergencies, kept smouldering as a fire-starter, or burned directly and its smoke wafted as a treatment for nightmares. Young Cheyenne men chewed the leaves of bitter perfume (*Monarda menthoefolia*) and blew them onto the manes and tails of favorite horses to impart a pleasing smell. They steeped the waxy berries and scaly leaves of red cedar (*Juniperus virginiana*) into a sedative tea and carved its pungent wood into flutes they played to woo their lovers.[19]

Using these resources involved more than just searching and gathering. Without actually cultivating them, Cheyennes and other plains Indians still managed the wild growth of the most vital plants. Nutritious wild rice grass grew in areas up to several acres that were protected from floral intruders and periodically burned to stimulate new sprouting. Although Cheyennes called groundnut (*Apios americana*) *ai'-is-tom-i-misis'-tuk*, or "tasteless eating," they liked it enough to transplant it into favored spots on the high plains, far west of its usual range on the prairies. There are indications that especially valuable species, such as prairie turnips, were brought into hospitable areas that were spaced strategically so nomads could count on extra food as they moved across the high plains in camps and on hunting and war parties.[20] On a larger scale Indians torched the riverine grassbeds to encourage freshly vigorous growth for their horses. Those burnings could also be a crude method of directing the rovings of scattered bison bands.

As they lived into the plains, the Cheyennes named its parts according to how they saw and used them. Rivers were especially telling. Nebraska's Niobrara was the Sudden or Unexpected River. The Platte was the Moonshell or Musselshell, the Arkansas was the Flint Arrowpoint, and the South Platte was Fat or Tallow River. They named the Solomon by its prolific game bird—the Turkeys Creek. The Smoky Hill went by its most welcoming feature: the Bunch of Timber River.[21]

The basis for this remarkable adjustment was laid during the first couple of generations after 1780. New leaders emerged during that time. Charles Mackenzie told of accompanying a Gros Ventre delegation to a Cheyenne plains encampment. Six miles from the camp they were met by a chief who galloped up on a large milk-white horse, accepted their offer of a pipe, then stripped himself and clothed the Gros Ventre delegate in his war dress before seating the man on his horse and leading the column to his camp, chanting and singing all the way. Soon afterward the trader Alexander Henry visited a camp on the Knife River. He was met by a friendly and outgoing chief dressed in a blue Spanish coat and wrapped in a striped Spanish blanket. The man rode skillfully a great black stallion. With him were many warriors on horses with heads painted to resemble bison and antelopes and with nostrils trimmed in red cloth.[22]

The isolated encounters suggest a quickening contact with distant trade centers, a blossoming self-assurance, and a deepening sense of possession of the country. Meanwhile the Cheyennes continued to drift to the southwest. Then, in the early 1800s, there was a new coalescence in the area of the South Dakota Black Hills. Just northeast of the Black Hills was a lovely steep-sided mountain that whites later called Bear Butte. To the Cheyennes it was Noaha-vose. Its significance can hardly be exaggerated. At Noaha-vose occurred the defining episode of modern Cheyenne history.[23]

The Cheyennes' guide and prophet on their trek onto the plains was Sweet Medicine, also called Sweet Root Standing. As the people approached Noaha-vose, a great door opened in the mountain and Sweet Medicine was called inside by Maheo, the All Being, whose lodge was within. The prophet remained there for four years. With the help of the four sacred powers and the four sacred persons, Maheo instructed Sweet Medicine in codes of law and behavior. In the end he gave him four sacred arrows, which conveyed power over enemies and the bison in the country surrounding Noaha-vose.[24]

From this point on Noaha-vose has been the holiest site in the Cheyenne world. It is the lodge of the All Being. The generous essence of Maheo, the people's spiritual sustenance, pours forth from the sacred mountain. A Cheyenne political and spiritual map would have Noaha-vose at the center, with its edges roughly at the Rockies and at the Missouri, Arkansas, and Yellowstone Rivers. The defining direction at the top of this map would not be north, as in European cartography, but southeast. The greatest of the four sacred persons, Esseneta'he, lived in that direction. Creator of light and life, Esseneta'he sent the sun into their world each morning and reaffirmed his blessing of the earth. Lodge entrances among the Cheyennes faced the southeast, toward Esseneta'he and the origin of life.[25]

That map is a reminder that the Cheyennes' move to the plains was more than an emigration. It was a fundamental reorientation of identity and reality. Taken literally or not, the story of Sweet Medicine tells that at some point in their journey the Cheyennes were changed so basically that they became a people apart from those who had lived before. The All Being granted the prophet's people true possession of the country around Noaha-vose. As in other spiritual traditions, Judeo-Christian among many more, this defining benediction was accompanied by another gift—a new name. This was proper and necessary. Maheo was proclaiming that the passage had transformed his chosen children. Their world's center had shifted, its horizons lay on a new pivot. They were now the Tsistsistas, the Called Out People.

UNFORTUNATELY, the move to the plains brought plenty of problems, too. The Cheyennes' vision had implications they did not fully appreciate until the costs began to mount. For one thing, others had the same ideas they had. The Cheyennes fought ferociously with other tribes drawn into the country by the new possibilities, especially by the wonder of horses.

Around Noaha-vose and the Black Hills they struggled with the Kiowas and drove them southward. Soon, however, they were pushed in the same direction by the expanding Lakotas, with whom they continued to fight intermittently for years. They formed a close and lasting alliance with the Arapahoes, but as they were pressed south they came into increasingly bitter conflict with three other groups. The Comanches, masters of the south plains, had allied with the Kiowas and the Plains Apaches. The three lived mostly below the Arkansas River but ranged north to hunt on the central plains. Especially after about 1825, as the Cheyennes rode more often below the Platte River, they clashed fiercely with these three formidable tribes.

The spilled blood finally encouraged both sides toward accommodation. In 1837 a party of forty-two Cheyennes, members of the Bowstrings warrior society, were killed on a horse-stealing raid against the Kiowas on the Washita (Lodge Pole River). When an expedition of Cheyennes and Arapahoes rode in revenge against the Kiowas the next year, a fight on Wolf Creek left many dead on both sides. With these twin calamities, all parties were more open to some settlement. Cheyennes, furthermore, were anxious to have safer access to the Arkansas valley, and Comanches and Kiowas were being pressed hard from the south and east by white Texans and tribes recently removed into Indian Territory from the other side of the Mississippi. Each side, that is, needed to occupy the upper Arkansas without being threatened by the other.[26]

The result was the great peace of 1840. Prominent leaders from all groups pledged friendship with an elaborate exchange of gifts at a crossing of the Arkansas the Cheyennes still call "Giving Presents to One Another Across the River." By then Cheyennes had forged an alliance with the Lakotas as well. The peace of 1840 led to a lasting amity among the high plains tribes— Cheyennes, Arapahoes, Lakotas, Comanches, Kiowas, and Plains Apaches. For twenty years Colorado east of the Rockies had been mostly a neutral ground, country that several groups wanted but none could fully control. In 1840 it became the common hunting and camping terrain of a broad alliance of former enemies.[27]

East of the 100th meridian, however, was still a bloody ground. All high plains tribes fought there with Pawnees, Osages, Potawatomis, Omahas, and others who lived on the low plains and ranged westward for bison, as villagers had for centuries before the horse frontier. Western Kansas was another neutral ground wracked by almost continual conflict for another twenty-five years. For the Tsistsistas, fighting and dying there became part of their annual cycle. Late each spring and in early summer warriors rode against their low plains enemies in revenge for past losses and to expand and protect vital hunting territory that eastern tribes also desperately needed. In the fall they raided again, this time mainly to increase their horse herds before the killing winter.[28]

Warfare became a natural extension of the plainsmen's feeling of expanded power. As had been true among most horseback societies, the cult of the warrior and the celebration of courageous killing took a central place among peoples on the hotly contested plains. War's importance was expressed in the very names of leaders. A man born at the turn of the century was known variously as Eager to Be First (in a fight), Brave, Impetuous, and Shot by a Ree (an Arikara).[29] Cheyenne traditions were filled with men of legendary prowess and heart. There was Alights on a Cloud, killed by an arrow into his right eye after he had counted coup on the Pawnees. He fell from his swift horse, clanging to the ground in his heavy iron shirt, the Spanish armor given him by Medicine Water. Enraged enemies stripped and butchered him and flung his bleeding parts to the wolves. Ice (or White Bull), after his disastrous assurance of victory over Sumner's troops, tried bravely for martyrdom against the Omahas when he was convinced he was slowly dying from an injury. But Maheo took pity and spared him, even though Ice rode directly between two Omahas, flailing his quirt as they shot at him with a flintlock and bow and arrow. And Mouse's Road was perhaps the bravest. Left afoot on a raid against Kiowas and Comanches, he held off 100 mounted warriors, killing several with only his knife and a lance taken from an attacker. Finally shot in the back and decapitated, he still raised himself up to sit in defiance. His killers fled in terror of the living corpse with a bloody stump at its neck, an embodiment of immortal valor.[30]

The costs of heroism, however, were enormous. From the 1820s to the 1860s, the central plains were probably the most viciously contested terrain of North America. The endemic intertribal conflict took at least as heavy a toll, and probably a much higher one, as later battles with whites. Behind the inspiring memories and moments of transcendent daring were an immense suffering and accumulated mourning. Raids and counterraids chewed at populations, ripped apart families, and upset crazily the balance of men and women. Cheyennes learned the truth behind the ancient tradition of many Old World cultures: Death rode a horse.

The bloody wars were only the start of their problems. Trade, and the lure of its wealth, carried the Tsistsistas in directions they could never have foreseen. If they gained far greater power over the bison herds, for instance, the Cheyennes also became dangerously reliant on this one wild ungulate. Their way of life was inextricably bound to the buffaloes' well-being—a shaky situation, as it turned out. Their great reliance on the bison trade, and on the hunting and military life generally, was especially unsettling for women. Before, in the riverine villages, women had controlled the produce of the gardens and the considerable income those foods brought through trade, and that had given them substantial economic, social, and spiritual authority. In the seminomadic plains life, however, the most valuable assets—horses and bison carcasses—were acquired and controlled by men. Power within the tribes shifted steadily toward males and away from females. Rather than producers, women became processors, in this case supplying the back-breaking labor of skinning bison and scraping, rubbing, and kneading the hides into pliable, saleable robes.

Everyone, of both sexes and all ages, soon faced some of trade's other implications. The plainsmen's greater affluence, for instance, was possible only by immersing themselves in an economic system subject to all sorts of forces beyond their control or understanding. The same had been true of every earlier people; moundbuilders and Querechos surely had little influence over decisions made in Ohio valley cities and Rio Grande Pueblos. Anyone who relies on trade is putting himself somewhat at the mercy of people and situations far beyond his edge of sight. The Cheyennes' situation, however, was different on two counts. They and their neighbors were considerably more dependent on trade goods and imported technologies than earlier plainsmen had been. And although they might acquire those goods through other Indians, the source of those products was a distant society unlike any that natives had ever encountered. By trading with whites, even indirectly, the Tsistsistas were locking themselves into an economic order changing more rapidly and less predictably than any that plains people had ever dreamed of, much less experienced.

In short, the Cheyennes were caught in another unanticipated irony. In order to chase their dream of independence and power, they found themselves dancing to others' tunes. Within a couple of generations they experienced a prime example of this when the fundamental structure of plains trade shifted under their feet. When they first moved to the plains, they had transferred British trade goods, garden produce, bison products, and horses back and forth between Indian villages on the middle Missouri and tribes on the southern plains. By the 1820s, however, the river villages were in steep decline, and the Tsistsistas faced the loss of one end of the profitable shuttle. But just then alternatives appeared. White trading companies established substantial posts or temporary entrepots at several locations on the northern and central plains. Quickly the Cheyennes reoriented toward these new outlets; soon they were trading primarily for goods channeled through those posts.

That switch, in turn, demanded two other adjustments. Although they continued to deal in some of the old goods, especially horses, the Cheyennes had to concentrate increasingly on what white traders wanted most—bison robes. That, of course, heightened the stress on that crucial animal. More important, this trade was no longer with other Indians. The Tsistsistas now dealt directly and almost exclusively with whites. Their vital exchanges were with a society that was at once more alien and far larger and more powerful than any native peoples. This change placed a high premium on secure, predictable lines of communication and exchange between two very different cultures.

The Cheyennes responded with a momentous adaptation. Its immediate focus was the family, but its true relation was between societies. Its key figure was the white trader, and its central institution was marriage. Cheyenne hunters transacted some business at posts or fairs, but much was conducted through white men who moved back and forth between trading entrepots and scattered villages, their horses and mules loaded with blankets, knives, muslin, coffee, foodstuffs, and other items. To ensure a reliable flow of goods, Cheyennes and other Indians married some of their women to these white men well connected within the trading network.

They could draw from a deep pool of possible husbands. Since the early 1820s white trappers, "mountain men," had worked the plains and mountains, earning considerable knowledge of the region and its peoples. They had dealt directly with white merchants. They had caught their prime prey, beavers, themselves and had prepared and swapped the pelts with firms operating out of New Mexico and Missouri. Some had taken Indian wives as helpmates and as a hedge against problems with the tribes, but Native Americans had relatively little direct role in the main business of trapping and exchange.

That changed around 1840. In that year—coinciding exactly with the great peace among the Cheyennes, Comanches, and Kiowas and the full occupation of the high plains—the beaver trade nosedived, the victim of overtrapping and collapsing prices. Mountain men shifted toward trade in a variety of animal products but especially in bison robes. Switching products also meant a change in production. The out-of-work beaver-killers found it far more efficient to rely on Indian men to kill bison and Indian women to turn skins into robes. Indian camps, that is, became the new production centers of the regional fur trade. To acquire those robes the former trappers thus became traders who carried goods from white outposts to Indian camps. Mountain men became middlemen. This new arrangement obviously required dependable, secure lines of exchange among the plains bands.

The match seemed perfect: precisely when Cheyennes and others were looking for reliable links to trade goods, former trappers needed sure access to what were suddenly the essential products of their business. The common ground of this mutual adjustment was the trade marriage. With amazing speed a marital network laced over the high plains and bridged native and white societies. The system already was well advanced in 1842 when John Charles Fremont found several of these families along the South Platte,

New Englanders who had come west to trap in the 1820s, then turned to trading, taken Lakota wives, and produced a crop of "little buffalo-fed boys" who frolicked around Fremont's camp.[31] There were many such unions in the Platte and Arkansas valleys and along the Front Range, including several among the loftiest families of both cultures. The daughter of White Thunder, the Cheyennes' keeper of the sacred arrows, married William Bent, builder of Bent's Fort. The sister of Red Cloud, perhaps the most respected Lakota of his day, married Marcellin St. Vrain, younger brother of Bent's partner, Ceran St. Vrain. Lakota women were taken as wives by virtually every significant trader with the larger outfits and other independents in the North Platte region.

The spread of trade marriages should not be seen as too stark a change. From one perspective this was just another variation on very old patterns. At least for generations—and by some evidence for centuries—potentially hostile native groups had secured channels of trade through marriages and adoptions. Even during war peaceful exchange was carried on by individuals who crossed between enemies over bridges of kinship.[32] Among the French, English, and Native Americans, of course, trade marriages had been vital to economics and diplomacy since the earliest contact, and during the beaver-trapping era such unions had given mountain men some security and help around camp. Marriages among traders after 1840 in this sense were natural outgrowths of old arrangements.[33]

But the number of Indian-white unions undeniably increased during these years. An old, tested system was expanded to satisfy the increasingly urgent needs of a new situation. Trader-husbands naturally became cultural brokers as well, interpreters in the fullest sense. They helped explain each side to the other, everything from sororal kinship and bookkeeping to facial markings and card games. With the help of these marriages the Cheyennes could still pursue their vision as the Called Out People. They continued to tap into the vigorous economic network of the plains, just as horses allowed them to draw more widely from the country's natural energy.

But as with their leap to horseback, this change left them open to other dangers. Through trade they linked themselves to a society that was immeasurably more powerful, wildly different, and not especially sympathetic to their own. By relying on intermarriage as their connective mechanism, they were handing over a crucial element of security to men who, despite their beaded buckskins and braided hair, were products of that other, potentially threatening culture. If the floor of the plains economy shifted again—more specifically, if white society should step in to redraw the lines along which power and resources and wealth flowed—the Cheyennes and other plains tribes would have to count on their white in-laws to speak for them. Trader-husbands would have to fashion some viable place for Indian peoples in whatever social order followed. Whether they were up to the job, or whether they had any interest in it, remained to be seen.

THESE PROBLEMS were external. The vicious competitions from other tribes, the specter of shrinking herds, the shifting economy, and vulnerability to outside power and further change—the dangers stood outside the Tsistsistas. The people would need to face them together. But by Cheyenne tradition, the gravest peril of these years had nothing to do with assaults from other tribes or pressures from whites. This threat came from within their own ranks. The same passage that gave them a new identity and a new name also ate away at their unity and common perception of themselves.

Part of the cause lay in the new economy. Trade at first pulled the Cheyennes southward to a more central position between the poles of trade in New Mexico and the middle Missouri. About 1815 or 1816 they were reportedly the primary figures at a great trading council on Cherry Creek, near the future site of Denver, where they exchanged British goods with French trappers and large delegations of "remoter tribes," including Arapahoes and Kiowas, who had come from the south with horses, "which they rear with much less difficulty than the Shiennes [sic], whose country is cold and barren."[34] In 1821 Jacob Fowler visited an enormous congregation of Comanches, Kiowas, Arapahoes, Snakes, Apaches, and Cheyennes along the Arkansas River, still farther south. He was stunned by the number of horses in the camps—more than 20,000, he thought. Fowler, one of the century's worst spellers, found the Arapahoes especially friendly: "More Sevelity Exsists amongst those Indeans than anny I have Ever knone." They were nevertheless horse-poor, "haveing last Sommer traided With Chians of the meurey [Cheyennes of the Missouri]."[35]

There was a price, however. Their move toward a better trading position took them farther away from Noaha-vose, their spiritual base. The Tsistsistas literally were drawn off-center. The aggressive Lakotas, who saw the Black

Hills as their own blessed homeland, also pushed them southward. By the 1820s this problem was compounded by the scrambling of the trading system—the decline of the Missouri villages and the appearance on the plains of white trading posts. The various bands looked for dependable connections wherever they could find them. Several gravitated toward American Fur Company posts on the North Platte.

Then, in the late 1820s, a portentous arrangement was struck with two brothers from a prominent St. Louis family, William and Charles Bent. The pair were operating a small post near the base of Pike's Peak when an emerging Cheyenne leader, Yellow Wolf, suggested that if the brothers would move their operations to a more favorable spot farther down the Arkansas River, his followers would stay close and trade with the Bents and their partner, Ceran St. Vrain. By about 1830 Bent, St. Vrain and Company had built an imposing adobe fort near present-day La Junta, Colorado. Bent's Fort became the preeminent trading entrepot of the central plains. Many Cheyennes began to depend on it as a market for horses and robes and as an access to outside trade. The move had the added advantage of a climate friendlier to people and horses.[36]

Not all leaders agreed with Yellow Wolf, however. Those who followed him became the Hairy Rope band (Hevhaitaneos), named probably for the rope halters used with the main items of their trade. Later they were joined by the Southern Eaters (Wotapio) and the Scabbies (Oivimana), their name reportedly a caustic comment on the other basic trade good, bison robes. Other bands, including the Aorta (Heviksnipahis), Northern Eaters (Omisis), Bashful (Totoimana), and Pipestem (Hisiometanneo), kept their home ranges farther north, along the North Platte and in the Powder River country of Wyoming. They traded at Fort Laramie and at smaller posts opening in the region.[37]

This was an unprecedented fracture. The opportunities of trade, part of their dream of new life, were pulling the Tsistsistas apart. After 1830 those remaining close to entrepots along and above the North Platte were known as the Northern Cheyennes. Those drawn by Bent's Fort and the lodestone of the southern horse herds became the Southern Cheyennes, who were committed to a home range along the Arkansas, on the far edge of the map centered on Noaha-vose.

The Cheyennes were fragmented still more by another force. The first threat to their unity was basically economic and split the Called Out People into two broad groups. The second was environmental. It splintered the people at a more fundamental level and kept them broken into far smaller units.

Earlier, in the river villages to the east, large numbers of persons could live closely together throughout the year, and in fact plenty were needed to defend the sprawling gardens and permanent dwellings. Nomadic life, by contrast, had a shattering effect. It was yet another paradox of the more promising life. Hunting by horseback offered greater affluence and power, but those greater resources could only support people who lived in much smaller groups.

The problem (another paradox) was also the nomads' chief asset—their horses. With eight to twelve horses for every person, the size of herds mounted quickly. A gathering of only forty people might have more than 400 animals grazing nearby. Each of those animals needed considerable forage, so even a smallish camp required a great arc of pasture around it. The addition of just a few more people, then, brought a considerable increase in the number of horses, the living tools essential to their new way of life, which meant a far greater demand for what those tools needed. Defense against horse thieves also became more difficult as the herds grew. The implications were obvious: the need *for* horses and the needs *of* horses put a practical limit on the size of nomadic groups. And that limit was reached fairly quickly.[38]

Weather compounded this difficulty. Summer, given adequate rainfall, brought out the plains' generosity. The giant pastures of buffalo and grama grasses permitted huge gatherings of horses and therefore of people. Herds of tens of thousands were sometimes reported. During winter, however, forage became much scarcer at the very time that the horses' energy needs increased. Especially during storms nomads had to keep their herds close to them, frequently in small, tight places along streams protected by bluffs and timber groves. During the cold months, when weather could change almost instantly for the worse, congregating in any significant numbers was extremely risky. From November to April, plains peoples had no choice but to break up into small groups.

The environment, in short, demanded a social fission. On the Missouri the Cheyennes had lived in villages of about 800 to 1,000 persons each. Within and among villages were smaller units, bands united by kinship and other groups bound by common functions. The environmental pressures on the plains led to a hiving off and the creation of several new bands as well as to some shuffling and realignment as people changed their allegiances from one group to another. At the head of each matrilineal band was a man, a "chief," considered its spokesman for trade and other matters. Increasingly the band became the focus of an individual's identity. Week to week, however, Cheyennes often lived in a still smaller group, a camp, or *vestoz* (literally, "that which has tipis"), a collection of a couple of dozen or so related persons.[39] A camp was the maximum number of persons—and just as important, of horses—supportable when the plains were at their stingiest.

Living in these small groups, year after year, naturally ate away at any sense of common spirit. Heroic efforts were made to nurture an identity as a single Called Out People. Because military societies drew from all the bands, they helped stitch the bands together. There was also one common institution, the Council of Forty-four. These highly respected chiefs were selected for their sagacity, courage, generosity, and self-control. Their traditional purpose was to resolve disputes and promote peace among the bands, and beyond that they provided some central authority and sense of unifying character. Once a year it was still possible for Cheyennes to act out their seamless collective identity. In highest summer, with the highlands an enormous banquet of grasses, their new home briefly allowed gatherings even larger than in the old villages. The various bands of the Northern and Southern Cheyennes converged. They performed their various unifying rituals, including their sun dance, appropriately honoring the ultimate source of new power and reaffirming the Called Out People's communion under the All Being. In those weeks their vision was most real.

Nonetheless, the stresses and fissures became increasingly apparent as time passed. Besides the formal divisions among the Tsistsistas, particular events shocked the people as signs that things were coming unstuck. In 1854 Walking Coyote, adopted son of the prestigious Yellow Wolf and prominent among the Bowstrings warrior society, killed White Horse, head of another warrior society, the Kit Foxes.[40] Murder was an almost inexpressibly heinous crime; it fouled the sacred arrows with flecks of blood and drove away bison and other game until the arrows were spiritually cleansed. Homicide by a man of status could barely be conceived.[41] Walking Coyote's reason—White Horse's theft of his wife—carried no weight. A responsible man remained unflappable in the face of personal loss. He would wave away an affront, perhaps with a traditional comment: "A dog has pissed on my tipi."[42] Walking Coyote's terrible crime was immensely troubling, both on its face and as a symptom of cultural shattering and moral atrophy.

The pattern was inexorable and devilishly perverse. Everything good about the plains had a way also of limiting or threatening the Cheyennes' new life. With the power of grass came grinding warfare. Economic opportunity laid them open to events far beyond their influence. The inspirations of a new identity—trade and an environment swelling with unimaginable energy—ate steadily at their cohesion and sense of kinship. As they acted out their vision of the plains, the Tsistsistas were losing sight of who they were.

IT GOT WORSE. Not only did the Cheyennes have to face unforeseen implications of the best of their new world, but they also miscalculated badly how well the plains could support their newly imagined lives. Their brilliant adaptations were undermined by three forces. The first was their own misunderstanding. Their prime error was a failure to see how fully their life was bound to the demands of the very objects that opened the country's possibilities—their horses. A later oral tradition tells that when traders first brought horses to the Cheyenne river villages, leaders asked the All Being for animals of their own. Maheo answered:

> You may have horses. . . . You may even go with the Comanches to take them. But remember this: If you have horses everything will be changed for you forever.
> You will have to move around a lot to find pasture for your horses. You will have to give up gardening and live by hunting and gathering, like the Comanches. And you will have to come out of your earth houses and live in tents. I will tell your women how to make them, and how to decorate them.
> And there will be other changes. You will have to have fights with other tribes, who will want your pasture land or the places where you hunt. You will have to have real soldiers, who can protect the people. Think, before you decide.[43]

The leaders chose horses, of course, and their decision brought all that Maheo predicted—and more. By becoming people of the horse, the Cheyennes were stepping into an ecological arrangement, a relationship among land, climate, and resources, that was more complex and precarious than they could have guessed.[44]

Horse nomads had to live by a rigid annual cycle. It was governed not so much by their own needs, or the requirements of hunting, but in service to their horses. In spring they had to be close to the rivers and streams that held midgrasses and tallgrasses, the first high plains pasture to green up for the season. After their herds fattened and gathered strength, the bands moved in early summer onto the highlands between the stream drainages. Well fueled on shortgrasses, the horses could carry hunters in pursuit of bison that congregated to mate and in raids against enemies also drawn to the bounty. This was also the season of the sun dance and collective renewal.

In early autumn groups began once again to fragment into small bands, their *vestoz,* or camps, and to drift off the highlands toward the valleys of creeks and rivers. This turn of the cycle was driven less by grazing than by the weather. In winter horses and people had to be close to the only shelter available, the river bottoms, with their bluffs, cutbanks, and canyons. Cottonwood groves along the streams gave added protection and essential fuel for fires, and in the worst weather horses could eat the green shoots of saplings. In these enclaves, as the veteran army officer Richard Irving Dodge wrote, "a day which would be death on the high Plains may scarcely be uncomfortably cold." Indians moved their herds close to these places as the weather cooled, and if a storm approached they would "fly to shelter at the first puff."[45] Even so the terrible cold and poor forage took a huge toll on the animals. Many died, and survivors were a mockery of the horseman's dream:

> He is a most miserable object, an animated skeleton. Exposed to the terrible cold and piercing winds of a plains winter, his scanty and innutritious food buried beneath the snow, he would undoubtedly perish, but that squaws cut branches from the cottonwood tree for him to browse upon. At this season, with coat long, shabby, and rough, matted with dirt and burrs, hips extended in the air, belly pouffed out with sticks and bark swallowed in the vain hope of appeasing the hunger that consumes him, forlorn and downcast, he looks an uncouth monster rather than a horse.[46]

Around early March, as the cold time eased, the camps would again be near the swards of spring grass to save the herds' famished survivors. With that, the cycle began again.

This was one more well-crafted adaptation, but at one point every year, the close pinch of winter, it posed serious problems. In those months when demands on horses and people were the greatest, the pastoralists and their herds had the fewest resources and least livable space available. They focused their hungriest need on a few limited habitats, all of them in river and stream basins, a small portion of the vast plains region. Often they lived as small camps tucked in canyons and cottonwood copses. Occasionally they gathered as crowds in the rare great stands of riverside timbers, like the gigantic trading camp Jacob Fowler found on the upper Arkansas in 1821. George Bent remembered as a child in the 1830s seeing Indian herds grazing for fifty miles along the river near Bent's Fort. In spring 1848, Thomas Fitzpatrick found a string of Lakota and Cheyenne villages with thousands of horses strung out for nearly eighty miles along the South Platte, plus another twenty miles up Lodgepole Creek. The next November an estimated 6,000 Indians, a clustering that easily could have included 20,000 to 25,000 horses, camped at the Arkansas "big timbers" in weather "cruelly, bitterly cold . . . , snowing and freezing."[47]

That intense occupation wore away at the very resources that made those enclaves valuable. Nearby forage was eaten down by horses trying (usually in vain) to keep their energy's intake ahead of its outward flow, as cold snaps pulled the heat from their bodies. More telling was the loss of trees. The cottonwoods and willows were steadily cut, burned, and eaten, year by year. The attrition advanced quickly. By one estimate, a camp with only thirty-eight horses spending three-and-a-half winter months along the Smoky Hill River would have consumed all firewood along the stream for nearly 600 meters and all pasture within an arc of more than a quarter of a mile.[48] Nomadic herders had to reckon with this tightest point of their yearly lives or die. Adjusting would have been difficult, even with no other problems at hand.

But a second problem was bearing down on the Cheyennes, compounding the effects of the first—an historical event far beyond their control. In the 1840s white pioneers began an emigration across the plains toward the Pacific Coast. They followed the main valley of the Platte River and the river's north branch to the Continental Divide and beyond. At first this movement of people and animals was barely noticeable, but it gradually grew and then exploded with the gold rush of 1849. The cross-plains traffic added to freighting on the Santa Fe Trail that had run along the Arkansas River between Missouri and New Mexico since the early 1820s. Great numbers of draft animals and huge herds of cattle and sheep accompanied the overlanders and freighters. The total of the two-legged and four-legged travelers was staggering. Between 1841 and 1859, more than 300,000 persons and at least 1.5 million oxen, cattle, horses, and sheep moved up the Platte road.

The impact was predictable. The thousands of outsiders brought an upsurge in one of the frontier's prime influences—epidemics. The year 1849, soon to be symbolic of opportunity and adventure to whites, was called the "Winter [Year] When the Big Cramps Take Place" by Southern Cheyennes who were devastated by cholera contracted from emigrants. The Flexed Leg band vanished, its minority of survivors absorbed by other bands.[49] The

Kiowas' pictorial image for the year was that of a man howling in agony with his knees drawn to his chest. Soldiers along the Platte reported terrible losses among Northern Cheyennes and Lakotas; some of the sick had been left to die and bodies had been wrapped in robes and laid out in abandoned lodges. At the eastern end of the trail an agent to the Pawnees reported 1,200 dead, nearly one-fourth of the tribe, with the epidemic still raging. The many unburied corpses were eaten by wolves.[50] The heavy traffic over the next decade proved an effective vector for spreading other diseases.

Other devastation, slower but in its way just as terrible, came from the streams of animals that moved annually up the roads. Every summer tens of thousands of oxen and other cattle ate voraciously at the grasses along the river trails. Iron-rimmed wagon wheels tore and crushed the earth, and emigrants and freighters felled and burned trees throughout the great Platte valley and along the Arkansas. This abrasion of resources was calamitous for plains Indians. In the autumn, after the last snaking wagon trains had passed through, the Cheyennes and other nomads left the highlands and headed for the river valleys. Now, however, they found many of those sanctuaries stripped of the timber and forage they needed to survive the winter. Some areas suffered less than others. The country between the Platte and the Arkansas roads—the valleys of the South Platte, and the upper Smoky Hill, Republican, and Solomon Rivers—was mostly untouched and unseen by whites. With the Cheyennes and their allies using it alone, this land showed some wear but still kept most of its resources. The wear was worst where Indians and whites overlapped the most, especially along the main Platte and North Platte and on the lower Arkansas. By the late 1850s these valleys were arguably the most overtaxed terrain in North America.[51]

A third and final force came not from human actions but from a return of an old natural cycle. Beginning in the late 1840s, just as the overland migration was really cranking up, a series of droughts hit the central plains. One blistered the Arkansas valley in 1849, another struck the entire region in 1855, and in the early 1860s two more, worse than the others, cooked the country from Nebraska to Indian Territory. The blows seemed even harsher because they followed a quarter century of generous rainfall that brought out the best the plains could offer.[52] The normally rich pastures took on a singed, balding look. The largest streams slowed, sometimes to a trickle, and the hundreds of seeps and ponds on the uplands shrank or disappeared.

Droughts were nothing new, of course. For centuries hunting cultures had adjusted painfully to the sudden loss of watering spots and plant life. The Cheyennes, however, had a much tougher time of it. Drought came as they were trying something never done before: building a new life based on another animal. Fundamentally, they were pulling power from a previously unavailable abundance, the grasses. Drought drastically reduced that pool of energy. The flow of power was suddenly choked off, and the meaning of the land and its animals changed. When grasslands were lush, a horse was an enormous extension of human strength and an expression of great wealth; without grass, a horse became a broken tool and an unsupportable burden.

Dry spells compounded the effects of the first two forces. As the highland grasses and ponds shriveled away, Indians stayed closer to the rivers and their forage—the same places they were overusing in the winter and that the white travelers and their animals were chewing, cutting, and burning between April and August. Making matters even worse, the bison, the Cheyennes' prime source of food, shelter, and trade goods and another great inducement for their shift to the plains, were disappearing. The reasons are cloudy. In part, however, the Indians' own prodigious hunting was surely to blame, and possibly diseases imported by overland animals. Certainly the degeneration of river habitats played a role; bison relied on those places as much as Indians and horses, and for much the same reason.[53]

A lifeway that had seemed pure allurement was turning out to be something more complicated, and as early as the 1830s some new arrivals were wondering about the implications. "I am traveling all over this country, and am cutting the trees of my brothers," Bloody Hand, an Arikara, told an army officer along the Platte in 1835: "I am travelling on their land and killing their buffalo before my friends arrive so that when they come up, they can find no buffalo."[54] That refrain became increasingly common, usually with the blame loaded onto whites who crowded the trails every summer. "Our women and children are suffering for food, . . . [and] we are now weak and poor," a prominent Southern Cheyenne, Old Bark, told Lt. J. W. Abert in 1845. "The whites have been amongst us, and destroyed our buffalo, antelope, and deer, and have cut down our timber."[55]

Old Bark pointed at only part of the problem. The Cheyennes were caught up in an old theme of gain and cost. As they broadened their command over valuable resources, they became absolutely reliant on the essentials they were helping to destroy. They found a dream of a people chosen for greatness, and with it an unstoppable cultural fracturing. They became some of the continent's finest warriors—and watched their men fall away in an almost continuous battling. They expanded their grasp over the land's energy and wealth; they became subjects of events they were powerless to affect. "Everything will be changed for you forever," the All Being had cautioned the Cheyennes when they asked for horses. Maheo's children were seeing the full truth of God's word.

THE SAME IRONIES were learned by every tribe drawn by the region's sudden new potential. Seen from one angle, the Cheyennes, Comanches, Kiowas, Lakotas, and others forged a stunning achievement. Western history traditionally celebrates the ability to exploit new challenges. The praise is usually reserved for white pioneers, but if we rethink the frontier as a general turbulence set loose by Euro-Americans, and if we bring all participants fully into the story, the Indians emerge as the champions of imaginative courage. Their shift to the plains was a masterpiece of adaptive fluency.

Like every frontier people, however, plains Indians brought along their own problems and contradictions. Those problems were compounded by natural and human forces beyond their view or control. They failed to grasp a fundamental ecological principal. In 1840, just as the Cheyennes were settling firmly onto the plains, a German scientist proposed what has been called Liebig's law, or the "law of the minimum."[56] It is deceptively simple: An organism's limits are set, not by the maximum profusion of necessary things, but by those things' minimum availability. To know how large something will grow, that is, or how successful a people ultimately will be, do not measure their essential resources at their most abundant. Look instead for how much is available when vital supplies are the tightest, lowest, and stingiest.

The rule sounds absurdly obvious, like telling a friend planning a long trip to pack for the worst weather as well as the best. But over and over in western history people have ignored what seems unignorable and have paid the price. For the Cheyennes and other nomads, that key measure was of pasture, wood, shelter, and water during the deepest winter, under the heaviest use, and when the droughts were most vicious. By the 1850s, after accomplishments as impressive as any on the unfolding frontier, plains Indians were feeling Liebig's law at its sternest. History and the weather were catching up with them.

Like everybody else on the frontier, they blamed other people for their problems. The obvious candidates were those who in fact were part of the trouble—the huge crowds of whites crossing their homelands and taking some of what the Indians needed most. Indians justified thefts and violence, an official wrote in 1849, "as a retaliation for the destruction of their buffalo, timber, grass, &c, caused by the vast numbers of whites passing through their country without their consent."[57]

This was the setting for the bloody incident at Grand Island in August 1856. In its aftermath frustrated Cheyennes lashed out at white travelers along the Platte road and angry young leaders called for further resistance. When Sumner set off on his campaign, an unprecedented violation of the newly won Tsistsistas' homeland, warriors were especially responsive to Ice's and Dark's promise of sacred support. And given all this, the moment of Sumner's call to "draw sabres" must have been profoundly demoralizing, a great twinge of doubt over the great dream itself.

Whites saw the clash on the Solomon in July 1857 as one more case of natives digging in their heels against civilization's vanguard. In fact, the battle followed from the Cheyennes' own pursuit of an audacious and dynamic vision. Their riding of the frontier had been masterful, but it also brought them into a tangle of unpredicted problems, some of their own making and others not.

The Indian perspective, the view from the plains eastward, was laid out clearly when several leaders met with Thomas Twiss, the agent on the upper Platte, in September 1858, a little more than a year after Sumner's victory. By "an Indian's reasoning," Twiss reported, the tribes' prospects were poor and getting worse. To illustrate their edgy mood and their "jealous care" of game and land, Twiss quoted a Lakota leader. As a young man—and he was then only fifty—the man had visited the Sac and Fox on the Mississippi, toured the great pipestone quarry, and celebrated the feast of green corn among the woodland Sioux. He saw no white people. Farther east among the Winnebagoes there were still no white faces. Only on the rim of Lake Michigan, in Potawatomie country, did he meet a few pioneers. Everywhere the tribes held dominion.

And now? Overlanders crowded the river roads. Agents asked for new agreements. All around the press on the tribes' territory and resources increased. "Our 'father' tells us the white man will never settle on our lands and kill our game," the Lakota man told Twiss, "but see! the whites cover all of these lands that I have just described, and also the lands of the Poncas, Omahas, and Pawnees."

The immediate future was even bleaker. Only two months earlier the Lakota leader had learned of another development more troubling than any before it. On the south fork of the Platte, he reported, "the white people are finding gold, and the Arapahoes and Cheyennes have no longer any hunting grounds. Our country has become very small, and, before our children are grown up, we shall have no more game." Twiss admitted that this "stated pretty accurately" the situation. Gold already was drawing hundreds of whites into country that Indians had kept mostly to themselves.

But even if the agent had wanted to halt the flow of events, and he definitely did not, Twiss thought it was too late. As he saw it, a combination of progress and fate—superior Anglo institutions, the rapidly growing white presence to the east, and the discovery of gold along the South Platte—had built into a momentum only a fool would confront: "It is beyond human power to retard or control it."[58]

Part Two:

GOLD RUSH

5

THE GOLD

To Buddhists and Christians gold is heavenly light and an earthly reminder of a call to spiritual perfection. It glows from the background of medieval icons and covers enshrined statues of Siddhartha, fluttering as thousands of scraps of thin, hammered leaf. Virtually every people who know it associate gold with purity. The English of Cromwell's time kept slivers of gold coin in their mouths to ward off plagues; Irish rubbed unwanted warts with gilded wedding rings. For alchemists, including Isaac Newton, gold held out the hope of enlightenment. Creating it from lead would show the way to a deeper transformation from base bodily urges to serenity and holiness.

As a help to physical labor, gold is virtually useless. It is a heavy, soft metal easily molded into jewelry but hopeless for implements. Its appeal comes from three qualities. It is rare. It is remarkably inert and will combine with almost nothing around it—the source of its "incorruptible" image. And it is shiny. In dozens of cultures gold's radiance links it intimately with the source of all power, the sun. Incas believed it was the solar essence fallen in fragments, "condensed light hidden in the shadows of the earth"; Aztecs called it *teocuitlatl,* "excrement of the sun." From this solar connection it also promised fertility, resurrection, and renewal. Sacrificial victims to Xipe Totec, the Aztec god of goldsmiths and spring rains, first were scorched black and then painted bright yellow as an annual plea from the earth for a new skin.[1]

Whether or not it replenished the fields of central Mexico, gold clearly had the power to reshape places, but not by adding directly to the strength of anyone or anything. Its force lay in its commanding cultural appeal, an allure that came close to enchantment. It did more than fog perception. Like the spellbinders of classic folktales, gold compelled those who held it to see the world entirely differently. Where people already looked at the land optimistically, that gave gold a special potency.

The American West had long been called the "golden land." The term expressed a general promise and a powerful, unfocused attraction. When gold was found in a particular place, that appeal took on a terrific, specific intensity, like light through a lens. The discovery of flecks of the metal in a millrace on the American River in California set off one of the century's great migrations to the continent's Pacific edge in 1849. Tens of thousands of persons were drawn across the continental center. The country they passed over, including the central plains, they considered a geographical hiatus, interesting and sometimes beautiful but finally a trial to be endured. Ten years after the rush to California, the power of gold was directed toward this American center. That region, and the nation, would be transformed.

WHEN EDWIN SUMNER AND JOHN SEDGWICK joined their forces on Independence Day of 1857, on their way to fight Cheyennes, they met in a place that had inspired a library of lovely fantasies. Rumors of gold along the South Platte and Front Range had been circulating for fifty years. The stories had been almost entirely ignored, and for good reasons.[2] Most were at least secondhand. The earliest published story came from Zebulon Pike. While being held by Spanish authorities in Santa Fe, Pike had met a trapper named Purcell who told of finding gold along the headwaters of the South Platte, though when pressed for proof Purcell said he had long ago thrown away his pouch of dust, "losing in his mind all the IDEAL VALUE which mankind have stamped on that metal."[3]

Most early reports, like this one, were from mountain men, by consensus the frontier's most accomplished liars. Similar stories floated out of the area during the next few decades, as Indian immigrants maneuvered for position on the plains. In 1823, as the Cheyennes were making their move for the

Arkansas, a party of adventurers reportedly found a silver mine in the Raton Mountains, just south of where the Arkansas left the Rockies. Ten years later another group of trappers were said to find good color along Clear Creek, a South Platte tributary in the neutral zone bitterly contested by Comanches and Cheyennes. The trapper Rufus Sage told of meeting an old French trapper who had found great flakes of gold in the same vicinity, but he had thrown them away and, "not being intellectually one of the brightest gems of nature's casket," had been unable find the original site. Sage also said he knew Arapaho warriors who had fought off a band of Pawnees with bullets smelted from gold they found in the dirt around their feet.[4]

More credible stories were mixed with the outlandish, but anyone could have heard much the same about any place between the Missouri River and the Sierra Nevada. For Indians, the country's potential was clearly demonstrated; they could watch others on horseback and see how the plains could be the source of greater power and wealth. For whites, on the other hand, nothing came from this country to make it anything more than a daydream. Much of the West was still the land of blow and buncombe. Creeks lined with gold dust, like caves full of Spanish treasure, seemed to be everywhere if one believed the tales. Sensible people listened with a wink and a smile.

A flurry of new reports came from the area after 1849. A variation of the overland trails ran out of northwest Arkansas and Indian Territory and up the Arkansas River to the Front Range. From there it followed the ancient road north along the base of the Rockies and finally joined the California Trail at the North Platte. Goldseekers and later cattle drovers took this Cherokee Trail to the Pacific, and some stopped to try the creeks along the way. Several fairly specific claims of gold trace came out of those trips. An Osage trader and trapper named Civil John claimed to have seen nuggets bubbling from a spring near a branch of the Arkansas River.[5] The timing was wrong, however. These were the years of the California hysteria. As the Sierra's mother lode poured out its millions, pioneers ignored possibilities closer at hand for the sure thing farther on. The Front Range was also politically unorganized territory and thus effectively beyond the reach of any government. Prospectors could expect neither protection from Indians nor any sure way to record their claims.

That barrier, at least, was removed with passage of the Kansas-Nebraska Act of 1854. During the next few years a flurry of new gold stories moved through Arkansas, Missouri, and the new settlements of Kansas. But other events intervened. Northeastern Kansas, the natural departure point for an expedition to the Rockies, was convulsed by the struggle between slave and Free-Soil forces and by a vigorous, sometimes violent scramble for townsites and rich prairie land. The upheaval, unusual even for a newly opened frontier, abated only when the territory voted resoundingly against slavery in August 1858.

There was also a fear of Indians. In the Treaties of Fort Laramie (1851) and Fort Atkinson (1853) Cheyennes, Arapahoes, Lakotas, Comanches, Kiowas, and Plains Apaches pledged not to molest travelers on the Platte and Arkansas roads, but within a few years they were restive, convinced that emigrants and freighters were responsible for their gathering troubles. They regarded the remaining trees, grass, and game along the roads with "jealous care," as Thomas Twiss put it, and in 1854 demanded that all traffic along the Platte road cease.[6] Just traveling those main trails seemed dangerous enough. Prospecting in the Cheyenne heartland between the Platte and Arkansas was beyond foolhardy.

Then came the troubles at Grand Island and along the Platte in 1856, the winter of growing tension, and Sumner's campaign that culminated along the Solomon River. Sumner's victory solved nothing; if anything it strengthened the hand of the more militant Cheyennes. The public perception, however, was of nomads beaten and pacified, and in fact the most belligerent were briefly demoralized by the stunning particulars of the defeat—Ice's and Dark's promise of godly favor, the high confidence in impotent rifles, then the charge of flashing steel. For a brief window in 1857 and 1858, prospectors were relatively free to chase down rumors that had floated around for decades.

The panic of 1857 in the meantime swept the East and Midwest. The economy slowed to a creep. As the new year began the depression worsened, especially in the Midwest and the middle border where the most frantic growth of the past twenty years had taken place. California no longer offered much of an opportunity; gold output there had declined by more than half since its peak in 1852. Meanwhile the seductive rumors persisted. Trace gold had been found near Pike's Peak, some Fort Laramie freighters heard in 1856, and the next year some Arkansas drovers, herding cattle up the Front Range on their way to the Pacific Coast, claimed to have found gold more plentiful than in California. Most recently, there was the party of Missourians found by Sedgwick during Sumner's campaign. Badly rattled after Indians stole most of their stock, they still insisted they had made lucrative strikes in the South Platte valley and even had given a bit to the Delaware scout Fall Leaf.[7]

Incentives were greater than ever. Barriers, if not removed, at least had been lowered. The middle border was full of restless men down on their luck and looking for a turn of fortune. Finally, a half-century after the first hints of gold in the Rockies, conditions were right for a thorough search.

In spring 1858 two very different expeditions set out for the Front Range. The Cherokee party was organized mainly by William Green Russell and John Beck. Both men were experienced goldseekers, and each had reason to believe the precious metal might be found in abundance along the Rockies' eastern face. Russell had spent his boyhood in the Cherokee country around Dahlonega, Georgia, site of the only significant gold rush east of the Mississippi. The bonanza in California sent him across the continent in 1849, and along the way he had panned a little gold in the Sweetwater River, in southwest Wyoming just east of the Rockies. During the next few years Russell moved restlessly—home to Georgia, back to the Pacific, then home again in 1852. Then he heard of John Beck. A Cherokee living in Indian Territory, Beck had also grown up in north Georgia before moving west. With other Cherokees he had traveled up the eastern face of the Rockies to California in 1850; and while camped along Ralston Creek, a small tributary of the South Platte, he and a few others had found traces of color. When Beck's story filtered back to Georgia through mutual acquaintances, Russell felt confirmed in his hopeful pan along the Sweetwater.

The obvious next step, a cooperative expedition to the Front Range, hung fire because of the same conditions that discouraged other goldseekers. Russell and Beck kept the idea alive, talking it up among relatives and neighbors, and by spring 1857 the pair were nibbling at the edges of the region. Beck and his son approached within sixty miles of Ralston Creek and once again found hints of gold before retreating in fear of Cheyennes and Arapahoes. Russell meanwhile took up land near Fort Riley, Kansas. Later he said that he had planned "a gold hunt," but the territory's political turmoil had held him back. With the coming of autumn, Beck left for Indian Territory, Russell for Georgia.

On the Kansas border, however, things were starting to bubble. A few weeks after Beck's and Russell's departures, a Missouri newspaper published a letter from George Butler, an Indian agent among the Cherokees, who retold the story of the find in 1850 along Ralston Creek, reported Beck's recent try in the area, and added Beck's opinion that the mineral region was "a fine country to live in." Reprinted throughout the Missouri and Mississippi valleys, Butler's letter drew considerable attention, in particular after Sumner's campaign. It was seductively specific, especially coming on the heels of a new rash of grand but fuzzy stories. The *New York Herald* had recently reported on "the very best authority" that all the central and southern Rockies were brimming with huge deposits of gold, silver, cinnebar, and "precious stones."[8] The new specifics about Beck seemed to prod into action many people who had heard those stories for years and now saw a chance to act.

Over the winter firm plans at last were made for a joint venture. In February 1858 Russell and eight others, including his two brothers, started for Kansas, where they picked up about a dozen more men. Beck formed a much larger company, mostly Cherokees. The two groups had trouble making connections, but Russell's party, helped along by a note scratched on a bison's shinbone, finally found Beck's just past the great bend of the Arkansas. On June 3 the united companies, about seventy strong, headed upriver and followed the Cherokee Trail up the Front Range. On June 23, as they rested on the South Platte, they were joined by twenty-seven Missourians stirred to action by Beck's story in a local paper. The entire contingent headed for their final destination, Ralston Creek. They arrived on June 25.[9]

At that moment, unknown to Russell and Beck, a second expedition was on the way. The Lawrence party had its start in a different chain of events. Sedgwick's column had brought back the Missourians' reports of gold along the South Platte, and the Delaware scout Fall Leaf had somehow received a few small nuggets he said were given to him by the frightened prospectors. Fall Leaf began to flash about this palmful of gold, tied up in a dirty rag. He embellished his story with a scene common in tales of the day; he said he made his find while stooping to sip from a mountain stream. However acquired, his scrap of nuggets was the first hard evidence of Rocky Mountain gold the Kansans had ever seen. Fall Leaf was well known and reasonably trusted. Some response was sure to follow.

During winter 1857–1858, as Beck and Russell were raising their companies, John Easter, a Lawrence butcher, was doing the same. He hired Fall Leaf to show the way, but at the last minute the Delaware backed out. In one story he feared the Cheyennes, in another he was stove up in a bar fight. He also didn't know where the gold had come from, of course, and so chose not to play the role of the Turk with Coronado. The Lawrence party headed west on their own, believing, as one put it, "that gold existed SOME-

WHERE in the Rocky mountains."[10] In late May they set out for the Santa Fe Trail and, beyond it, probably the only landmark they had ever heard of—Pike's Peak.[11]

This group differed from Russell's. Neither Easter nor anyone else in the group had any experience hunting gold. They were a collection of grocers and clerks, liverymen and farmboys who had recently come to Kansas and were suffering from the tight times of the depression. The company's sudden creation suggested both the region's changed circumstances and the early signs of a crowd mentality. Before 1858, departure for the Front Range was a careful and calculated process. Now leavetaking had a lighter, spontaneous spirit. "We anticipated a real 'joy' trip," a chance to see some new country and maybe shoot a buffalo, one of them wrote later.[12] Julia and James Holmes joined on the spur of the moment, not from economic interest but "animated more by a desire to cross the plains and behold the great mountain chain of North America."[13] The party grew as it went along. A California-bound family threw in with them after a visit around the Kansans' campfire. People seemed to go along essentially because others had. The ruling question was no longer "why?" but "why not?"

By June 12 they had reached the Arkansas. Earlier the party had organized into messes and elected a captain, J. H. Tierney. Duties were assigned and a daily routine developed. Some travelers sought their western adventure. "Every solitary wolf or mound of earth in the distance, was transformed by some of our most anxious and imaginative hunters into a buffalo," Julia Holmes wrote in her diary, but "a few short pursuits of these delusive objects served to render our braves more cautious." The men poked around Cheyenne funeral platforms and found two young eagles, barely fledged and "a pure, beautiful white."[14] It was a trip of new sights but no serious difficulties. They celebrated Independence Day by drinking their remaining whiskey at the base of the Rockies.

At this point more than 150 whites were straggled along the Front Range, far more goldhunters than had ever scoured the area at any one time. The immediate results were unencouraging. Most of the Lawrence group had the interest but no competence. Some conducted a desultory search near the base of Pike's Peak, not sure of what they were looking for. At that point there appeared from the north a large contingent who had left the Cherokee party. They joined some of the Kansans to follow a Mexican guide of dubious ability to explore South Park, several days into the Rockies, and three men went even farther west. They returned with nothing but frustration and a handful of iron pyrite. Those who never intended to hunt gold spent their first weeks admiring the scenery. Julia and James Holmes climbed Pike's Peak in early August. "I feel that I would not have missed this glorious sight for anything at all," she wrote her mother from the summit.[15]

For the rest of her time, Julia Holmes was deeply, painfully bored. Only the initiated, she told her diary, can imagine the "disgusting inactivity" of camp life.[16] By then the Kansans' quest was all but dead. Scratched and scraped after exploring the hills and canyons, their hands raw and chapped from testing the icy creekwater, most had given up. They spent what was left of the summer lounging in camp, carving pipes and finger rings from soft white limestone and playing cribbage and euchre. With no gold for gambling, they wagered for more leisure time, the losers taking on the winners' guard duties.

The Cherokee party had not fared much better. Although they found gold almost immediately along Ralston Creek and other nearby streams, the quantities were pitifully small. Beck and Russell began to pay for their puffery. Beck in particular had made grand claims while trying to raise an expedition. A day of panning gravel, he had promised, would pay twenty dollars or more. In fact, a man squatting for several hours in a frigid stream earned about fifty cents, barely enough for a plate of beans in Kansas City. The party was a mix of expertise and naivete. The leaders and several friends had prospected in Georgia and California and so knew the need for persistence, but most of the rest apparently were farmers who expected plenty, and fast. Grumbling began almost immediately. On July 2 the first few defectors headed south, saying that "they had farms and niggers at home, and home they were going."[17] Two days later the majority of the company, including Beck, all the Cherokees, and most of the Missourians, joined the exodus. Some of them prospected briefly with the Kansans. Seventeen more, tired and fearful of Indians, announced that they were giving up on July 6.

From a bit more than 100, the expedition had dwindled to Green Russell and a dozen others. They stayed, apparently, from a combination of experience, loyalty, and family ties. Russell was clearly the key figure. The group members, which included his two brothers and two cousins, had either come with him from Georgia or had joined him in Kansas. Russell doubtlessly argued that two weeks of searching were not nearly enough for a final judgment. The few accounts of him suggest a confident man who inspired trust. In a later portrait he has a direct, drowsy-eyed look of assurance.

Whatever his appeal, Russell convinced the others to stand against the tide.[18] On the afternoon of July 6 the "apostates," as one of Russell's followers called the last departing group, started homeward. The final thirteen prospectors immediately moved farther up the Platte and camped on Dry Creek, a small tributary, about eight miles above the mouth of Cherry Creek.[19] Within an hour they found color. A day or two later they were gathering up to ten dollars a day per man, roughly twenty times the yield of any place tried before.

THIS WAS THE TRUE DISCOVERY of gold in the Pike's Peak region. Many other people had previously found traces. A few, notably the Missourians who met Fall Leaf and Sedgwick's troops, may have located it in substantial quantities. But among all the tales of gullies full of nuggets and banks of cinnabar, only Russell's find met the three specifications of effective discovery. He located gold in reasonable amounts, enough at least to provoke an immediate interest. His strike was precisely located; with adequate instructions, anyone could find it. Finally, the find shortly would be verified and reported by a neutral observer. These criteria satisfied the minimal skepticism of the thousands who looked westward for a fast road to riches.

Russell's strike, however, was not particularly rich or promising. He had found placer gold, an erosion from the mother deposits in the mountains. Gold originates deep in the earth, and most of it stays there—thus the first element of its appeal, its rarity. When mountains are formed the process of hefting them upward generates enormous subterranean heat. In the fracture and lifting, magmatic force squeezes molten rock, some of it carrying gold, up into fissures that vary from filigree-thin to a few feet wide. The liquid rock cools and forms veins; gold veins typically also carry white quartz. The gold remains in veins for a while in geological time, and in human terms for an unimaginable period (in the Rockies about 75 million years). Gradually, however, water, wind, and ice are wearing down mountains, even as they are being built. While the earth is pushing part of itself up, erosion and gravity are pulling it back toward the plain below. Gold comes out with everything else, flecked off from veins usually in tiny amounts. Some of it washes down in creeks, tumbling with the boulders, stones, gravel, dirt, and sand. Here its second elemental appeal, its inert incorruptibility, comes into play. Although pumped up as superheated liquid, cooled within quartz, eroded, and flushed in frigid water, gold nonetheless combines with virtually nothing it bumps into. It stays pure. Because it is also heavy, it sinks to the creekbed as the stream slows and levels out. Then its final appeal, its shininess, attracts the eye of a prospector like Green Russell as he washes it free of the surrounding gravel and dirt from the bottom of a stream like Dry Creek.

Placer gold is the most accessible form of the precious metal. It has come out of its hiding place and sits literally at the feet of anyone looking for it. It can be mined with only a pan or with systems built by the simplest carpentry. These aspects made it the prospector's favorite: "placer" is from the Spanish word meaning "pleasure."

But placer gold is only a tiny portion of the original source. It represents crumbs brushed from the table. The real feast remains to be found and taken. Not all placer gold is alike, furthermore. Tumbling among the rounded creek stones, gold dust is pounded and ground. The farther it travels, the finer it is. Russell and his men discovered "flour" gold, exceedingly light and chaffy. That had two implications. This dust obviously had come a long way; its mother deposit could be anywhere within the creek's watershed, a giant arc reaching high into the peaks that rose to the west. And although it occasionally occurs in concentrations that yield well for a short time, flour gold is rarely found in large amounts. Russell knew that the dust he found would be quickly gone.

Sure enough, the return from these first diggings began to decline sharply after several days. The party made the next logical move, testing several other streams in the area, trying to gauge the extent of the placer beds and hoping to find some that would continue to pay. They discovered others like the first. One creek provided up to eighteen dollars a day for one man's labor, but none promised a sustained yield. The land teased the prospectors.

On the last day of July, a small group rode up to Russell's camp near the site of his original discovery. Among them were several mountain men and John Cantrell, a Westport trader. Cantrell had been at Fort Laramie, selling whiskey and supplies to travelers and trappers, when he heard that men were panning on the Platte, and he decided to come down for a look. The Georgians readily showed him one of the most lucrative runs of gravel, which he dug out with a hatchet and washed in a frying pan.[20] Cantrell soon left with a pouch of dust and a few bushels of unpanned dirt. Three weeks later he was in Westport, where he was well known. In a dramatic demonstration on a prominent street, Cantrell washed some gravel from his bag. The crowd could look down and see the glitter. Immediately the word went out:

THE NEW ELDORADO!!!
GOLD IN KANSAS TERRITORY!!
THE PIKE'S MINES!
FIRST ARRIVAL OF GOLD DUST AT KANSAS CITY!!!

This report, published in the *Kansas City Journal of Commerce* on August 26, was elaborated by newspapers throughout the Missouri valley. By the first days of September, the "yellow fever" had reached Cleveland, Ohio, where William Salisbury, an unemployed college dropout, read the news, his eyes widening at the thought of making fifteen dollars a day just by bending over and picking it up.[21] By October 1 the word had made its way to the Pacific Coast via Panama. Soon the Overland Mail Company, which was opening its transcontinental service during these same weeks, was carrying regular reports to San Francisco, and from there inflated rumors crackled by telegraph into the mountain camps: a man had made $600 in several days, Californians heard, and a child had found $1,000 in a few weeks.[22]

Outfits already were organizing in Kansas towns for a trip to the mountains. This emigration was necessarily limited. It was late in the season for westering, so only people living in the closest zone of border settlement—eastern Kansas and Nebraska—could consider taking the trip. In all, a few hundred made the crossing between September and January. They were a diverse lot. The majority were young men, many set adrift by the depression and all of them on the scent of income and excitement. "Sam has the 'gold fever' and is almost carried away," a member of a prominent Missouri family wrote of his brother after they heard that a prospector had quickly gathered $40,000 in dust. Sam was determined to go, which was just as well: "He will not lose much . . . as he is making nothing here."[23] Winter prospecting would be difficult, but those on the scene would still be in position to grab the richest pockets at the first thaw.

There was, in any case, not much time for thought. In Rockport, Kansas, twenty-two-year-old J. C. Baird heard a man walking the streets and calling out, "All aboard for Pike's Peak, Cherry Creek, and the Rocky Mountains!" A day later he had joined a party of thirteen headed for Russell's diggings.[24] Most of the white population scattered along the Front Range also gravitated to Cherry Creek. The Lawrence party had grown tired of loafing and carving limestone gewgaws and had already abandoned their camp at Pike's Peak. Some had drifted back to Kansas; others had moved south to Fort Garland and Taos. When word spread of Russell's discovery, those in the area immediately headed back to the South Platte and settled in.

Meanwhile Russell's party had been busy. Some explored the Platte nearly 100 miles into the mountains, struggling up canyons thick with underbrush and jumbled with boulders. Next Russell led an expedition northward up the face of the Front Range to an area along Medicine Bow Creek, near where he had found color a decade earlier. A later foray tested the country southward along the mountains into New Mexico. In this wide reconaissance Russell's party found plenty of placer gold, but, as one of them wrote, "The main question yet remains unsolved, viz: THE SOURCE WHENCE THIS GOLD HAS DRIFTED."[25]

Odds of an immediate solution were dwindling fast, however. By September most of the best placer locations had been found and the mining season was coming to a close. A placer operation had to have water to wash the gold dust free of its dirt, and as summer passed into autumn, the creeks and rivers steadily dropped, nearing the low point of their annual cycle. Within several more weeks what water was left would start to freeze, and mountain storms would halt most prospecting in the high country. Chances of a good and quick return would have to wait until spring.

AT THIS POINT the attention of the Platte campers began to slide to other matters. Between September and November many went back to Kansas, some to stay and others to spend the winter more comfortably before returning for another try. A core remained. By October they were making preparations for the cold months ahead. They stocked forage for their animals and hunted to put in stores of seasoned meat. In virtually the same motion, they began to claim and lay out towns.

The change was not nearly as abrupt as it might seem. There were hints that some emigrants had planned from the start to engage in town promotion if gold was found. Expedition organizers had given vague enticements of long-term settlement—John Beck had called the area "a fine country to live in"—and some rank and file had come equipped for the tasks ahead. One Kansan brought equipment to survey sections, streets, and lots. This is not to say these men had come with hidden purposes. They were products of a time and place in which speculation, especially in land, was almost second nature. The middle border in the mid-1850s was full of "magicians" who knew how to turn a prospective town site into a paper fortune, Henry Villard wrote, "but the revulsion of 1857 knocked the enchanting wand out of their palsied hands." For these men the news from the Rockies promised a speculative revival, and many on the South Platte, Villard noted, were the sort who "desired not to pitch into, but onto the land."[26]

Another impulse was at work. Within a few weeks the emigrants would have company—lodges of Arapahoes and Cheyennes. Prospectors had known from the start that this was Indian country. There may have been others besides Indians. An early history of Denver noted offhandedly the story that Mexicans, in partnership with the trader John Simpson Smith, had prospected and mined at a site on the South Platte known as Mexican Diggings, about three miles above the mouth of Cherry Creek.[27] Although there is no mention of Mexicans in the area at this time, the Kansans and Georgians probably had heard of earlier expeditions from the south, and they certainly knew the Platte was easily reached by the old road from Taos. In short, the newcomers understood that others had been in this place before, knew it better, and at least in the short run could bring in considerable numbers of their own. Laying out a town was like driving a cultural stake. As easterners competed among themselves, they reached out to bring this country into their common grasp, and the central ritual in this act of faith was the survey. Notice was given: Society from the Missouri valley, with its grids of streets lined with mercantiles and saloons, would control the area.

The center of action shifted. If the miners could be said to have a base, it had been close to the first serious panning around Dry Creek, but as interest drifted to town sites they looked farther afield. Hopeful settlements appeared over the next several months on the Cache la Poudre River, Clear Creek, Boulder Creek, Plum Creek, and to the south along Fountain Creek at the base of Pike's Peak. The best spots would combine accessibility, strategic location for future development, and attractiveness. The trick was to guess where those places were.

In this effort, several among the Lawrence party were on more familiar ground. They were from the Missouri border, the trenches of American urban promotion, and they could see an opportunity before stumbling over it. Quickly they set to work.[28] Some laid out Montana City on the banks of the Platte upstream from Cherry Creek at a spot where they had begun some tentative panning. A few then reconsidered. Four miles downriver the trading road from New Mexico to Fort Laramie passed by the mouth of Cherry Creek. There, they thought, was the obvious site for a commercial entrepot. One of these men, William Hartley, was the civil engineer who had brought the surveying equipment. This group immediately laid out two sections of land in the angle formed by the south bank of the Platte and the east side of

Cherry Creek. Soon several streets were staked out in the town site they called St. Charles.[29]

Several Georgians also were interested in town promotion. The most prominent, Dr. Levi Russell, brother of William Green, discussed with some of the Lawrence group possible sites for another entry. Just then a fresh wave of immigrants arrived, the first of those who had heard the golden news in the Kansas border towns. On November 1 an amalgam of early prospectors and new arrivals approved a constitution for a new town on the west side of Cherry Creek, across the stream from the St. Charles site. Its name, Auraria, both recalled a Georgia town near the Russell home and promised a glittering future in the new land. An observer wrote home the next day with typical optimism: "It is going to be the place."[30]

These hopeful townmakers, however, were about to meet their master. The autumn tide brought William H. Larimer. A native of Pennsylvania, he had been on the border for three years, boosting a variety of projects. First had been LaPlatte, Nebraska, on the Platte River near its mouth. It was a frontier town like many others: a good location, a fine prospectus, and virtually no people. LaPlatte suffered credit problems, then the river it celebrated washed most of it away. Larimer left for other speculations in Omaha and Leavenworth, where he and his sons heard of Russell's strike. Probably Larimer was less impressed by the wondrous talk than by the fact that so many people were talking. He quickly decided to go.[31]

Larimer showed his shrewdness and initiative even before his first step toward the mountains. He knew, as did every western promoter worth the name, that the best guarantor of a frontier town's success was a superior connection to the outside world. Accordingly, Larimer paid a call on one of Leavenworth's most prominent citizens, William H. Russell, a senior partner in the West's greatest freighting and stage firm, Russell, Majors, and Waddell. The two men ended their visit with an understanding. If Russell's firm should decide to establish a stage route to the gold fields, Larimer's town site, wherever it might be, would be the line's terminus.[32]

That done, Larimer, his younger son, and four others set out following the Arkansas River route on October 1. They soon met another mountain-bound group from the Kansas capital, Lecompton. The travelers gave Larimer some exceptionally welcome news. These dozen men carried a decree from the governor of Kansas, James W. Denver, organizing the general area of the gold strikes into Arapahoe County. Governor Denver had named several members of the Lecompton party—H. P. A. Smith, Edward "Ned" Wynkoop,

Hickory Rogers, and Joe McCubbin—as officers of the new county. And for treasurer, Denver had chosen William Larimer. His appointment might have been a stroke of luck or yet another case of Larimer smoothing his own way; Denver later wrote that he simply knew of the Leavenworth promoter and that he was going to the new settlements. Solicited or not, the appointment made Larimer part of the area's first power structure. He also heard alarming news from Green Russell, whom he met hurrying eastward along the Arkansas on his way to Georgia. After praising the area's potential, Russell reported that boomers already were laying out town sites. Urging on his newfound fellow officeholders, Larimer pressed forward. The party arrived at Cherry Creek late on November 16.[33]

Larimer was up before dawn the next day, stamping around his chosen spot. By the time his son found him he had cut four cottonwoods and laid them in a square. It was the first "improvement" of his rising city. The site was on the east side of Cherry Creek, looking from slightly higher ground across at Auraria's scattering of cabins. Immediately he started soliciting allies among earlier arrivals, and within five days he had founded a town company.[34]

Larimer had a problem, however. His site was already claimed for the future city of St. Charles. Once again Larimer showed his experience and varied skills. First he worked the time-honored frontier tradition of preemption. None of the founders of St. Charles, he noted, was on the site. Most had headed home to Lawrence a few weeks earlier to gather supplies and more settlers. Along the way, after meeting several parties moving toward the mountains, they had sent one of their number back, fearing their site might be jumped, but that man lost momentum after raising the walls of a cabin. That was not enough to hold the land, Larimer and his supporters argued; if the St. Charles group had earlier preempted, they had later deempted. To help make their point, the new claimants soon had a surveyor setting posts at their town's boundaries and laying out streets, along which they quickly constructed cabins of their own.[35]

Larimer turned also to another common maneuver. He absorbed the competition. Two members of the St. Charles company had remained in the area. John Simpson Smith and William McGaa (or Jack Jones) were mountain men and traders who had worked the region for years. With their Cheyenne and Lakota wives they had gravitated to the diggings when they heard of the strike, and both had joined in the bid to establish St. Charles. Larimer and his cohorts quickly moved to pull Smith and McGaa into their own venture, which must have seemed like a better bet than a town with an absentee population. Smith and McGaa were quickly aboard. When the principals of the St. Charles enterprise eventually returned, they found their town site occupied and their partners defected. Larimer, having seized both the ground and the initiative, offered the cup of consolation—shares in his town company. The St. Charles group accepted.

Larimer's performance was masterful. His town site's location was the best on three counts. It would be the first reached by anyone traveling either the Platte or Arkansas roads. It stood also along the traders' path from New Mexico to Fort Laramie. And, assuming the mother deposits lay within the Platte's mountain sources, the town's position was ideal as a transition point between any future mining camps and the world to the east—an advantage he had anticipated, even before leaving home, in his deal with Russell's stage and freight business.

Larimer believed his city-in-embryo needed more, however. Official confirmation was essential, he thought, and political favor much desired. Two weeks after his arrival Larimer sent Ned Wynkoop and a friend back east to secure support from Lecompton authorities, including the man who had been governor when they left, James Denver. Wynkoop soon learned the dangers of winter travel on the plains. As he moved down the Platte a norther dropped the temperature to twenty below zero and raked the two men with razor winds. Wynkoop made it through with badly frostbitten feet and a better understanding of weather in Nebraska. The news in Lecompton wasn't good, either. The legislature had recognized the St. Charles company, and James Denver, the man Larimer considered a benefactor, had resigned and been replaced.[36]

As it turned out, by the time this news made it to the mountains the Larimer group's possession of the Cherry Creek site was too firm to challenge. Distance, winter weather, and the pace of events gave the people on the scene the advantage over those who went home. Before that was clear, however, the company left a lasting reminder of the pioneer impulse to look east for approval. In a long discussion prior to Wynkoop's frigid dash to Kansas, they debated what to call their town. They considered several euphonious options but settled on a simple, politically resonant name for their metropolis of cottonwood logs: Denver City.

BY THE TIME Denver was named, the first author of these changes had determined it was time to look toward 1859. William Green Russell counseled with his loyal dozen and decided to return to Georgia with his brother Oliver and one other. He was sure the next year would bring much richer strikes in the mountains, but they would need help. Back home he would recruit prospectors and buy supplies to build mining equipment. As reinvestment he took everything his company had to show for a summer in El Dorado: a pouch of dust worth between $300 and $500. The three set out about October 1. Except for a few bumpy spots—like the night wolves chewed in half the rawhide tethers of the men's horses, which then ate most of their supplies—they completed the trip safely and set to work.

The rest stayed to hold their claims and to try their hands at townmaking. To find winter supplies Levi Russell took a wagon south to Fort Garland, although he had no dust or biting money. He tried some panning along the way but earned little, so when he entered the sutler's store he could only barter with what he had. As Americans from Boston to San Francisco read breathless reports of nuggets like hen eggs, as thousands gathered their kit and dreamed of finding fortune with the lucky argonauts already rich beyond imagination, Levi Russell sold his last asset, a gold watch, to buy a few bags of flour and dried beans.[37]

6

THE GATHERING

Tom Sanders remembered well the day the news arrived. For several years his family had worked their farm near Girard, Illinois. None of them had found it easy. Tom's father especially had sagged under mounting debt and drudge labor, slipping lately into dark, clinchjawed moods. Then, in fall 1858, word came of gold at Pike's Peak.

"The effect was electrical," Tom recalled. His father "forgot his own worn out condition and hard work and became all fired up again with the ambitions of earlier years." Within days the man made up his mind: they would go, all of them. His wife begged him to reconsider, for God's sake and the children's, but Tom's father sold the farm and most of their belongings and packed what was left into a converted farm wagon. A month after hearing the first rumors, they were on the road.[1]

Thousands of others joined the Sanders family on their impulsive journey. The panic of 1857 and the deepening depression already had shaken many Americans loose from their roots. "The disposition to emigrate has reached every class of society," a Kansas editor had written months before the strike. Frustrated and desperate, armies of the displaced were ready to "cast their lots with the people of the west."[2] Sumner's victory, coming virtually at the same moment as the financial collapse, suddenly opened the door for a safe passage to one of the closest regions of the new country, the Front Range. Then word arrived of Green Russell's strike by the foothills of the eastern Rockies. El Dorado waited barely 600 miles west of the Missouri River.

The news spread by telegraph and mail and was passed along city streets and down corduroy country roads, into market towns and hamlets tucked deep in woodlands and mountain hollows. Hopes of a new bonanza spread like a reviving breath across the stricken East. Some editors inflated the slightest rumors. The Cherry Creek diggings, according to the *Democrat* of Carrollton, Maine, were the richest the world had seen. The *New York Times* was more cautious in its first report on September 1, but it soon speculated that the discoveries might give the economy a jog that would be of "profound interest."[3] The word crossed the Atlantic by ship—Cyrus Field's cable had begun operations in early September but had shut down after two days—and the London *Times* broke the story on the thirteenth, soberly telling of "considerable excitement" in Kansas after a couple of men with the simplest equipment made $600 in a week.[4]

Now the restless victims of the depression had a focus and a destination. "There is scarcely a village west of Ohio in which some are not fitting for and impatiently waiting the day when a start may be prudently made," reported the *New York Tribune* in late January.[5] In Amboy, Illinois, a sizable contingent that included the mayor was ready to go. They would join companies from Joliet, Sycamore, and scores of other towns across the state. The farther west one moved, the more frenzied the activity. "Nearly every man you meet is bound for the Peak in a 'few weeks,'" an Iowan wrote in his diary.[6]

The great gathering was under way.

THIS NEWEST EMIGRANT SURGE began another transformation of mid-America. Towns along the eastern edge felt an economic jolt and began to rethink what they might become. The gathering spawned a vigorous, sometimes ruthless competition among economic interests as far away as the Atlantic Coast. That competition in turn began a subtler process full of implications—a change in the way Americans pictured that great wedge of prairie and plains between the Missouri River and the Rockies.

During the previous few generations Indian peoples had dreamed this same country into a new shape. They brought their thoughts to life and maneuvered the land and its animals into other arrangements. They conceived new stories to explain the present and to inspire their future. They found a measure of glory, even as they came to face some of the uglier consequences of their imaginations.

Now another vision was taking its turn. The events it set in motion once again remade the plains and moved the lives of its people and creatures in another direction. Soon the Republic at large would begin to see itself differently, as Indians and whites fought to control the meaning of the continental center.

At the heart of this story were the routes that emigrants would use to cross the plains from the Missouri valley to the Rocky Mountains. These trails were more than part of the landscape; they became actors themselves. Travelers saw them as friends and adversaries; editors canonized and vilified them; over time their characters changed for better and for worse.

Although a few Californians came in from the west along the old California Trail and a trickling of Texans moved up from the south, crossing the Red River in the vicinity of Bonham and ascending the Canadian River and the Arkansas to the mountains, the huge majority of goldseekers came west from the Missouri and Ohio valleys, the middle Atlantic states, and the upper South. They traveled by several combinations of road, rail, and water. Most who came from the South and the southern portions of Ohio, Indiana, and Illinois gravitated toward St. Louis. From there they could go by steamboat up the Missouri to any of several departure points—Kansas City, Westport, Leavenworth, Atchison, or St. Joseph—or by rail to St. Joseph via the newly laid Northern Missouri and the Hannibal and St. Joseph Railroads.

Travelers from the northern sections of the Ohio valley states and from Pennsylvania, New York, New England, and Canada naturally moved as directly westward as they could, tending toward points farther up the Missouri from St. Louis. They might stay entirely on the roads, especially if funds were short, but many took advantage of railroads built during the previous twenty years. Some rail lines took them through Chicago into eastern Iowa, and from there they went by foot, hoof, or stage to Council Bluffs or other towns well up the Missouri River. Many emigrants, however, chose a route that took them more to the southwest to the Mississippi ports of Quincy, Illinois, and Hannibal, Missouri, since these offered a rail connection all the way to the

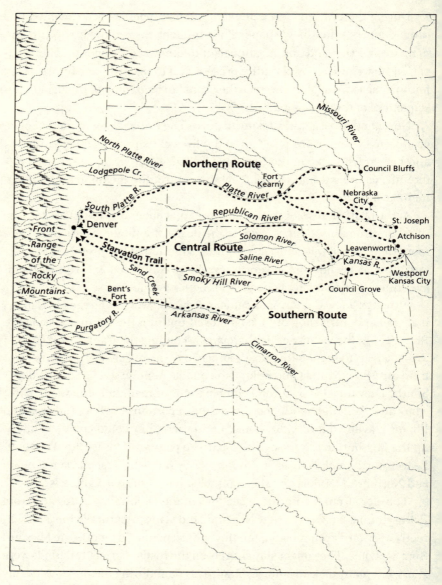

Routes to the Colorado Gold Fields

Missouri River at St. Joseph. A traveler could then proceed upriver or down, toward Council Bluffs or Leavenworth, or could take a stage west to Lawrence and other Kansas towns.

A traveler was then at his jumping-off place, some border settlement where he would make final preparations. Between him and the Rockies stretched more than 600 miles of prairie and plains. It was time to choose his route.

Three possible ways lay before the emigrants: the northern, southern, and central routes. Each actually had several variations. Although they converged at the same point—the diggings around Cherry Creek—their eastern ends usually had several approaches feeding in from various departure points, so on a map each resembled a rope neatly wrapped at one end and badly frayed at the other.

The northern trail followed the Platte and South Platte Rivers upstream through southern Nebraska and present-day northeastern Colorado to the new settlements of Denver and Auraria. Its main trunk began at Fort Kearny, where three feeder roads converged. One of these began at a string of towns well up the Missouri—Council Bluffs, Omaha City, and Plattsmouth—and ran southwestward along the Platte. Another went from Nebraska City, on the Missouri, due west to Kearny. The third was actually a weaving of trails angling northwestward from St. Joseph, Leavenworth, Westport, and assorted Kansas towns. Since the early 1840s overlanders had moved up these gathering strands to follow the great Platte River road, the major route to Oregon and California. For much of its course, up to the point where the South and North Platte converged, the northern route was a well-marked highway. The Platte "assumes an unequal importance among the streams of the Great Prairie Wilderness!" Thomas Jefferson Farnham wrote in 1843; "The overland travel from the States . . . will find its great highway along its banks."[7] At the junction of the North and South Plattes, argonauts of 1859 would turn off the old road and follow the South Platte southwestward toward Cherry Creek.

The southern route also ran over familiar terrain for much of its course. It followed the Santa Fe Trail through eastern Kansas, then moved upstream along the Arkansas River. The old road led to New Mexico, either along the Cimarron cutoff, which left the river in far southwest Kansas, or by the "mountain route," which turned south from the Arkansas above Bent's Fort. The goldseekers' path, however, turned sharply northward up the Front Range along a trail used by cattle drovers, traders, and, most recently, the prospecting parties of the previous year. Inadvertently, they were also taking perhaps the oldest path in North America, following where the people of the blue ice may have walked at least 12,000 years earlier. The southern route, like the Platte road, had several eastern approaches. The best known was the traditional New Mexican freighters' trail that ran southwestward from Kansas City and Westport through Council Grove to the great bend of the Arkansas. A newer route began farther west, at Lawrence, and sloped down to meet the older road at Council Grove. Yet another variation ran westward from Lawrence and Topeka along the Kansas River to Fort Riley before turning southward to join the main route.

The central route lay between the first two. Also called the Smoky Hill–Republican Trail, it ran directly westward up the Kansas River from Lawrence and Topeka to Fort Riley, where the Republican and Smoky Hill Rivers merged to form the Kansas. From there one trail ascended the Republican in a long arc before striking west, crossing a series of creeks and divides to the diggings. Another option, the most direct route of all, went from Fort Riley up the Smoky Hill to its origin in eastern Colorado. From there a traveler pushed westward to Sand Creek (or Big Sandy), then veered northwestward up that valley and over a divide to Cherry Creek.

Sketching out a trip on the central route, however, was an act of bravado. What little was known of the country along the Republican was based on military reports and a scattering of vague descriptions, mostly from surveyors. Knowledge of the Smoky Hill was even skimpier. A few editors confidently gave directions, complete with estimates of mileage, but in fact they had only the bleariest notion of what anyone would find. The Spanish had rigorously avoided this country, then the domain of nomadic Querechos; and French, English, and white Americans too had stayed away from its disorienting terrain, erratic streams, and bewildering distances. The northern and southern roads were deep with ruts and heavy with folklore, but the central route, especially that of the Smoky Hill, was a speculation, a trail of surmise and printer's ink.

The rush promised to lift the economic gloom from the middle Missouri River valley where all the routes began. The *New York Times* predicted that a "busy population" soon would fill the continent's interior if reports of healthy deposits were true.[8] Some businesses felt an especially sharp excitement. Among these were railroads, particularly the newer lines laid across the Midwest during the previous decade. Overbuilt and underused, these roads had suffered terrible losses since the panic of 1857, and their officers, frantic for traffic to stave off disaster, began to court the thousands looking for the quickest and easiest way to the mountains. Besides these executives, the businessmen of the Ohio and upper Mississippi valleys, whether merchants, hostlers, bankers, or farmers who offered rooms by the night, were excited by the thought of an emigrant army moving through.

The river towns themselves were the most obvious beneficiaries. Everyone moving to the Rockies would pass through at least one of them, and trade among outfitters, liverymen, dry goods merchants, wagoners, restaurateurs, and others was sure to boom. For the past few years these towns had engaged in a vigorous rivalry that sometimes had turned ugly. Businessmen from St. Louis to Council Bluffs were determined to maximize their profits—and that meant pulling as many emigrants as possible away from their neighbors. As early as mid-September 1858, Leavenworth businessmen held a strategy meeting to devise ways of drawing the crowds. First they formed a committee to advertise the town's advantages. Then, early in February, they learned that St. Joseph, Atchison, and Kansas City had paid runners in St. Louis to steer emigrants their way and to denigrate Leavenworth. One thousand dollars was raised for a two-man mission to protect local interests.[9] The episode suggested the tone and tactics of these rivalries.

To compete, however, every town needed a selling point, something to set it above its rivals. The most obvious possibilities were the various trails that stretched out toward the mountains. So it was that each town tagged its fortunes to one or two of the routes across the plains.

Council Bluffs, Omaha, Plattsmouth, Nebraska City, and St. Joseph, for instance, were closest to the northern route up the Platte River. Spokesmen for those towns described the Platte Trail as the safest and most tested as well as the most direct for the hordes coming from the Ohio valley, Great Lakes region, New England, and Canada. Atchison boosters also smiled on the Platte, but they urged strong consideration of the central route, which argonauts could easily reach by heading south and west after emptying their purses in the town's emporia and wagon yards.

Leavenworth sat directly east of the central road, so its business leaders stressed that the Smoky Hill and Republican Trails were the shortest and quickest roads to fortune. Boosters in nearby towns agreed: "Let Hercules do what he may / The Smoky Hill Route MUST have its day."[10] From Kansas City and Westport, long the twin gateways to the Santa Fe Trail, came lengthy arguments that the southern road up the Arkansas was the only one worth considering. It was the oldest, surest, and easiest way. Besides, with the grass up by late March along this southernmost route, its travelers would have a jump on the competition.

Two other towns—Lawrence and Topeka—had a serious problem since they sat on the Kansas River, away from the Missouri's steamboat and railroad connections. Both turned their problem into a selling point. Perched well to the west, they stood as a kind of pivot from which emigrants could choose any of the three roads after moving through the area and mulling over the options. Part of this was a bluff; any traveler choosing the northern route almost certainly would approach it from elsewhere, from St. Joseph or towns on the Missouri above it. So promoters in Lawrence and Topeka pointed more vigorously toward the Arkansas road and, above all, to the central route that began directly to the west.

Border boosters understood that in westward expansion geography was, if not destiny, at least the best help toward it. The way they applied this lesson pointed toward something much larger—the changing meaning of mid-America. As promoters trumpeted St. Joseph or Kansas City or Council Bluffs as the obvious gateway to the Rockies, and the Platte or Smoky Hill as a natural highway connecting the Missouri with the rising towns to the west, they were creating a radically different perspective on the continental center. Before 1859 they had seen their towns first as commercial centers for the Missouri valley and farms of the far eastern plains, and second as departure points for the long trek to the Pacific. The plains and Rocky Mountains were only a great space to cross; their towns' value lay in helping people get past that country as quickly and painlessly as possible.

Then, virtually overnight, what had been simply distance quickly took on value in itself. River towns were no longer the last safe ground for launching over a threatening void. They became part of a continuum. They were gateways to an opening promise that began on their streets and spread westward unbroken to the Continental Divide. A new vision was being born. The Missouri, the plains, and the Rockies were seen as bound organically into an economic whole. The simple unity of the region's parts, the country's soaring possibilities, and the best ways of passing through it were suddenly described as self-evident. Anyone who failed to see must be a dolt.

THE WINTER GATHERING of emigrants and entrepreneurial energy produced a considerable promotional literature. Broadsides, pamphlets, bundles of news articles, and books of short gestation were circulated throughout the nation and across the Atlantic. They urged the venturous westward with a blend of practical advice, gasconade, and bald lies.

The appeals appeared first in the bordertown newspapers but soon went much farther as items were picked up by papers from Maine to Virginia. Border editors felt the tug of various motives and emotions. They were caught up in hopes that the new strikes would bring back prosperity and fuel America's steady rise to greatness, but they also felt some obligation to give an accurate appraisal of the gold fields. Ultimately, these editors looked to their towns' and advertisers' interests. American journalism was a generation away from professional organizations and a professional canon, and the line between reporting and advocacy was blurry. At their most objective, editors tended to sift through reasonable truths to pull out the one that fit most snugly their local needs.

Not surprisingly, opinions swung about erratically. A lot of editors at first were derisive. The *Leavenworth Times* classed the rumors of gold with stories of huge pearls taken from the White River.[11] Within weeks the mood was changing, however. A Kansas City editor wrote of seeing a nineteen dollar nugget that "made his pocket beat with the Placer pulsation." Certainly journalists were aware of local benefits from traffic to the mountains. By the end of October the anticipation of a rush already was giving a boost to businesses most directly affected. Speculation had driven up the price of mules to awful levels, an army purchasing agent wrote his boss from Fort Leavenworth: "I seen how it would go as these P.P. [Pike's Peak] men were looking at them before the sale."[12]

A glance at any newspaper showed the range of enterprises that would profit. Merchants and carpenters offered long toms and rockers for work in the diggings. A Kansas City gunsmith devised a "gold washer," and a St. Louis shop had a "Pike's Peak Gold Auger" to test for deep deposits. Advertisements for wagonmakers, livery agents, hostlers, steamboat lines, clothiers, and general merchandisers appealed to crowds preparing for a dash across the plains. An emigrant was urged to get his hair cut by H. H. Thomas of Leavenworth and to stock up on "Pikes Peak Wares" as well as some chewing tobacco from the vast stores shipped in to meet the overlanders' needs. For the road a traveler could buy "Pike's Peak Saddles!" to put on one of the "Pike's Peak Mules." He could take "gold country medicine chests" packed with expectorants and liniment, quinine and salves, hair tonic and morphine, and pills for dyspepsia, worms, and liver complaints. He could hedge his bets with "Pike's Peak Life Insurance."[13]

Most editorial opinion came around by Christmas. The *Leavenworth Times* proclaimed that the diggings "exceed any [gold] discoveries yet made . . . in the world," and its competitor, the *Weekly Herald,* declared the mines "a fixed fact." The *Missouri Democrat* of St. Louis thought that the entire region, from the interior parks of the Rockies to the upper valley of the Rio Grande to the San Juan Range to the west, held the richest deposits on the planet.[14] Calls for caution slackened and took on a perfunctory air. After the first of the year most papers published special editions filled with descriptions of mines, reports on the mounting migration from the east, advice for the inexperienced, and poetic tributes to gold and to democracy:

> Hurrah for Pike's Peak! where the breezes of Heaven
>> Waft the glittering dust on their far sweeping wings;
> Where Rank is unknown, and no station is given
>> To men in whose veins flows the life tide of kings.
> Who cares for the bliss which society gives,
>> Or the love which we find at our hearthstones alone?
> Society spurns him who moneyless lives,
>> And bears in his pockets no "rocks of his own!"[15]

Columns were also crowded with reports and letters carried back from "the Peak" by travelers and freighters. This correspondence, reprinted throughout the East, was the prime source of the public's portrait of the diggings, which made the letters controversial. Within months many people were charging that the rush to the Rockies was cynically engineered by businessmen and speculators hoping to dupe the gullible goldseekers. As early as January, in fact, some correspondents in Colorado were warning of "broken down land speculators from Iowa, Nebraska and Kansas" puffing the possibilities far beyond what was justified: "The reports you see in the papers, I warn you not to believe. . . . There is nothing here to pay for coming."[16]

The truth, however, was more slippery. Some reports were certainly outrageous. One had a man setting a horseshoe in a creek at sundown and finding it gilded by morning. Another told of a Mr. Robinson mining a "kettle of gold" worth $6,000 or $7,000, another of a vein yielding $3,000 in less than a month, still another of gold found "everywhere you stick your shovel." These correspondents were usually anonymous or unidentifiable, so the letters might have been speculators' concoctions.[17] But men who signed their names rarely put out such gush. Samuel Curtis predicted privately that miners would make twenty-five to seventy-five dollars a day, yet in letters meant for the press he was conservative: "What I write to the papers I consider as certain," he assured his brother, namely that gravel paid from a penny to a nickle a pan—hardly claims to entice the multitudes.[18]

Sam Curtis was no shill. High hopes were his natural tendency; he leaned into optimism. Most who wrote from the mountains were like him. An early merchant, John Ming, was astonished at the level of optimism ("I have seen nothing yet which will warrant such an excitement"), yet he and other businessmen praised the area's long-term promise, especially in the infant cities.[19] "Everything is wanted here from a needle to an anchor," Larimer reported in February, and others echoed his shimmering predictions of Denver's greatness.[20] Boosters wrote more about the rasping of whipsaws than of the cries of "Eureka!"

Readers could have found just about anything they wanted in the dozens of letters. A few correspondents were liars, but most stood somewhere along a spectrum of confidence, from modest fancy to derangement, typical of the frontier. A more obvious point was the unchallenged agreement that *something* grand was sure to happen in country that months before was called a distant wilderness. If there was a conspiracy, it was diffuse, and it involved virtually everyone in the region trying to convince himself that Colorado was the new hope of the West.

Emigrants could also turn to a small library of guidebooks for the trip across the plains. Like earlier guides to California and Oregon, these claimed simply to tell travelers how to get where they wanted to go with maximum speed and minimum risk. Far more than the earlier books, however, they were creatures of commercial and urban interests. Many were equal parts promotional documents and travel manuals. They were as much about departure points as about destinations.

Of nearly thirty known guidebooks, a couple appeared late in 1858, the rest during the first half of 1859. Some books were only a few pages long, but most ranged from twenty to eighty pages. A few were published in Missouri valley towns. Most, however, came from eastern and midwestern cities—New York, Chicago, Boston, Cincinnati, and others. None was from the South. Their origins suggest they were pitched to regions hit hardest by the depression, where the largest crowds were ready to move. Only a few authors had been to the mountains. Luke Tierney and William Parsons had played prominent parts in the Russell and Lawrence parties, and a few others apparently had gone to the mines and returned during the autumn. Most authors apparently relied on news accounts, reports of others, rumor, and pure imagination.

In some guides readers could find useful and reasonably accurate information. Tierney's, Parsons's, and a few others gave good and practical descriptions of roads along the Platte and Arkansas. *Allen's Guide Book and Map* provided itineraries of nine ways to the mines, each chopped into increments of only a few miles to show landmarks, camping places, water and fuel sources, and difficult spots.[21] Other books had tips on handling stock, coping with the weather, and dealing with medical problems. To ward off scurvy J. W. Reed recommended a pleasant noontime drink of water, sugar, and vinegar.[22] Some books included detailed lists of supplies needed to cross the plains and to set up operations on the other side. Parsons gave a short course in placer mining methods.[23]

Many books were also propaganda tracts, showcases of the suasive arts. Their tone was self-assured and level-headed. Some began with historical sketches of the region and its gold discoveries. We know the country, they seemed to say, and therefore know your business. Writers pointedly warned against excessive hopes and reminded readers that any rewards would come only after plenty of work. Anyone comfortably situated should stay home, one wrote, while John Pratt and F. A. Hunt made it clear that "we have carefully avoided recommending any man to go to the gold mines." But the rhetoric around this hard-nosed advice spoke differently. Pratt and Hunt's guide brimmed with accounts of hundreds of strikes and fifty dollar nuggets, followed by their own opinion that the Rockies offered *"the purest gold that has ever been discovered on this continent!"*[24] Like theirs, most guides reprinted letters that had appeared in valley newspapers; one book was composed entirely of them. Only the most encouraging correspondence was used, however. Readers were left with opinions sifted clean of doubt.

This air of credible confidence was essential to the real goal of many guides—a convincing endorsement of a particular departure point and route to the mines. Half a dozen or so were either published by railroads or relied heavily on railroad advertisements. These rail lines funneled into the upper Mississippi from the Ohio valley and the Great Lakes, and some had direct links to the Hannibal and St. Joseph Railroad, the only rail connection to the Missouri River. Every railroad's last stop, that is, was on or close to the upper stretch of the Missouri, north of Atchison. It was no surprise that these guides strongly endorsed the northern route up the Platte from St. Joseph, Council Bluffs, and other towns between.[25]

Other guides showed economic allegiances to one city or another. The *Guide to the Gold Mines of Kansas* had handy rail schedules from several eastern cities. No matter which schedule a traveler followed, however, he would end up at Atchison, and every route shown in the guide began there. The *Guide*'s authors were Atchison's city engineer and chief freight agent.[26] L. J. Eastin, author of *Emigrants' Guide to Pike's Peak,* was editor of the *Herald* of Leavenworth. With the Platte River traffic flowing to the north and the Arkansas River crowds to the south, Eastin concluded that the "BEST ROUTE TO THE GOLD MINES [is] THE SMOKY HILL FORK . . . [with] LEAVENWORTH CITY THE STARTING POINT." Although published in New York, the *Guide to the New Gold Region* obviously had close ties to two firms based in Leavenworth—the freighting giant, Russell, Majors, and Waddell and its close relative, Jones and Russell, which soon would offer stage passage to the diggings. After showing how emigrants could outfit in Leavenworth (a "youthful GIANT" second only to San Francisco in its rapid, "almost magical" progress) and still make their way easily to the three major routes, the *Guide* agreed with Eastin that the central road, up the Smoky Hill or Republican, was the wisest choice.[27] An ardent booster of Lawrence and other Kansas River towns, William B. Parsons blithely ignored the usual approaches to the northern and southern roads and advised travelers to make their way up the Kansas to Fort Riley. From there they could branch to the Platte or Arkansas or, best, head west on the middle route.[28]

Authors trotted out the usual arguments. The Arkansas road was the oldest and surest and the first to sprout grass; the Platte was shorter and better watered; the Smoky Hill–Republican route was the shortest and the only choice for the man of gumption. To back up opinion they sometimes mangled facts. The *Complete Guide to the Gold Mines,* promoting rail traffic to St. Joseph and towns above it, claimed the trail from Plattsmouth to Cherry Creek was 489 miles, about 120 miles shy of the truth.[29] More often authors artfully arranged known facts to suit their position. The result was a snarl of advice, an informational briar patch. The true distance along the Platte from Fort Kearny to Denver was 385 miles. But the *Guide to the New Gold Region,* which boosted Leavenworth and thus opposed the northern route, declared it was close to 500, a sum calculated by routing travelers well up the North Platte to Fort Laramie, far past the usual turnoff, before sending them south to the mines.[30] Another book showed the road from Westport along the Arkansas ("the best route by far") was 624 miles from start to end. The end, however, was at Pike's Peak, eighty miles from the placers.[31] These maneuvers left rivals gnashing their teeth. "They have changed the course of rivers, removed mountains, lengthened streams and made bleak hills and barren sand wastes smooth, and even highways," wrote a Kansas City editor of a Leavenworth-based guide.[32] He exaggerated only a little.

One result was the Battle of the Maps. Although several guides reprinted detailed, accurate maps, such as those of the New York firm of J. H. Colton and Company, others drafted their own, often with some sleight-of-hand to push one route over the others. Some simply ignored competitors. One could look on many railroad-sponsored maps without an inkling of any road except along the Platte.[33] Another tactic was the cartographic brushoff. A map distributed by the town of Lawrence showed a broad road sweeping boldly up the Smoky Hill to the Rockies. The old Oregon Trail up the Platte, by contrast, was a whisper of a line; this, the trudging ground of tens of thousands, seemed barely a goat path.[34] A guide backed by the Chicago, Burlington, and Quincy Railroad added another touch: plastering the railroad's name over its closest competition, the central route.[35]

A few guidebooks were guilty of appalling incompetence or outright fraud. A guide by William Byers featured a map with the Smoky Hill originating about sixty miles east of the Rockies, at least fifty miles closer to the mountains than was actually the case. The Republican was shown rising even closer to Denver. It flowed from the large (but nonexistent) Kansas Lake. A broadside published by the Toledo, Wabash and Great Western Railroad argued that the northern and central roads were incomparably superior to that along the Arkansas. To help make the point the Smoky Hill was shown rising virtually within sight of the mountains. The trail along it was labeled "Gen. Kearney's Route," suggesting that the road must be well known if Kearney's command had used it for its march to New Mexico during the Mexican War. In fact Kearney had followed the Arkansas, not the Smoky Hill. Many travelers worried about the lack of protection and supplies. This anxiety seemed to give an edge to the Arkansas road, which had a few posts along it. Draftsmen favoring the central route met the problem head-on. They took two Arkansas posts, Fort Atkinson (which had been closed for five years) and Bent's Fort, and simply moved them northward to the Smoky Hill and Sand Creek.[36]

A close look at these guidebooks would leave a traveler bewildered. A quick reading could be dangerous. Economic ambition and perception bled into one another in a grand display of Victorian boosterism. More than that was going on, however. As border towns and various interests tried to shoulder one another aside, they also pictured the continental center as a region of diverse parts knit naturally into one. Vigorous river towns and the newborn mountain settlements were not so much separated as bound together by safe and sure arteries of commerce. Mid-America was being remade through a mix of reasonable truths and bent reality.

THE SWEEP OF COUNTRY between the border towns and the Front Range began to look like a different place. A secondary theme in this promotional literature told of agricultural and pastoral opportunities in western Kansas and eastern Colorado. Muted but still heard under the soaring hymns to gold fields, cities aborning, and smooth highways to fortune, it also played its part in reshaping the region's meaning.

The image of an agrarian wonderland was not as old as the dream of gold, but a beginning had been made by the time of Russell's strike. Military reports had good things to say about some of the country. On his expedition of 1843–1844, John Charles Fremont told of well-watered, handsomely timbered land with rich, black soil in the bottoms along the lower Republican and Solomon. On the middle Smoky Hill he found "far-stretching green prairies, covered with the unbroken verdure of the buffalo grass."[37] A dozen years later Lt. Francis Bryan toured the Republican valley. Settlers would soon be crowding into part of it, he predicted, drawn by stands of hardwoods and fertile prairies much like those in eastern Kansas.[38]

The same men added that much of the land west of the 100th meridian was treacherous and forbidding, sandy and arid, and with little nourishment for animals and the men who rode them. The "streams" were undependable tricklings often walled by high banks. Later publicists, however, tossed out the warnings, kept the compliments, and used the officers' authority to paint the whole region, from Fort Riley to the Rockies, with the broad brush of praise.

Glowing accounts of the plains were increasingly common once Kansas and Nebraska were opened to settlement. The focus at first was on the most accessible areas, but almost immediately attention shifted westward to the country between the Platte and the Arkansas. A pamphleteer of 1855 supposedly offered a first-hand description, although much of it seemed either invented or lifted from military accounts. The Republican River valley was a fertile prairie of "rich, black vegetable mould" (Fremont's exact words). The Smoky Hill's soil was the same, only deeper. For building material settlers could find abundant white limestone, clay for bricks, and thick stands of black, white, and red oak, hickory, poplar, beech, ash, and other hardwoods. The land also held veins of coal and rich deposits of gypsum, lead, tin, zinc, and copper. The upper Arkansas was similarly blessed, and the higher reaches of the Platte in southern Nebraska were prime grazing lands where huge herds could live year-round on native grasses. The plains of western Kansas and eastern Colorado would "soon be swarming with active, industrious inhabitants," with church spires and courthouse towers "lifting their heads among the hills."[39]

The newspapers of Lawrence and Topeka, gateways to that alleged garden-land, soon picked up the refrain. Stories of parched wastes high up on the Smoky Hill were simply wrong, wrote a correspondent to the *Lawrence Herald of Freedom*. Several others agreed. Above the junction with the Saline one could find productive soil, plenty of timber, and the "hidden treasures" of minerals. "There is no better country in the world," one writer concluded.[40] Railroads boosted the agrarian dream. A long letter and article praising the new Hannibal and St. Joseph Railroad ended by pointing ambitious farmers toward the Kansas interior: "I deem it 'a good opening for a young man,' as the whale remarked to Jonah."[41]

By then individual impressions were filtering in. Augustus Harvey worked with a government survey team in the middle Republican valley in fall 1858. He had no economic stake in the region, yet like Sam Curtis in the gold fields, he was caught up in the western dream. His personal journal reads like a publicity tract. Soil on the beautiful rolling hills was as fertile as along the Missouri and "capable of producing any crop." The valleys were lush with timber, the streams full of fish, the earth graced with coal and iron. In land teeming with wildlife, including swans, Harvey's party dined on bison steaks, duck, and snipe potpies seasoned from deposits of salt so fine you could pinch it from the ground and sprinkle your dinner. Here was "the richest portion of the United States and when as well settled and improved as some of the older states, will be the wealthiest of the Union."[42]

Even as he wrote, word of Russell's gold was dispersing through the East and Europe, and the first parties were scurrying toward the mountains. At first that was troubling news for those who had tied their interests to an agrarian empire. Four months before Green Russell's discovery, the editor of *Freedom's Champion* of Atchison had prayed that gold would never be found in Kansas, for everywhere else it had lured men away from more lasting enterprises and thus retarded economic growth by at least a decade. With the first confirmed reports in September, a writer for Lawrence's *Herald of Freedom* counseled all readers to put their money into a much surer investment: 100 acres of rich Kansas soil. The *Leavenworth Times* agreed: "We have that in Kansas which is better than gold—our coal, iron, lead, and fertile plains."[43]

Quickly, however, that tune faded and another rose. Visions of gold and of grain were not in conflict; they were in harmony. Miners had to eat, so a growing population at the Rockies would provide an expanding market for farmers and shippers of eastern Kansas. That in turn would draw cultivators farther west to occupy the valleys of the Platte, Arkansas, and the streams between. Around the gold camps themselves was land for fields and pastures. Such production might bite a little into the profits of eastern farmers, but in the long run this new agrarian region would market its surplus through the Missouri valley border towns. Mining and farming would feed one another. Promoters of both decided they were really in two facets of the same enterprise.

The gold fields, then, would be "the evangel to a new commerce," wrote a St. Louis editor. As the mountains gave up their wealth, the plains would offer opportunities almost as great. Farm boys would become cattle barons and "the buffalo path will turn into highways for hurrying merchandise."[44] Many letters and guidebooks praised the plains' agrarian potential. "That the Platte and Arkansas bottoms will yield abundantly to the industrious farmer, there can be no doubt, neither can it be excelled for cattle," wrote D. C. Collier from Denver. Another writer reported that every valley around the diggings already was being readied for cultivation, and no wonder, since other correspondents told of a mild climate, bounteous timber, and soil that could produce any crop common to that latitude.[45] Parker and Huyett's *Illustrated Miners' Hand-book* gave as much space to farming and ranching as to prospecting. Quoting the oldest white inhabitant as authority, they assured readers that natural grasses along the Front Range could sustain "millions of cattle" in all seasons.[46]

Predictably, each author usually keyed his praise to the town and route he favored. Redpath and Hinton's guide, which generally reflected Leavenworth interests, spent fifteen pages on farming in east Kansas before discussing the way west. Chicagoan William Horner's book boosted the northern route; it included a chapter, "The Great Unoccupied Northwest," predicting vast agricultural and pastoral development up the North Platte from Fort Laramie. With interests both around Denver and in Lawrence, William Parsons made astounding claims about the eastern and western ends of the route up the Smoky Hill. Vegetation along streams around Denver "recalls the luxuriance of the tropics, or the magnificence of the ideal world of old navigators," and the valley of the Smoky Hill already was thickly settled by farmers 200 miles west of Lawrence.[47] (In fact, a traveler in those months had gone barely half that distance before he "left the white man for a long tramp in the wilds of Kansas."[48])

This bucolic vision—of vigorous, well-tended fields and lush pastures speckled with cattle—never overshadowed the grand claims about the gold fields. But the rhetoric was rarely absent, either. No reader would have missed it. And once in a while it would soar, as when one author predicted that on the bounteous plains "the plow and the scythe will yield a better return . . . than the pan and the pick."[49]

THE BLIZZARD of letters, editorials, and guidebooks blew over America during winter 1858–1859. Of its enormous audience, tens of thousands were preparing to move toward the Missouri River by the first of the year. In the weeks ahead they took to the roads.

It was a mixed crowd. Some, like Daniel Witter, took off spontaneously and traveled light: "I start with a bag of Clothing, a valise, a gun, revolver, and my dog Fido, with about $250 in money."[50] Many emigrants had much less than that. Charles Hull had been a carpenter in New York City when the panic took his job. He hunted work for weeks until Mother Fletcher, the owner of his boarding house, closed her doors and forced his hand. "To return to the monotony of my father's farm was undesirable," he wrote later, so Hull floated west to Wisconsin, where he found demeaning employment at occasional grunt work. When he heard the first reports from western Kansas, he left for the mountains with hardly a second thought.[51]

Men with more at stake took time to judge the odds. Sylvanus Wellman wrote several letters to Kansas, then recorded in his diary the various steps of disengagement—leasing his land, cleaning his house, selling some oxen and all his turnips—before joining a company headed west.[52] The hardest choices confronted men with broader responsibilities. A midwestern merchant checked with a Kansas farmer for a view close to the action:

> Friend Colamore,
>   I take the liberty to write to you for information respecting the gold mines at pikes peak as you will know more about it than any one that I am acquainted with. . . . I am in minnasota now but there is nothing doing in the business line a great portion of merchants have failed here if there is a chance for me and

wife and one little girl eight years old I would like to come out there and go to the peak. . . . there is great excitement in this place about the gold there I wish for some information from you that would be more satisfactory to me than all the storys.[53]

Thousands like him decided on several months of "baching it" in hopes of making enough to rebuild their shattered fortunes. After trying his luck in California and Iowa, Alexander Rooney despaired of making a place for himself and his fiancée. "This thing of waiting for something to turn up I fear is abridging our hapiness," he wrote her. Colorado seemed their best chance. If his luck turned, the pair could "look forward to a bright future whear thear shal be no breaking asunder those cords of afection." Men like him took whatever they could scrape together. They sold everything but their clothes, wheedled from friends, borrowed from in-laws. Deals were struck. A surviving contract shows an Illinois merchant providing a wagon, tools, and a year's provisions for two young men who pledged, sharecropper-style, to pay back either half their earnings or $5,000.[54]

Just getting to a jumping-off place could be a trial and an adventure. Traveling by rail was quickest but not always pleasant. The only direct connection to the Missouri River was by the Hannibal and St. Joseph Railroad, barely completed in time to serve the crowds of 1859. In fact, the rails were laid so hastily, doubtless under pressure to ride the rush, that the Missouri Public Works Board almost immediately condemned the construction. The grades were too steep, the cuts too narrow, the trestles and bridges unsafe.[55] Emigrants complained for years. "It beggars description," one wrote in 1864. "It seemed as though it was built in a hurry and had not been repaired since." The service was appalling, the facilities filthy, and when it rained "the mud in or out of the cars had little difference as to depth." After hours of agony, he delivered the ultimate complaint, thanking the fates when the train hit a soft spot and derailed: "We lay there until daylight which gave us a good opportunity to sleep, which we needed."[56]

Many travelers went by rail to St. Louis, then churned upriver on steamboats. A Leavenworth paper claimed up to 1,000 persons a day were disembarking there.[57] Passengers stood on deck and caught glimpses of border life— acres of wild geese, thick groves of cottonwoods, isolated cabins, and "ragged girls" in hoop skirts drawing water on the riverbank. For amusement men shot at ducks, organized dances, and held mock trials.[58] They grew irritable at surly stewards and the close confinement with bad company: "One man drunk and robbed. One threatened to shoot another and that one was myself."[59]

The largest number came overland, some with only knapsacks, some pushing wheelbarrows, some in wagons used to haul corn and hay a few weeks before. The crowds funneled gradually onto routes converging on the middle border. A crush of travelers moved through Illinois, Missouri, and Iowa on badly worn roads soaked by melting snow and then pounded by early spring storms. "Never have I seen such mud," one recalled of the trek over Iowa's soggy troughs and hills.[60] Wagons sank up to wheelhubs. Hikers slogged along beside the road, trampling the shoulders and widening the corridors of muck.

At the end of this first stage of the trip, temporary emigrant camps appeared on the edges of every border town. People, oxen, mules, horses, and dogs milled about on land soaked by rain and snowthaw. J. S. Baker figured more than 10,000 persons were waiting for the grass and trees to green. He felt his own sap rise: "I like the Western country verry well. . . . I am well and as tough as a bear."[61] Others chafed at the delay. With the grass soon eaten or trampled, camps became sinking sloughs. Residents labored their way calf-deep through mud, garbage, and manure. The camps were splendid cultivators of contact diseases, with travelers from throughout the country and much of Europe coming together in close quarters and wretched conditions. Children, as always, were most vulnerable.

Here the emigrants made their final adjustments for the jump westward. Some parties had followed the pattern of the thousands who had taken the trip to California and Oregon, gathering most of their provisions before leaving and packing them closely in wagons. Many, however, took advantage of a decade of changes. With improved transportation leading to new mercantile centers along the Missouri, they chose to move as quickly as they could to their departure point, where they bought what was needed for the rest of the trip. These relatively cash-heavy emigrants were the flutter in every booster's heart.

"Those who are flush purchase cattle, mules, and wagons, and go well provided," a reporter observed. "The next class takes the hand cart and wheelbarrow, while the poorest, and, I fear, the most numerous, take it on foot."[62] Besides the means of travel, emigrants bought supplies. Guidebooks recommended at least six months' rations—flour, bacon, salt, coffee, sugar, dried fruit, beef, beans, and more—as well as utensils, camping gear, and a mining kit of gold pans, shovels, axes, saws, and other essentials. However else authors might fuddle the facts, this advice was usually sound. The reasonable traveler carried at least flour and beans, crackers, and some dried fruit, perhaps with some coffee and sugar. Most came well armed. No outfit was complete without a revolver, a diarist noted, although he doubted one man in a dozen could have shot anyone twenty paces away.[63] Some found room for molasses, cheese, and a few personal weaknesses. A few went beyond the basics. A winter party took off in November with one wagon full of barley and shelled corn to feed the oxen and a second with two years' provisions, not only clothes, equipment, and bedding but hams and bacon, corn, potatoes, fruits, beans, peas, flour, coffee beans, even condiments, cream of tartar, and dehydrated foods.[64]

Emigrants shuttled to and from the camps, working their way along the crowded streets, comparing and bargaining and spilling funds in local emporia and liveries. "This is a very brisk business place," a new arrival wrote, "an immense amount of buying and selling."[65] The guidebook of Oakes and Smith thought four men could get by for six months with an outfit costing just over $500; Pratt and Hunt's estimate was $668. Most figures fell between those two, tending toward the lower one. The estimates were reasonable, and they represented a considerable boon for merchants. A single Leavenworth firm claimed to have outfitted more than forty parties in a few weeks, which translated into at least $20,000 in trade.[66]

The layover served another vital purpose. In a practice common on the roads to the Pacific, previously unattached parties joined into larger companies. Besides protection from Indians and a general hedge against the unexpected, many tasks were best done collectively—watching over animals at night, fording streams, and repairing wagons and equipment. For women like Julia Lambert's mother, traveling with three children and no husband, the need was even greater. Some parties formed loose unions pledged to help one another when the need arose. Or, exercising the national passion for process and politicking, they lay down precise roles and lines of authority. A captain might be elected to choose camping spots and to oversee the enterprise generally and a captain of the guard to organize evening watches. Perry Kline's party also chose a wagon boss, a company cook, and a secretary to keep a journal. Smart companies looked for men with special gifts. One traveler was known as "the Jack Screw" for his ability to lift and hold a wagon while the wheel hubs were greased.[67]

Solitary travelers prowled the camps trying to link up for the crossing. Thomas Wildman found a freighting outfit that would feed him and carry his goods for fifty dollars. Some agreed to work their way to the diggings in exchange for food and protection.[68] Eventually there was nothing to do but wait and think about the moment. A man wrote from along the Missouri:

Dear children,

 I am soon going over a great big river, and then away off to a place where there ain't any people living. . . . That is the place they call Pike's Peak. There is lots of gold there, and that is what money is made out of. I will get some when I go there, and bring some home to you and ma. . . . I look at your pictures every day, and ma's, and Bon's and Bonpa's too. You must be good children and think about pa. You must take care of the little general. I send you a seed to plant. It is for you both.[69]

Still the camps kept swelling, and every approach to the border was clogged. Steamboats were filled to the rails, and long columns of wagons and "carpet-bag boys" turned every road into a quagmire. When the rains broke and the sun hardened the mud, emigrants killed thousands of rattlesnakes that slithered out to warm themselves in the ruts. There were unexpected alarms. "The pigs nearly ate Dick and Jo up last night. Tore an awful hole in the tent to get at the bag of oats," a diarist wrote; another found the "pigs . . . almost carried us off."[70]

As the hogs testified, these were lean years for farmers, and locals saw a chance to recoup losses. E. H. N. Patterson found little grain and hay when crossing Iowa: "It is almost impossible to get either, and when we do secure a little it is at an exorbitant price." With corn selling for seventy-five cents a bushel and hay for up to one dollar for 100 pounds, the approach to the border was soon known as a gauntlet of gougers. Hustlers prowled the campsites. "A sharp fellow came to us & we trayded westfall's gun and mine coat for a watch & oilcloth," wrote one emigrant, obviously stung. Here were "the biggest lot of cut-throats . . . that ever I saw in any country," an overlander thought, and when a farmer charged Patterson thirty-five cents for five sticks of firewood, he raged, "He is a professing Christian—but heaven save the mark, if such men are to become our exemplars!"[71] Travelers struck back, sometimes ingeniously. Henry Kingman would pause by a farmhouse and toss a baited line over his wagon's side. When he felt a bite, he would reel in his catch, wring its neck, and have stewed chicken for dinner.[72]

 Trolling for chickens, jostled in railcars, fending off pig attacks, they made their way to the Missouri. "A bigger army than Napoleon conquered half of Europe with" was passing through Des Moines, and from St. Louis to Council Bluffs, hotels were jammed and streets choked with goldseekers.[73] In the emigrant camps arrangements were transacted, outfits put in final shape, discomforts endured. By early March travelers were chafing to leave, as much to escape these sodden bivouacs as to find their fortunes.

Six hundred miles to the west a few hundred men huddled along the South Platte and Cherry Creek. Where the earliest residents had hunted mammoths and camped in hide tents, the newest sketched out the latest meaning of the place. They laid out streets, swapped town lots, and worked in the frozen mud to hammer together long toms and to build stores and grog shops. Behind them the Front Range loomed "like a steamboat in the fog"; to the east they looked across the plains and thought of the coming hordes.[74]

Hopes of various sorts—town-site speculators and busted farmers, freighters and merchants, down-and-out laborers and railroad executives—had been drawn to the middle border and to the straggle of settlements at the base of the Rockies. Now they were like two poles of charged ambition. Between them a lot of energy was crackling, ready for release.

William Green Russell. In July 1858 a party of thirteen men
led by this Georgian panned some placer gold from a small
tributary of the South Platte. It was a pivotal moment in the
modern history of mid-America. (Courtesy of the Colorado
State Historical Society)

RETURNED PIKE'S PEAKERS.

Struck by the Yellow Fever. Response to the news of gold in the Rockies was especially vigorous, coming soon after the panic and depression of 1857 had left many thousands of persons unemployed and uprooted. (Courtesy of the Colorado State Historical Society)

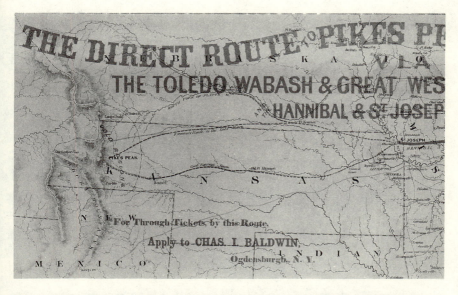

Battle of the Maps. Border promoters fought to control the emigrants' images of the plains lying ahead of them. A champion of the central route (top) moved forts from the Arkansas to the Smoky Hill River and drew that stream far larger and longer than it actually was. The same country was concealed by the logo of a railroad favoring the northern route along the Platte (bottom). (Courtesy of the Beinecke Library, Yale University, and the Denver Public Library)

"How Do You Go?" With only six hundred miles of plains to cross, goldseekers piled into all sorts of conveyances: carriages, buggies, ambulances, carts, and wagons drawn by oxen, mules, horses, and even dogs. A handcart (bottom) cost as little as five dollars, but its owners were left exposed to spring blizzards. (Courtesy of the Colorado State Historical Society)

The Master Booster. William H. Larimer stands before his cabin on the
site he chose for Denver. Mixing shrewd manuevering with bombast,
he established the town as the center of the region's new economy.
(Courtesy of the Colorado State Historical Society)

Bonanzas for Real. As reports that the Colorado gold fields were humbug
filtered back to easteners in early summer 1859, William Green Russell and
others were finding true gold strikes higher in the mountains, like this one
in Russell's Gulch. (Courtesy of the Colorado State Historical Society)

Bound for El Dorado. One of a hundred thousand argonauts who set out for the Colorado gold fields in 1859. The changes these goldseekers helped set loose, and the gilded dreams they embodied, transformed mid-America and undercut the life of nomadic Native Americans. (Courtesy of the Colorado State Historical Society)

THE RUSH

After filtering into the Missouri valley throughout a gray and blustery winter, the wash of emigrants had grown to a flood by early March. A correspondent in Kansas City described the human wave breaking over the border:

> Here they come in every steamboat, hundreds from every place—Hoosiers, Suckers, Corn crackers, Buckeyes, Red-horses, Arabs and Egyptians—some with ox wagons, some with mules, but the greatest number on foot, with their knapsacks and old-fashioned rifles and shotguns. . . . Enthusiastic, merry, with light hearts and a thin pair of breeches, they calculate to accomplish all their fondest hopes. Many have sold out all their homes, all their valuables, to furnish themselves with an outfit for Pike's Peak mines. . . . [They] blindly rush headlong into the wild delusion of glittering sands full of golden eggs.[1]

It seemed that every life-form on the border had caught the fever. A Topeka editor reported that "large companies of catfish and gar are daily seen passing up the Kaw, *en route* for the mines."[2]

More than 100,000 persons headed for Colorado that spring, far more than had ever taken to the overland trails in any previous year, even at the height of the California hysteria. It was quite a show. The rush revealed much about midcentury America, East and West. It was also a crucial moment in the long history of the central plains and Front Range. After several generations of quickening transformation, this new onslaught, muscling its way westward, set loose changes of a new order. Few creatures, human or otherwise, escaped the consequences.

TRAVEL ACROSS THE PLAINS never stopped during the winter. Some people who had gone to the mountains the previous summer returned east for supplies, and a few new parties, determined to steal a march on the competition, struck out for the camps during the weeks after Christmas. A new dribbling departed for the mountains on horseback in January. Most emigrants, however, waited at least until late February, and most of them longer than that.

The timing of departure was tricky. Leaving early offered the best chance of finding the choicest claims at the end of the trail, but starting too soon, before the grass was up and the road dried from the snowmelt, led to nothing but trouble. If emigrants waited too long, on the other hand, they not only would give up their edge in the gold fields; they also would find the trails overgrazed and on some stretches the water supply dangerously low. Each party figured its own odds, but most departures took place within a couple of months, and the fiercest rush was compressed into a few weeks.

By early March the roads out of Westport were crowded. Outside Council Bluffs a "steady tide of hoofs and horns, covered wagons and stalwart bipeds" was moving toward the Platte, and a month later 600 wagons were passing through the town every week. By May Day travelers clogged the first stretches of all roads. The Santa Fe Trail thronged with persons from all classes and every region. A diarist found 700 people camped on a small tributary of the Kansas River: "The waggons are so thick, it looks like a village." West of Nebraska City 1,000 wagons stretched for three miles along a creek. For 100 miles beyond St. Joseph, on the road toward the Platte and Fort Kearny, every stream and stand of timber was "alive with the tents of emigrants," a journalist wrote, and at night, another added, "the smoke of ten thousand camp-fires curled to the astonished clouds."[3]

A smattering of older hands and children were along, and during the next few years families became increasingly common. When Charles Clark crossed the next year, "Old and wrinkled age was there, and rosy youth, and, withal, the mewling infant in its mother's arms," and six years later Bayard Taylor wrote of columns of emigrant wagons with "sunburned women and wild-looking children . . . stored among the piled household goods,—there was no end to them."[4] The initial surge of 1859, however, like earlier rushes to California, was overwhelmingly male, as shown in a tally of traffic through Council Grove:

men	5,214
women	220
wagons	1,351
oxen	7,375
horses	632
mules	381[5]

Virtually all the emigrants were white, and most were between eighteen and forty, sporting far more peachfuzz than grizzle. Within that spectrum they generally were ordinary examples of Young America, but the action also drew a different crowd—sharpers and thugs, gyps and quick-blades, the shiftless and the unhinged. Besides practiced crooks there were many travelers devastated by the hard times, hungry and disheartened and looking for a way to get by. Border town boosters, after doing their best to portray their towns as cradles of hope, were outraged when a lot of desperate people showed up. The editor of the *Nebraska City News* railed at "the shiftless, lazy, lousy, scurvy, profane, insane and idiotic herd of rapscallions, nincompoops and ninnies" who passed through his town, "rushing headlong, they knew not where nor whither."[6]

Many emigrants did indeed seem astonishingly ill informed or unconcerned about what lay ahead. A tall man in a butternut suit passed through Leavenworth with twenty pounds of cornpone, a slab of meat, and a violin. Ragged, flap-booted farm boys marched off dangling small carpetbags from shovels. A German immigrant, after walking from St. Paul, hiked out of Council Bluffs with a rifle, a butcher knife, and the clothes on his back. Like him, many showed up with little except desires and illusions. A journalist interviewed a group of twenty men about to leave with a tired horse and fifty pounds of hard bread. How would they live for the next several weeks? They would kill wild game, they said, and sleep in sheds they thought Indians had built for buffaloes.[7]

Most people were better prepared than that, although the options seemed endless. "The most common question on meeting," a journalist found, "is

not 'How do you do?' but 'How do you go?'"[8] Whenever possible the overlanders, especially families and groups of men, chose simple farm wagons
topped with canvas pulled taut over wooden bows. Work wagons were among
the most common possessions of rural Americans, and once transformed they
were the cheapest means of travel. A ton or more of tents, tools, and food fit
into the fifty or so square feet of a cargo bed. Ingenious farmers maximized
the possibilities by building false floors and storing goods under them. Bennett
Seymour's father raised his wagon bed, extended it over the wheels, and built
walls with windows and a door that was removed to serve as a table. The
interior was warmed by a cookstove at the wagon's rear. Many other variations could be seen along the road. If the wagon survived reasonably intact,
it would be reconverted at trip's end to serve in new enterprises.

Oxen were the beasts of choice to pull these wagons, as they had been on
the treks to the Pacific. Masters of plod, they dominated the road, for although
much slower than horses and mules they had far greater strength and endurance. For a normal-sized emigrant wagon, four oxen worked best; occasionally more were used, and many owners tried to get away with fewer. Some
enterprising travelers brought extra cattle, both to relieve their draft animals
and to sell or use in the diggings. All told it was quite a bovine crowd that left
the Missouri camps, with more four-legged emigrants than two-legged. The
columns snaking out of each border town approximated the range of human
conditions in eastern society. It was, an emigrant remembered,

> such a sight! A few ox teams, then some horses, then a mule team or two and
> then, perhaps, more oxen. Some of the wagons were covered with clean, white
> sheets, some dirty dilapidated ones. All had high bows with sheets stretched tight
> and tied back and front when they were in trim, but some were dirty and ragged,
> tied by one corner, and the other flapping in the wind. Some teams had a lame
> horse or ox and on nearly every wagon sheet was written, generally with a piece
> of charcoal, such mottoes as: "Bound for the Peak," "Pikes Peak or Bust," "On to
> the Promised Land," "Bound for Denver."[9]

Wagons, however, did not begin to exhaust the alternatives. The peculiar circumstances of the Colorado rush colored every aspect of it, including
how its people moved over the land. Compared with the trip to the California mines—2,000 miles over brutal deserts and two mountain chains—this
one seemed more like a stiff hike, barely 600 miles across an area described
as easy terrain. Some emigrants showed up riding only a whim. Some saw a

chance to try the most fevered schemes; others came with slapdash improvisations pieced together from hope and barnyard leftovers.

A range of vehicles was pulled by whatever beasts were at hand—buggies, ambulances, hansoms, grocers' carts, phaetons, decrepit wagons powered by plow horses and milch cows. There was "a sort of Jersey cart, drawn
by a jaded mule."[10] One wagon was hitched to a cow and a horse, another to
six dogs: two Newfoundlands, a pair of hounds, and two pointers in the lead.
The pioneer anthropologist Lewis Henry Morgan, touring Indian communities in eastern Kansas, met a couple of young men riding in a two-wheeled
cart pulled by a small pony, with ash poles for thills and with hames made
from a collection of straps, strings, and yarn.[11] A Kansas City correspondent
saw a light wagon drawn by a small white bull with Pike's Peak Lightning
Express painted on its side; several days later he spotted the vehicle in Council
Grove, this time with the bull missing and its six owners in harness.[12]

Sprinkling the crowds were other improvisations: a long and narrow piece
of sheet iron, called a Tebogia, piled with supplies and pulled by two men.
There was a wheelbarrow with a sail and another with pontoons. Many
embarked on foot—or, as a journalist grandly put it, by "the mode independent." Albert Richardson watched crowds of these men tramping along, bent
forward, "each a domestic Atlas, with his little world upon his shoulders."
Hundreds of "carpet-sack and devil-may-care boys" started up the trails with
little thought or preparation; a diarist watched scores begin "without anything but a blanket and a brazen face."[13]

Hundreds more were part of the "handcart army." For as little as five
dollars, an emigrant could buy a two-wheeled cart like those that Mormons
had pulled to Utah in the late 1840s. With room for a few hundred pounds
of baggage and supplies, a cart had two poles extending forward from its sides.
One, two, or three persons propelled the vehicle by pushing against a cross-
bar connecting the poles. Even some families used these devices; a Westport
correspondent saw a man driving an overloaded wagon while his wife pulled
their sick child in a cart.[14] Companies were organized, with several persons
to a cart, taking turns at bending their backs to the task. Handcart columns
were a familiar sight over the next few years, including one in 1861 crewed
entirely by women whose children trotted beside them.[15]

Among this hodgepodge were occasional fantastic contraptions built by
entrepreneurs hoping to exploit a unique opportunity. A lot of people wanted
to move as quickly and as effortlessly as possible across country they thought

was flat and uncomplicated. A few customers would probably pay for the prospect of jumping the competition. Here was a chance to experiment with devices catering to Americans' passion for speed and gadgetry.

Several "wind wagons" were launched toward the Rockies, the largest built in Westport in April 1859. Tall masts with sails rose above a body designed like an omnibus and wheels twenty feet around. Its inventor claimed this land ship, literally a prairie schooner, would cruise over the grasslands at a steady 100 miles a day, carrying two dozen passengers to the Peak and back in less than two weeks. Designers, however, badly underestimated the difficulties of plains navigation; as a sea of passage, the central plains made most oceans seem relatively easy to deal with. The wind blew a lot, but not necessarily in predictable patterns or in desirable directions. Even with expert tacking, captains had to move over land sinuous with draws and hillocks and made up of various soil compositions.

Charles Post saw the Westport vessel barely into its initial run: "[It] cast anchor in a deep ravine where the wind failed to fill the sail, and she stopped." Border townsfolk found it all a great show. A local poet wondered why the wind wagon was becalmed, given the promotional rhetoric:

> Why do not the ponderous wheels revolve?
> And why idly flappeth the sail?
> For surely you've furnished wind enough.
> What need of a stronger gale?[16]

More modest attempts continued over the next couple of years. Intriguingly, one diarist reported a "sail wagon" far up the Platte, almost to the diggings, in late May 1860, although he was unclear whether the rig was heading to or from the mountains. The next year a pony express rider saw another on the road from Kansas to Fort Kearny. Its crew of four reported trouble with uneven ground and sandy draws.[17]

More technologically ambitious, and even more farfetched, was the "prairie motor," a steam-powered vehicle built in New York City and shipped to the border in summer 1862. Its front wheels were six feet in diameter. Four engines, burning a cord of wood every eight hours, powered a shaft that turned the ten-inch driving wheels at the rear. Nearly 25,000 pounds of freight supposedly could be carried about four miles per hour. This daring enterprise came to nothing, although the details of its failure are not known. A pilot, an engineer, and a fireman were on board when the motor chugged westward from Nebraska City toward the Platte in July. Then it disappeared from sight and the historical record.[18]

These contrivances might seem laughable, but they were fringe examples of a broad, intoxicating faith in technological wizardry among emigrants who, after all, had seen their nation dramatically shrunk by steamboats and railroads. Many goldseekers had ridden sternwheelers and rail cars to the edge of the plains. Was it so outrageous to buy a ticket on a new machine promising a quick trip over the final stretch? Wind wagons and the prairie motor in one sense were fantasies made briefly real, anticipating by a few years dime novels such as Edward Ellis's *The Huge Hunter; or, The Steam Man of the Prairies*.[19] They were also only slight exaggerations of a people perfectly at ease with reimagining the West in terms of mechanical mastery, shrunken distances, and limitless possibilities.

TRAVELERS HAD TO LEARN QUICKLY the basics of trail life. Women who had worked in kitchens for twenty years still might know little about cooking over an open fire in a stiff wind, or watching over restless children who bounded in and out of wagons, or cooking and washing in water thick with sediment. Young men puzzled for the first time over a hundred trivials of daily survival: how to soak beans, how to darn a sock and fix a boot, when to pull a dutch oven from the coals, and how to roust lice from the bedding. Men and women alike faced the new challenges of wrestling with tents, packing and unpacking an overstuffed wagon, and drawing drinkable water from a brackish pool.

Some of the most difficult—and comical—adjustments came when untrained wagoneers first dealt with unbroken oxen. In the border towns unwary travelers often bought animals that had never known a yoke, and when the newly drafted oxen first felt the weight they balked and bellowed and pulled any direction but forward. Getting the animals rigged, a job done quickly by seasoned freighters, might take two hours. Then came ludicrous attempts at travel. One first-timer estimated that for every five miles gained his animals weaved around for twenty-five. He and his friends were unamused: "If a man had come along and offered us three dollars apiece for the outfit, we would have sold out."[20]

Once the most troubling kinks were smoothed out, parties fell into a daily routine. A young overlander described his:

All hands up together in the morning—Hileman goes after the mules which bear the following euphonious names "Club" (the favorite) "Split-ear"—"Dolly" "Dandy" "Tom"—Redfield begins by packing the beds & striking the tent & Judd gets after the coffee & grub —Breakfast over & plunder packed—Judd takes the lines & off we go—the drive is shortened by anecdotes & song watching and speculating on the accompanying emigrants—at noon Hileman puts out the Mules on picket—Redfield starts for novel & Judd for water. Sometimes a short nap comes after dinner but oftener we call upon or are called upon by our neighbors—The eve camp is like the noon only the tent is pitched & bed made for the night—we retire as soon as dark & "Consign to Heaven our cares & woes / Then sink in undisturbed repose" & get up refreshed—strong and hearty[21]

Duties were usually distributed among the company. Men normally rotated assignments in guarding livestock at night from Indians and from other travelers "with confused ideas of *meum* and *tuum*."[22] Efficient travelers rose early enough to eat, break camp, hitch up teams, and be on the move by dawn. Men took turns driving the oxen or mules, if they had them. By late morning the parties were ready for a long layover, up to three hours, usually with a cold meal saved from breakfast. Then it was back on the road. When a halt was called in late afternoon, some fetched water while others set up camp or built a fire and cooked as best they could. Some slept in tents or in the wagons, but many preferred the open air. Most were rolled in their blankets by full dark.

For food, travelers typically relied mostly on what they brought with them. Experienced farmers sometimes gathered fresh greens and occasionally wild fruit from the spring profusion. Although many men apparently intended to hunt, few did well, for hunting was a specialized, place-specific craft, and they were entering country very different from what they had left. Men especially looked forward to bagging a bison, an almost mythical beast in the public mind, and at the first view of the shaggies hunters jumped to the chase. One leapt on his horse with a piece of breakfast bacon still in his mouth. Their huge quarries, however, were faster than most horses and extraordinarily quick-footed, and a gunshot to most parts of their heavily muscled bodies would hardly slow them down. Unless unusually skilled or very lucky, hunters generally returned with nothing to show for the effort but exhausted mounts. One man's horse looked "like the tail end of a hard winter."[23] Some did not fare that well. After chasing a bison more than two miles, Charles Post dismounted and fired. He wounded the buffalo and frightened his horse. Both animals ran off, and Post trudged back to camp, humiliated.[24] At best, hunters brought in one or two animals during the trip; most killed none.[25]

After feeding on folklore of the great overland journeys, many men anticipated a grand adventure leavened with genuine danger. They found plenty
to widen their eyes, but the dominant memory would be of fatigue, relentless labor, and, for parties with livestock, loss of sleep from long night watches.
The limited food, often cooked poorly, left even the hardiest with dwindling
reserves after the first couple of weeks. The heat wore them down and the
cold sucked precious energy. The work of rising, packing, walking, unpacking, cooking, and herding was as rigorous—and the monotony as relentless—
as in most jobs the travelers had left behind. Few reacted as dramatically as
the Iowan who lay down and refused to speak or get up, but not many could
resist some grousing. Most travelers would have seconded a bachelor's comment, about halfway down the road: "This going to Pikes Peak only for fun is
souring on me *fast;* I begin to long for the quiet walks of life."[26]

As for dangers, there was little to fear from Indians, at least during the
rush of 1859. The few recorded deaths from Indian attacks came very late
in the year along the southern road. Men had more reason to fear themselves
and the weapons they brought to fend off Indians. David Lindsey saw a young
Kentuckian killed when his rifle fired as he was pulling it, muzzle first, from
the wagon. Two weeks later another pair in Lindsey's party were shot in two
separate accidents; both survived but one lost his arm.[27] Although rattlesnakes
were a common sight—one party saw twelve in 100 yards, another sixty in a
day—bites were extremely rare. There is no record, in fact, of a death or
serious injury from any wild animal during the year of the great rush.

Emigrants who chose the northern and southern routes up the Platte and
Arkansas Rivers were following the footsteps of nearly 200,000 other white
overlanders who had plied these trails for four decades. Native peoples had
used these roads for centuries as hunting and trading routes. The passage
along the Arkansas was genuinely ancient, used long before Coronado crossed
it at the river's great bend in search of gold and pyramids. The first official
observer from the United States, Zebulon Pike, found the trail dotted with
old Spanish and Indian camps.

Both trails deviated in their last stages from the well-worn routes to the
Pacific and New Mexico. The Platte road, instead of staying on the North
Platte to Fort Laramie, turned southwestward along the South Platte to
Cherry Creek. The southern road followed the Santa Fe Trail's old mountain branch along the Arkansas nearly to the Rockies, but instead of turning
south to New Mexico, argonauts headed north up the face of the Front Range,
over a divide to Cherry Creek. Neither of these variations was new, however.

The South Platte was a familiar byway of trappers and traders and a busy wintering ground of the Lakota, Cheyennes, and Arapahoes. The path that ran north along the base of the Front Range was part of the Cherokee Trail. For hundreds of generations before Coronado nomadic hunters and traders had passed up and down the trough below the Front Range.

Fifty-niners thus may have fantasized about launching into the unknown, but on the northern and southern roads they traveled first by trails centuries old, then turned onto North America's most ancient axis of movement. They were always close to water and rarely more than a few days from some military or mercantile establishment. Getting lost was virtually impossible; they needed only to follow the region's largest rivers and tallest mountains. For most emigrants, crossing the plains turned out to be less dangerous than crossing a street in New Orleans or New York.

But there was one significant exception. The trip was safe, if grueling, only for those who moved west along the Platte and Arkansas Rivers. Between those two roads was another, the central route. The emigrants who chose that road found that they had made a much chancier, perhaps even fatal, choice.

The central trail began in Leavenworth, Topeka, and Lawrence and ascended first the Kansas River and then either the Republican or Smoky Hill. In the last stages travelers were to cross a region of roughly 1,000 square miles in far western Kansas and eastern Colorado to reach Cherry Creek and the Rockies. Most guidebooks gave only general instructions for this part because nobody except the Indians knew much about the place. Few white explorers had ventured there, and none had followed the recommended route. An honest map would have shown this country smooth and clean of any crinkles of information.

Nonetheless, the central route's champions promised vaguely that the way was clear and the country full of whatever travelers needed. This claim rested above all on a particular view of the Kansas River and its tributaries, especially the Smoky Hill. Boosters said the Smoky Hill rose in the Rockies, or within sight of them, and flowed vigorously eastward to join other branches of the Kansas. Parker and Huyett's guide, for instance, described the Smoky Hill as fed by a cluster of creeks originating "within three miles of the base of Pike's Peak."[28] These writers probably were drawing on earlier promoters of plains settlement. One had assured readers that the Kansas River system began "far up among the Rocky Mountains" and tumbled across the plains between grassy banks dense with timber. He added that the Smoky Hill's flow was so healthy that small boats could navigate its whole length. Another map of 1857 had gone further, predicting that steamboats would soon be churning westward up the Kansas and Smoky Hill to dock at the Rockies near the site of future Denver.[29]

If these claims had been anywhere close to the truth, the central route would indeed have been easy, safe, and fast. Moving west would have been much like ascending the Platte or Arkansas, only on a more direct line to the diggings. This happy vision of a short and simple road to the mountains was pushed hardest by towns closest to the central route, Lawrence and Leavenworth in particular. Competitors warned that the trail was untried, but in March the *Leavenworth Times* heard from William Larimer, Denver's founding father with Leavenworth connections. Larimer announced that a small party, led by A. H. Bacon, had made the crossing in January via the Smoky Hill. Even in winter they had found plenty of wood, water, and game. They arrived "delighted." The value of the central route seemed confirmed.[30]

Larimer, however, was once again bending the facts. Bacon's group had indeed made it through without losing anyone, but the trip had been far from easy. With terrible timing, they had set out at the start of the most treacherous time on the high plains. For the next few months water was especially scarce and the land subject to killer storms. Nomadic Indians knew the dangers of crossing open country during that time, when the Cheyenne's Cold Maker controlled the plains, and they stayed almost entirely in their protected enclaves. For the first week the group slogged miserably through cold rain and deep mud. As they passed the Republican and Saline and proceeded up the Smoky Hill the weather cleared and turned colder. They admired the prairie grasslands, the chalkbeds, and bluffs, and as they edged onto the high plains they at first were charmed by the spacious sweep and the grandeur of a plains sunrise. "The glorious Orb of day has rose with redoubled splendor," Wilbur Parker, eighteen, wrote in his diary on December 1. But that evening a snowstorm's blast left Parker frigid and terrified ("Oh heavens my hearts blood almost froze within me") and nearly killed their teams.[31]

By then the terrain was tricking them. Farther up the Smoky Hill they found that it rose not in the mountains, as claimed, but on the plains, just west of today's Kansas-Colorado border. Marching up the stream's north fork, Bacon's party watched the river dwindle and fade to sand. Where then? They would have to cross a broad watershed and find other streams to follow to their destination. This watershed was no simple and distinct saddle, however, but a slightly rolling plain, like a badly warped table top. The sandy creekbeds and arroyos did not point the way but bled off in all directions. The highest points of reckoning were occasional stubby nipples of eroded limestone. Even with a compass the travelers got badly boggled until some Indians, probably Plains Apaches, pointed them in the right direction.

They pressed on, although there was virtually no forage and they had to melt snow for drinking water. "[For] 4 days . . . our lives have been suspended on a single hair," Parker wrote on December 16. Soon they reached timber and water, but even then, within reach of the mountains, they came close to disaster. With two others Parker set out on a hike to get their bearings, but they were caught in heavy snow and became badly disoriented. As Parker weakened his friends left him and tried to find help. "I am afraid it will not be a very Happy New Year to me," he wrote in his diary; "am on the Plains of Kansas, with only one meal in my Pack, and Lost." Stumbling along on frost-bitten feet, hallucinating, and followed by wolves, he somehow managed to find his way back to camp. Two weeks later the group was on Cherry Creek, telling Larimer of the frightening passage he subsequently described as a delightful, untroublesome tramp.[32]

Lured by sunny reports such as Larimer's, a sizable minority of emigrants in the spring chose this route, which, after all, *looked* like the most direct way. By late May alarming reports were floating back to the river towns. Travelers found "a dreary waste as far as the eye could reach" beyond the head of the Smoky Hill, a disorienting desert more than 100 miles wide. Many veered north or south to try to reach established roads. For days one man followed what he thought were wagon ruts only to discover they were tracks from Indian travois; after more thirsty wandering he made it to the Arkansas, although he left behind five French companions he assumed were then dead. Others staggered into camps on the Platte and Republican, reporting "a number of bodies" on the trail behind them. Two men told of seeing many graves and at least ten unburied corpses. More persistent emigrants kept pushing westward, reckoning as best they could by compass and stars. They found only the thinnest grass—one man fed his oxen flour—and virtually no water. When rations ran out they ate prickly pear, rattlesnakes, wild onions, and ravens.[33]

Or worse. At the end of May, news broke in the Kansas newspapers of the horrifying ordeal of Daniel Blue. The Illinois native and his two brothers, Alexander and Charles, had left Topeka with a small party. Three weeks up the trail their packhorse ran away with most of their provisions. Their condition soon was desperate. Three men left to find help—they were never accounted for—leaving the Blue brothers and an Ohioan named Soleg. The weakened travelers agreed that if any died the survivors would eat from the remains for the strength to go on. Soleg died first, and the brothers took nourishment, although, Daniel remembered, "it went very hard against our feelings." When Alexander succumbed, the remaining pair ate some of him immediately, packed the rest of their brother on their backs and set out again, but quickly their energy ebbed. Charles died, and Daniel consumed most of the corpse before an Arapaho found him and took him to his lodge, then to a stage station. Skeletal, nearly blind, and somewhat deranged, Blue was taken to Denver, where he told his tale of sequential cannibalism.

The last section of the central route, where events turned frightful for the Blue brothers, came to be called the "starvation trail." How many died there in 1859 cannot be known, partly because the sketchy evidence was distorted by emigration rhetoric. Kansas City newspapers, prime champions of the Arkansas River route, filled their columns with descriptions of terrible suffering. An angry mob of 100 reportedly lost their way, wandered down to the southern trail, looted a trading post, and manhandled its owner before continuing to Colorado with stolen sacks of flour and corn on their shoulders. Journalists passing to the north of the trail told of crowds camped along the Republican River, regathering strength after abandoning the Smoky Hill and marching in desperation toward the Platte. Some told of going seventy-five miles without water, and all denounced the central trail as a dangerous snare.[34]

THE SMOKY HILL SUFFERERS, however, were far outnumbered by travelers on the two other roads. Looping to the north and south in long ellipses, they eventually made it to Cherry Creek, assuming they chose to see it through. They became the latest among tens of thousands to know one of the most distinctive and revealing experiences of nineteenth-century America—an overland journey. The Colorado rush, however, had its unique qualities and tone. It was a briefer, telescoped version of the forty-niners' trip. Its unprecedented numbers brought together more travelers from a broader social range than in any previous crossing. It threw more outsiders than ever into contact with the novel world of the central plains.

Their introduction to this new world came gradually. As they left Westport, Leavenworth, or St. Joseph, emigrants entered a zone of transition, ecologically and perceptually. For roughly the first quarter of the trip, 150 miles or so, the landforms and climate were much the same as the prairies of the lower Ohio and Missouri valleys. Travelers found the country striking but not strange. There was nothing to jar their senses.

They moved first over low hills that gradually flattened as the land opened toward the true plains. On steeper hillsides, where water had cut and the wind had blown away the topsoil, there were outcroppings of white and cream-colored limestone and sandstone, like bones of the earth breaking through soft green skin. Prairie fires kept the hills and higher ground mostly treeless, but shallow erosional wrinkles had tracings of brush and shrubs, dogwood and sumac especially. These grew thickly, taller than a man's head. Fat-trunked cottonwoods sometimes stood in the more pronounced draws. The deepest valleys that were drained by rivers and larger creeks held stands of willow, locust, hackberry, oak, elm, hickory, and other hardwoods.

This was part of the far western border of the mixed-grass prairie, a grassland of more than 50 million acres that covered Iowa and much of Minnesota, Missouri, and Illinois. As travelers moved toward its edge they entered the Flint Hills, well watered with usually more than thirty inches of rain a year. The small creeks that filtered through the unbroken prairie sod ran clear and cold. Larger streams that fed into the Arkansas had banks thick with trees and clotted with vines and brambles. It was close in those bottoms, abuzz with gnats and flies. By summer it was stifling, and travelers seeking shade found little relief from the heat. Swimming in the sluggish water, one man wrote, was like soaking in warm milk.[35]

There was much to please them, however. "We have passed over a splendid country today," a freighter wrote from along the Big Blue.[36] The perceptual balance was ideal. The land was familiar yet unsettled enough to give a taste of wildness, a sense of touching new potential. And by passing through when they did, the overlanders saw one of the continent's most glorious shows. The prairie was home to an extraordinary profusion of grasses and flowers; an acre might host more than 300 species. The shorter ones blossomed in early spring, taking in sun and drawing pollinating insects before their taller neighbors rose to have their turn in summer. With a moment's glance one could taste the visual feast—gayfeather and blue wild indigo, blazing star and butterfly milkweed, nodding lady's tresses, daisy fleabane and rose verbena, purples and reds and brilliant whites, yellows and burgundies and blues, all of it blended and swirled as the wind moved over the hills.

Travelers were enchanted. Their diaries are sprinkled with midcentury romanticism. "O, it is perfectly splendid," a young woman wrote; "we enjoy it ever so much."[37] Ellen Hunt was delighted to find her tent floor dotted with wild daisies and strawberry blossoms. The dominant grass was big blue-stem, which grew so thick and lush that Charles Post's oxen "came very near bursting" from eating it. Thousands of quail, spooked by the creaking wagons, scattered and flew low over the knee-high grass. There were irritations. One mother remembered sweeping snakes each evening from the family tent, and a soaking spring rain or late snowstorm lowered the spirits of the happiest traveler. But in this benign setting even the weather's nastier surprises left them pleasantly impressed. Anson Bradbury marveled at a hail storm that scattered the campers' tents, killed scores of birds, and flattened the grass along the next seventy-five miles of road.[38]

After two weeks on the road parties were approaching the end of the journey's first stage. Those on the Santa Fe route had passed through Council Grove, with its stores, smithy, and Methodist mission, and had crossed 100 sandy miles to the great bend of the Arkansas. On the old Oregon road out of Atchison and St. Joseph, emigrants had ascended the Little Blue to Fort Kearny; those who chose the central trail had moved up the Kansas River well beyond Fort Riley. The country opened up. There were longer vistas and a bigger bowl of sky. Along the creeks were thinner stands of timber, with hardwoods giving way increasingly to cottonwoods and willows. Dominant grasses grew shorter. The air was drier.

Just about here, around the 99th meridian, travelers crossed into fundamentally unfamiliar topology. They were edging onto the plains proper. The land rose above 2,500 feet, a year's average rainfall dropped below twenty inches. Beyond this boundary the perceptual basics—light, mass, space, color—suddenly shifted in ways both obvious and indescribable. Before, the land they called "wild" was really attractive on terms neither surprising nor threatening. Now, looking around, they were suddenly less sure of themselves. The high plains left them perceptually off balance.

The land evoked varied responses. Some travelers marveled at new sights—beds of bright cactus flowers, the plains afire to the horizon, mirages of lakes and islands. Sunlight refracted through the shimmering heated air, so distant wagons seemed suddenly to lift off the ground and bob along like sloops at sea.[39] Mostly, however, travelers were impressed by what was *not* there, the sheer immensity of unbroken sweep. A minority were attracted, yet floundered at descriptions of the treeless, wind-scoured, dun-colored country that had nothing they had been taught to call beautiful. Julia Holmes wrote vaguely of grandeur, tried a comparison with the ocean, then gave up:

"It is impossible for me to describe."[40] William Lockwood seemed puzzled at his own admiration after he climbed a bluff and looked up the Platte valley:

> It was a right welcome sight, strange too, and yet it had not one picturesque or beautiful feature about it, nor had it any features of grandeur other than its vast extent, its solitude and its wilderness. For mile after mile a plain as level as a frozen lake was outspread before us; here and there the Platte, divided into a dozen different little streams, was traversing it, and an occasional clump of wood rising in the midst like a shadowy island, relieved the monotony of the waste. No living thing was moving throughout the vast landscape.[41]

Although this country would soon be drastically re-envisioned, these travelers were mostly repulsed by what they saw. They looked forward to the mountains, but they described the land they crossed in terms common among outlanders, from Coronado onward. The plains seemed just short of nothing. After a morning's march along the Arkansas, Charles Post was certain he had "never traveled over so desolate and uninteresting eight miles of road in my life." Others wrote testily of "an ocean of land, the same day in and day out." When they came across a break in the monotony, many projected onto it memories of what lay behind them, sometimes in astounding detail. Along the Platte, James Owen gazed at a bluff and saw "a Lady in full dress . . . indeed one could not help thinking it a real object. The Lady was drest in a Rich Black Satin Dress richly flowered with Satin figures a Cape of silk with green fringe, the right arm laying hold of the left a little above the elbows and the left hand pendant[,] the hair Black and done up . . . the Shoes and stockings to be seen." Travelers had praised the prairies as ripe for the plow—but not the plains. E. H. N. Patterson thought the place was fine for buffalo, but the soil was wasted otherwise. Erosion was a merciful act, he thought. Looking at the gullies and draws draining into the Platte, he decided that "the great Creator had made this vast desert as a sort of storehouse of materials from which he is day by day transporting them to other regions, where they can be made more available for the use and to the benefit of man."[42]

The rivers, like the land they carried away, left travelers reaching for adjectives. The Platte, Arkansas, and Kansas, churning and muddy from springtime runoff, were valueless except as a source of water and as an assurance that one was moving in the right direction. The Platte, "the most peculiar river I ever saw," according to one traveler, drew the harshest criticism.[43] Its turgid waters lay thinly over its broad, flat valley, nearly a mile across in some places and rarely more than six feet deep. It could hardly have been more different from the deep, green, tree-lined rivers easterners had grown up admiring. Most travelers would have agreed with an army officer's description from 1849: "It is unfit for navigation, bad to ford, destitute of fish, too dirty to bathe in, and too thick to drink, at least until custom habituates one to it."[44] Thomas Knox thought the Platte looked magnificent at a distance, but "like many a loud-mouthed declaimer, it lacks sadly in depth; it has not sufficient water to afford safe navigation to a good-sized cod-fish."[45] Mark Twain saw the river farther upstream. His is the classic dismissal:

> We came to the shallow, yellow, muddy South Platte, with its low banks and its scattering flat sand-bars and pigmy islands—a melancholy plane, and only saved from being impossible to find with the naked eye by its sentinal ranks of scattering trees standing on either bank. The Platte was "up," they said—which made me wish I could see it when it was down, if it could look any sicker and sorrier.[46]

Then there were the animals. Overlanders were not surprised to see new species of beasts; they would have been disappointed had they not seen a bison. But the actuality of these creatures jarred them. They were unprepared for the bison's size; it was, after all, the continent's largest life-form. Beyond that their impressions varied, sometimes wildly. A woman found her first bison "the impersonation of a prairie god," fierce and majestic, "with beard enough for a dozen French emperors." A man thought a running bull looked like a fat hog in a rush, maybe the ugliest beast alive. When seen in their thousands, however, bison always left the travelers agape. "The nearest ones were so close that we could see their eyes, and the farthest were like waves of the ocean," recalled a woman who had crossed the plains as a girl. Another remembered being almost deafened by a roar like a cataract when the galloping animals plunged into the Arkansas. Almost as impressive was what was left behind: this was God's barnyard, one farmer thought, with millions of acres deep in manure.[47]

Antelopes left observers slightly giddy. Groups of sleek pronghorns stared at the wagons in saucer-eyed startlement, then bounded away in what one woman praised as "lofty and intelligent motion." When hunters gave chase, the animals cut away at sharp angles, accelerated, and, as one diarist put it, "gave [the hunters] a beautiful pair of heels." Pursuers were frustrated, observers amused. Antelopes were "like some of the young ladies," a Texan wrote, "hard to come up with, and harder to bring down when you do get in reach."[48]

Wolves were more familiar, but overlanders had never seen them in such numbers. The plains were home to scores of thousands of true wolves (sometimes called lobos) and coyotes (or prairie wolves). They swarmed along the roads, hoping for stray calves or sheep and feeding on garbage and offal. Symbols of nature's dark side, they convinced some travelers that they finally had stepped beyond civilization. "Surrounded by wolves and wilderness," one told his diary.[49] By day the animals trotted and loitered at the edge of sight. Then, with night, came the howls. A soldier in western Kansas later told his wife of walking to his camp's perimeter to listen to

> the big wolves and the little wolves, the prairie wolves, the timber wolves, grey wolves, blue wolves, coyotes and all; to hear more distinctly the snapping of the teeth, the piteous "yowls" and dismal howls, the barking of half a dozen or so and then the dire yell!—the grand chorus in which every wolf participated as if the grand period—the special moment for which he had been born—and had long awaited—had at length arrived, and it was his especial business to "let out."[50]

Like him, some travelers made light of the eerie wailing: "I am entertained every night by the wolves. No need of getting lonesome or sleepy." Others were unnerved. "Wolves and coyotes make nights hideous," one wrote; "saw a grey wolf larger than a newfoundland dog."[51]

Just as unsettling was the erratic, sometimes treacherous weather. Luckier travelers faced only long and soaking rains during the first weeks. "Tonight everything is wet, and everyone cross and used up," a young wife wrote. "It is almost beyond human endurance at such times as these to keep amiable." After driving his team through a four-hour downpour, Hiram Allton swore he had "never before put in such a day. . . . I am mud up to my eyes."[52] Storms that struck on the plains proper, however, went far beyond irritating. Emigrants described them as a force beyond anything they had known. First lightning came in sheets and snakes, with deafening thunder and the sizzle of static electricity, then the torrent ("RAIN is no name for it") and wind that overturned wagons and tossed tents like scrap paper.[53] Even worse were hailstorms, which inspired a terrified fascination:

> Suddenly, we saw ahead of us a dense cloud moving swiftly along the ground, towards us. . . . There was no thunder or lightning, but a loud roaring. The edge of the cloud was well defined, and it was grand, as I sat helpless in the wagon, to watch it rush across the prairie. My four companions, each seizing a pail or food box to cover his head, sprang for the team, and hastily unhitching the mules from the wagon, separated them as much as possible from each other, each man hold-

ing onto a mule. Before this was entirely accomplished, a furious storm of hail was upon us, varying from the size of walnuts to almost as large as goose eggs. The pieces were not rounded like ordinary hail, but it was as though a field of ice had been put through a powerful crusher, and then rained down upon us. . . . Fortunately, the roar and the pouring hail passed almost like an express train, and all was still as before the storm struck us.[54]

Blizzards might bellow out of the north even in April. "We went to bed last night in Nebraska," one man wrote, "but as we awaken this morning, we may easily imagine ourselves in Siberia." Those with wagons or tents had minimal protection. Anyone on foot must have suffered considerably: "Heavy snow storm in the afternoon," wrote an emigrant huddled under canvas; "a handcart and wheelbarrow co. passed at 1 pm. Wind NW, cold and blowing hard."[55] The temperature next might rise seventy or eighty degrees in a few days. The sandy soil, which seemed to draw the sun "with the strength of a burning glass," blistered feet through the bootsoles and left oxen moaning in agony.[56]

But hot or cold, storm or shine, travelers had one complaint in common. "Most windy day I ever saw; cannot keep dishes on the table," a woman wrote on her first day on the plains. The trails had been grazed free of vegetation, and when the incessant wind swept over bald soil pounded by hooves and wheels, the result was a refrain running through diary after diary: "The wind blows the sand and dirt dreadfully"; "the wind blew very hard and filled our eyes with dirt"; "the wind blew furiously . . . small stones and sand"; "the dust is dreadful!"[57] An Ohio farmer compared the clouds of debris to chaff and dirt belching from a bowl-head thresher. Travelers soon were caked with grime. "That would be a keen-eyed mother who could recognize her own son at a glance under the dirt and disguise of plains-travel," wrote a journalist along the road. At mealtime the wind filled a cook's eyes with smoke and ashes and seasoned the food with sand. Everything, even scrambled eggs and gruel, crunched.[58]

When the wind lulled, the bugs moved in. "O, mercy, the mosquitos. Thought they would devour us," Rose Bell wrote along the Platte. They swarmed in such clouds along the southern route that A. M. Gass thought they must have been generated spontaneously from the elements. Gnats and sand flies stung the travelers' faces and hands and drove the stock nearly mad. Lavinia Porter recalled skimming a glaze of drowned insects from her coffee between sips. Sleep brought other problems. "The other night some insect crawled into my ear and I thought it would kill me for an hour or two,"

Alonzo Boardman wrote his wife. The pain finally stopped when he filled his ear with medicine, but a mysterious fluid oozed from the opening for days. The experience left Boardman "nervous."[59]

ALONZO BOARDMAN was one of thousands shaken by the trip over the high plains. But even as their surroundings unnerved them, in other ways they carried their own environment with them. This imported setting was social, not physical. Emigrants were walking bundles of values and belief; cultural particulars were embedded in their thoughts and manners, institutions and biases, language and fears, in how they dressed and ate and prayed and in what they named their mules. The overland rush was a loud shout westward, a way of life projected through the plains to the Rockies.

Not that imported attitudes were always in harmony. Travelers were part of a society more angrily divided than at any time in its national past. The situation, in fact, seemed almost specially designed to set the emigrants at each others' throats. Nowhere else in the nation were so many people of such varied backgrounds thrown together so quickly and so closely. At a time of unprecedented sectional tension and gathering paranoia, only two years before the onset of civil war, streams of northerners and southerners converged in, of all places, eastern Kansas, the one spot in the country where opponents and champions of slavery had already begun killing each other. Three years earlier John Brown had murdered five slavers in Osawatomie, twenty miles south of the southern trail, and proslavery forces had burned Lawrence. Now people from all parts of the country and of all shades of opinion were funneled into battered country still warm from the fighting. But travelers did not have to be politically opposed to feel the tension. The road ahead tested the firmest friendships and the sunniest spirits.

The Yankee majority occasionally chafed at being tossed together with southerners. "Got into a log shantee amongst a vulgar low set," a Bostonian wrote of a roadhouse full of Mississippians: "I backed out and slept at a free state man's."[60] Some were stunned at southern habits, especially among borderlanders. Lavinia Porter fell in with Texans and Missourians who were, she thought, the champion swearers of the world: "They swore at their wives, at their horses, at each other, at the wind that blew, at the stones in the road. The air was constantly filled with their curses." Neighbors at another camp were at least as bad:

Sitting around their wagons were other unkempt soiled and bedraggled women, most of them lean, angular, and homely, nearly every one of them chewing on a short stick, which they occasionally withdrew and swabbed around in a box containing some black powder, while a muddy stream oozed from the corners of their polluted mouths. It was evident to the most casual observer that they were snuff dippers from Arkansas or Tennessee.[61]

More homogenous groups also felt the stress. Riding with the Lawrence goldseekers the previous year was the handsome Julia Holmes, daughter of a Free-Soil settler and wife of a John Brown disciple. Several fellow travelers were from the South. They were insulted when she demanded, in the name of sexual equality, her rightful turn at nighttime guard duty and were shocked by what she considered practical clothes—Indian moccasins, a man's hat, short dresses, and bloomers. They called her a dangerous crank. She sniffed at them as "quasi-moralists" and "croakers against reform."[62]

Given the circumstances, however, the emigration was astonishingly peaceful. The record shows virtually no serious violence among the parties, either in 1859 or during the following years when Americans elsewhere were slaughtering each other as never before or since. Perhaps the experience showed the conservative, unifying tendency of westward expansion. As overlanders bundled along traditions into new and disorienting country, perhaps they saw how much cultural ground they shared. More likely they were peaceful because of the daily grind of travel. After fifteen hours of hard work, emigrants were too tired to fight.

They usually had energy for fun, however. Reading was the least taxing. Literature, high and low, was valuable cargo. "Anything in the shape of print was greedily devoured," Lavinia Porter remembered. Freighters and teamsters, neighboring campers and old trappers pestered her family for periodicals and the yellowing newspapers they had brought. Novels were loaned and reloaned; precious volumes by Shakespeare and Byron were protectively hidden away. Travelers wove reading into their work and leisure. "Went swimming, . . . washed shirts, socks, overalls, towels, hdkfs., etc.," Charles Post wrote one Sunday; "read four chapters of Proverbs, part of 'As You Like It,' shot at mark five times, two hundred and thirty yards; ate supper and went to bed." And from a Mrs. Creel: "I made myself tidy and spent the remainder of the day with Mrs. Jones, I sewing while she read aloud, 'Locksley Hall.' I do not know when I have enjoyed anything so thoroughly. I forgot all bodily fatigue in the delight the poem gave."[63]

Music was even easier to bring along. A traveler with no room for books could still carry a tune. Many brought whatever instruments they could. At any stopping place one might hear guitars, banjos, flutes, fiddles, tambourines, and bones. A band of Indiana musicians fully outfitted with "saxhorns, trombones, kent-bugle and bass drum" passed through Kansas City in April 1859 and a brass band from Illinois two months later. One family packed a legless piano in the bottom of their wagon, and although they later had to jettison other supplies, it stayed. Campers held impromptu dances with neighbors. A man wrote of visiting Missouri bullwhackers, ragged and loose-jointed fellows who organized a cotillion among themselves, with "women" designated by strips of canvas tied on their left arms. Musical styles and songs varied as much as the instruments. Besides sentimental favorites ("Gentle Annie" and "Hazel Dell") there were plantation melodies ("Uncle Ned"), sailors' chanteys, and war ballads ("Nicodemus"). With new neighbors each night, all things were possible—"Nellie Bly," "The Girl I Left Behind," "The Irish Immigrant," or "I Am Captain Jenks of the Horse Marines."[64] And more. Along the Arkansas a woman awoke to a chorus from *The Barber of Seville* performed by nearby soldiers:

> Bravo, bravissimo, Figaro, Bravo!
> Tutti me chiedono
> Tutti me vogliono

A doctor on the same road was startled to hear airs by Beethoven and Mozart played around a nearby campfire, "strangely out of place in this wild waste."[65]

The hours spent in relaxed amusement were cultural exhibits—contemporary, traditional, ancient. E. H. N. Patterson described his camp: "The boys are occupied in cooking antelope meat, mending clothes, reading, writing, singing, telling yarns, arguing politics, discussing religious topics, and the like." In the trip's first stages travelers could attend minstrel shows and circuses. Later they passed evenings at whatever diversions were possible: playing cards, yodeling, composing poetry, learning to dance the Pigeon Wing and the Double Shuffle. Alden Brooks, appointed the company phrenologist, spent hours feeling and analyzing his companions' heads.[66]

Travelers also carried their society's fundamental institution—the family. This part of the story was especially revealing about what did and did not change in the move west. It might seem that the strange world of the trails would challenge and reshape people's most basic notions of family. Every society has elaborate rules, evolved over centuries, that state the different duties and prerogatives of men and women, adults and children. These rules imply different traits of character and spirit of male, female, younger, and older. Life on the trail was a sort of laboratory where people were often thrown into new familial roles, especially that first year when young single men or heads of households temporarily "baching it" suddenly had to try their hand at "women's work." After several weeks over cookfires and washboards, they might be expected to question the fundamentals of a normal household.

Life on the trail did not undermine family structure, however. It reinforced it. Instead of trying to master a few domestic skills, men did women's work only when it was utterly unavoidable, muddling through with a minimal effort. The experience generally taught them just how much they hated those duties, and as soon as possible they handed them back to available women. The sudden absence of wives, children, and younger siblings also brought out in men the most romanticized Victorian sentiments idealizing home and hearth and the woman as domestic angel. As a result, the standard rules that defined the family were, if anything, more rigid and insistent in the towns where these men landed at the trip's end.

Men's attempts at female labors on the trail became a pathetic floundering. "Burnt the beans—burnt the apples—burnt our hands," Daniel Witter reported after his first try at cooking; "had a general burning time."[67] A bachelor's diary from 1863 is a culinary horror show. Day after day he ate crackers and uncooked bacon and drank coffee "strong enough to float a four pound wedge." Trying something slightly more ambitious rarely worked: "Burned my hand on the spider [a skillet]—got mad at the potatoes and wouldn't eat them." He sank finally into starved despair:

> I never was half so hungry in my life. But good lord deliver me from all such grub as we have—Bacon and crackers for one meal and then for the next—crackers and bacon—and then we will have them in a promiscuous manner. When we started from St. Jo I thought we should live fine and fatten right along. . . . but Oh flesh potts of Egypt, how I sigh for ye.[68]

Not surprisingly, in families that did make the trip the traditional arrangement of responsibilities and power remained solidly intact. Husbands and other older males directed the march, decided when and where to stop, and oversaw the routines of camp. Familial work roles were basically unchanged. Men did the equivalent of field work—driving and caring for the animals, repairing wagons, and standing watch at night. Women assumed the domestic duties of making fires, cooking meals, making and breaking camp, and caring for the young and the sick. Children drew water, gathered fuel, and helped with lighter tasks.

The trip held quite different meanings for males and females. Women, after all, were embarking (sometimes against their will) on an exhausting, uncertain enterprise in which they would have relatively little control. There was, besides, a fundamental inequity in the load of work. Although both husbands and wives left some tasks behind them—working the fields and fencing for the men, scrubbing floors for women—wives took relatively more of their labor on the road. Besides cooking and childcare, they were expected to wash and mend clothes, nurse the sick, keep all goods well packed and the wagon tidy, and generally maintain an orderly household. Doing domestic jobs on the move was relatively more challenging. Herding oxen was much the same on the trail as on a farm, but building an open fire of bison chips, then cooking in a steady wind while wearing long skirts that occasionally caught fire—that made women look longingly back to a kitchen and a cast-iron stove.

Mothers with young children felt the strain the most. During the day they sat packed among the shifting cargoes in the swaying, groaning, stuffy wagons, trying to pacify babies who, understandably, were rarely in good humor. They had to stay constantly vigilant, lest older sons or daughters topple out of the wagon and under its wheels. At night they cared for their youngsters while managing their rolling households. The inevitable childhood diseases wore them down more. "Babies very sick all night," Ellen Hunt wrote of her two infants, and the next evening: "All the children complaining."[69] On rare days of "laying by" the men lounged about and regathered their strength, but women were expected to catch up with work undone while on the move. "We have to roast and bake, and clean up generally, as the men will not stop of weekdays," one wife wrote of her first Sunday on the trail. "There are 6 of us to cook for." A few weeks later her company paused on a Thursday. She was at first relieved that "we have decided to rest for one day," but remembering the women's work, she quickly caught herself: "Rest? Where *is* rest for us?"[70]

In countless other rituals and social passages, emigrants carried west the collective habits of the Republic. Courtship, the prelude to family, continued. The famished bachelor who longed for the "the flesh potts of Egypt" managed a series of flirtations. The day after he *"gassed a little"* with three women, his eye was drawn to a young stranger who "skipped over the prairie like a young fawn to pluck a prairie flower." Then she cooked him a meal, and his heart was hers: "I love her." The next day, however, he was drawn to a curly-haired beauty and her mother (a "fine looking old lady and great talker"), and a few days later to several women who serenaded him with guitars.[71]

A considerable number of newlyweds took the trip, especially after 1859, seeing the chance to begin their lives fresh in the new country. A marriage's first weeks of mutual discovery took place on the rutted, dusty roads and in crowded campsites. Byron and Mollie Sanford had been wed barely a month when they left Nebraska for Colorado. Sexual intimacy must have been difficult, sleeping in a small tent with two others, but they found time for solitary walks, long conversations, and flower-gathering. They tested their roles and each other's tolerances, got tired and irritated, fought and got over it. They began the accretion of memories that were friendship's tissue and the stuff of family tales: the turbulent crossing of the river that drowned their rooster, Mollie's crying bitterly after Byron cursed the oxen, and Byron's rising thirsty from their bed for a long pull from a water bucket in which Mollie had set his muddy socks to soak.[72]

At trail's end, after weeks on the road, younger travelers might arrive with a bluster. "I tell you Baldwin a 36 days trip over the plains with d___d Indians prowling around, wolfs howling, Rattlesnakes neighborly, sleeping on the ground with Boots for a pillow and Revolver under your head ready for use tends rather to dispel any feelings of fear," one wrote home. "It became so monotonous after a while that I would have welcomed an Indian fight if awake." Most, however, would have agreed with Samuel Mallory: "We arrived here . . . safe, sound and healthy; dirty, tired and awful hungry," he told his diary; "I think this journey will be remembered by all of us as long as life lasts." Like it or not, it now was time to retrain their thoughts toward what lay ahead. "Tomorrow our long march will be ended," Mollie Sanford wrote, looking back on her extraordinary introduction to married life and a new land. She drew a simple lesson for herself and her husband: "I am thankful we are alive. I ought to think more of this than other affairs."[73]

THE SANFORDS' TIME ON THE ROAD was a rough metaphor for the rush itself. Like all newlyweds, emigrants set off in a chaotic scramble into the utterly unpredictable. Buoyed by naivete and grand expectations, they dreamed of turning their lives for the better. Travelers carried a social hope chest of deliberate belief and expectation, and with it an extensive baggage of subtler attitudes and biases about the world and its parts—a load that would shape, intentionally or not, new lives in a new place.

Those who moved with the rush of 1859 and the few years following watched a culture in its fullest meaning—an evolving whole of artifacts, customs, values, and habits—carried into the country as rapidly and thoroughly as ever in history. They saw a young nation's ambitions, its confident projections of domination, its fantasies of mastering space and time. They also lived through quite a story.

But like every story, it had its own perspective. It was told from east to west. Others were living the same experience from another angle—from west to east, from the plains outward. The same events looked quite different when seen that way. The people living on the plains understood instantly that the march of the "merry" and "light-hearted" argonauts was part of a shuffling of power and resources that raised some up and devastated others. One group's opportunity was another's disaster; what seemed an emigration to some was to others an invasion. Every moment along the trail was full of these various meanings. In March 1859 some overlanders were caught in a spring storm. One of them recorded their response to an uncomfortable evening:

> Last night Rogers cut down a lone cottonwood tree, high up in the branches of which was tied a dead Indian. On my protesting that such sacrilege would bring down the whole Sioux nation upon us he replied that he was going to have a fire if he had to fight every Indian on the South Platte. As the tree struck the ground, bones, blankets, red ochre and trinkets flew in all directions.[74]

Part Three:
POWER

8

PATH OF EMPIRE

On the afternoon of September 21, 1859, as miners and merchants in the diggings were starting to think about the coming winter, two Kiowa men entered George Peacock's store at Walnut Creek Station, a prominent stopping place along the Arkansas River road. Satank and Pawnee, both subchiefs, reportedly were slightly drunk. They demanded goods from the clerks, who told them to leave. The two stomped out, furious, but Satank was not finished. He grabbed a sheep, slit its throat, and filled his mouth with the spouting blood. Then he strode back into the store and spit the blood into a clerk's face. After a brief but spirited fight, Satank withdrew but then climbed onto the roof and began tearing and throwing the sod. He soon left, promising to destroy the post.

The next day Pawnee was shot and killed by soldiers sent to investigate the episode. When a larger force marched on the Kiowa camp they found it deserted: "We were much disappointed," a young officer wrote, "as we expected a fight." The Indians had not fled the area, however. Within forty-eight hours Kiowas had attacked a mail stage and had killed four prospectors returning to the states. Over the next weeks other incidents were reported at several spots along the road.[1]

As usual, some whites had a simple explanation: Indians, being Indians, caused trouble, and if given the chance they killed people. The real situation was more complex and revealing. Only a year earlier the many Kiowas, Comanches, and Cheyennes crowding close to the road had been uniformly friendly, but the gold rush and its many repercussions were transforming the central plains. From the Missouri to the mountains, the land was being rethought and reshaped. For Indians, as the incident on Walnut Creek suggested, the changes were much for the worse. Satank's gesture spoke of defiance, a world whirling downward, and bloody times ahead.

INDIANS WERE ANGRY for a lot of reasons. A main cause was the blossom of white settlements along the Front Range, the western flank of the nomads' range. The season's first overlanders arrived on Cherry Creek late in April, most on horseback or on foot, some pulling handcarts. They found about 200 log cabins with turf roofs and mud-and-daub chimneys where several hundred men and a few women had shivered away the winter.[2] Denver and Auraria had a few general merchandise stores, some liveries, several ragtag saloons, and a scattering of other businesses. Over the winter Denver's first tinsmith built the town's first stove, which he sold to the first hotel. For most people, one man wrote, "the principal amusement . . . [was] card playing, telling yarns, and drinking most execrable whisky."[3]

The immediate economic outlook was poor. A little powdery dust could be panned after a lot of squatting in icy streams, but experienced miners had stressed from the start that any significant deposits would be well up in the South Platte tributaries. A little prospecting was done during the winter, with a few provocative finds to the north along Boulder Creek. Generally, men sat on their claims and waited for someone to make a move. An early arrival wrote his wife that land was taken up for ten miles around every paying site, and prospects were "any thing But flattering."[4] A young man who stumbled in from the Smoky Hill Trail was first disillusioned, then desperate. "No man can make ten cents a month," he wrote his father; "if you don't send some money, I will starve to death."[5]

Discouraging reports soon hit the border towns like a dash of cold water. Two engineers had labored forty days; one cleared forty-five cents, the other, three. They built a tiny flatboat barely a yard wide, floated down the Platte to the Missouri, and sold their craft for two cents more than their combined income in the new El Dorado.[6] Letters from the mines told that the best sites, with plenty of water and worked by experienced hands, yielded two or three dollars a day. Most claims would not pay for the scantiest provisions. There were rumors of better chances in the mountains, but the hard facts were grim. The Pike's Peak craze was "the humbug of humbugs," the *Hannibal Messenger* concluded in early June: "It has no parallel in the history of civilized nations, unless we except the famous 'South Sea Bubble.'"[7]

Almost immediately the emigration was affected. Disgruntled first-comers, tramping back toward St. Joseph and Westport, complained bitterly to travelers on their way out. The result was a volatile collision of moods and expectations. "Raining and storming," one man wrote the day his party heard the discouraging news. "Chambers & Clark forfeited all their stock & turned back to the states." He too felt the urge: "I took a caper and thought I would go along with them [but] when we had our bundles on our backs I thought mine was too heavy. I whelled [*sic*] right short round and went west & left them go East. Made up my mind to go to the peak if the lord would spare my life."[8] Plenty of others, hungry and weatherblown, gave up the chase. One party was determined to keep going, but after counting 107 wagons in a day going in the other direction, they wavered: "This has given us all the blues and what to do we dont know, but time will tell." Most turned around the next day.[9] Some argonauts traveled less than fifty miles before reversing their course.

They were dubbed the "go-backs." By one account they outnumbered those persisting for the mountains by five to one, but a better guess is that about half who started the trip turned around along the way or after only a brief stay on Cherry Creek. A small minority chose to turn up the North Platte and take the longer journey to Oregon or California, but most put their faces toward home. Alden Brooks and his friends composed new words to the gospel hymn "Jordan" to capture the scene:

> I looked to the west & I looked
>   to the east,
> & I spied the pikes peakers a coming.
> Some on horse back some on foot
> & some a running.[10]

New slogans on wagon covers replaced the earlier bluster: "Are going home, can't stay in the wilderness. Go way trouble." Many shuffled along in fatigue.

Some begged for crackers. Back at the trail's start a Nebraskan wrote that for weeks the roads were filled by "a continual stream" of thousands of go-backs, "disappointed, dissatisfied, and exhibit[ing] much bad feeling."[11]

Tension indeed was high. A few shrugged off the whole affair. "I have had a good chance to see a good deal of the country and it has not cost me much but my time," a young midwesterner mused the day he returned home; "I have had good health and have enjoyed myself first rate, if I have been a little Humbuged."[12] Most were less generous. After reading into early reports whatever they wished to hear, they were outraged when reality refused to cooperate. Blaming themselves would be painful, but they could still find scapegoats.

The main candidate was D. C. Oakes. A "yon-sider" who had returned from California prospecting to open a contracting business in Iowa, he had gone to Colorado in fall 1858. He knew from experience that much better prospects probably waited in the mountains. Oakes returned to Iowa with the journal of Luke Tierney, one of the Russell party, and published it under Tierney's name and with a map attributed to himself.[13] Then he bought a sawmill with two partners and in March started up the Platte. Oakes's emigrant guidebook was only one of many, but because he was actually on the road, moving slowly with his mill and therefore meeting dozens who passed him on their way west, he became well known.

At O'Fallon's Bluff Oakes left others with the mill and set off by horse to choose a site. Immediately he began to meet disgruntled go-backs, men who were "in no good humor, you can be assured." As he later told it, he offered to bet all his funds that better times were coming, but the contrary tide grew steadily and the mood turned so surly that friends warned Oakes he was in danger. One day, after he had started back for his mill, he saw a crowd standing around a newly dug grave. He walked up to pay his respects, looked down, and saw that he knew the deceased: it was himself. Angry emigrants had buried him in effigy and scribbled bitter epitaphs on tombstones of bison bones: "Here lies the remains of D. C. Oakes, / Who was engaged in this damned hoax." And: "D. C. Oakes *dead* and buried and in hell."[14]

Symbolic harm was the worst Oakes had to fear. Cranky go-backs felt no true rage because they had no real commitment. Most had little notion of what emigration involved and so were stunned by the first jolt of reality. They turned back as they had left—on a whim. A scornful Nebraskan watched them return: "So the world goes. No doubt there is gold plenty there scattered over the country, but it requires labor to get it; they must dig and work for it. The gold won't come in their pockets without."[15]

The larger lesson of the go-backs was less obvious. The disillusioned thousands who washed back to the border towns were vivid testimony of how the plains, relatively removed until recently from shifting moods to the east, had become vulnerable to the fantasies and mercurial impulses of millions who now had easy access to the region. Physically, culturally, and emotionally, the plains and its peoples were on white America's doorstep.

Ironically, the first ebb tide of go-backs coincided with the first truly significant gold discoveries, west and north of Cherry Creek. During the winter George Jackson, a yon-sider, had found excellent color up Clear Creek, also called Vasquez Fork. In the spring he and others ascended the churning stream, which emerged from the foothills where the town of Golden would soon appear, and fought their way up its narrow canyon, later nicknamed "Toughcuss." Early in May they hit paydirt on a branch about twenty miles up Clear Creek. Other strikes soon were made in the neighborhood of their camp, Chicago Bar, named for the hometown of several in the prospecting party.[16] Northwest of Denver a rich vein of gold-bearing quartz was found at Gold Hill, high in the foothills on an affluent of Boulder Creek.

By far the richest find of the spring was between these two places. Jackson and the Chicagoans had moved up the main branch of Clear Creek. Another party of four led by a Georgian freighter, John W. Gregory, pushed up the snow-clogged canyon of the creek's north fork to a gulch near the stream's head. Four days after Jackson's discovery, the men found dirt yielding up to eight dollars a pan. Gregory, who had a reputation for low energy and spotty attention, reportedly was so addled by his good luck that he sold his claim within weeks. After drifting around the country for a couple of years, he checked out of an Illinois hotel and vanished from the record.[17] His name remained with one of Colorado's true bonanzas. A cluster of camps soon sprang up in and around Gregory Gulch; Central City was the largest.

Another find, almost as rich, was made nearby. Green Russell, leader of the party that made the first discoveries a year earlier, had left his brother Levi and returned to his native Georgia over the winter to visit family and to recruit more goldseekers. Green returned to Denver soon after Gregory's strike, and his seasoned intuition told him that the surrounding terrain was full of promise. With brothers and colleagues he left immediately for the mountains in early June. They dug several prospect holes in a ravine just south of Gregory's, and in each they found paydirt that was more than respectable. Within days seventy-five sluices were operating in what they called Russell's Gulch, and by early fall 900 men were finding $35,000 in dust a week.[18]

Veterans like Russell had said all along that the pockets of flour dust in creeks around Denver were only invitations, with payoffs for the persistent higher up the mountain streams. There, too, would be the mother veins running through deposits of quartz. Now, after all the panic and retributions, those first predictions proved true.

The discoveries on Clear and Boulder Creeks had four consequences that reverberated far beyond the men who worked the gulches. First, they confirmed white settlements along the Front Range and guaranteed their rapid growth. All talk of humbug was over by autumn. Between $200,000 and $500,000 in gold was taken out in 1859 and at least $1 million the next year.[19] That brought a new and steady emigration to the Rockies. Word of Jackson's and Gregory's strikes, in fact, moved eastward along the trails not far behind the deflating news of the nay-sayers, so that some travelers became double turnabouts and headed once more for the mountains. The strikes, second, determined that mining in the mountains would be quite different from the panning camps around Denver. The richer gravels were worked with elaborate placer systems with long toms, sluices, and more. Quartz (or lode) mining demanded far more that that—equipment to blast and bore tunnels, machines for sorting and initial processing, stamp mills and perhaps refineries, an elaborate community of machines and support for them.

Third, a supply center would be needed to receive and channel material in and out of the mountains. Transition points appeared throughout the montane West during the second half of the nineteenth century—Sacramento, Boise, Helena, and other cities. These towns were close to the mining action but were more accessible to transportation and were situated at lower altitudes, away from the vicious mountain winters. The Colorado camps needed such a place, a town to be the funnel's neck for people and materials flowing back and forth. The strikes thus virtually ordained a significant urban center on the western edge of the plains.

Finally, these effects were full of implications for the country to the east. Not only would many more people, goods, and animals move across the plains, but also the nature and meaning of this movement would change. Before, traffic along the Platte had been mostly emigration to distant places, people trying only to get somewhere else and to return home. The new developments demanded a continuous current of commerce and supply between the Missouri ports and the mountains. When people in the East looked toward the Rockies, the plains appeared less like a place to suffer and pass through. Suddenly that land seemed the middle ground of an economic whole, a vital membrane of exchange.

SEVERAL TOWNS had popped up by summer 1859. "The first thing Americans think of when they emigrate," Ned Wynkoop decided, "is to lay out a town-site, expecting of course that their own town will some day . . . become the metropolis of the world."[20] Maps show an impressive urban sprinkling of up to twenty-five towns: Arapaho, Pike's Peak City, Montana, Highland, St. Charles, Colona, Nonpareil City, and several others. Most were cities of gas. A member of Green Russell's party wrote that the towns were indistinguishable from New York City—except that they lacked people, wealth, and buildings. A few, however, took root, and two, Denver and Auraria, soon emerged as places of substance.

Both settlements were helped by muscular promotion. The boosting was not from the men who had given the towns a reason to be; Green and Levi Russell and most other prospectors hunted for paydirt in the hills. Instead professional town-puffers took the lead. William Larimer continued to push the Denver site he had chosen the morning after his arrival the previous summer, and he was joined by several others. William M. Byers, founder of the *Rocky Mountain News*, worked for both Denver and Auraria. Before coming to the mountains Byers had written a guidebook as popular as that of D. C. Oakes, and for a while Byers was equally reviled. Besides promising "gold . . . found all around," Byers added a promotional wrinkle. Fifty miles up the South Platte, his map showed a road that swept westward up Lodgepole Creek, through a great break in the mountains, then on toward the Pacific. "To Salt Lake," read a caption beside it. Such a route could in fact be taken, but it was nothing like the grand highway implied. To the uninitiated, the central plains seemed a broad avenue of western progress, with Denver and Auraria just off a major continental thoroughfare.

The boosters greeted word of the mountain strikes with "told-you-so" boasts of greater things to come. Outsiders, especially anyone threatened by good news, scoffed at first. Given the Kansans' habit of "downright, square, out-and-out lying," the *San Francisco Evening Bulletin* wrote, the new reports from Colorado should be tossed aside. Publicists answered with salvos of the boldest claims. "Why, bless your soul . . . , there's nothing but gold here," a correspondent wrote to the *Leavenworth Times* about Gregory's diggings. Miners averaged seventy-five dollars a day, and "in truth the mines have turned out richer than we ever believed they could. California can't hold a candle to Pike's Peak."[21]

Some stroke still was needed to banish the skeptics, however. It came with the arrival of one of the most familiar figures of the era. Horace Greeley—reformer, prominent publisher, prophet of western growth, and general spouter of opinion—arrived early in June on the first leg of a grand western tour. With him were two lesser luminaries, Albert Richardson, a well-known Illinois journalist, and a twenty-four-year-old Bavarian, Henry Villard, a journalist from the *Cincinnati Commercial* who became an executive and a brilliant promoter of western railroads. When they toured Gregory's Gulch, what they found must have set Greeley's famous muttonchops aquiver.

Greeley declared almost all claims to be paying operations, with some producing nearly $300 in a day. Just as impressive was the speculative spiral. After paying $500 down on a $2,500 claim, two men were offered $10,000 while still building sluices.[22] In a jointly written report the three journalists soberly cautioned against another "infatuation" and reminded readers of the need for hard work and patience, but in the mood of the day this was like telling a circus crowd to exit slowly from a burning tent. The "Greeley report" was just the ammunition the boosters were looking for. After the *Rocky Mountain News* published it as an extra on June 11 it was immediately sent East for wide publication.

By September, with additional strikes in South Park and elsewhere, Colorado was confirmed as a major mining region. The question then shifted: What lucky town would be the transition point between the mountain mines and the world outside? That town would harvest part of the investment sent to the Front Range and some of the gold that came out. It would market locally produced goods and serve as a storage and holding area for bulkier items, the tons of groceries, building materials, hay, and machinery demanded by a growing mining economy. It most likely would become the region's administrative and governmental center.

From the first weeks some emigrants moved instinctively away from goldseeking toward these new possibilities. The mining career of Samuel S. Curtis, son of a prominent border family, lasted only moments. "It is very hard work," he wrote home in 1858, "and after I had washed one pan full I concluded [gold] was here, but that I was not adapted to digging it." Instead he advised his brother to bring goods so they could find their fortune in banking and in selling mules, sugar, whiskey, and Hawken rifles.[23] Many hoped to profit from the lift of property values that came with the boom. Some worked on site, some from afar. Two New York City businessmen gave a young relative, Thomas Bayaud, full powers "to buy and sell real estate or personal property . . . and to make and execute deeds and legal conveyances."[24] Any individual might combine these various interests. While Bayaud was dealing in financial ephemera for his East Coast backers, he was also establishing a lumber business and becoming a pillar in the Episcopal church.[25]

In appealing to such men as Curtis and Bayaud, Denver and Auraria promoters had huge advantages. They built on the appeal already established—a prime location astride older and newer roads, their superior leadership, and political connections. Soon they had unique freight and stage connections to the Missouri valley.

A key maneuver was the early appearance of a newspaper. The gold rush happened during an emerging communications revolution. Americans increasingly relied on information transmitted telegraphically and dispersed in journals that could be established easily with new, cheap, technologically improved presses. The result was a proliferation of newspapers in eastern America. A frontier like Colorado, however, had only one or a few, at least during its first crucial months. This temporary imbalance gave promoters a valuable edge. As a curious world got its facts from dozens of newspapers strung together by copper wire and the postal service, what they learned about Colorado came from a sole journalistic source at the place itself. Whatever interests allied with that lone newspaper could influence uniquely the larger perception of the region. The spring snows had barely melted when William N. Byers appeared with press and print. He worked fast. Six days after his arrival (having printed up the front and back pages before he left Omaha) he published the first number of the *Rocky Mountain News* from an office above an Auraria saloon. With Solomon-like diplomacy he soon moved his press to a building in the middle of the boundary between Denver and Auraria, the dry bed of Cherry Creek.[26]

Some letters called Denver a shamble of small, poorly built houses in a vast sop of mud. They reported inflated prices, the first murder and hanging, drifting crowds of Mexicans, Indians, and eastern hard cases. But others noted the first signs of more cultivated life. At least ten white women had arrived, according to one midsummer report. There were some civilized dinners and the Christian burial of a good man—an Ohio dentist who died of bilious fever. Stores were springing up, and both towns held their first theatrical productions on the same October night.[27] New Mexican whiskey, a clear, gut-searing liquid that hit the brain like an artillery shot, was slowly giving way to brandy and Kentucky bourbon. Charles Post was "very much disappointed to find so large and flourishing towns." Instead of the expected frontier oddities he saw "lots of men, women and children all busy and apparently as contented as people in Decatur."

Denver's and Auraria's champions were walking a line. They had to set their towns apart and above their immediate competitors, yet their appeal rested on the sure prosperity of the region as a whole. Always, explicitly or indirectly, boosters pictured not only the mountains but also the foothills, Platte valley, and plains to the east as country destined for economic and cultural bloom. They enlarged on the promotional themes that ran through the first emigrant guides. Enormous herds of fat cattle would graze in the shelter of the Front Range. Cleanly plowed fields of corn and wheat would soon border the full length of plains rivers, with neat towns along the way, spaced in a civilized rhythm. Back on the Missouri border, boosters played up the same images. The Hannibal and St. Joseph Railroad, luring settlers to its colony in northwest Missouri, looked beyond St. Joseph (the "Young Giant of the West" perfectly positioned to dominate trade from mountain and plains) to the fertile valleys of the Platte and Arkansas. The view from the Missouri was of superior land rapidly filling with farms and ranches.[28]

A brave pattern lay westward, like a carpet unrolled. Already some individuals saw it as part of a larger inevitability. Notice, wrote Albert Richardson in the *New York Tribune,* how the central plains, Denver, and the new diggings sat along a broad parallel with Philadelphia, Baltimore, Washington, D.C., Cincinnati, St. Louis, St. Joseph, and San Francisco. The main thrust of expansion had always been along that line, and there it would continue to build. Before long the passes west of Denver would be gates of passage for a railroad linking Atlantic and Pacific, and mid-America would be a lasting home to hundreds of thousands. Border towns, the Platte and Arkansas, Denver, and the mountain camps were squarely within this great "PATH OF EMPIRE."[29]

Essential to this process was setting down narrative roots. To lay true claim, any society needed its own story. It had to retell the country's past in a way that made itself authentic, a believable and welcome historical outcome. Some of the first guidebooks included sketches of early prospecting, followed by glorious predictions, as if placing two chronological points, backward and forward, made a plotted line of events algebraically certain. Denver leaders picked up the responsibility. They had hardly established a post office and had not yet named any law officers when they founded a historical society.[30]

An image of regional destiny was crystallizing. Vigorous promotion and genuine finds together created a momentum of presumption. From the Missouri River to Gregory's Diggings and beyond, the whole expanse was headed for grand things. Only the particulars were undecided. The new vision was summed up nicely in a directory of Denver and Auraria published barely eighteen months after dust was first panned on Dry Creek. It began with a brief heroic history of gold discoveries, early governments, and social development. After that came a map of well-planted towns, a commercial prospectus, and lists of businesses, churches, and fraternal societies. Readers could find all the requisites of an American city. Denver had a past, a future, a chess club, and fourteen lawyers.[31]

THE BOOSTERS HAD HELP. In the frenzy of townmaking some of the most enthusiastic participants were white traders who had lived in the area for years. Virtually all of them were connected through marriage with Cheyenne, Arapaho, and Lakota bands, and in that capacity they had served as invaluable cultural and economic liaisons between white and Indian societies. How they responded to the gold rush told a lot about them and their historical role. It also made amply clear just how grim the Indians' situation had suddenly become.

Most traders had recently lived as beaver-trapping mountain men, figures who stand in the popular mind as fiercely independent, happily at home in a free-roaming world beyond civilization, proud in their isolation from civil ordinances and soft beds. Supposedly they viewed the coming of pioneers with contempt, if not open hostility. We remember them as running away from cities, not building them.

This view is one of the great contortions of western history, as the case of Colorado showed. When gold was discovered, every trader who had the chance jumped into the flow of development. Some jumped out again, usually not by their own choice, but others stayed to play key roles in remaking the high plains and mountains. All of them helped destroy the way of life that, according to tradition, was the only home for their anarchic souls.

In December 1857 John Simpson Smith outfitted for trade at a post on the Platte, and during the next spring, as the Russell and Lawrence parties probed along the mountain face, Smith apparently conducted business as usual. In mid-June 1858, just as the Georgians were approaching the South Platte, he brought more than 200 bison hides back to his outfitting post. On July 7, the day after Russell's first promising pan on Dry Creek, Smith left again for the field, loaded with coffee, muslin, tobacco, and other items for swap. This time, however, he returned the day after Christmas with only a single hide. Shortly after setting out to trade, Smith had found the excited prospectors on the South Platte. Immediately his interest shifted to a new course.[32]

John Smith fit the rip-roaring image of a mountain man. In 1830, at age twenty, he had fled a job as a tailor's apprentice and soon was trapping and carousing with the luminaries of the fur trade. Since the 1840s he had lived among the Cheyennes, who called him Blackfoot or Saddle Blanket. Lewis Garrard fixed on Smith as a typical white exotic when the two met along the Santa Fe Trail in 1846. Garrard wrote of the mountain man lounging and smoking in camp, eating marrow pounded with cherries, and bison boiled with fungus from decaying logs. Smith had his peaceable side—he enjoyed backgammon—but still was a true member of the trapping fraternity, Garrard wrote, "rough men . . . aliens to society, . . . strangers to the refinements of civilized life."[33]

Yet when townmaking began, Smith was in the thick of it. He was named as one of five officers in the Auraria Town Company. He took this job at least a little seriously; residents of Montana City charged him with luring new-comers with free draughts from a large whiskey barrel. Before that he had been named treasurer of the St. Charles board of trustees. The town's back-ers probably expected him to defend the townsite when they headed home for supplies, but when William Larimer and his backers made their move, Smith surrendered it and accepted his third post in two months: a director of the Denver City board.

A fellow director was William McGaa. McGaa's origins were shadowy and his reputation appropriately depraved. No one was sure of his name; he went also by Jack Jones and sometimes claimed descent from an En-glish baronet or a lord mayor of London. Camped nearby at the time of the first strikes, McGaa too joined the St. Charles Company as vice-president and was given title to the town's first lot, but when Larimer made his move, he went with Smith onto the Denver board of directors. Later he claimed the Denver City crowd plied him with whiskey and made dark threats of violence. The Denver Company's first meeting, on the other hand, was held in McGaa's cabin.[34]

Other traders mixed in where they could. Baptiste (Big Bat) Pourier reportedly hauled the first load of logs to Denver. Richens (Uncle Dick) Wootton was responsible for a hallowed landmark, the town's first dram shop, consisting of a plank between two barrels of raw corn whiskey he had hauled from northern New Mexico. The Kentuckian John Poisal had full credentials as a mountain man, having been arrested for smuggling in Santa Fe and having traded along the Front Range for a quarter century. In fall 1857 he had camped on the site of Denver to barter with Arapahoes and Cheyennes, and when he heard of the strike a year later he hurried back. "Bring picks and shovels, groceries and provisions," he wrote his son-in-law from Auraria, adding the merchant's favorite chorus: "They are in demand, and sell at high figures."[35]

Although these men did little or no prospecting, one of them took part in another significant production. On March 8, 1859, as the rush was really gathering steam, William McGaa's Lakota wife bore a son in the couple's cabin, the same one where Larimer and friends had organized their town company. It was the settlement's first baby. The father chose what he must have thought was a propitious name: William Denver McGaa.

The gesture was revealing—and rather pathetic. The name suggests that McGaa thought his reproductive timing would signify and seal a bond among McGaa, his family, and the emerging white society. He probably assumed, that is, that William Denver would be in the new order what fur trade babies had been in the old—a link between cultures. The weeks that followed, however, told a different story.

In Indian societies, as in every culture, power flowed along well-worn routes, some of them determined through sex. By marrying into plains tribes, all of them matrilineal and matrilocal, traders had gained valuable economic connections and considerable personal status. Native American families in turn expected their white in-laws to provide trade goods and to speak for their interests. Virtually every trader in early Denver had at least one Indian wife. John Poisal was married to Ma-hom (Snake Woman), sister of the influential Arapaho peace chief Niwot (Left Hand). John Simpson Smith had been married among the Southern Cheyenne for many years while trading with them, the Kiowas, and the Comanches.

By 1858 these marriages had produced dozens of mixed-blood children like William Denver who were central to an increasingly elaborate relational web among whites and Indians. Chivvy-say (Maggie), daughter of John Poisal and Ma-hom, was the recently widowed wife of the prominent mountain man, trader, and Indian agent, Thomas Fitzpatrick. When Garrard met John Smith in 1846, he wrote fondly of Smith's toddler son, Jack, throwing tantrums and clinging shyly to his Cheyenne mother's leg. By the late 1850s Jack was old enough to begin taking part in the trade with his father.[36] These sons and daughters were living expressions of a fusion of cultures and an accommodation that bound Indians and whites in the world of the plains fur trade, and for their fathers they were reminders of rank and influence. McGaa seemed to expect the same arrangement would hold in the town whose name he linked with his own through the infant now suckling in his cabin.

He was wrong. Such an idea rested on two faulty assumptions. First, McGaa apparently assumed that Indians—and therefore their white liaisons—would continue in some significant role of power. It must have seemed so, with townmakers like Larimer coming, hat in hand, to invite him into one company after another. The new power brokers, however, had other plans. They courted traders like McGaa out of concern only for the immediate future. Boosters worried that their settlements—isolated, poorly provisioned, and untrained for serious fighting—would be exceptionally vulnerable to native hostility. They were especially nervous that first winter. Just as their numbers thinned and the weather cut them off from help from the east, Arapahoes and Cheyennes returned from their summer hunts to spend the cold months along the South Platte and Lodgepole and Boulder Creeks. Nothing in the record suggests any serious threat, but white campers were probably worried, if not about attack, at least about loss of food, draft animals, and other basics. The conjugally connected Smith, McGaa, Poisal, and others seemed the best hedge against trouble.

Once Denver and other towns had taken root and gathered strength, however, a marital union's protective purpose was over. New enterprises meanwhile quickly pushed the fur trade to the edges of the new economic order, so a trader's access robes and other goods no longer counted for much, either. Marriages such as McGaa's lost almost all their strategic and economic value. Even then, those unions might have seemed useful as bridges of understanding between two cultures feeling their way toward accommodation. Such a purpose, however, assumed that marriage would continue to work as it had in the fur trade era—as an institution that defined power *within* both societies and channeled the flow of power *between* those societies.

But this second assumption was also flawed. The invading white society did indeed arrange itself partly through families, and it drew its lines of power partly through marriage and the roles of males and females and the fruits of sexual intimacy. Anyone along the trails to Colorado could watch those values acted out—in the bachelors' comic blunderings, in husbands and wives dividing their work, in women bending to brutal labor while Womanhood was idealized as a fragile saintliness. Sex, gender, and marriage, that is, were as important to whites as to Indians. But the particulars differed.

Euro-Americans, to start, were patrilineal, and because they located themselves and assessed a family by looking to the father's side, not the mother's, they saw nothing inherently prestigious in a Cheyenne or a Lakota wife, no matter who her parents or uncles were. As a road to status, a man's marriage to an Indian was a dead end at best. To most new emigrants, it was much worse than that. Native Americans might be allowed some fuzzy, abstract nobility, but face-to-face, as potential neighbors, they were considered somewhere between marginally tolerable and barely human. Certainly they would not be allowed any significant role in the emerging society, and anyone communing with them on a level of equality paid a price. In Victorian America, furthermore, the emotional weight of human contact rose immeasurably when it passed from the social to the sexual. A white woman who voluntarily bound herself intimately to an Indian man could hardly be imagined, and a white man married to an Indian woman was not much better. He was a "squaw man," a term, as historian Janet Lecompte has put it, that "carried . . . a little whiff of dirty blanket and boiled dog."[37] The attitudes could be seen and heard along the trails in the same camps where travelers acted out their own gendered arrangements of power. Sarah Hively, a newlywed crossing the plains in 1863, found that nearly every post along the road illustrated a survival of the old social order, a household with a trader, usually French, and his Indian wife. She was disgusted: "What a shame and disgrace to our country."[38]

Interethnic marriage, then, changed almost immediately from a proud social asset to the badge of a pariah. With the relative decline of the fur trade, only a marriage's protective function was left, and when that disappeared, there was nothing else to commend it. By early spring 1859 it was clear that Indians posed no immediate threat to Denver, Auraria, or nearby towns. Boosters began thinking more of their image in society back East. They had their eyes on emigrants looking for both opportunity and polite pretentions, men and women who wanted money, sidewalks, and churches. Households of whites and Indians were now "a shame and disgrace" and mixed-blood children an embarrassment.

So traders such as McGaa and Smith might have thought they were earning seats of influence for themselves by helping found and promote towns like Denver, but in fact they were chopping at the roots of their own power and prominence. Almost overnight they found their positions reversed. An intimate alliance that had been an advantage was suddenly a hindrance. They fell fast. In early spring 1859 McGaa was expelled from the company leadership, supposedly for dissolute habits his partners surely had seen from the start.[39] Poisal faced growing hostility and soon left Denver to return to trading. Smith was ousted both from the board and from Denver itself after he was accused of wife beating—a charge of breathtaking hypocrisy, given the miners' attitudes toward Indian women. He also resumed his trade among his wife's people. A year after the first gold dust was panned, every trader-townmaker had been squeezed from the ranks of power.

But this was only part of the story. Other traders jumped just as eagerly into the commercial fray. Their trajectories, however, rose as sharply as the first group's fell. And their success reveals just as much about the new society and its lines of power.

Antoine and Nicholas Janis, Missouri natives who had come west as young men in the 1840s, worked the same area as Smith and McGaa. Antoine later wrote that he had been smitten by the valley of Cache la Poudre, north of Denver, when he first saw it in 1844. Invented or not, the story describes well enough what happened. Antoine was at Fort Laramie when he heard of Russell's find, and he immediately went to the Cache la Poudre to hold the spot. The next year, as fifty-niners flooded in, he and Nicholas formed a town company with several other traders and new settlers. By autumn the town of Colona was surveyed and fifty houses built, and within a few years it emerged as a farming and ranching center.[40]

The brothers' partner in the Colona enterprise was Elbridge Gerry, another mountain man with a background typically clouded by contradiction and boasts. He was probably born in New England. He said his grandfather was the famous signer of the Declaration of Independence, Federalist politician, and source of the term "gerrymandering," although the claim was shaky. In the 1830s he may have been a free trapper, or perhaps a sailor; he may have married and sired his first children back East, or perhaps in the West. What *is* clear is that by the mid-1850s he was trading out of Fort Laramie and at his own post on the South Platte. It was Gerry who outfitted John Simpson Smith on the eve of Smith's plunge into townmaking, and like Smith he moved quickly with the changes brought by the rush. His account books show that in 1859 he began to shift his trading post inventory toward the emigrant market, although he continued to outfit traders. In 1860 "Little Gerry" moved his South Platte operation farther upriver to the mouth of Crow Creek, an ideal position to work with nearby Denver while selling to travelers on the last stage of the trip. Gerry's Ranche became one of the route's most prominent way stations, and its owner would later be called the first settler in Weld County.[41]

Not far from Gerry's post, Geminien (Jim) Beauvais operated Star Ranche, the only other outlet on the South Platte in 1858. Beauvais had worked as a field agent for the American Fur Company before opening posts at Fort Laramie and at the South Platte's Old California Crossing. By one account he sent up to 50,000 robes a year to Atchison and St. Joseph. In 1859 he expanded his Star Ranche into a principal stopping place for travelers, and his substantial business shot upward. Large, quiet, and distinguished, Beauvais was a classic bicultural man, well educated and well positioned in St. Louis social circles and enmeshed in the Indian and mixed-blood society he had helped shape for twenty years. The changes after 1858 moved him to choose between the two worlds. Besides, the emigrants reportedly bored him silly. Beauvais turned most of his business over to his mixed-blood son Edward and retired to St. Louis with his considerable fortune. He was barely fifty.[42]

Like Smith, McGaa, and virtually all traders, these men had taken Indian wives as entrées into native communities, and they used their connections to ease their way into the new order. Beauvais parlayed marriages to several Lakota women into one of the largest trading operations on the central plains. His son and successor, Edward, found a measure of security for Star Ranche in his relatives and those of his wife, a mixed-blood daughter of the Robideaux trading dynasty. Gerry, called White Eye by his in-laws, had two Lakota wives, and one of his daughters married the mixed-blood son of his partner, Seth Ward. He supplemented his new businesses with continued exchange in robes; he was the only white allowed to trade with the Cheyenne militants, the Dog Soldiers. These ties gave him a measure of protection when relations soured and raids began in the 1860s. The Janis brothers were married among the Arapahoes. They received permission to found Colona on the Cache la Poudre from Bald Wolf, probably an in-law.

These men, then, were identical in most ways to McGaa, Smith, and Poisal. No obvious traits of character separated one from another. They all had worked the southern Rockies and central plains for years, had lived at Hardscrabble and Bent's Fort, shuttled in and out of Taos and Santa Fe, traveled many times the old Front Range road to and from Fort Laramie. They knew the plains, mountain passes, and parks just as a master New England fisherman knew the soundings and currents of George's Bank. They were seasoned figures in the alignment of interests, centering on the fur trade, that had set the patterns of labor and wealth for thirty years. When gold was discovered, every man sensed that those patterns would shift. They moved quickly, without a hint of hesitation, to take advantage of events. Some, however, rode the changes to success while the others slipped into the cultural gloom.

There was one obvious difference. When the gold rush began, Gerry, Beauvais, and the Janis brothers had the essential stuff of power in the new Colorado—property, and well-located property at that. Gerry and Beauvais were operating South Platte posts when the first dust was panned, and Antoine and Nicholas Janis grabbed prime sites along the Cache la Poudre before anyone could challenge them. Using their Indian kin at first for protection, they built their strategic holdings into a secure place in a system that was rapidly swamping the old one. Smith and McGaa, on the other hand, had only what was given them by the newcomers. They held paper partnerships with nothing behind them but the boosters' goodwill, and apart from that they offered only some familial security during the settlements' first months. They had no property or other convertible wealth, only a kind of marital capital that rapidly devalued. When it sank low enough, white society could judge these men however it wished.

The very different sets of stories measured the displacement of one order by another and the redefinition of power and respectability. Every trader with economic weight in 1858 died wealthy and honorable. Gerry, William Bent, and some others kept their Indian wives beyond the first few years, but they did so out of affection, not advantage, and with their wealth and property they apparently did not worry about public criticism. The men without property, on the other hand, were shoved with their Indian kin to the fringes of a new social world. It happened with astonishing speed. At one moment Smith, McGaa, and Poisal were flattered and wooed because they had married Indian women; in the next they were thrown away because they were squaw men.

ALTHOUGH THE STORY turned out to be mixed for the white traders, for their Native American in-laws it was uniformly calamitous. Purely hypothetically, men like Beauvais and Gerry might have helped negotiate a genuinely bicultural society, and their children might have pioneered a way of life in which Indians and whites shared both genes and power. In reality there was little or no chance of such blending. Fur trade marriages were the latest expressions of an ancient arrangement that had stabilized economic life and promoted peace for centuries. They had flourished because practical economics required them and prevailing values honored them.

As the fur trade faded, however, the captains of new enterprises—mining, freighting, ranching, and farming—had no reason, measurable in cash, to cultivate relations with Indians. They had good cause to avoid intimate contact, as Indians slid to the bottom of the social scale. As a cultural credit became suddenly a debit, the intermarried elite had no time to adapt its miscegenist arrangement to the new reality. The change could not have been worse for plains Indians. Earlier, marriages with traders had given them a route of influence to a foreign, potentially menacing society. Now that society swept into their country on more troubling terms than most could have dreamed, and as it did the marital lines of contact were rudely and quickly severed. Cheyenne, Arapaho, and Lakota leaders lost their social middle terrain. Their mixed-blood children lived surreptitiously in respectable white Colorado or moved to its margins.

In a second fundamental way Indians also were being pushed to the fringe. Plains tribes already were in deep trouble before gold was discovered. Partly by their own errors, partly from events they could not control, the horse nomads were finding it increasingly difficult to squeeze out the means of supporting the life they envisioned when they made their move to the plains. This was a crisis of resources. Though they enjoyed an abundance of some things, other essentials were in short supply—and getting shorter. Access to the rest was growing harder.

The gold rush instantly deepened their predicament. Troubling conditions became suddenly ruinous. If the story of white traders told how Indians were being cut off from lines of social power, these environmental developments showed them increasingly isolated from the shrinking basics of physical survival.

The first prospectors had found no Indians along the Front Range in summer 1858. None, in fact, had been seen during the final weeks of their trip west. A few visited the diggings during August, but only after summer had passed did sizable numbers of Arapahoes and Cheyennes appear and set up camps close to the goldseekers' cabins and along Boulder Creek to the north. Their principal spokesmen were Little Raven and Left Hand, both Arapahoes who favored friendly relations with whites.

The Indians' summer absence and autumn arrival were part of an annual pattern, one more adaptation of thousands fashioned since the earliest occupation. This pattern, however, was very recent. Just fifteen years earlier John Charles Fremont had found an "extremely populous" Arapaho village "with a great number of children" on the South Platte in early July. They were living well with "a regular supply of the means of subsistence" taken from the huge numbers of bison he saw in the area.[43] Arapahoes and Cheyennes had been able to hunt in this country without fear, however, only since their peace with the Comanches and Kiowas in 1840. Before that, the plains along the Front Range had been a neutral zone—dangerous land that no group controlled absolutely. This competition among humans had made the area a kind of game preserve. Because worry of war limited the hunters' access to the region, bison and other game found a measure of protection. Then in 1840 the great peace suddenly ended the animals' security. Within ten years the freer hunting, coinciding with other factors, had severely reduced the bison herds. Surviving animals withdrew eastward, eventually more than 100 miles from the Rockies, into an area still bloodily contested between the Pawnees and high plains tribes. In this country, another neutral zone, human warfare still gave the grazers some relief from predation.

Because the South Platte and the Front Range were swept nearly free of buffaloes by the 1850s, Indians could not live there year-round. (The first prospectors who saw no Indians did not find any bison, either.) To find the animals they required, high plains tribes moved eastward each spring. From about June to September, they hunted among herds to the east, performed their rituals of annual renewal, and fought with their enemies. In winter, however, they returned westward to the protective trough along the base of the mountains. The land along the Front Range became a refuge for the horse nomads, as it had for native peoples for at least seven or eight millennia. The drainages offered good grass, timber, and shelter and a climate kinder than on the open plains. By about October some bands of Cheyennes and Arapahoes returned here to hunker down for the next several months. Others retreated to the upper Arkansas and to the North Platte.

The land where Green Russell found gold, then, was considered absolutely vital by the Indians. It might have been empty of people when the prospectors arrived, but the Cheyennes and Arapahoes had left it only for a few months for their summer hunt to the east. They did not consider the South

Platte unoccupied, any more than a St. Louis bank teller would think his house was abandoned while he was at work.

Given that, Little Raven's and Left Hand's bands could not have been pleased when they returned to find new neighbors on their usual wintering spots. During the next several months their survival would depend on access to the very limited resources being used by men laying out streets and building long toms. "Go away; you come to kill our game, to burn our wood, and to destroy our grass," Left Hand supposedly told the miners he found camped on Boulder Creek.[44] The quotation cannot be verified but the sentiment was true enough. William Bent, then agent for the upper Arkansas, wrote that the Arapahoes "want you to do something for them Concerning thair country. The whites are about taking possession of it . . . , laying off town lots." He was doing his best to keep the peace, Bent wrote, but he added poignantly that he had no idea what to tell his friends and kinsmen.[45]

What, indeed? First their own overhunting had helped kill off the bison along the mountains and had forced them eastward every summer to fight Pawnees and others for the shrinking herds. Then their winter sanctuaries were invaded. Both developments seemed inexorable. Bent wrote again in mid-December that Cheyennes and Arapahoes "are very uneasy and restless about their country." Emigration to the diggings was already large, and still the goldseekers came. Boomers were "laying off and building Towns all over the best part of their country," on the upper Arkansas as well as on the South Platte. Nothing had been done to compensate native peoples or to protect their interests, and "that goes rather hard with them." Once more Bent warned that he was not sure how long he could keep the peace. Some Indians "have been talking very hard against the whites." Time was running out.[46]

Left Hand and Little Raven also tried to dampen hostility. Both were "peace chiefs" whose task was to reconcile conflict among their people and to an extent with others. They also seemed to have a hardened knowledge that their people could not win a nose-to-nose confrontation with whites. Although the evidence is sketchy, Left Hand, his wife, and children may have taken a remarkable odyssey as far east as western Iowa in summer 1858 in an effort to learn about agriculture and white society by working as field laborers and harvesters.[47] Whether or not Left Hand took the trip, he and Little Raven had a fair grasp of the demographic and technological forces arrayed against them. They apparently concluded that their best course was by some middle way—if there was one.

There were several moments of concord that winter on Cherry Creek. Drawn by the noisy Christmas festivities, a delegation of Arapahoes and Cheyennes paid a visit and stayed to eat and race their prize trotting mule against some of the miners' horses. Shortly after the new year whites returned the visit, roasting two oxen in the Indian village and serving great heaps of dried apples to about 500 men and 300 or 400 women and children. Occasional gestures continued well into the spring. When Little Raven was feted at Denver's express office in May, Henry Villard was impressed; the Arapaho was sensible and friendly and "he handles his knife and fork and smokes his cigars like a white man."[48] Whether whites were working toward long-term harmony, however, is doubtful. Correspondents said they feared an Indian attack throughout these months, and in April one of them looked back and wrote that "we had to feed [the Indians], rather than have a difficulty with them."[49]

In fact some Indians did expect—and call for—trouble. Opposing Little Raven and Left Hand were younger men who saw no future in compromising with whites. These men were dedicated and enthusiastic warriors, and they were especially furious to find the prospectors' tents, horses, and mules along the South Platte when they returned for the winter. The more adamant among them, such as Heap of Whips, argued that white miners must be driven out or killed. (Perhaps Heap of Whips was a little pacified at the January feast. "I have never seen men eat till now," an observer wrote of him; "I verily believe [he] could eat a whole ox.")[50]

The discord between Heap of Whips and Little Raven was part of one more troubling change among the plains tribes. Besides being socially isolated and shut out of the new power structure, in addition to losing critical territory along the South Platte and the Front Range, the plains tribes were increasingly divided among themselves. This fragmentation had several causes, but lately one division was preeminent. Cheyennes, Arapahoes, Kiowas, Lakotas, and Comanches were torn between the leaders who called for accommodation with whites and others advocating confrontation, or at least a studied disengagement. The gold rush aggravated forces already threatening to pull each tribe apart.

The case of the Cheyennes once again shows the stresses felt by each group. From the start environmental forces threatened the Cheyennes' unity. Except during summer the plains usually could not support large gatherings of them and their horses, so they lived for most of the year as bands or in smaller camps, *vestoz*. Some bands had also been pulled steadily southward by a warmer climate and the denser horse herds along and below the Arkansas River; others stayed to the north along the forks of the Platte, closer to Noaha-vose, their sacred mountain and lodge of Maheo. A new trading system, centering on white outposts, splintered the people further. Northern bands stayed near trading entrepots on the North Platte, the southern bands along the Arkansas and Bent's Fort. In dealing both with the land and with white merchants, the Tsistsistas watched themselves being pulled apart.

Yet another division ate at their sense of unity. Trade involved much more than the question of where to exchange robes for goods. By the 1830s Cheyennes were debating the very meaning of and wisdom of trade itself. Because it touched so much of native life, trade inspired a constellation of questions about material, political, social, cultural, and spiritual matters. Other Native Americans had faced similar issues from their earliest contact with Europeans. Now it was the Cheyennes' turn. Trade became both a practical concern and a symbolic issue of terrific emotional intensity.

No one denied the need for trade. As part of the bargain struck by moving to the plains, the tribes had to reach out for what their new environment could not give them—foodstuffs, utensils, tools, and other Euro-American products that had become part of their daily lives. Disagreement arose over how much trade was proper, and beneath that the question of how much contact with whites and white influence should be tolerated.

From the 1830s through the 1850s, several prominent chiefs cultivated trade with a special vigor. Old Tobacco (Cinemo) consistently worked for close relations with men like William Bent, who operated out of Old Tobacco's tipi when trading in his camp. Yellow Wolf, a celebrated warrior in raids against the Comanches and Kiowas before 1840, urged Bent and St. Vrain to open a post on the Arkansas. Thereafter he was consistently among the leading advocates of expanded trade. At the time of the gold rush another respected warrior was ascending to leadership and speaking for peace: Black Kettle.[51] It was these bands, and others of a similar leaning among the Arapahoes and Lakotas, that had reached outward to white society by marrying their sisters to such prominent traders as John Simpson Smith, Elbridge Gerry, William Bent, John Poisal, and John Prowers.

Inevitably, economic connections became embroiled with political and diplomatic issues. Trading chiefs almost always favored compromise and accommodation. Old Tobacco, Black Kettle, and others consistently took the role of conciliators and liaisons. Their motives were a mix of economic interest, affection, kinship, and certainly a practical awareness, gained through greater contact with whites, of the power that Indians were up against. Slim Face, another trading chief, had traveled to St. Louis in 1844 with one of Bent and St. Vrain's trains. He was equally impressed by the crowds on the streets and the riding he saw at a circus. Back home he reported the un-countable numbers of people bulking not far to the east. Some leaders, like Yellow Wolf, even said they favored the government's insistent dream of the nomads taking up farming, although it is debatable how serious his overtures were.

Every tribe, however, had other leaders who argued with growing passion that relations with whites had to be limited. Partly the opposition grew from distrust of individual traders and from past grievances, partly from knowing how contact undermined the independent, roaming vision that had blossomed with the nomadic life. Regardless of the origin, doubts about too much contact with whites were widespread by the 1840s.

To no one's surprise, those feelings were sharpest among men whose inclinations and status lay with waging war, especially leading figures in the six warrior, or military, societies: the Kit Foxes, Crazy Dogs, Bowstrings (or Wolf Soldiers), Elk Scrapers, Red Shields, and Dog Soldiers (or Dog Men). Most of these societies had been around long before the Cheyennes became the Called Out People, but they grew increasingly influential in the years after Sweet Medicine (who by tradition named them) led his followers into their new homes. Warrior societies were voluntary and ungraded; any male could join, and although some members were especially admired, there was no formal system of ranks. Because each society drew from different bands, the groups became bonds that helped hold the Tsistsistas together. Dedicated to military traditions, seeking respect by warring with outsiders, the members of these groups naturally took the hardest line toward any external threat—and by the 1840s, as more and more Cheyennes blamed whites for the dwindling bison, vanishing trees, and diminishing grass, traders and their enterprise seemed a source of terrible danger.

Feelings for peace, on the other hand, usually found their focus in another institution—the Council of Forty-four. This group also had roots deep in Cheyenne history. Like the military societies, it drew on all the bands and so helped hold them together. Members typically were older men chosen for their wisdom, insight, experience, and restraint. The council members' prime purpose was to promote harmony among their own people, but given their character and their role they also tended to rein in those pushing too hard for war. The forty-four knew about fighting. Often, in fact, they had been respected figures in the warrior societies, but when chosen for the council they always left the military groups. The reason was basic. Everyone recognized that friction was unavoidable between the two countervailing forces of warriors and councilmen.

The council and the warrior societies stood as two sides of an old, creative tension. This inbuilt conflict could do its good work, however, only if the two forces were roughly equal, and only if the Tsistsistas saw themselves in a larger sense as indivisible. Without that rough equality and that faith in coherence, healthy disagreements could become a dangerous social sickness. By the late 1830s there were signs that something was terribly wrong.

In 1837 the Bowstrings wanted to raid the Kiowas for horses. Recently, however, a murder had been committed, which always left the four sacred arrows stained with blood and without power to protect the Tsistsistas. The arrows, a sacred gift of Maheo, had to be cleansed in a lengthy ceremony conducted by the most respected holy man, the Keeper of the Arrows. White Thunder, the keeper in 1837 and also a council member, told the Bowstrings that he would perform the ritual soon, but the impatient, hot-tempered young men demanded immediate action, and when White Thunder refused they beat the old man brutally with the leather thongs and bone handles of their quirts until he agreed. This appalling violation took its toll when Kiowas killed forty-two of the forty-four Bowstrings.[52]

The shocking episode showed vividly how life on the plains was upsetting the balance between the two poles of influence within the Cheyennes. Conditions fostered a cult of militancy and a celebration of the warrior. The fierce competition for hunting and camping grounds cultivated all the martial skills. Fighting fed a heroic folklore that inspired further tries at daring and sacrifice. Beneath it all was an emanation of power that came with horses and the room to run them. Under these circumstances warrior societies naturally grew in prestige and influence. Because they were voluntary organizations open to any man, their numbers swelled with the years. Eventually their power and independence challenged the very structure of Cheyenne society.

The precipitating incident was a murder. The Dog Soldiers were perhaps the most ardent military society. In 1837 their leader, Porcupine Bear, and some of his kinsmen murdered Little Creek in a drunken brawl. Porcupine Bear was a man of legendary courage and forceful personality, a reputation enhanced still more when he and his followers fought bravely (and in defiance of custom) during a raid on the Kiowas the next year. Because of their double violation—the unspeakable social crime of homicide and the disobedience to tradition in the raid—Porcupine Bear and his followers were forced to live apart from the other bands. In earlier years they would have been shunned and isolated, but now, astonishingly, they began to attract other followers. When cholera killed more than half of the Flexed Leg band, the survivors merged with the Dog Soldiers, who lost only a few to the epidemic. The exile continued, the dissidents drew more supporters, and gradually the Dog Soldiers emerged as their own band, separate and distinct from the others.

Yet as a hybrid, still part-warrior society, they remained fully open to anyone wishing to join. Shifting allegiance to this new band, in other words, became a political statement at a time of rising debate. The Dog Soldiers, as a band, cultivated their reputation for militant resistance; they allowed only a few trade connections, mostly with Elbridge Gerry, and they firmly opposed any whiff of accommodation. Among them the veneration of the warrior reached its zenith. There was, for instance, the tradition of the Dog Ropes. These four holy objects were spiritually renewed during each summer's sun dance and worn by the four men recognized as the band's bravest. Each rope was actually a ten-foot sash of bison skin elaborately decorated with quills and feathers. The sash was slit at one end so its wearer could drape it over his right shoulder and under his left arm. At the other end was a thong with a red stake. If things went poorly in battle, a Dog Rope's wearer was to dismount, pound the stake into the ground, then stand and fight on his sacred tether until killed or until another warrior pulled up the stake and drove him from the field. The tradition had enormous appeal, both as drama and as a symbolic statement of standing firm against compromise or retreat.[53]

Equally significant, the Dog Soldiers withdrew increasingly from the Arkansas and Platte roads. As the plains environment forced all bands to pull apart from one another, this newest one spent most of its time by the 1850s on the upper Republican, Solomon, and Smoky Hill Rivers and on the South Platte. Here they became friendlier with two of the more bellicose Lakota bands who came often into this middle country, the Brules and Oglalas. The Dog Soldiers chose their home for two interlocking reasons. It was the area farthest removed from white contact; it was consequently the country resembling most closely the lovely and heroic vision of the Tsistsistas.

This was an extraordinary development. From the two basic divisions, the northern and southern branches, the strains on Cheyenne unity had created a third. Pulling apart from the others, the Dog Soldiers carved out their own territory and began establishing their own identity. But this was not merely another hiving off from environmental pressure and economic strategy. The Dog Soldiers had a unique political and cultural meaning; they became a gravitational center for men of particular persuasion and belief. Before, warrior societies had provided an invaluable cohesive force among the bands. Now one of them was its own self-contained band, but it combined that identity with a military society's rules of joining, its allegiance to the warrior's code, and its commitment to the nomadic greatness of the Called Out People. Finally, the Dog Soldiers gave this new arrangement a geographical home, the central plains heartland, country increasingly linked, in practice and symbol, to resistance to whites and a loyalty to the old ways. Simply by riding to the Republican or Smoky Hill, a Cheyenne man could focus three identities—of band, society, and political stance—into one. It was a heady possibility and a powerfully divisive force.

The Dog Soldiers stayed increasingly in the middle country. After 1856, John Prowers later testified, they never drew annuities or traded on the Arkansas. They harangued the southern bands repeatedly to return to their first homes in the north and to break their close bonds with the whites.[54] To increase their independence and prowess they even began to reverse the usual exogamous requirement—that men always marry outside their band and move away to live with their wives' families. Now men chose women from the outside but required their wives to live with them. They also pressured their sisters to marry promising warriors from other bands, then have their new husbands play by the old rules and live in the Dog Soldier camps.[55] And in the emotionally charged arena of trade, they were committed to the hard line and symbolic gestures. "The Dog Soldiers have always been mean to white traders, always wanting to make the traders trade as the Dog Soldiers pleased," Prowers remembered; "they have often thrown the traders' goods into the fire."[56]

The Dog Soldiers embodied as purely as possible the vision of man and horse united and set loose into the open country. They became a kind of consecration. With brilliant clarity and sense of theater, they acted out their chosen story—of the plains as a dreamland of liberation, the Tsistsistas as centaurs of the spirit.

Something similar was happening among the other high plains tribes. Some leaders reached out to trade with whites and gave assurances of peaceful intent. Others—Satanta and Satank among the Kiowas, for instance, and Heap of Whips among the Arapahoes—argued that resistance was the only sensible response. The worse the conditions became, the more the tribes were polarized, and during the 1850s the situation was grimmer every year. Cheyennes, Arapahoes, and many Lakota "are actually in a *starving* state," Thomas Fitzpatrick wrote in 1853. "Their women are pinched with want and their children constantly cry out with hunger." Two years later Thomas Twiss agreed that those groups were "suffering—starving," and in 1856, the year the Dog Soldiers pulled back for good into the middle country, he repeated that the bands he knew "suffer for want of food [and] become actually emaciated; the very old people and young children frequently die from starvation."[57]

Ten months later Colonel Edwin Sumner and the First Cavalry marched into Dog Soldier territory along the Solomon River, killed several warriors, and burned nearly 200 lodges. Sumner's intent was to intimidate the most resistant Cheyennes. Border town residents thought he had, and some were confident enough to go looking for mountain gold. The battle on the Solomon, however, deepened the rage among the Cheyennes and strengthened the Dog Soldiers' appeal. As border residents reassured themselves that the Cheyennes were chastened, more warriors gravitated to the militants' camps and to their vow of heroic contention. Anger was higher than ever, and hunger was deeper.

THIS WAS THE SETTING for the gold expeditions of 1858. Within weeks of Russell's strike miners occupied the splendid wintering grounds along the South Platte, and soon afterward boosters, helped by traders who had been the Indians' best allies, were describing the valley as ordained for cities and busy commerce. Beginning in December and continuing through the summer, overland travelers marched through the previously inviolate valleys of the Smoky Hill and Republican Rivers. It was a perfect script for crisis.

Some Indians responded with pleas for help, others by turning defiant. On September 18, 1859, Thomas Twiss met with several Cheyenne and Arapaho leaders near Fort Laramie. He commended them for keeping away from the goldseekers and leaving them to their digging, but an Arapaho replied with a common lament: "Our old people & little Children are hungry for many days, & some die," he said; "our sufferings are increasing every winter. Our horses, too, are dying, because we ride them so far to get a little game for our Lodges." Then came the simple, elusive petition: "We wish to live."[58]

Two days earlier William Bent had met with Kiowa and Comanche leaders at the great bend of the Arkansas. More than 2,500 warriors were camped nearby. The leaders professed peace, but Bent felt sure that "a smothered passion for revenge agitates these Indians." The causes were clear: "[It is] the failure of food, the encircling encroachment of the white population, and the exasperating sense of decay and impending extinction with which they are surrounded."[59]

Five days later the Kiowa Satank rode into Walnut Creek Station, confronted the clerk in George Peacock's store, and spit blood into his face.

' BUSTED BY THUNDER !'

The Unwitting Financiers. The vast majority of goldseekers ended up "busted," but in the process they poured out money to build a new society along the Front Range. (Courtesy of the Colorado State Historical Society)

Enterprise Digs In. Filthy, dark, and noisome whiskey holes and stopovers were the vanguard of profound changes. Within a few years the Platte valley was lined with commercial outposts supporting a continuous traffic across the plains. (Courtesy of the Colorado State Historical Society)

The Bullwhacker. His wild and profane image to the contrary, the freighter was a key figure in transplanting eastern culture—and in seizing the energy resources Native Americans needed to live out their own vision of plains life. (Courtesy of the Denver Public Library)

Carriers of Empire. Thousands of wagons carrying millions of pounds of freight made real the new vision of the Missouri valley, plains and mountains bound together into a land of plenty. (Courtesy of the Nebraska State Historical Society)

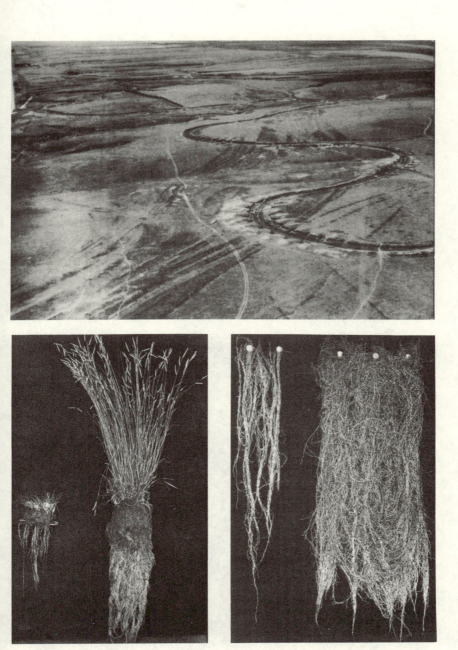

Ruts and Roots. Top: Surviving overland ruts, hundreds of yards wide, dwarf a modern highway, irrigation canal, and jeep trail. Bottom: Massive overgrazing by emigrant stock and Indian horses left vital plains grasses and their dense root systems fatally stunted, as shown by experiments on blue grama grass (left) and little bluestem (right). (Courtesy of the Nebraska Department of Commerce and Tourism, and the Ecological Society of America)

Conquering Waters. Where nomadic bison hunters had made their winter camps along the South Platte, white settlements were fed by farms and ranches sustained by irrigation projects, like the Denver High Line ditch. (Courtesy of the Colorado State Historical Society)

9

ON THE ROAD TO A FLOURISHING

MOUNTAIN STATE

Richard Francis Burton once wrote a cross-cultural study of farting. With that kind of voracious, slightly bent curiosity, Burton could hardly resist a chance to visit the American West. He arrived at St. Joseph in early August 1860, already famous at thirty-nine. The Irish explorer had visited Mecca disguised as an Afghan Muslim, then had become the first European to enter the East African city of Harar, another Islamic holy site forbidden to nonbelievers. He came to the United States in the middle of a furious controversy with John Speke over their common search for the source of the Nile and their respective discoveries of Lakes Tanganyika and Victoria. Unlike many adventurers, Burton looked the part. His fierce, dark expression and his drooping mustache, twirled at the ends, gave him a wild brigandish look heightened by great facial scars earned when a Somali tribesman thrust a javalin into his left cheek and out the other.

Presumably Burton had come to see another holy city, the one built by Mormons beside the Great Salt Lake. The trip may have been more impromptu; he wrote in his diary of a longtime friend inviting him to "come with me and drink through America."[1] Whatever the urge, Burton made his way to the Kansas border, paid $175 for stage passage to Utah, and set off into what he thought were the true American wilds. The first entries of his travel journal, *City of the Saints,* from his departure on August 7 until he passed the Platte forks five days later, described the central plains at a crucial moment in their history.

Nothing escaped Burton's attention. He discussed plains grasses and speculated (incorrectly) on the origin of the term "grama." He described not only the long trains of freight wagons, "like lines of white cranes trooping slowly over the prairie," but also the freighters, who in their large green goggles reminded him of giant crabs. He compared bison chips to the dung of three continents and judged the sweet morning air as "brisk as a bottle of *veuve Clicquot.*" Over and over he compared what he saw with his African adventures. The high plains were as "sere and tawny as a jackal's back." Cottonwoods were like birds in Arabia and monkeys in the jungle: they signaled the presence of water. He compared plains Indians to Bedouins and added that the Pawnees, "African-like, will cut the throat of a sleeping guest."[2]

The Pawnees and some other tribes were slipping faster than others, he thought, but "the [whole] Indian race is becoming desperate, wild-beast like, hemmed in by its enemies." Burton doubted they would be replaced by farmers, at least on the high plains. Instead the region would soon be "the great grazing grounds" of America and the world. Besides cattle, the country might soon host herds of Tibetan yaks, Andean llamas, and African koodoos, a variety of antelope.[3]

The five-day ride revealed the ancient world of the plains once more becoming a new place. Burton's account caught the dynamics of change, both physical transformations and new assumptions taking hold. In 1860, as states in the East edged toward crisis and war, his passing glimpse showed that another American story was unfolding in the continental center, a shuffle of power and economic shifting as swift and deep as any in the region's history.

BURTON ENDED each day at a stage station. Most were "foul tenements." In one he peered through an atmosphere of smoke and mosquitoes to see drunken men and women heaped together with several dogs and sheep. The food was execrable—old meat, greasy bacon, "suspicious eggs," and milk "not more than one quarter flies." Even for this veteran of African safaris, the journey was a trial. His list of travel necessities included a revolver, Bowie knife, umbrella, poncho, carpet bag, cigars, cognac, and opium. The last item, he wrote, was "invaluable when one expects five consecutive days and nights in a prairie wagon."[4]

Wretched as they were, the stations measured the dramatic pace of change along the road. The rush to the Rockies gave a vigorous boost to economic activity along the Platte and Santa Fe routes. Established businesses increased their trade; fresh competitors sprang up to challenge older firms; entirely new enterprises and services appeared to meet the needs of this evolving economy of transit.

The most common businesses were mixed mercantile operations that travelers called "road ranches." Their basic function was to supply emigrants with necessities and a few frivolities, although many owners milked travelers in other ways. The earliest had appeared in the 1840s to serve the crowds moving back and forth to the Pacific and New Mexico, but in 1858 they were still few in number. On the Santa Fe Trail travelers would find the Walnut Creek Station 132 miles beyond Council Grove and Bent's New Fort at what was left of the big timbers, near the mouth of Sand Creek. The latter was quite an establishment; a fifty-niner was impressed to see Bent selling dress hoops. On the old overland trail, there was little between Forts Kearny and Laramie except two road ranches a short way up the South Platte before the trail turned north.[5]

The surge of fifty-niners quickly changed that. In November 1858 the experienced trader Andrew Drips, trusted agent of Pierre Chouteau at Fort Laramie, was sending wagons of goods from Ash Point to the diggings and was looking into merchandising the following spring.[6] By the time E. H. N. Patterson reached the South Platte the next May he could visit five trading posts in six days. Businesses sprang up along the Santa Fe Trail between Council Grove and the Arkansas and at Ash Creek, twenty-six miles beyond Walnut Creek.[7] The great sprouting, however, came during the next few years, once the value of the mines was proven. As he passed Fort Kearny in June 1861, H. M. Judson wrote that "here we are to bid adieu to civilization . . . no more to meet . . . [the] habitations of civilized man." This was an exaggeration even then, but two years later another traveler seemed disappointed that stations and road ranches lined most of the road to Colorado: "We have yet . . . to see the untrodden West that the poets sing about."[8] Two trips by E. M. Stahl, two years apart, showed dramatically what was happening. Heading west in 1860, Stahl mentioned only a couple of stores along the trail; on his return in 1862 he could stop at a road ranch at least once a day between Denver and Ft. Kearny to eat, shop, sleep, drink, or jaw with the locals.[9]

Road ranches were the closest contact points between whites and Indians. One diarist called Julesburg in 1859 "a little town on the South Platte, inhabited by ten dogs, four Indians and one family." If things went well between the two peoples, these posts might continue their role as pivots in the declining robe trade, but they had the most to lose if relations soured. Not surprisingly, the old system of intimate politics survived here longer than almost anywhere else. Some of the first stores were operated by white traders—Jim Beauvais, Elbridge Gerry, Bernard Blondeau, and others—as they hurried to make a place in the new order. These men kept their Native American wives and tended their friendly relations with in-laws. A few figures stepped in to cultivate these traditional roles. The founder of the Walnut Creek Station, William Allison, died in April 1859, just as the rush was getting under way. His successor, George Peacock, had none of Allison's knack for getting along with Indians, as suggested by the blood-spitting exchange the following September. Almost exactly a year later the Kiowa Satank killed Peacock. The store's next owner was a German immigrant, Charles Rath, who had freighted and traded along the Arkansas for a few years. About this time Rath married Making Out Road, or Roadmaker, an unusually well-connected woman among the trade-oriented bands of the Southern Cheyennes. She may have been the sister of Owl Woman, William Bent's first wife. The birth of a daughter, Cheyenne White Girl (called Cheyenne Belle by whites), helped solidify Rath's place in the interethnic economic and social network. When trouble started, the marriage served him well.[10]

Others did not bow so deeply toward traditional ways. Charles McDonald arrived in late 1859 and established a prosperous business at Cottonwood Springs. He traded with Lakotas and hired seasoned hands with Indian wives, but he himself stayed maritally aloof. John Burke, a German immigrant, opened a store nearby after he was temporarily marooned by Indian troubles a few years later. By the late 1860s he was one of the valley's leading entrepreneurs. Like McDonald he worked at amicable relations with Lakotas and Cheyennes but kept them at a certain distance.[11]

The changing society was on display in these strings of businesses. Road ranches such as Rath's and Beauvais's were islands of an older world where Indians and whites worked with each other to mutual gain. Old liaisons sur-

vived because they still served some useful purpose, because they were protected by powerful men like Gerry, and because they existed outside the close
orbit of the new white settlements, where "squaw men" were shouldered to
the edges of tolerance. Outfits such as McDonald's acknowledged the older
ways while leaning firmly in other directions. Other entrepreneurs barely
recognized Indians, except as irritants and potential problems. They were
harbingers of what was soon to come.

Physical facilities also ran a range, from crude to polished. There were
adobe hovels, low, dark, and smoky, no larger than a homesteader's first
soddie. Just down the road might be something more ambitious. Near Fort
Kearny a fifty-niner found a trim, newly built frame building with a sign:
Pennsylvania House. A woman answering the door with her two children
explained that her family had recently come from western Pennsylvania and
laid out an entire town, although this would-be hotel so far comprised the
entire community.[12] Sprinkled over the whole route were wretched whiskey
holes. A traveler in 1860 described them:

> They were queer structures, partly tent and partly cabin. A few rough posts would
> be driven into the ground. These supported a ridgepole, across which some old
> pieces of canvas and ragged sailcloth formed a rude and primitive shelter, large
> enough, however, to hold several barrels of whiskey. On a dusty shelf above a
> counter made of board resting on two empty barrels were a number of broken
> and cracked glasses, some half-emptied bottles, a few cans of oysters and sar-
> dines, and this constituted the entire outfit of the so-called "Tavern." Probably
> the Boniface of this crude establishment knew his business better than we did
> and had decided not to squander his capital in articles that were not considered
> a prime necessity.[13]

The horrific "wet goods" soon were the stuff of folklore. By local tradition
the whiskey sold to travelers at Jack Allen's gin mill was made from alcohol,
water, chili, tobacco, old boots, rusty bayonets, soapweed, and cactus thorns.[14]
In the withering competition proprietors tried any device to gain an edge. A
pair of young men passing a primitive saloon along the Little Blue River were
taken up short by an inverted human skull nailed to a post and filled with
tobacco. "Help yourselves, boys!" a voice called from inside the dim tavern.
"A pipeful is free!"[15]

Some businesses soon offered a widening array of goods. To such basics
as wheel rims and flour they added ax handles, sugar, and lashes, then
workpants and hats, matches, and whiskey, then horseshoes, tobacco, boots,
and baking soda. Merchants began to anticipate various needs, as suggested

by this entry from the ledger of Penniston and Miller's store: "W. H. Welty, Dec 12 1866: Cocane 1.00." Within a few years inventories had expanded enormously. Day books included sales, among other things, of bacon, brooms, padlocks, nails, mustard, pickles, chalk, ham, pepper sauce, calico, bar soap, panes of glass, stomach bitters, shovels, augers, kettles, sacks of coal, gate hinges, Young America liniment, ground pepper, glass tumblers, rope, resin, playing cards, gum drops, potatoes, rifles, ox bows and yokes, dutch ovens, crosscut saws, cordial tonics, pipes and pipe stems, soda crackers, canned sardines and oysters, schnapps, silk shirts, wine, nuts (in and out of shells), butter, neckties, and cravats.[16] The outfitting and mercantile business of the border towns spread westward along the roads, easing travel and binding the regional parts into a whole.

These enterprises, whatever their condition, offered minimal shelter, so they were potential stopover sites for travelers. This service, almost an afterthought in many cases, had momentous consequences. Once businesses were spaced roughly twenty miles apart, travelers could assume a roof and floorspace, if not actually a cot, would be waiting at day's end. Suddenly different means of travel were practical. "You might go all the way on your pony," with maybe a night or two in the open, a veteran wrote a friend in 1860.[17] In another year or so regular passage by horseback and buggy was common. Because they could usually find some food at each stop instead of carrying their own, travelers could go lighter and faster. They had to pay, of course, but by spending less time on the road and less money on supplies at the start, the cost of transit dropped. A man crossing from Fort Kearny to Denver in 1863 stayed nineteen nights in road ranches, paying as little as $.40 a night on the eastern end and as much as $3.25 farther on. His total outlay was just under $36.00.[18]

The month of that trip—January—tells of an even greater change. Before 1860 winter travel had been crazily dangerous except for the hardiest, best-provisioned few. The next year an enterprising Missourian set off in November with two mules and a horse and wagon, betting that the cold weather would preserve his valuable cargo of fresh butter and newly slaughtered pork. He slept in road houses, haystacks, and express stations as he made good time over bare ground hard as pavement. The food arrived unspoiled.[19] He saw few others on the road, however; express riders rose high in their stirrups and gawked at him as they galloped past. But barely a year later, and only four years after a handful of brave or ignorant souls had taken off for the gold fields in the coldest weeks of 1858–1859, the trip over the Platte road in December and January had become a safe and commonplace jaunt.

Almost immediately, in fact, even faster travel to the mines was possible for those who could pay for it. This development had implications that ran much beyond the rates and ease of transit.

Before leaving for the mountains in summer 1858, William Larimer had secured a promise from the freighting kingpin William Russell that if Russell should establish coach service to the new settlements, the line would end at Larimer's town—which turned out to be Denver. Russell soon decided a stage line was a good bet, but his more conservative partners, Alexander Majors and William B. Waddell, thought that pouring resources into such a dream, especially before the mines had proved themselves, was beyond risky. Russell persevered. He formed a partnership with a prominent subcontractor, John S. Jones, and traveled to New York to float stock and to drum up business for the new company. He bought 1,000 of the best Kentucky mules and ordered a route surveyed and stage stations built. The new partnership, Jones, Russell, and Company, announced that the Leavenworth and Pike's Peak Express soon would offer quick and frequent passage from the Missouri to Cherry Creek. Fast freight also would be available at reasonable rates.[20]

The plan was especially audacious. Instead of following the favored Platte River road, the stage line used a variation of the central route. From Leavenworth coaches would ascend the Kansas River to a point twenty miles east of present-day Abilene, then angle northwest to the Solomon River. After moving up the Solomon valley the route would cut to the west across several tributary creeks of the Republican before following that river's south fork. From there stages would cross to Sand Creek, move north and then directly west to Cherry Creek. The appeal, of course, was the route's seeming directness. Russell's coaches, however, would be crossing an unfamiliar, potentially troublesome region, as others were finding out. Even as the surveyors were marking their course, the Blue brothers were lost and starving to death near the Smoky Hill, not far to the south.

One hundred and twenty persons and forty wagons, some with 5,000 pounds of material each, set out to plot the route and to build the support facilities. In a little more than a month twenty-seven stations were set up, roughly one every twenty-five miles. Most were tents—adobes and cabins were planned before winter—but they could accommodate stationkeepers, fresh mules, and basic supplies. The entire enterprise unfolded at an astonishing clip. Surveyors moved out on March 15, stationbuilders thirteen days later. On April 18 the first two stages—shiny Concord coaches, the first ever seen in Kansas—left Leavenworth. They rolled into Denver May 7 to loud and liquored salutes by hat-waving locals, who right away voted Leavenworth "the greatest city in the East." Three days later the coaches started home. When they arrived after a passage of ten days, the editors went wild: "NINE CHEERS FOR LEAVENWORTH . . . The City in a Tumult!!" and "Bring Out the Flags, and Let the Cannon Roar!" There followed a two-day celebration of parades, dinners, and soaring bombast.

Any passenger with $125 then could race to the mountains in not much more than a week, with up to twenty pounds of baggage in the boot. Stages left far less often than advertised, sometimes only once a week, and the trip had its uncertainties. A mule team once ran off with some bison and plunged the coach into an arroyo. Jones and Russell's line nonetheless offered by far the fastest passage available. The running of the Leavenworth and Pike's Peak Express also demonstrated how much could be done and how quickly once serious money was brought into play.

Service over the Republican River route lasted only about two months. As the Concords were making their inaugural trip and Leavenworth orators were declaring a new era, the two partners were redrawing the entire operation. For $144,000 they agreed to assume the contract of John M. Hockaday to deliver mail weekly from St. Joseph to Salt Lake City. This meant abandoning their newly blazed route and following the overland road through Fort Kearny, as stipulated in the government contract. The shift had great advantages, however. The new arrangement, in effect a federal subsidy of an expensive operation, was tasty enough to bring in Majors and Waddell. The two firms agreed to a simple division of responsibilities. All parties would have a hand in the first stretch, from St. Joseph through Fort Kearny and up the great Platte valley to the river's forks. Routes and commitments then would diverge, with Russell, Majors, and Waddell carrying mail and passengers up the old Pacific road to Salt Lake City while Jones and Russell took their stages up the South Platte to Denver.[21]

With that, one of the West's greatest pools of capital, plus the support of the federal government, was committed to an overland transportation system far more elaborate than anything yet seen. Buoyed by the infusion of funds, Jones and Russell soon had facilities established along the northern route, with two dozen stations between St. Joseph and Denver and others spaced up the North Platte and over the Continental Divide. Leavenworth was not abandoned; a branch was run from it to Fort Kearny. The first stages set off along the new route on July 2, only days after the last trip up the Republican River. Quickly the new system proved its worth. The trip to Cherry Creek was longer but the road was far better—the best natural highway in North America, some thought. As stations were completed and the trip finely tuned, the Missouri and the Rockies were drawn steadily closer to one another. By summer's end the time of transit was cut to a week or less.

Boosters at both ends saw in the dusty stages a confirmation of the fabulous future of the Front Range settlements, but even their grand gush missed the significance. The enterprise showed how quickly the clout of capital, and in this case the paired entrepreneurial styles of Russell and Majors, could bring profound changes. Stage lines to Denver and along the California–Oregon Trail, with the other road ranches and mercantile clusters, created a nearly continuous thread of posts throughout the valley of the Platte and both its branches. By 1862 there were fifty-one stage stations between the Missouri and Denver, averaging nearly one every ten miles. These stations also served independent travelers, and so encouraged a far larger number of emigrants. New businesses—smithies and grog shops, hay dealers and grocers—appeared beside the more prominent outposts to work the swelling crowds.

Stage service was also a vital step in reimagining the region. It seemed suddenly more natural to picture the river towns, plains, and mountains not as distinct and widely separated entities but as parts of a geographical and economic whole. In the delirious parade after the first stage trip to Denver, one of Russell's coaches carried a sign: "Leavenworth Catches the Golden Echo from Her Mineral Mountains." Until that point of view was established, other changes would never occur. Once that perspective was set, however, the plains and their edges were literally re-vised. Further change took on an inevitable air. The string of tent stations, an orator announced at the twelve-hour celebration, was introducing "civilization, cultivation, and refinement" into what had been thought a desert. And next? The routes "could not but become the . . . iron arteries of inland commerce . . . over which the iron horse would yet snort on his road to the Pacific."

ANOTHER BUSINESS swelled in a vigorous surge with the gold rush—freighting. Commercial hauling had been part of plains life since the 1820s, and by 1858 the Missouri valley towns from Westport to Council Bluffs had become the transfer points in traffic between the growing Republic to the east and its young provinces of the Southwest, Great Basin, and Pacific Coast. After 1859 that trade changed dramatically in two ways. Its volume grew enormously along both the Arkansas and Platte routes, especially the latter.[22] Freight shipped by Atchison's three major outfitters doubled in the first year after 1859, from 4 million pounds to more than 8 million pounds, and in 1860 a single Leavenworth company shipped out 3.5 million pounds in twenty-one trains of twenty-seven wagons each, a huge increase.[23] Most of this new trade, furthermore, was bound for a new destination, Denver and the other towns of the Front Range. Of the sixty-six trains sent out from Atchison in 1859, fifty went to Colorado. The volume received in Denver the next year, between 15 and 20 million pounds, was a huge jump from the year before, but by 1866 the total had risen to more than 100 million pounds.[24]

The reason for this surge and shift was simple: Denver and vicinity provided an utterly new kind of market. California, Oregon, and the Mormon settlements of Deseret were so far away that only a narrow range of goods, those valuable and easily transported, were profitable to carry; otherwise, the distant communities had to provide for themselves. New Mexico was closer, but it was an old, well-established society with ties to the south and with many of its wants supplied locally. The Front Range towns, by contrast, were close by and almost wholly dependent, at least at first. Although the market was small at the outset, Denverites and their neighbors soon relied on eastern Kansas for a wide range of goods, from machinery to tobacco. Border merchants instantly saw the unprecedented opportunity.

Looking back, the link across the plains might seem odd. The camps, after all, already sat along one of the continent's oldest trade routes—the north-south road that ran from New Mexico along the Front Range face to the northern plains and northern Rockies. Since before the Christian Era trade goods had moved along this path that linked the plains ultimately to Mexico and perhaps to Central America. At the time of Coronado it was used in the bison-maize exchange essential to both plainsmen and Rio Grande villages, and most recently *comancheros* had kept the lanes of commerce open. In the year of Russell's strike a party of *comancheros* was seen bartering flour with Indians on the Platte.[25] White outposts on the North Platte drew on this connection for more than trade. In an echo from the Apaches learning to garden from displaced Pueblos in the seventeenth century, an officer at Fort Laramie in 1850 sent an agent to Taos to hire a dozen New Mexicans to start the post farm. Cultivation was possible only by irrigation, he explained, "and I have no one who understands it."[26]

The north-south route along the mountains in fact did supply the earliest needs of the first prospectors and townmakers. During their first winter they drew the wherewithal of survival—food and whiskey—from Taos and Santa Fe merchants, and during the next few years they continued to import corn, beans, wheat flour, onions (useful against scurvy), and Taos Lightning from the south. The well-established Anglo-American community there explored the possibilities of expanding that trade.

The shrewd correspondence of two business partners, James Josiah Webb and John M. Kingsbury, tells of their calculation. On site in Santa Fe, the younger Kingsbury was first enthusiastic ("We have nothing here except favorable reports") when the first gold dust arrived in fall 1858.[27] In February word came that the Missouri border was "perfectly crazy" over the mines. As New Mexican parties organized to go north, Kingsbury squirmed to get in on the profits. Webb looked on from the more conservative distance of his Connecticut offices and nearly a quarter century of experience with bursting bubbles. Contain yourself, he wrote Kingsbury, and keep your eyes on your plate: "Our business is in New Mexico." If the rumors turned out to be true—something he doubted—gold probably would be found throughout the region, and the stake they already had would fatten nicely: "Perhaps by 'holding on to the willow' the wave will roll down our way and our property [will] yet become very valuable." In the meantime, Webb wrote his partner, sell to reliable men who are willing to take the chances, but otherwise stay where you are and play the odds we have.[28]

It was good advice. Webb was worried that the unpredictable swirl of action would swamp the market and depress prices throughout the area, and that indeed happened. In July 1859, as the full wash of goods hit the Colorado camps, Kingsbury wrote that business in Santa Fe was "rather squally" and stores badly overstocked, mainly with groceries diverted from the glutted market to the north. Imported food was being offered at cost, plus freight, but still no one was buying. He hoped for a turnaround and meantime was holding fast.[29] Webb and Kingsbury never did try to break into the Denver market. Two years later, in fact, they dissolved their Santa Fe enterprise and disengaged entirely from western trade.

Webb understood the limits of the New Mexico–Denver axis. Close as they were, Santa Fe and Taos could not offer the breadth of goods and support available through the Missouri valley. Besides, the growing American presence in the Southwest already had begun to align the region with the Missouri valley; most New Mexican firms were financed from the East, so income immediately fled to St. Louis and elsewhere.[30] Now emigrants to settlements in the Rockies would also come mainly through the middle border. Their natural inclinations, and any business links they already had, would turn their heads back to the east, not to the south. By the time gold was discovered, in short, a new pattern was mostly laid down. Lines of commerce and capital would follow its implications.

New Mexican freighters did play some role in the new activity. "We met a train *of Greasers* of almost every variety of color," A. T. Bartlett, an Illinois argonaut, wrote in his diary along the Platte in 1860, and a few days later he saw several other trains, most driven by "Mexicans." He and his friends stood extra guard over stock and possessions, wary of the sinister ethnic presence.[31] Seasoned Hispanic bullwhackers continued to work the Santa Fe Trail for years. In general, however, the southwestern presence was felt only slightly, and barely at all in the mounting traffic along the great Platte road. The cross-plains shuttle, east and west between the Missouri and the Rockies, quickly became the region's preeminent economic bond.

Rates fluctuated wildly during the first year or so, from as much as ten to twenty cents a pound to as little as five. By 1862 they had stabilized somewhat, usually at around eight cents a pound between April and November. These were only averages, however. From a freighter's perspective bulk and space were more important than weight; his costs were about the same whether he carried sacks of sugar or inflated balloons. Consequently rates might range from under ten cents a pound for flour to more than thirty for furniture. Weather and events also affected charges. Long winters and Indian troubles sent rates up, balmy Novembers pushed them down.[32]

As freighting bound the mountain settlements more closely to the border, it became a year-round enterprise. Large cattle-drawn trains began leaving for Denver with the first hint of spring and typically made two roundtrips a year. When outfits began wintering their stock around Denver, they could add a final half-trip from the border to the mountains in late fall, with ox-drawn trains still arriving in Denver well into November. "Fast freight" continued through the winter. Trains of smaller wagons powered by six or eight teams of horses and mules could make the crossing in a month or less. They stopped only for the worst winter storms. The rates, however, were usually twice those of summer—ten to twelve cents a pound, sometimes more—so fast freight vas profitable only for high-priced, compact commodities like sugar, candles, coffee, and, during winter, flour, sausage, eggs, and other edibles. Still, demand was vigorous. On his first run in 1861, Percival Lowe left Leavenworth on St. Patrick's Day and pulled into Denver barely three weeks later. Charging between twelve and fifteen cents a pound, he cleared $5,000.[33]

Lowe was one of many independent operators who jumped into the business, some with little more than a wagon and an impulse. A pair of innovative Germans loaded canned oysters into a farm wagon in February 1865, poured water over them, and hauled the frozen conglomeration to Denver. The boisterous trade produced some remarkable success stories. In a single year one newcomer expanded from two wagons with two horses each to seventeen large wagons and more than 100 ox teams. After drought burned him off his Nebraska farm, James Ralston Porter started freighting with three wagons, each with a yoke of oxen. Four years later he had thirty-six wagons and more than 400 oxen. From the start, however, a few giant firms dominated the traffic. As Russell and Jones were organizing the first stage line to Denver they also sent out the first freight outfit, twenty-five mule-drawn wagons that arrived early in June 1859. Russell, Majors, and Waddell began shipping a month later. When that firm went bankrupt, Alexander Majors carried on, and in 1865 he and another large enterprise, Jones and Cartwright, hauled more than half of all goods freighted to Denver. Between them they had more than 1,250 wagons.[34]

Shipments increased in breadth as well as in size. The earliest cargoes of food—smoked bacon, sugar, coffee, and especially flour, which came in sacks by the tens of thousands—quickly diversified to include prunes, succotash, strawberries, worcestershire sauce, and canned peaches, pineapple, and oysters. Enormous amounts of liquor sloshed up the roads. A single train in 1864 had eighty wagons with 1,600 barrels of whiskey and 2,700 cases of champagne. New construction demanded paint, nails, glass, hardware, and assorted house and mercantile furnishings. As society matured boots and shirts were joined by dinner jackets and wedding dresses, kegs of nails by bathtubs, ornamented grillwork, and corsets. The development of lode mining required much heavier machinery, especially stamp mills to crush the ore for processing. The first mills were almost toys, with stampers (the weights that pounded the rock) under 100 pounds, but within a few years mills were operating with up to fifteen stampers, each more than 500 pounds. Powerful steam engines were needed to drive the crushers. One large mill needed fifty pairs of animals to pull it.[35]

Facilities were quickly built to hold the freight and to satisfy the team
sters' appetites. Denver's first brick building was a warehouse for incoming
goods. The town's largest clutch of businesses in 1859 was the Elephant
Corral, which included a gambling hall, a saloon, and the leading hotel, the
Denver House, as well as stables and other facilities for animals. Similar
places were built over the next few years to handle the growing trade. Saloons
and brothels lined the muddy streets to meet the hungry demand for the full
complement of male vices.[36]

Freighting shaped as well the mercantile community along the trails.
Commercial and private traffic supplemented each other. Road ranches,
emporia, and stage stations were founded mainly to serve private travelers;
once in operation, they also catered to the growing number of freighters. The
combined business of freight and individuals encouraged more stores, which
made private traffic easier and less risky. The results were dramatically dis
played by the end of 1861—a well-rooted, briskly growing transit establish
ment all the way from eastern departure points to the Rockies. The road was
open year-round, with beds and food, however flea-full and greasy, readily
available. A freighter in 1864 recorded facilities of various types no more than
five miles apart for most of the trip.[37]

A FULL FREIGHT TRAIN in motion was one of the great sights of
the day. "We first see the white wagon tops looming up," a traveler wrote,
"and as they come nearer, before we see the cattle drawing them, they make
us think by their slow majestic motion, of a line of white elephants lumber
ing along."[38] Standing by the road, one would watch the ponderous sway of
these behemoths for more than half an hour before the entire train passed.
Wooden joints groaned, chains clanked, and the huge oxen let out occasional
deep moans as they strained forward with their peculiar stiff-legged gait.
Immense wheels dug into the dust. Beside each team a man walked with a
lash, gripping its thick handle and letting its fifteen-foot braid trail behind
him, ready for use.

A full-sized train had between twenty-three and twenty-six wagons, each
pulled by five or six teams of oxen, plus a small commissary wagon. Promi
nent eastern firms—Murphy, Espenshied, and Studebaker—constructed
freight wagons especially for plains travel, wide-bodied with heavy, durable
iron-rimmed wheels almost as tall as a man. White canvas was stretched
tautly over the arching bows. In front were high double boxes where men

might sit while teamsters drove the oxen. A Murphy or Studebaker carried about 7,000 pounds. It loomed over an emigrant wagon like a plow horse over a newborn colt.[39]

These famous prairie schooners traveled as part of outfits that were nearly as elaborate as small ocean fleets. Each wagon usually required seventeen to twenty animals, enough for oxen in harness plus extras to spell the weaker ones and replace those that went lame. A small remuda of horses was needed to herd the draft animals. One man was usually hired for each wagon as well as a wagon master, sometimes an assistant, and always a cook. Although teamsters provided most of their own basics, the company allowed a daily ration that was slightly better than a soldier's. It was long on bulk and short-term energy and sure to swell in the gut: two pounds of flour, a pound-and-a-half of bacon, an ounce-and-a-half of coffee, two-and-a-half ounces of sugar, and some dried apples and beans.[40]

Trains brought a large inventory to keep the operation rolling. An equipment list for twenty wagons in 1860 included 165 yokes, 149 chains, 24 double sheets, 27 ox lashes, an animal medicine chest, 5,000 pounds of flour, and 1,118 pounds of bacon; soda, soap, tallow, salt, rosin, frying pans, kettles, coffee mills; 30 plates, 9 wagon boxes; chisels, shovels, rasps, wrenches, goose necks, pincers, lariats, washers, water kegs, wagon tongues, coupling pins, linch pins, picket pins, tongue pins, king bolts, lap links, saws, hatchets, shoe hammers, knives, augers, and much more.[41] It added up. The entire outfit of goods and support often amounted to more than 175,000 pounds of cargo.

Ideally a train moved over the plains at an efficient tempo. The crew was on the road by dawn, with a short stop after about half an hour to allow the cattle to urinate and catch their first good breath. About ten in the morning came a rest of two or three hours. The "evening drive" lasted from early until late afternoon. In good weather an outfit covered fifteen to eighteen miles a day. In camp the wagons were drawn into the distinctive freighters' corral. Once the first wagon had led half of the others to form a long half-ellipse to the right, the middle wagon led the rest in making the formation's left side, halting about twenty-five or thirty feet shy of the first wagon. The result was an oblong corral with a gap at each end. Each halted wagon was turned with its tongue outward. Its team then was unyoked and led to pasture while the wagons were joined by their chains, right rear wheels to their neighbor's left front ones, to form a tight enclosure for holding the cattle and, if necessary, for defense. When breaking camp several men encircled the animals and drove them into the corral for yoking. The order of pairs in each team was critical. The most trustworthy animals were yoked in the lead and the next most disciplined put at the other end, closest to the front wheels. Between the "leaders" and "wheelers" were the greenest and most worrisome cattle. It was an elaborate procedure, but with experienced teamsters and well-trained stock it went smoothly. Alexander Majors once timed a crack crew as they yoked up twenty-five teams of twelve oxen each. It took them sixteen minutes.[42]

Not all trains operated so tightly. The fabulous demand for workers and cattle brought many that stumbled and balked through their first weeks. "Yoked up wild cattle. Had lots of fun. One got so cross we had to shoot him," the green teamster G. S. McClain wrote his first day on the road, and three days later: "Got started about noon. Some of the teams run off—broke the wagons to pieces so that we only got two miles." The next few weeks were a catalog of comic mishaps. The cattle ran away during the night; four teams spooked while crossing a bridge, smashing four wagons; four wagon tongues were broken in a day. McClain turned sarcastic: "Made a drive of 10 miles today . . . not much bad luck. Only broke 2 wagons." Gradually his crew found their legs, and accidents dropped to only one every couple of days.[43]

As McClain learned, freighting was a subtle craft. Yelling and cracking the lash were fine on the road, but when cattle were corralled they had to be gentled and soothed with a baritone "whoooooaahhh" and later driven slowly from pasture and yoked only after several minutes of "quieting in." Ox chains had to be properly wrapped or they would cut the spokes, and wagons well greased with dabs of lubricant in critical joints. River crossings were especially difficult and dangerous. Maneuvering a huge, top-heavy freight wagon over the shifting stream bottom, trying to keep the current's push away from the flat wagon side, working the terrified oxen to safety called for experience and luck, especially when larger streams were high. One freighter remembered using twenty-six teams to pull each wagon over.

Ruling the whole operation, commander of the fleet, was the wagon master. For his pay of up to $150 a month he was fully accountable for all stock and equipment. He kept the records and saw that rations lasted the trip. With these duties came considerable authority. A company's book of regulations stated that the men were "subject to the full control and orders of the Wagon-Master."[44] He kept track of debits for extra goods advanced, and he could dismiss any employee, which meant the loss of everything issued by the company. He had plenty of leverage to make a man's life miserable. His control was balanced, however, by the need for teamsters, experienced if possible but ultimately any young bodies willing to learn a considerable job of work.

A few teamsters already had experience in eastern companies, but most drifted into the job after arriving on the border. Many had chased gold in Colorado before turning to the surer income of the road; others took jobs to work their way to the gold fields, then kept at the business for years. Later, as the Civil War wound down, soldiers floated west to fill the ranks, often doing tasks well learned in the army. Novices learned from veterans in the old manner of guilds—the tying of hitches, gentling cattle, a hat brim's proper angle, splicing a wagon tongue, gauging the docility of animals and their place in a team, handling the lash, fitting tautly the wagon sheets and wrapping the lock chains snugly with gunny sacks.

As in every such arrangement, beginners learned and formed bonds within a creative tension of workers and bosses. The first regulation in a wagon master's official instructions stated flatly that "swearing, gambling, and intemperance will not be allowed in camp or on the Plains." Teamsters were required to observe the Sabbath and, when possible, to "hear preaching [and] embrace it." They were to act with full respect toward everyone met on the road, white and Indian. Whatever the purpose of these rules—an effort to tone up a public image, perhaps, or a lever of power if the master needed one—full enforcement was not part of it. As in most crafts of men working for weeks in semi-isolation, wagoneering came with its code of imprecation, rude conduct, and swagger. Initiates took lessons in a fantastic oral literature of vile jokes and curses so gloriously profane that awed bystanders gazed upward, expecting the heavens to crack open. Wagon masters understood and exploited the pull and tug between their authority and their workers' resistive pride. If the train kept to its mark, accommodations were made. The book of regulations that began with a stern prohibition against swearing and drinking ended with the master's careful accounts of whiskey dippered out to his teamsters on credit.[45]

Green freighters became the latest inductees into the overland experience. Because they kept to the road for more than half a year, they felt the full range of discomforts. In June 1864 Solomon Edwards wrote of rain that stopped the oxen in their tread and mired the wagons up to the hubs. July 8 brought a "small hericane," and three days later the cattle were stampeded and some wagons smashed by "the worst hale storm I ever seen." (An apprentice a few years earlier wrote that "it blowed so hard that I could not sit on my mule.")[46] Soon afterward Edwards suffered through a day as hot as any in his lifetime. The dips and swings continued. In late September it "rained like Scissors," then rained some more before turning "so thundering Cold we did not go any further to day."[47] Another teamster endured hammering hail and blistering heat before being caught in an October blizzard that froze the Arkansas nearly across. He wrote in his diary: "If we get away from here you will hear from me."[48]

In sheer exposure, freighting surely introduced more persons more fully and rapidly to the high plains than any other experience. The demand for teamsters rose on a steep curve after 1859. Besides the Colorado trade, business to New Mexico, Salt Lake, and the Pacific continued to grow. When gold was discovered in Montana and Idaho in 1862–1864, a fresh flood of goods moved up the Platte valley, this time to turn north and ascend the Bozeman road to the northern Rockies. The growing military establishment relied on millions of pounds of imported supplies, most of it shipped from the Missouri border. By one estimate the freighting businesses in Nebraska City alone employed 8,385 men in 1865. More than 5,000 teamsters worked for Atchison's twenty-seven firms and nearly 8,000 in Plattsmouth.[49] To put the numbers in context, the census of 1860 set Colorado's non-Indian population at 34,277. Five years later at least that many freighters were working the central plains.

Simply counting workers, however, barely begins to register their significance. Cross-plains freighting was a paradox: continuous motion that helped create an unmoving place. Freight routes were cords of binding energy. The steady press of huge wagons and the shuttle of fast freight fused the young towns of the mountains to the river towns and the broader culture of the East. Freighting encouraged dozens of posts and stations in a mercantile stitching that by 1862 ran the breadth of the plains. Wagoneering might have been a workingman's subculture, a masculine cult of bravado and esoteric skills, and the slouch-hatted, big-booted teamsters might have given travelers some of their favorite scandalous memories, but despite their raw reputation, these men had far more in common than not with the clerks and farmwives who stood slack-jawed at their blasphemy and rough ways. Virtually all were part of an east-to-west wave with Anglo and Germanic roots. Thousands of freighters moved on to prosaic occupations on the plains and in the mountains. They helped fix the behavioral basics of the new order—the assumptions of what the place was supposed to be, the skeletal structure of attitudes, definitions of the good life, the biases that left only the thinnest room at the social edges for Indians, mixed-bloods, and "greasers."

A freight train was a coalescence of forces remaking the country. In the goods it carried and in the men who worked it, it was a cultural invasion. The wagons and equipment were an impressive display of technology and capital, bulling their way westward. In its particulars, its sheer bulk, and its consequences, a freight train summed up the vision of a seamless region of mountains and plains. In that, it was a rolling undeniability.

THE LONG LINES of swaying, groaning wagons told something else about the changing country—and about the threats facing the native peoples already there. Consider the raw numbers. The volume of freight to Colorado rose from between 15 and 20 million pounds in 1860 to at least 105 million pounds in 1866. Rates varied by products and conditions, but shippers usually charged at least ten cents a pound in the early years and about eight cents by the mid-1860s. By these crude measures, the money spent to carry goods across the plains rose from at least $1.75 million in 1860 to a minimum of $8.5 million six years later. Because assessments were conservative, the actual figures might have been a lot higher.

These amounts raise puzzling questions. Goods were carried to the mountains to build and supply new settlements dedicated to the extraction of precious metals. In measuring the productive worth of those settlements, the key gauge was the output of gold. Estimates of gold production are as rough as those of freighting, but most reliable figures set the amount at around $25.5 million between 1859 and 1866.[50] This figure seems impressive, but when the two sets of values—the costs of freighting and the production of gold—are put side by side, the comparison is astonishing. Year after year, freight costs surpassed the worth of the product that supposedly was the reason for the settlements' being there in the first place.

This seems to make no sense at all. Colorado was not a charity. Businessmen sent money and goods there because they expected to get back their investment, plus some profit. The shipments east to west might go as a direct investment, such as funds sent to finance a mine or, much more commonly, money brought by thousands of hopeful prospectors. Or goods might go as a simple exchange; products were shipped to a Denver merchant, who sent back his payment on the return stage. Or investors might bring capital and commodities westward to establish businesses that would turn a profit; they moved to the mountains with money and materials, set up an enterprise, then hoped to take in enough local money to support themselves and to send back East for more goods. In all cases Colorado was expected to generate at least as much wealth as was being sent from the world outside.

But in fact the imbalance was fantastic. Much more was going east to west than returned west to east. The economic dynamic, of course, was more than a simple exchange. By the "multiplier effect" the money sent west paid for many times its face value. A shovel, worth a dollar, was shipped to a merchant in Denver. A miner in need of tools took the shovel and gave a dollar to the merchant, who used the money to buy his dinner from a restaurateur, who in turn paid his grocer, who bought a bottle of Hosteter's Bitters at the Elephant Corral or maybe lost a buck at a round of faro. One item—a dollar's worth of shovel—had financed a considerable economic activity. Ultimately, however, the value sent west had to return east if the person who sent it was to be satisfied. If the dollar continued rattling around Denver and never went home, its original contributor would suffer—and probably would not send another shovel out to the Rockies.

Perhaps gold was not Colorado's only valuable export. By the mid-1860s ranching and agriculture had developed enough to begin sending cattle and foodstuffs back East and elsewhere in the West. Little or nothing of those products, however, was sent out during the territory's first years; indeed, much of Colorado's food had to be freighted in. Gold was early Colorado's only significant export. Given that, perhaps production estimates were low. But that seems unlikely. Calculations would have to be consistently and wildly understated over several years to balance the trade between East and West. The preceding comparison, after all, matches gold exports with the costs of freighting, not with the value of what was being shipped west. In other words, the expense of simply carrying goods to Colorado surpassed the value of the reported gold coming back. When the cost of the cargoes themselves is thrown in, the gap becomes a chasm. Eventually the difference would narrow, as the Colorado economy diversified and matured, but for at least six years after the first strike, the worth of goods taken from the Missouri valley to the Rockies was probably two or three times the flow of wealth coming back from the mines, perhaps more.

The conclusion seems inescapable. From 1859 to at least 1866, Colorado was a major losing proposition. Lucky individuals might profit, of course, but region to region the Front Range was sucking huge amounts of capital from the middle border and the nation to the east. Year after year many people were willing to send valuable goods and vast sums of money to a place that gobbled up investments and gave little back. Part of this flow came as money to develop mines and placers and to build the towns, their businesses, and residences. Part came as stock for store shelves and equipment for emerging enterprises. Probably the largest portion came in the pockets and satchels of men and women who passed over the trails looking for the main chance, wherever it lay, and who spent their dollars prospecting, feeding, and clothing themselves, finding shelter, and chasing whatever else caught their fancies.

Cash brought to the settlements passed from hand to hand; goods and labor were exchanged for money and barter; assets bounced and rebounded like billiard balls on a busy night. But in the final regional tally, the worth of what came west continually outweighed what went back to the east. Investors presumably lost much of their stakes, and the thousands who came to Colorado apparently left most of their money there, thrown into the ground or onto merchants' counters and roulette tables.

It is not surprising, in that golden age of plunging, that a lot of Americans took economic risks. What is remarkable is that so many continued to pour such a concentrated stream of capital into a place that sopped up money like an unquenchable sponge.

The most obvious lesson is gold's seductive power to remake the country, starting with its mental shape. The process started well before the rush. There were persistent stories of gold washed out of the Front Range, Thomas Fitzpatrick wrote the commissioner of Indian Affairs in 1853. If the rumors proved true, and if free access to the mountains were allowed, he predicted, "the inducements . . . will soon people it with thousands of citizens, and cause it to rise speedily into a flourishing mountain State."[51] Then came the first strikes. Emigrant guides and newspapers amplified the theme of an inevitable rise to greatness. It was not just the belief that any place with a little gold must have a lot; it was the assumption that any country that had gold must have everything else. That conviction apparently drew money and goods steadily to the mountains, even in the face of bad odds.

Prophecy eventually became fact. The Rockies and high plains did have plenty of resources. Mines, farms, and ranches brought some prosperity, albeit erratic. But those later good times were bought with an early unrequited gush of funds. That money built business blocks, sawmills, corrals, stamp mills, toll roads, and much more. The physical basis for Fitzpatrick's "flourishing mountain State" was financed by people faithfully shoveling capital across the plains into an area that gave them little reason to expect much back. It was something like an act of mass self-hypnosis.

Colorado, then, was an economy of fantasy. Its story had its own wrinkles, but much of the mid-Victorian West experienced something similar. Whole regions were being reconfigured at an enormous cost. The price was paid by tens of thousands of persons, mostly middling sorts who carried or sent money not in large bank drafts but in thin sheaves tucked into wallets or folded in their boots. Colorado and the West were transformed less by well-heeled capitalists than by a whole society paying dearly to dream the land into another shape.

As collective bravado, this monumentally expensive fantasy was impressive. For Native Americans, on the other hand, it measured the enormity of the crisis they faced. Plains natives suddenly confronted an expansionist economy that dwarfed anything they could have imagined. Their opponents, after all, were simultaneously paying for the greatest disaster in their history. Hundred of millions of dollars were being spent on the nation's costliest war. The economy that invaded Colorado was so powerful—it generated and applied such extraordinary wealth—that it could still afford to create from scratch a large island of its own people and everything they needed. Whites could pay the Civil War's bill and still throw money across the plains, largely at a loss, in an effort to chase faith toward reality. The Cheyennes, Lakotas, Comanches, and others could resist that power for a while, heroically and at a terrible price. Finally, however, they had little to match that weight of capital and will.

Even that expansionism did not begin to cover the plains tribes' problems. Besides these circumstances—the economic juggernaut, the traders' defection, the freighting and the blossom of roadside businesses, the invaders' intolerance—Indians also watched the fundamental elements of survival steadily erode.

Cheyennes, Arapahoes, Comanches, Lakotas, and Kiowas had fashioned a brilliant scheme of living by taking some of what Europe offered and using it to push outward the ancient limits of one of the world's great grasslands. Some limits, however, they could not escape. They had to reach out through trade to get what the plains could not give them. They needed access to relaively rare sites that provided essential resources, especially during the dangerous winters. They had to meet the needs of the living tools that were the keys to their new power—their horses. This system boiled down to a dual strategy required of everyone who had ever lived on the plains throughout their long history. To use the country's many scattered essentials, horse nomads had to move unhindered over large areas. And when the time called for it, they had to occupy key places that could satisfy the vital needs of the moment.

Being able to move when they wished, and being able to stay in one place when they had to: these were the twin requisites of plains survival. The nomads' magnificent rise to military and material power was a history of artful maneuver within those two demands. Their rapid fall was a story of how their arrangement unraveled.

Well before the gold rush their difficulties already were mounting. The greatest threats were to the second of their two requisites—access to vital sanctuaries. A few wondrous spots—much of the Purgatoire and upper South Platte valleys and the big timbers of the Arkansas, Smoky Hill, and Republican Rivers—could hold thousands of people and horses for weeks at a time during the deep cold of winter. Dozens of smaller protective islands of timber, water, and forage were scattered around the high plains in gullies, stream valleys, and feeder canyons of larger rivers. From November to March, when living safely on open land was a contradiction in terms, these habitats were the only places the nomads and their mounts could survive. By the late 1850s, however, many refuges could not offer them much help.

The Indians themselves were partly to blame. They badly underestimated how much damage their horses did to grasses and especially to the cottonwood groves that gave them fuel and blunted the killing wind. "This stream affords fine wintering ground for the Indians, on account of the abundance of deer that are found along its banks," Lt. J. W. Abert wrote of the Purgatoire in 1845. "We were astonished at seeing great numbers of fallen trees, but afterwards learned that the Indians are in the habit of foraging their horses in winter on the tender bark and young twigs of the cottonwood."[52]

Those winter campgrounds were still largely intact when Abert saw them; he described lush grassbeds and stands of "ancient cottonwoods." But by the early 1850s some of the best sites were terribly worn. The famous big timbers of the Arkansas had stretched more than sixty miles, from near the mouth of the Purgatoire almost to the present-day Kansas state line, when Zebulon Pike came upriver in 1805. By the 1840s they had shrunk nearly by

half. The thickest run of the timbers thinned over the next fifteen years. In
1846 Susan Magoffin compared them to luxuriant growth along the Missis
sippi, but in 1853 an army officer wrote that the trees were "not thick enough
to obstruct the view."[53] The nomads who wintered in the timbers by the thou
sands did most of this damage, since most white traffic left the Arkansas River
well downstream to take the Cimarron route to New Mexico. The same was
true of refuges on the South Platte, Smoky Hill, and Republican Rivers, which
were showing the effects of the nomads' winter occupation by the mid-1850s.
Pasturage, too, was suffering from the intensive grazing during winter, early
spring, and late fall.

The consequences were far worse in areas used heavily by both Indians
and whites. Where thousands of nomads were pasturing tens of thousands of
horses in winter, emigrants and freighters were cutting surviving timber for
fuel and driving hundreds of thousands of animals in summer. Trade increased
steadily on the Santa Fe road, and after 1850 the number of oxen, mules,
horses, and sheep along the great overland route surged as well. By late in the
decade there were twelve or thirteen animals using the trail for every person
making the crossing. The combined impact was horrific. An expedition in 1835
had found thick groves scattered along the Platte and abundant timber in the
side canyons, but in 1849 an army officer wrote that any tree "might be looked
on as a curiosity," and in 1855 a woman wrote that throughout the Platte val
ley "there was not a stick in that distance large enough for a switch."[54]

Pasture dwindled year by year. Along the Platte and on the Arkansas below
the Cimarron cutoff forage was thin by July and virtually gone by September.
The greatest damage was out of sight and underfoot. Foraging and light tree
trimming at first stimulated vigorous new growth, but overgrazing and
overtrimming stole energy from what grass and trees needed most to sur
vive—their roots. The starved and withered root systems in turn left the
grasses and trees terribly vulnerable during the frigid, arid winters. Surviv
ing plants began the next year weakened and less likely to hold up under the
double assault, first of freighters and emigrants, then of wintering Indians.[55]
The costs accumulated. By the mid-1850s overlanders in late summer often
had to take their weary oxen a mile, and sometimes four miles, off the road
to find enough to feed them. The crush of wagon wheels, the plodding hooves
of animals, and the millions of human footballs tore the denuded road into
a swath hundreds of yards wide, a "whitened . . . trail as far as the eye could
reach" that was "as broad as eight or ten common roads in the States." Ruts
sometimes eroded into yawning gullies.[56]

A rare account from fall 1857 gives a vivid image from the end of a travel season after years of massive overgrazing. In mid-October Lt. Col. Philip St. George Cooke led a large column of troops, horses, mules, and ox-drawn wagons up the Platte toward Utah as part of the Mormon War. Grass was so scarce that his bags of supplementary feed were soon gone. By the forks of the Platte, with the only forage far from the river, the horses were stumbling. They soon began to fall by the road. With the cold deepening, facing the worst, Cooke wrote bitterly in his journal: "The earth has a no more lifeless, treeless, grassless desert; it contains scarcely a wolf to glut itself on the hundreds of dead and frozen animals which for thirty miles nearly block the road."[57]

Cooke described conditions at their worst, along the most overused route in mid-America, but the barren valley was only an exaggeration, and often only a slight one, of widespread disaster. Every fall plains Indians returned from their highland hunting to find the situation along the protecting streams worse than ever. The crisis deepened when an abnormally wet period after about 1825 ended with drought on the Arkansas in 1849 and throughout the region in 1855. Some areas fared better than others, but throughout the central plains the Indians' essential refuges were feeling the stress by the end of the 1850s.

Then, six months after Philip St. George Cooke led his command through the "lifeless, treeless, grassless desert" along the Platte, the Russell and Lawrence parties set off for the Rockies. In October 1858, a year after Cooke watched the frozen bodies of his horses pile up along the road, the first wave of speculators and goldseekers washed up the same trail. When Arapahoes and Cheyennes returned that fall to one of their best remaining sanctuaries, the South Platte valley, they found the cottonwoods and cedars cut to build cabins and sluices and corrals for the oxen and horses eating the grass their horses had to have.

The next spring 100,000 persons crowded up both of the old roads, but now the traffic continued up the Arkansas past the Cimarron cutoff, through the big timbers, and on to the mountains, and at the great fork of the Platte emigrants turned not up the North Platte but onto the South, along the valley where a decade earlier Thomas Fitzpatrick had seen wintering villages strung out for eighty miles. The emigration of 1859 began earlier and continued much later than usual. People and animals washed back and forth along the trails—optimistic goldseekers, discouraged go-backs, revitalized go-back-backs who turned around when they heard of the true strikes in the mountains. The effective number of persons actually crossing the land one way or another probably approached 150,000.

Fifty-niners wrote that the lower Arkansas valley now was stripped virtually bare of trees; two men called the big timbers the first shade they had found for 175 miles. That once magnificent grove was reduced to barely 200 low and scrubby cottonwoods. Pasture was sparse. Grass had been failing for more than 100 miles, George Willing wrote in his diary as he approached Bent's Fort. Ellen Hunt described conditions in the same stretch: "Sunday—no grass"; "camped late, very poor grass"; "desert plains and sandy, stony hills . . . Cattle nearly starved for grass."[58]

On the Platte Thomas Patterson complained that except for a few spindly copses, mostly on islands, the whole valley was treeless. (The next year Richard Burton reported that even the islands were stripped clean. The only trees he saw were dwarf cedars high on the bluffs, "distant black dots . . . which are yearly diminishing." He recommended burning the bison bones that were heaped along the valley.)[59] On the South Platte a party's oxen were so famished for lack of forage that the men threw away their tent to lighten the load. "The country [is] a desert, no fuel except dry grass," one of them wrote. A passing freighter, who refused to sell them corn, had problems of his own. With no trees for miles to cut for fuel, he smashed and burned one of his wagons to warm himself and his animals in the bitter cold.[60]

The full disaster of what followed for the Indians—the growing number of travelers, the two-way year-round traffic, the running of stages, the road ranches, and the enormous swell of freighting—has to be seen in this context. The flurry of action did not just stimulate changes in the Rockies and energize business on the Missouri border. It profoundly altered the land between. Besides drawing and supporting thousands of invaders, it drastically undercut the Indians' capacity to sustain their own lives.

Every wagon was a reminder of this oldest theme of plains history. From one perspective a freight train was a dramatic innovation that gave whites mastery over the invaded land—a self-contained mechanism that rolled over the plains, directed by humans and powered by animal flesh as it hefted and hauled its 8,000 or 9,000 tons of groceries and gunpowder, hinges and sawmill blades, stained glass and whiskey. But from another angle that was an illusion. No person or animal is independent of its immediate setting. The ox teams and the landscape they crossed affected one another. Murphy wagons remade the trails; the altered terrain changed how the teamsters drove the wagons and what their animals could find to eat. The new businesses seemed to grant travelers autonomy, but emporia and whiskey dives could serve the emigrants only by drawing some of what they needed from the land around them. By doing so, they added to the country's endless evolution and subtly shaped the alternatives of owners and customers.

People never master their environment; they bargain with it. The freighters' agreement with the land had its own costs, penalties, and debts, as did every one before and after it. Whatever its balance, however, their bargain methodically displaced another one—the arrangement that the Indians were trying desperately to make work. Whites, that is, did not have the power to command the land, only the power to control negotiations with it, and the deal they struck left little room for any other.

Wagon trains, as great grass-gobbling machines, devoured much of the remaining forage along the major routes. For the first time, furthermore, white overlanders ventured up the valleys between the Platte and the Arkansas, country virtually untouched and unseen by outlanders previously. The effects were immediate. The Kiowas called summer 1859 the time of the "timber-clearing sun dance," because when they gathered for their annual ritual on the Smoky Hill, they found that a large familiar grove of sheltering trees at Timber Creek had been cut.[61] Russell and Jones lined out their stage stations through this country, and although they soon shifted to the Platte, further wearing away that river's resources, the message was clear that the middle ground along the Republican and Smoky Hill was no longer exempt.

The rapid depletion along the roads, of course, meant that freighters and emigrants soon were short of fodder, too. Here, however, the new users had an insurmountable advantage. As part of an enterprise stretching far beyond the plains, they could carry their own fuel and fodder or import and cache it strategically along the way. Since the mid-1850s giant "corn trains" had plied their way over the trails, lines of wagons with deep beds loaded to the top with shelled corn as feed for oxen and horses.[62] Most at first went to military posts, but after 1860 some carriers were stashing their loads at ranches on the trail to feed the growing cross-plains traffic. At his post at Cottonwood Springs near the Platte forks, for instance, Charles McDonald stored up to 100,000 pounds of corn at a time. Some was contracted to the government. Most was kept for private firms, especially Russell, Majors, and Waddell, and doled out to freighters according to telegraphed instructions. Part was put aside to sell to emigrants and other freelancers who could not feed their stock on available pasture. By 1864 the corn trade was a major part of McDonald's business.[63]

Importing feed soon drove up the expenses of commerce and travel. As early as 1861 independent freighters raised rates between October and April to cover costs of imported fodder, and soon overland diaries showed how travelers were paying for the consequences of overgrazing. Silas Hopper came up the Platte in early May 1863. Traditionally this was prime season for forage. The bottomlands should have been thick with bluestem and other favorites of cattle and horses, but Hopper wrote monotonously day after day of "no grass," "wood none, only what you buy," "no hay or grass," "no wood and poor grass," and "no wood or grass." Instead he bought corn at two dollars a bushel, hay at one dollar a day, and wood at fifty dollars a cord.[64]

Travelers, shippers, and freighters found these costs irritating. But for Indians they signaled a full disaster. Silas Hopper, paying two dollars for a bushel of corn, was an accomplice in an abduction of energy. When the horse nomads moved into this country, they had to reach outside for some essentials, just as others had for centuries, but the basic sources of power they had to find at home. In particular they relied on the grasses that, through their horses, magnified their freedom to move and fight.

Now, along the most-traveled streams, where Indians had found some of their richest horse fuel, new residents took most of what was left, then held their ground while they imported what was needed to power their own animals. It made sense. As they saw it, the plains were knit tightly to regions on either side, so why not use something from one part to supplement another? The system was not meant as a blow against the Indians, but in truth it was. For a slight boost in travel costs, whites captured exclusive control of a resource Indians could not live without.

WITH THAT CONTROL, the Cheyennes and others saw a desperate situation get much grimmer. First they had lost the South Platte and the generous trench below the mountains. That pushed them eastward. Then the boom along the roads took most of the leavings along the two great rivers of the central plains. Steadily, they were losing some of the best of the essentials that had drawn them to the country. The boom of white business drove them more and more into the middle ground between the Platte and the Arkansas.

The further this process went, the greater the practical and symbolic value of that middle country, the valleys of the Smoky Hill, Solomon, and Republican, with their sheltering groves and large bison herds. That ground was worn, but not nearly as badly as elsewhere. Environmental pressures were overlaid with political ones, for this heartland, the best of what was left, was also the terrain of the Dog Soldiers and others most adamantly resistant to white contact.

Indians were "becoming desperate, wild-beast like, hemmed in by [their] enemies," Burton wrote from one of his dingy stage stops in 1860. Their desperation grew as the forces on display along the roads created a new country with no place for Indians in it.

10

THE PEOPLE OF THE CENTRE

William Gilpin was a summation of mid-America's transformation, a synopsis that walked like a man. The tall, bearded Pennsylvanian had traveled with Fremont, served in the Mexican War, and in 1847 had commanded a cavalry unit along the Arkansas road. His tour of the Rockies and plains convinced him that the whole region brimmed with resources, especially mineral, and throughout the 1850s he predicted glorious possibilities for anyone with spine enough to look. By 1858, Gilpin's vision had risen far beyond mere gold. His eye was on latitudes and destiny.

Not that gold wasn't waiting, and plenty of it. In a widely published speech given a few weeks after the big news from the South Platte, Gilpin told a packed Kansas City hall that the mountain West was "everywhere auriferous."[1] Within three years pioneers would find not only "gold in mass . . . and infinite in quantity" but also "all the precious metals and precious stones . . . in equal abundance." To prove it he cited elaborate principles of thermal power and mineral displacement, presenting them with his characteristic "nervous temperment and . . . French gestures."[2] Gilpin used simple, vivid metaphors to explain the earth's generous roil: Wealth burbled inside mountains, he said, like rice boiling over a campfire.

Gold and emeralds, however, were only the beginning, as anyone looking at the past and a map could plainly see. The truth lay in symmetry. The American nation was rising roughly midway between the thick populations of Europe and Asia, and the settlements coming with the gold rush would sit squarely in the middle of the young Republic. The region around Pike's Peak also sat equidistant from the equator and the Arctic, along the "isothermal axis" where "the principles of revealed civilization make the circuit of the globe." Every great city—Jerusalem, Athens, Paris, London, New York, Baltimore, St. Louis, and others—could be found in these latitudes. North to south, the interior West rested along this belt of historical cultivation. East to west, it was perfectly positioned to benefit from—and to dominate—the declining cultures on either side. History and geography had done their part. Now gold would be the final element "to unite, to complete, to consummate the rest."

The American moment had come. An empire of mountain and plain soon would rise up to become the locus of world power. Citizens of the Republic were "emphatically and, *par excellence*, THE PEOPLE OF THE CENTRE!" And the focus of gathering greatness, resting at the crosshairs of historical and geographical destiny, was the South Platte and its gold fields.

Abraham Lincoln named Gilpin governor after Congress created Colorado Territory in February 1861, and after heading west through the first rumble of civil war, the prophet of the new order arrived in Denver on the afternoon of May 27. As he climbed down from his Concord coach, Gilpin could properly say he was setting his boots on his rightful domain. At that moment, as he waved to the cheering locals who packed the dusty street, the flamboyant expression of mid-America's new dream achieved power in its formal and familiar sense, the grasp of high office.

As it turned out, Gilpin's tenure suggested more. He was a disastrous governor. He issued warrants without authority, ran up gargantuan bills, and committed laughable political blunders. He seemed to rule by self-inflicted illusion. In less than a year he was gone. Politics, the most fleeting and unstable expression of power, was also the most sensitive gauge of the new vision's profound flaws. The fallacies of imperial fantasy soon were as clear as Gilpin's ineptitude.

The changes continued nonetheless, carried by their own momentum. With enough support behind it, the dream of a land free of limits could be sustained for a while. Road merchants and freighters were the first to act out Gilpin's vision. Others took it up and carried it further.

GOVERNMENT WAS BIRTHED with the usual ruckus, more heated than usual perhaps because it came at the start of the nation's most terrible crisis. An effort to form a Jefferson Territory had aborted. There were borders to argue about, especially the eastern boundary with the mother state of Kansas and the northern line with Nebraska. Above all there were offices. William Larimer had coveted the governorship, and most people thought he would get it, but Washington, not the public, chose territorial officials, and with powerful support from Missouri Gilpin got the post. Already some people were calling for statehood, while others strongly opposed it. Within a few years the first showdown over this perennial frontier wrangle took place.

The population was growing at less than a Gilpinesque clip, however. The few new strikes were not enough to establish the Rockies as the new California, and the diggings that paid were beyond the grasp of newcomers. There was a constant outward wash, especially when rumors arrived of action to the southwest. "At present many Pike's Peakers are passing through here," the merchant John Kingsbury wrote from Santa Fe; "they are a hard looking set of people and mostly broke."[3] Some headed for Arizona, all of them out of Colorado. Measured strictly by numbers, the new territory was having trouble holding its own.

Denver grew sluggishly, but even so speculation was rampant. By one account a piano, hauled in for $200 in freight charges, was swapped a year later for fifteen city lots, which were sold after a few more years for $15,000.[4] City fathers cultivated a more settled look. Besides warehouses, wholesale outlets, noisome liveries, and foul grog shops, there were new hotels, invariably described by some variant of "first-class" or "well appointed," as well as theaters, bakeries, and apothecaries, one of them boasting the "longest and tallest doctor in the country." There were missteps. Near Fifth Street, between Uncle Jake Smith's meat market and a general provision store, were the remains of what was to have been a "stupendous hall." Unfortunately, as the Rocky Mountain News grandly put it, during the last stage of construction "it fell from lack of strength."[5] Nonetheless, the capital's overall appearance improved.

The citizenry resembled a bit more the mother society to the east. In June 1859, when Albert Richardson described a "most forlorn and desolate-looking metropolis," he had seen virtually nothing in a dress: "There were five women in the entire gold region; and the appearance of a bonnet in the street was the signal for the entire population to rush to the cabin doors and gaze upon its wearer as at any other natural curiosity."[6] The disparity offered women limited opportunities if they could bear the work. Ellen Hunt had hardly unpacked her family wagon when she began baking to supply the ravished market of wifeless men. "Weary days of labor and pain," she wrote in her diary of the last two weeks of July 1859; "have made 175 loaves of bread and 450 pies. Taken all the care of the children and done all the house work but the washing." And the next month: "All through August nearly worked to death."[7]

Denverites continued to cleanse the city of Indians and their white kinsmen. John Poisal visited occasionally to bring friendly assurances from his Arapaho kinsmen, but after some drunken miners tried to rape Ma-hom in their lodge, he no longer brought his wife. In 1861 or 1862 he was found dead in a small cabin behind the city's main hotel. William McGaa settled in the Cache la Poudre communities founded by the Janis brothers but also came often to drink in the town whose name he had given his son. He died there in summer 1868 when locked up for drunkenness in a stifling, unventilated room.[8] Architecture reflected the new attitudes. Owners of the Elephant Corral built a thick, eight-foot cactus-topped wall with gun ports around the complex of liveries, stockyard, hotel, gambling saloons, and brothels. With ethnic lines drawn and tensions growing, Denver protected its horses, whiskey, whores, and oxen.

Younger members of the old mixed-blood order were uncomfortable in the new towns. Edward Guerrier, son of prominent trader William Guerrier, had been born in a Smoky Hill village of his Cheyenne mother, Tah-tah-toisneh. He had lived with her until her death, then with his father at Fort Laramie before being sent to college in St. Louis. He was there in 1858 when word arrived that his father died in a Lakota camp when a coal from his pipe dropped into a powder keg. Ed returned to Colorado just as the wave of goldseekers hit the mountains. He tried a bit of mining and freighting but soon broke with the new ethnically sorted communities. By 1861 he was back with his mother's people. Ed Guerrier eventually found a wife in that mixed society—Julia Bent, William's youngest child, and one of his wildest. Even if Edward had been accepted in towns like Denver, marrying someone like Julia would have been a tense proposition as pressures for Victorian respectability grew with the population of white women. A guide on the Sumner expedition of 1857, Slim Routh, had married a young Lakota woman that year at Fort Laramie, but in 1861 he took a white wife in a church wedding in Denver. A friend happened to look up to see Routh's Indian wife on the porch, watching the ceremony through the window.[9] Like her, the few Indians with ties to Denver society stood on the outside looking in.

By 1861, with Denver's ethnicity more ordered and its balance of the sexes closer to center, boosters could rightfully claim the new capital had moved closer to national norms. Its physical pretensions were more convincing and its claims to permanence ensured. There was still plenty to set it apart from its urban models to the east, but Denver's social tone was at least a blend of the refined and the rough. The city even had a Parisian blacksmith named Garnier.

Other transformations continued around Denver and across the plains. The first changes, the instant sprout of road stores and the surge of freighting, flowed with barely a ripple into another enterprise—ranching. A few people had predicted grand things for high plains cattlemen during the years before the gold rush. Then boosters picked up the refrain. "No part of Kansas Territory can offer greater inducements to stock raisers," claimed an emigrant's guide, and a Missouri editor agreed that in the new country any farm boy could become a successful rancher. The natural fodder could sustain tens of thousands of contented cattle and horses and meet the inevitable demand for beef as the mountains filled with miners.[10]

Freighters saw the possibilities first. Elsewhere on the high plains wagoneers had already discovered that weakened animals left to die usually survived and plumped up over the winters, grazing on the cured grama and buffalo grasses. Two early arrivals on Cherry Creek, A. J. Williams and Jack Henderson, learned the same lesson when they set loose their exhausted oxen on an island in the South Platte and along Bijou Creek over winter 1858–1859. In the spring they found the animals fat and sleek and ready to haul.[11] The next step was obvious. For a minimal cost freighters could maximize a season's trade by making a final trip from the border to Denver in midautumn and pasturing their stock for the winter along the South Platte and its tributaries. At the start of the next season they could harness the animals for work or sell them to competitors who needed more power.

In the entrepreneurial scramble someone was bound to take advantage of this insight. The pitch appeared in the earliest issues of the *Rocky Moun-*

tain News: "Cattle Ranch! . . . on the Platte River . . . where we have built a large and secure 'Correll' in which the stock put in our care will be put every night." Other operations appeared along the Platte and Clear Creek, usually charging one dollar a head per month. The herds mostly grazed on open range, with supplements of hay during storms, and at night were kept corralled against thieves and predators. Jack Henderson commandeered a grassy, well-timbered island in the Platte where cattle and horses could be confined with plenty of feed on its 300 or so acres. With the help of 100 tons of hay he kept 2,000 head of cattle his first winter.[12]

A similar enterprise was happening along the roads. Freighters and overlanders often found themselves with oxen and other cattle drained to uselessness after pulling wagons for 300 or 400 miles. Worn-out animals usually were turned loose or eaten, but soon travelers could sell or board their tired cattle at stores and buy others in better shape. Elbridge Gerry was caring for at least a few animals for freighters by 1860. The ledgers of another store owner, Charles McDonald, are full of entries of cattle boarded for $2.50 per month per head. The sales markup was huge. One party found themselves selling several lame and haggard oxen to a merchant for $2.50 each and "paying him $100 for fresh and fat ones to take their place." Some merchants may have sweetened the arrangement even more. Jack Morrow was strongly suspected of hiring Lakotas to steal stock from emigrants who stopped at his store at the junction of the North and South Platte. Morrow then sold replacements at bloated prices.[13]

These businessmen were dealing in energy. A cow began the trip fully loaded with vital power, which gradually dissipated as exertion outpaced the calories it took in from grazing along the way. When the gap was too great, the animal's reservoir of strength ran dry and its owner had to sell the depleted cow to a store operator and buy another, an energized replacement. The road merchant then held the emptied animal as it gradually rebuilt its reserves by ingesting and storing the raw solar power growing around its hooves. The grass was free, and cattle reportedly gained back as much as 25 percent of their weight in a few months.[14] Once the cow's potential had been recharged, the merchant could sell it to a passing freighter or emigrant for several times what he had paid, perhaps taking in another emptied animal in the exchange. The lucrative give-and-take appeared to involve only cattle, but merchants essentially were selling fuel, the power to move and haul, and beyond that they were marketing the energy that poured out of the sky.

Animal refueling could turn a considerable profit when done on a large scale. In 1863 a Denver merchant bought a herd for $4,000 and hired a man at $40 a month to pasture them sixty miles down the Platte. As the seasons passed he sold off a few animals to pay the herdsman. After two years he resold the herd, increased by twenty-one calves, to a freighter for $15,025.[15] Most businessmen could not expect that level of profit—close to 400 percent after twenty-four months—but the opportunities were impressive, certainly compared to mining.

A natural extension of these businesses was haying. The taller grasses of the stream swards were cut in late summer, cured, and kept for sale to passersby or hauled where they were needed. Denver quickly became a center of the trade. One of the area's first ranchers opened a corral and hay yard in 1865. In time he sold more than 4,000 tons of hay in a season. Besides in cities and the nearby countryside, there was an enormous demand in the mountains. Huge shipments left Denver to feed the thousands of oxen, mules, and horses working in the mining towns and in the mines themselves.[16] Those animals were basically aliens to the high country. They could live only through massive imports of cured nourishment from their natural habitat, the plains, and hay dealers met that need. Ultimately mining, freighting, and ranching were tangled in the use of the same sources of energy. Wagon trains of dried grasses laboring toward the Continental Divide were one more instance of the region's parts being bound together by a common vision of interactive resources.

People, too, needed the energy found in sun and grass. They couldn't graze on grama and bluestem, but energy brokers could sell the plains' vitality, as stored in the bodies of cattle, to men and women needing calories. Denver and its vicinity provided a hungry market for meat. Hunters made good livings for a while selling quarters of venison at one dollar each, bear meat at thirty to fifty cents a pound, and ducks and grouse at fifty cents a pair, but the demand quickly surpassed the dwindling supplies. Few bison were hunted. The vigorous hunting since 1840 had left the Front Range virtually bare of buffaloes. Denver hunters had to go 100 miles to the east before finding them in significant numbers.

"Who will supply the demand" in this booming population of hardworked miners, a promoter wondered, "for though the land were literally paved with gold, the stomach must be fed!"[17] Carnal energy obviously would have to be imported, then raised locally. Some individuals tried innovative answers. A man bought a large flock of turkeys in Missouri and with the help of two boys began herding them to Denver. The birds ate grasshoppers along the road, supplemented with shelled corn carried in a six-mule wagon. With a good following breeze the gobblers could make twenty-five miles a day. Head winds, however, were a problem.[18]

It would take more than turkeys to quiet the thousands of growling stomachs. One obvious source was at hand—the herds of cattle used to haul wagons overland. Some of these animals apparently were culled and butchered from the earliest waves of the great rush. By midsummer 1859 meat markets had opened in Denver and Auraria with both wild game and beefsteak, which sold usually at eight to ten cents a pound. One of Denver's first dairymen, Daniel Holden, raised cattle for slaughter as soon as he realized the possibilities. At least by 1862 a slaughterhouse, Buttrick's Abattoir, was buying stock at five-and-a-half cents a pound on the hoof. Most or all of the butchered cattle seem to have been working stock, probably the ones worn out by their labors. Chewing must have been a challenge. Nonetheless business boomed. Joseph Bailey, soured on prospecting, turned to butchering and in eighteen months in 1864–1865 cleared more than $30,000 in beef sales to emigrants and miners.[19]

Freighting, boarding, cattle raising, and butchering were interlocking businesses that dealt in animals and that captured, used, and sold the plains' abundant energy. Workers and businessmen moved easily among the enterprises. Eugene Munn, a teamster for Russell, Majors, and Waddell in 1860, was put in charge of a winter herd of 700. The next spring he signed on with a new outfit, drove teams from Kansas to Central City, then went back to another winter of herding, shifting the cattle around various pastures before selling some for beef and herding the rest back east. After leaving the army for freighting, Percival Lowe began selling the goods he carried. He also sold off part of his mule and cattle teams to would-be herders and during slack times put his men to work cutting hay, which he both used and marketed. It paid well. By moving profits from each enterprise into the next, he expanded his freighting operations from six to thirty-six teams in three years.[20]

Lowe traded some mules and perhaps some cattle to a Denver merchant, John Wesley Iliff, for a stock of food. It was an early transaction in Iliff's path to becoming one the West's most successful cattlemen—a career that illustrates the patterns and rapid development of high plains ranching. Iliff had grown up as the son of a prosperous Ohio farmer and stock raiser. At twenty-five, after studying science at Ohio Wesleyan University, he headed for Kansas with $500, helped found Ohio City, and opened a store there.

Early in 1859 he sold the business, took his profits of $2,000 or $3,000, bought a wagon, an ox team, and an inventory of food and supplies, and left for Cherry Creek. With two partners he opened an outfitting business for miners.[21]

Sometime during the next two years Iliff decided that, while selling shovels and pants was a better way to make money than mining, raising cattle was far ahead of everything else. He traded animals for provisions, as he had done with Lowe, and by fattening and reselling cattle he must have seen the larger possibilities. By 1861 he was listed in the Denver directory as "Cattle Dealer." At a cow camp on Crow Creek near its junction with the South Platte Iliff built crude corrals and hired cowboys for a little over one dollar a day. He bartered for cattle with passing emigrants, by one account swapping tobacco and swigs of whiskey for "a broken-down cow or tottering steer" and later reselling the rejuvenated animal for a handsome profit.[22] He watched his investment closely, kept his losses low, and worked his income back into a business he kept lean and fit. By shrewd tactics, work, luck, and help from experienced neighbors like Elbridge Gerry, Iliff avoided the worst consequences of the drought of 1863 and the intensifying Indian troubles. He was poised to turn a successful business into an empire.[23]

Iliff showed what could be done by someone who could see and exploit the developing patterns of power in two of the word's meanings, as economic connections and as evolving uses of the plains' colossal store of energy. Like the freight lines and the Platte River stores, the new ranches reshaped the region's sum and substance and built up further the connective economic tissue binding mining settlements to border towns.

Within a few years ranching was developing along the other main route to the east, the Arkansas valley and southern Front Range. Actually cattle had been raised earlier in the general vicinity of today's Pueblo and in the valley of the Huerfano River by longtime residents such as Alexander Barclay, Charles Autobees, Joseph Doyle, and Richens (Uncle Dick) Wootton. William Bent had tried his hand at ranching along the river near his fort. Their markets were local settlements and trading posts, New Mexican villages, and Fort Union, founded in 1851 at the junction of the Cimarron and mountain branches of the Santa Fe Trail. Those enterprises had all but disappeared, however, when the gold rush suddenly provided a new and far larger market.[24] Three years later several ranches were operating in the basins of the Huerfano River and Fountain Creek. Cattle raised and fattened there could be sold in the towns that appeared along Fountain Creek and on the southern Front Range or driven over the low divide to Denver and other towns.

By then the emerging cattle king of the south had taken his first steps to dominance. John Wesley Prowers had come to the area in 1856 while still in his teens. His early career was another instance of an innovative culture-jumper moving from one opportunity to the next. He worked first for the Indian agent Robert Miller, then with the old master of trade, William Bent, selling and swapping with Indians at Fort Lyon and later traveling for Bent throughout the region. After the Civil War he worked for five years freighting government goods from Kansas to Fort Union. Meanwhile Prowers was establishing a more independent position. He freighted on his own and accumulated considerable capital. He forged friendships among the Indians, learned their languages, and in 1861 married Amache, the fifteen-year-old daughter of the prominent Southern Cheyenne Ochinee, called One-Eye by whites.

As in the posts along the roads, such marital alliances between whites and Indians survived much more openly than in Denver and other towns, and for the same reasons. A ranch and a merchant outpost were exposed and vulnerable; both could profit by trading with Indians for robes and horses. With good reasons to nurture good relations, other Arkansas valley ranchers married into the native elite. In 1860 Robert M. Moore, soon to be a prominent cattleman and civic father, married Mary Bent, daughter of William Bent and, more important, of Owl Woman, with her incomparable matrilineal connections. Another rancher, Ben Keith, was husband to Mary Poisal and thus an in-law, through Ma-hom, to the best-known Arapaho peace leader, Niwot (Left Hand).[25] These conjugal alliances lost most of their practical value within several years, but as in the households of some road ranches, the Cheyenne and Arapaho women remained as respected matriarchs. In the protective embrace of powerful and wealthy men, the marriages stood as rare survivals in a changing world.

Yet even as these men established valuable links within the old system of native trade, they were ushering in the new economic order. The year that Prowers married Amache he put down his savings of $234 to buy 100 Missouri cattle. He pastured them along the Arkansas near the mouth of the Purgatoire River and soon was selling regularly to markets on the Front Range. Shrewd and knowledgeable and well connected, Prowers began rapidly to exploit a range of pastoral opportunities. Thus began what became southern Colorado's largest ranching enterprise.[26]

The two entrepreneurs with the same Methodist surname, John Wesley Iliff and John Wesley Prowers, moved quickly to take advantage of possibilities suddenly opened by the transforming vision of the plains. They followed the two basic routes of the new order. One came with the fifty-niners and moved quickly through a mercantile entry into stock raising. The other parlayed connections and capital acquired at the end of the trading era into a firm base for ranching operations. Both men understood instinctively the movement of events and how to ride them.

ILIFF AND PROWERS were more than shrewd businessmen. They also understood the first rules of succeeding on the plains. No one ever prospered in that country without learning to rank resources and to control the most vital ones. Despite their different origins, both men grasped and applied that principle, and it served them well.

Iliff first chose some land along the north bank of the South Platte and established a cow camp on Crow Creek. A few miles away, at the creek's junction with the river, was Elbridge Gerry's store. Iliff thus had close at hand one of the area's most experienced residents and a man closely connected to lines of Indian power. He was also following Gerry's lead in settling on promising terrain. Crow Creek flowed vigorously through a grassy basin, and with the emigrant road close by, Iliff picked up hoofworn animals on the cheap, fattened, and resold them. His investment, according to a writer at the time, grew "at a rate before which even the twenty-four and thirty percent per annum which western banks in those days gave for ready cash deposits were as nothing."[27] Within a few years Iliff developed a breeding herd with shorthorn bulls brought in from Iowa and Illinois.

When a withering drought came in 1863, Iliff set up a cow camp down the South Platte at Fremont's Orchard and the mouth of Kiowa Creek. A fan of sixteen streams, large and small, drained into the river from the south within a few miles of that spot. It was a rare watershed of dependable flow and reliable grass, even in that dry time, and Iliff emerged from the drought largely unhurt. He soon expanded, setting up other cow camps at key locations. At first he held these points by occupation, but with the rapid development of ranching in the 1870s he began buying land outright. By his death in 1878 he owned nearly 16,000 acres in the South Platte watershed.

His holdings, however, were in no sense a "spread" as portrayed in the popular image of a cattle king. Iliff, in fact, could hardly be said to own a ranch at all. His land was composed of more than 100 pieces. None was more than 320 acres; most were less than 160; many were less than 15. These parcels were distributed within more than 7 million acres, an area 100 miles long and 60 wide. Iliff's 16,000 acres, that is, were in small fragments within an area more than 400 times as large. But they were not scattered randomly, like dry toast crumbled and tossed. The sites were shrewdly selected, and they had one thing in common: they contained or bordered water. Several were along the South Platte and prominent tributaries like Crow Creek. Others enclosed some of the ponds and small lakes that dotted the highlands.

Iliff realized that the key to dominance was not how much land you had, but *what* land you had. Years later an observer explained: "Grass, in order to be eaten, . . . must be near water in summer and shelter in winter. There are . . . millions of acres of the finest pasture in the West which are never grazed over by reason of remoteness from these vital necessaries." Of the three essentials—pasture, water, and protection—the first was the most plentiful and noticeable, the other two much scarcer. Success depended on controlling some of these three in the proper combination, a feat that was difficult under usual conditions and especially hard when weather and climate were unpredictable. Iliff's choice of Crow Creek and his move to Fremont's Orchard and Kiowa Creek were shrewd maneuvers to keep those elements available during troubled times. His later purchases applied the same strategy as he sought out wallows and water holes, the best riverine sections, protective enclaves.

This gave him a sharp competitive edge. Iliff did not need to buy vast acreages of grasslands to stave off rivals, because even the best and largest pastures were useless without the other vitals of water and shelter. Other ranchers could operate only if he granted them access to streams and ponds that he controlled. By owning the best of the scarcest, Iliff became the effective proprietor of far, far more.

Prowers was doing the same in the Arkansas valley. He began with grazing land along the Purgatoire and along the Arkansas between the Purgatoire and Caddoa Creek. It was prime pasturage. The stretch along the Arkansas was immediately upriver from what was left of the big timbers and both the Purgatoire and Caddoa had healthy stands of cottonwoods. Over the next fifteen years Prowers steadily expanded his control over, and then formally paid for, more land in the upper Arkansas valley. He first settled in three stone buildings on Caddoa Creek, and in 1868 he moved his growing family (eventually nine children) to a fourteen-room adobe house at Boggsville, just upstream from the Purgatoire's mouth. By then he had started farming as a partner in the valley's first irrigation project. In 1873 he moved to West Las Animas to open what became a highly successful mercantile business. In barely a dozen years Prowers's herds had grown from fewer than 100 head to more than 10,000, and he had built up holdings of 80,000 acres, an empire five times larger than Iliff's, all of it along the Arkansas and its tributaries. As with Iliff, every acre he owned in the basin brought with it control of many more away from the water. By common estimate Prowers's 80,000 acres gave him de facto possession of .5 million more.[28]

Many others tried to follow Iliff's and Prowers's lead. Not only was Colorado's climate and scenery divine, a man wrote his wife, trying to lure her out, but $1,000 invested in ranching would bloom into $15,000 in five years. Men from all walks of life chased the dream. Among the new ranchers an Englishman found former trappers and scouts, petty civil servants, clerks, hostlers, and railroad conductors trying their hands at ranching.[29] From 1859 to 1866 Edward Creighton pastured freighters' working stock along the Platte. He added cows and calves and set them to breeding and four years later had 8,000 head. By 1864 Weld County officials began registering brands to sort out the multiplying herds along the river. South of the Front Range divide, more ranches quickly appeared in the valleys of Fountain Creek and the Huerfano and upper Arkansas Rivers. Some immigrants simply took the land and began working it, but more than sixty cattlemen had filed claims in the Pueblo land office by 1867. By then the Denver Board of Trade estimated that the upper Arkansas watershed was producing 29,000 cattle and nearly 50,000 sheep annually.[30]

The first sites chosen, naturally, were the best endowed in year-round grasses. Prowers's daughter recalled neighbors working with her father to cut great heaps of indigenous hay for winter feed. Soon cattle raisers supplemented forage by planting oats and other grains. On the Platte many of the first ranches appeared where stores had been. Those early merchants, after all, also had needed the pasture, wood, water, and shelter. Some traders simply expanded their business to include ranching. Edward Beauvais, Jim's mixed-blood son, began raising stock, first at the Star Ranche post and later in Red Willow County, Nebraska. Elbridge Gerry concentrated on raising horses and mules around his store at Crow Creek. Other merchants sold out. Iliff's holdings covered what had been several Platte River stations: Wisconsin, Washington, Ashcraft, Dennison's, and others.

It was good business—and a variation on the oldest theme in plains history. Like every survivor before them, these latest users were cobbling together essential resources. The trick, as always, was to be able to turn and find what they had to have in the worst times. For thousands of years, hunting nomads had to know the streams and seeps that offered shelter and water among the bounty of the herds, and early farmers had stayed in the floodplains while foraging the highlands. The appearance of tamed grazers expanded hugely the rewards of the plains, but pastoralists still had to worry about their animals' needs as well as their own. They had to move easily among different habitats, which in turn placed enormous value on holding a few places with the vitals of life.

The horseback Indians also grasped the pattern and put it to use. Almost as quickly they faced other problems that came with the gains, but before they could find their way out, the gold rush and its changes washed over them. The first ranchers preempted some of the best habitats that had sheltered the horsemen and, before them, hundreds of generations of plainsmen. They redirected the surviving resources to a new purpose—raising animals to power the flow of people and goods and to feed infant settlements of the new society. The transition was complete in a few years. It was an energy grab as rapid and complete as any in the region's history.

Like every variation before it, this one also had its own lessons. Ranchers faced the old, unbending limits of the law of the minimum. They could expand no further than the smallest dependable supply of what they had to have. A few of these newcomers, however, looked beyond this restriction and found an opportunity. When Iliff and Prowers selectively seized a tiny portion of a vast domain, they were acting out a positive corollary of Liebig's law, one especially pertinent to pastoral capitalism. Abundance may be meaningless without the bare essentials when times are hardest. But if, on the other hand, you have sole command of rare and needful things, everything else is yours.

THE LINE BETWEEN farming and ranching was as blurry as those among ranching, freighting, and roadside mercantilism. Each enterprise fed and was fed by the others. They tied the central plains to country on either side. Farming, however, differed in one important way. It promised—and delivered—changes greater and deeper than any before it.

Boosters often wrote as much about farming as mining. The earliest emigrant guide used three of its five pages to praise the South Platte valley, which was said to have superb soil four feet deep, and the huge region of rich, black loam that lay in gently undulating hills to the southeast.[31] The land along the Front Range, another claimed, was as fertile and beautiful as any on earth: "The climate is balmy and healthful . . . with all the natural resources of a great agricultural brotherhood. . . . At no distant day [this will] be one of the exuberant garden spots of the world." The widely distributed guide by Parker and Huyett assured readers that the country around Denver "is as fine an agricultural one as you will find anywhere," with soil that was "light, mellow and quick."[32]

A correspondent from the diggings in January 1859 wrote that every valley from the Cache la Poudre to the South Platte canyon already was claimed for farms—and no wonder, since another writer called the land along the range "the nicest farming valley . . . I have yet seen, and capable of producing everything common to this latitude." Larimer chimed in, predictably, and others added that "the Platte and Arkansas bottoms will yield abundantly to the industrious farmer." Businessmen at the eastern end of the trails soon were pitching to this dream. The Great Western and Pike's Peak Outfitting Establishment offerred everything for "the Miner, Farmer, Sailor [!]," not only picks and shovels, carpenter tools, cutlery, and mill saws but also plows, mowers, haying tools, reapers, corn mills, and straw cutters.[33]

This merchant selected his goods "with a view to the peculiar wants of that large extent of country." By then those wants included a considerable demand for food, besides meat on the hoof. Almost immediately agrarian go-getters moved in to satisfy it. In its first issue the *Rocky Mountain News* predicted that anyone who stayed to cultivate farms around Denver would find greater profits than those chasing gold in the mountains.[34] Many agreed. Large gardens were planted in early spring 1859, and the produce quickly sold at good prices.

Although some farmers relied strictly on rainfall, most recognized that some irrigation would be essential. The fifty-niner David K. Wall, an experienced Indiana farmer, set up one of the area's first modest systems and was marketing the produce within a year. James Wanamaker and James McBroom also opened operations along area creeks during the early months of the rush.[35] A far more ambitious project was started the next year. Ten miles above Denver water was diverted from the South Platte into a channel nine feet wide. In 1865 the Witter, or Capitol Hill, Ditch was finally opened. Besides feeding farms along its route, it furnished water for surviving placer mining and, for immigrants yearning for green eastern landscapes, it began

Denver's "era of general tree-planting [and] lawn-making." Farming, mining, townbuilding, and the broad transplanting of culture drew on the same vitals and fed one another.[36]

From 1860 to 1865 irrigated farming spread as rapidly as ranching up and down the South Platte valley. The river became a stark boundary between the two economies. Creeks that drained out of the plains from the east and south supported nice beds of grass, but their flow was too erratic for agriculture. Their drainage became cattle country. Streams from the west and north came from the Rockies. Snowmelt and mountain rains usually kept them vigorous through the planting and growing seasons of spring and summer. Because these creeks and rivers ran through gravelly beds and rarely meandered, they made for dependable irrigation. Drawn by good land and a hungry market, farmers prepared fields up to one half-mile deep on either side of every eligible watercourse. Riverside farms spread quickly up each mountain-fed stream, like green fire up a fast fuse.

Euro-American farming had an older history in the Arkansas valley. The first was in the 1830s, and for years a few settlements on the upper river and Fountain Creek sold large amounts of corn to Bent's Fort. Corn was also traded to (and stolen by) plains tribes, and in 1854 the Utes, mountain rivals of the nomads, destroyed the most prominent farming outpost, Pueblo (or Napesta). Within a couple of years, however, Charles Autobees was trying again. The rush of 1859 jolted this sporadic cultivation into vigorous life. The first irrigation project was begun that year, and several others soon were under way. By the end of 1859 Denver merchants were receiving wagonloads of corn and onions from the upper Arkansas as well as flour ground at a mill on the Huerfano River. During the next few seasons farming and ranching expanded simultaneously in the upper Arkansas watershed.[37]

Ranching, in fact, often depended on local agriculture. Especially along the Arkansas and downsteam on the Platte, where businesses catered more to immigrants and freighters than to urban markets, farmers grew oats and hay, corn and cabbage. These "stock farms" were basically agricultural and after 1862 were often claimed as farms under the Homestead Act, but they also ran cattle and raised fodder and hay for their own use and for sale. In the dry year of 1861 Percival Lowe was driving 600 army horses from Leavenworth to Fort Union. The road through the dwindling big timbers was nearly bare, but on the Purgatoire he found a young man, probably Prowers, raising and selling a large crop of oats. He gladly paid $900 for 3,600 bundles of the grain to feed his famished animals.[38] Similar enterprises could be seen along the upper reaches of the river roads.

Ranchers often rode point in the drive toward agriculture. In partnership with several others, Prowers, Robert Bent, and Thomas O. Boggs, a former Bent trader, constructed a seven-mile irrigation canal, the Tarbox Ditch, which poured onto more than 1,000 acres on the west side of the Purgatoire. Neighbors built an even larger project in Nine Mile Bottom. The irrigated valley produced corn, barley, buckwheat, oats, and a variety of vegetables as well as grass and hay for the growing herds of cattle and, by the mid-1860s, large numbers of sheep.[39]

In 1862 Gov. John Evans estimated that farms on Fountain Creek alone produced more than 40,000 bushels of corn, 25,000 of wheat, and 20,000 of potatoes; Arkansas valley output was several times that. Just five years later estimates of corn and wheat production were approaching 1 million bushels annually. The grain yield of the Platte valley, meanwhile, had risen above 1.3 million bushels, with wheat now the major crop. By then mining was sagging a bit, but the farming and cattle economies had matured to the point that survival of the new economic order was ensured. By one estimate 35,000 persons, one of every two in the labor force, worked at some form of agriculture in 1867.[40]

Change came more slowly to the eastern side of the plains. After some hesitation, Kansas boosters predicted that the Missouri basin soon would enjoy a surge of prosperity by feeding the hardy miners 600 miles to the west. That optimism was never realized. Crop production first plummeted when troops of local farmers took off for the gold fields, then the ugly droughts of 1860 and 1861 devastated much of the eastern plains. As many as 30,000 stricken farmers, roughly as many whites as were living in all of Colorado, fled the area. The blistered fields could not feed their own communities, much less fill the storerooms in the mining towns. By the time conditions improved in a few years, the farms along the Rockies were meeting the demand of Denver and the mountain towns. In time the region's development and the interactive stimuli of various enterprises helped trigger an agrarian push onto the central plains, but the gold rush's immediate influence on low plains farming was mostly blunted.[41]

In a few places, however, cultivators benefited nicely. The luckiest worked close to the main roads west. Emigrants were desperate for fuel, both human and animal, and farmers who could raise at least some crops sold all they produced. Good profits were possible, as shown by the howls of pain from travelers who complained of gouging, especially in the gauntlet of Iowa farmers. On the eastern edge of the plains settlement was much thinner, but recent arrivals in the lower Platte valley and along the Santa Fe road east of Council Grove enjoyed a modest boom. It was a welcome break.

A small colony of German settlers was among those rescued by the rush. They had started farming along the Platte near Grand Island in 1857. At the end of their first winter they were reduced to eating their starved, nearly meatless oxen. "Everyone is losing weight . . . and we all have a miserable appearance," one of them, Heinrich Egge wrote in his diary: "I am so weak that often I cannot work all day." Life improved when they found jobs driving wagons at Fort Kearny, but then came a series of disasters. The price of corn collapsed, and most of their men were unemployed after losing military contracts for corn and hay. A prairie fire destroyed eight of their houses.

The diary then fell silent from December 1858 until the following October. Egge resumed with a survivor's gratitude: "Much, yes very much has changed during the time that I have not written in this book but, thank God, every thing has turned out for the best. . . . The want and misery have come to an end . . . , and we see good times ahead." Gold strikes had brought "an enormous trade" through the valley, and it was still was growing. By selling to the passing crowds, the Germans had stabilized their position. They were not prosperous, but they were eating. Egge could afford to look back and marvel at the transformed land, real and perceived: "Before 3 years ago all this was a solitude and waste land that white man hated, and now all this magnificent intercourse." Telegraph wire led westward along a march of poles at his farm's edge. By winter, he thought, it would bind the plains and mountains and bring the colony "in closer union with the civilized world." The spin of events left him dizzy: "How rapidly things change in America."[42]

THE INDIANS must have agreed. As Egge wrote of heavy traffic and newly strung telegraph lines, plains tribes were being pushed into narrowing choices with unpromising possibilities. Already facing dwindling resources and their own dilemmas, they lost much of what was left. Settlements seized the prime country along the face of the Rockies. Road ranches, grog shops, and hostels, then ranches and farms took firm possession of the Platte and Arkansas valleys, now filled with a continuous flow of freight and travelers. The nomadic life still was possible, but only in the central plains heartland, the country east of the mountains, west of the low plains enemies, and between the two great rivers.

A tour by army surveyors gave a rare view of this country on the eve of the rush. In September 1856 Lt. Francis Bryan and a small cavalry company moved southeast from the South Platte. The highland beyond the headwaters of the South Platte's feeder creeks was a flat, thick carpet of buffalo grass interspersed with rain-fed ponds. At the beginnings of the Republican River Bryan found wide steam bottoms, often deep within sheltering banks and mostly covered with rich grasses. Lower on the river were stands of cotton-woods, some quite dense. Bryan had seen only an occasional bison on the South Platte and the highlands, but on the Republican's headwaters he reached "the region of game." There were first antelopes and deer, then a profusion of meat on the hoof: "The bottoms on this river afford subsistence to immense herds of buffaloes and elks."[43]

Signs of Indians were nearly everywhere. Remains of winter quarters were along the South Platte. The highlands were cross-hatched by drag marks from hundreds of travois. Bryan found many camping grounds and several trees with robed corpses on ritual platforms. Farther east was evidence of vigorous sum-mer use. The Republican basin was "the very home of the Cheyennes, who claim this valley as their particular hunting ground," Bryan wrote. He found dead fires of many camps along a well-worn trail beside the river. Except for some wagon tracks from a trader's visit, nothing hinted of a white presence.[44]

The description is especially powerful when set beside that of Philip St. George Cooke barely a year later and less than 100 miles to the north. The North Platte had been one of the continent's finest pastures and corri-dors of travel, but in October 1857, after years of use and at the end of an emigrant season, Cooke found it a "lifeless, treeless, grassless desert" that could starve a wolf, not to mention a horse and rider. The desolation made the country Bryan saw even more appealing and rare.

If the nomads were to make a stand, it would have to be here. Unfortu-nately, the heartland was hotly contested even before the gold rush. Since 1840 the Cheyennes and their high plains allies had fought bitterly for this terrain with Pawnees, the Sac and Fox, Osages, Potawatomies, and others from the low plains and Missouri basin. This middle country had been a neutral zone, desired by all but controlled by none. Warring groups hunted and fought there in summer, then repaired in winter to enclaves on safer ground. As the bison disappeared to the west, the herds in the vital center were about the only ones in the region. The competition sharpened.

In the 1850s there were more butcheries and new acts of legendary courage and sacrifice. In 1853 a party of Cheyennes, Kiowas, Lakotas, and Arapahoes killed more than 100 Pawnee men, women, and children they caught
between the Smoky Hill and Republican. Near the same spot a major Kiowa
chief was killed when a small group of Sac and Fox used rifles to pick off
their surrounding attackers. The furious western allies assembled on the
Arkansas River the next year. Out of this camp, with more than 1,200 lodges
and 40,000 horses, an expedition of Kiowas, Comanches, Cheyennes, Plains
Apaches, and Arapahoes moved north, determined to drive their competitors once and for all from the contested terrain. Instead they found disaster
and humiliation. Along the Kansas River they encountered another party of
Sac and Fox, and once more the beseiged took a heavy toll with their rifles,
wounding more than 100 and killing 16, including the prominent Apache
Bobtail Horse.[45]

The fighting intensified during the next few years. To match their enemies' firepower, western tribes asked (unsuccessfully) that their annuities
be given partly in rifles and powder. Whatever weapons they and their enemies were using, they were effective. A census in 1855 reported only two
men for every three women among the Southern Cheyennes, Arapahoes, and
Comanches.[46] There could be only one explanation—horrific death rates from
hunting and fighting. The situation was even worse among some eastern
tribes. (The Civil War, the bloodiest conflict by far in white American history, did not approach this carnage. About 660,000 men died in that conflict. To reduce the ratio of men to women to that of the Cheyennes, the toll
would have been between 2 and 3 million men. Put another way, a family
among the horse nomads was three or four times more likely to lose a husband or son to fighting in the mid-1850s than a corresponding white family
during its own tribal war several years later.)[47] The core of the central plains
was not just the only hope for Indian independence. It was also the cockpit
of the bitterest, most vicious struggle among plains tribes.

The discovery of gold placed this heartland squarely in the path of the
most muscular push of the midcentury frontier. For the first time overlanders
invaded the central valleys between the Platte and the Arkansas. Overly
anxious, poorly informed, hoodwinked by maps drawn from ignorance and
lies, thousands moved up the Kansas, Smoky Hill, and Republican Rivers on
what seemed the most direct route to the mines. Some made it through, many
turned back, and some died on the plains. In April the Leavenworth and Pike's
Peak Express ran its first stages through the Republican valley. William Bent,

having played a pivotal role in drawing the Cheyennes fully onto the plains, then watched events bear down on his Cheyenne kinsmen. At the end of 1859 he wrote his superiors:

> The prominent feature of this region is the recent discovery and development of *gold* upon the flanks of the Great Cordillera and its spurs protruding out over the great plains. I estimate the number of whites traversing the plains across the center belt to have exceeded 60,000 during the present season. The trains of vehicles and cattle are frequent and valuable in proportion; postlines and private expresses are in constant motion. The explorations of this season have established the existence of the precious metals in absolutely infinite abundance and convenience of position.
>
> The concourse of whites is therefore constantly swelling, and incapable of control or restraint by the government. . . . [The] numerous and warlike Indians, pressed upon all around by the Texans, by the settlers of the gold region, by the advancing people of Kansas and from the Platte, are already compressed into a small circle of territory, destitute of food, and itself bisected athwart by the constantly marching lines of emigrants.[48]

After 1859 the rush through the center slowed down, cannibalism being bad for business. Hardy souls could give it a try, the *Rocky Mountain News* suggested, and "if they get through without eating each other up, some adventurous individuals may be induced to follow."[49] Traffic moved to the older, longer, safer roads, and Russell's early stage line soon shifted to the Platte. Emigration by the central road never entirely stopped, however, and border towns close to it, especially Leavenworth, were determined to rehabilitate its reputation.

In 1861 Leavenworth hired the father of the gold rush, Green Russell, to survey the Smoky Hill route. He spent most of April 1861 ascending the river with thirty-six men, crossing to Sand Creek and then to Denver. His report, generally favorable, inspired a more ambitious expedition later in the summer by two respected surveyors and engineers, who followed Russell's route to about present-day Limon before turning southwest to Colorado City at the base of Pike's Peak. The second report was classic bombast. Leavenworth "more than any other city on the Western Continent [illustrated] the spirit and energy of the American people." The town stood as the gateway to the shortest and best route to the rising civilization of the mountains—a hard, flat highway with plenty of grass and water all the way. As for larger possibilities, the whole region was flush with year-round pasturage. The lower Smoky Hill, rich in coal and alluvial soil, could easily support a large farming population. Farther west the soil was poorer but still boasted a "peculiarity . . . that, in a severe drought, enables it to withstand the absence of rain."[50]

Promotional salvos did not help right away. Traffic kept to the Platte and Arkansas for the next few years. The campaign continued nonetheless to imagine white communities into the region. The whole central plains were being re-envisioned as a piece into an empire of fused blessings: rich mines, prodigal fields, bustling commerce, contented cud-chewers, and towns of clapboard and Methodism. No part was exempt. The vital center, the terrain of last hopes for the nomads, felt the pressure soon enough.

GIVEN ALL that was happening, the Indian response was remarkably restrained. There were dark rumors of violence on the Smoky Hill route, mostly told by champions of the other roads. Kiowas and Comanches killed six whites along the Arkansas after Satank's rage at the Walnut Creek Station and the killing of his friend Pawnee.[51] Elsewhere, however, Indians helped the overlanders much more than than they hindered them. An Arapaho saved the starving, delirious Daniel Blue by carrying him to a newly established stage station. After a snowstorm during a winter crossing in 1858, a party was given food and water and pointed in the right direction by some Indians on the dangerous stretch between the Smoky Hill and Sand Creek. A "very prety young squaw" even gave them a language lesson.[52] The first vulnerable settlers on the South Platte, despite their worries, had no difficulties when Arapahoes and Cheyennes camped nearby.

Much of the contact along the roads in fact was remarkably friendly during the first few years. After feeding a large group of Indian horsemen biscuits and cold bacon some argonauts amused them by standing on their heads and turning somersaults. The Indians were greatly pleased but disappointed when the women travelers declined to do the same. When a woman in another party threw away a hoop skirt, an Indian visitor put it on. "As the skeleton hoop composed the larger part of his attire, he was a sight to behold," the woman wrote. Emigrants expecting the exotic often found something else. E. H. N. Patterson's group meant to dazzle a visiting Cheyenne with watches, a revolver, and fiddles. Bored with these familiar items, the man entertained his hosts with a selection of tunes on his Jew's harp, then showed them several ambrotypes of his children.[53]

The lighter moments hid a darker reality, however. Unless they could find some way to support their chosen life, the horse Indians would have to redefine who they were. There were few options. One possibility was to draw more of what they needed from whites crossing the plains. In camp along the Arkansas, Daniel Kellogg's party was approached by a large band of Kiowas and Arapahoes looking for buffaloes. "They swarmed into our corral and insisted that we feed them as toll for passing through their lands," he wrote. Food was laid out, but when "we saw that they would eat us out of house and home," the men quickly hitched up and took off, leaving the visitors "sullen and threatening."[54]

This was a time-tested ploy. For years Indians had asked for or demanded food and supplies and often had stolen stock from overlanders, who sometimes commented with surprise that natives seemed to consider what they took as a toll. In one variation several chiefs first had presented their agent, Thomas Fitzpatrick, with written testimonies from travelers that the Indians had not harmed or stolen from them; then the chiefs had demanded the government reward them for their good behavior.[55] The outraged Fitzpatrick (who paid up) saw this as extortion, as did travelers who complained of lazy beggars holding out hands for a dole. Indians, however, probably considered it reasonable recompense. Overlanders, after all, were taking from them. They were consuming huge amounts of nomadic necessities. They were also carrying into and across this country substitutes for what was lost—food, animals, and other pleasurables. Modest repayment seemed only fair.

From this angle the gold rush might seem a boon. Roads became deep rivers of goods to be dipped from, and Indians crowded in to wheedle for food, tobacco, and whiskey. They also bartered for goods. Men brought bison robes for swap. Emigrants in camp visited villages along the road to trade for exotica. Sometimes they got more than they hoped to bargain for. Perry Kline entered a tipi to trade for a pair of moccasins but backed out quickly when he noticed the woman sewing them was chewing the end of animal entrails piled beside her.[56] There were hints of small-time prostitution. The argonaut Wilbur Parker met his first "wild Indians" along the Smoky Hill. Turning later to his diary, he wrote discreetly in code (easily broken) of an interesting moment: "While comeing through the encampment a good looking squaw came to me and said if I would give her my hankerchiy she would let me lay with her." A guide book of 1859 was more direct. At O'Fallon's Bluffs on the South Platte emigrants could find "an abundance of wood, water, grass, and squaws."[57]

This roadside commerce was grotesquely imbalanced, however. Indians came to whites for what they needed to survive; whites received Indians as momentary diversions and sources of colorful memories and souvenirs. The exchanges could never give the nomads what they needed. They were instead a nasty mockery of what had helped lure the Indians, especially the Cheyennes, onto the plains and into the life that was turning against them.

Trade initially had brought power and had fueled the dream. Cheyennes first had played the middleman between poles of Indian commerce and later had reoriented their trade toward white markets and demands. That, too, served them well for a while, but by the 1850s this system was in crisis. Bison, the staple of trade, were disappearing, while the habitats that supported the tribes and their horses were degenerating. Nonetheless, despite its troubles, the Indian-white robe trade was still the dominant economic system of the plains in 1858.

Then the torrent. Besides propelling forward every threatening trend already under way, the gold rush quickly undercut the basic structure of native trade. The Indians' links to white society, the traders who conjugally bridged the two cultures, either joined the new action or were soon marginalized. With breathtaking speed the flood of population brought new enterprises that redrew the region's economic structure and redefined the meaning of its resources. The robe trade continued. Now, however, it was an adjunct to other business, and often a minor one. The ledgers of Charles McDonald, proprietor of the Cottonwood Springs road ranch, show him sending a lieutenant, Samuel Watts, to barter for robes with nearby Lakotas and Cheyennes. The books make clear, however, that the primary traffic was with emigrants. The robes seem almost an afterthought, tossed into supply wagons to Omaha and shuttled to Denver with loads of ax handles, whiskey, oysters, coffee, baking powder, liniment, and neckties.[58]

What had been the lifeblood of commerce was at most a sideline and often a kind of puttering. Before 1859 posts had been the equal signs between two sides of an economic equation; they had no purpose without the Indian trade. Now that trade could vanish in a day without merchants feeling the ripple. In scarcely a blink the new order had pushed aside the supporting economy of the plains tribes. The horse nomads were no longer just in trouble. They were irrelevant.

The government's policy had always been the demand that Indians surrender their vision and adopt that of the whites. Specifically, they were told to abandon hunting, gathering, trading, and raiding for a life as sturdy farmers. Agents must push the Indians away from their present doomed life, one official wrote. They would soon see the advantages, another agreed, and "instead of being roving and predatory bands they would become *settled,* and dwell in fixed and comfortable *homes.*" If not farming, some said, they might choose something better suited to the "peculiar tastes and habits of the wandering hordes." By turning from hunting bison to herding cattle, an agent thought, the Indians' passion for a life on horseback could be absorbed into the new order: "We could make them the Tartars of America."[59]

Both alternatives might seem reasonable. Some high plains tribes had been farming peoples for most of their earlier histories, in some cases only a few generations back. The Cheyennes had shown their adaptive genius in their leap to horseback and the plains, and they might reconvert to farming just as smoothly. Some Indian leaders said they were interested, even eager, to make the shift. "In settling down and raising corn, that is a thing we know nothing about," the Southern Cheyenne Yellow Wolf told Thomas Fitzpatrick in 1847, but "if [the Great Father] will send some of his people to learn us, we will at once commence, and make every effort to live like the whites." A year earlier he had said the same to J. W. Abert, adding that his people also wanted to raise pumpkins and tend cattle.[60]

But the situation was murkier than that. The change would depend ultimately on the spirit with which all sides approached it, and looking back, the attitudes are not so clear. Indians may have said only what they knew whites wanted to hear. Yellow Wolf began his conversation with an almost comic obsequiousness: "My father, we are very poor and ignorant, even like the wolves in the prairie; we are not endowed with the wisdom of the white people." After such a start his plea to be a corn farmer loses some of its clout. After sending Yellow Wolf's remarks to his boss, Fitzpatrick cautioned: "Circumstances and necessity may seem to change their disposition; but ingratitude, low, mean cunning, cowardice, selfishness and treachery, are the characteristics of the whole race."[61] Many in the invading army of farmers, ranchers, merchants, miners, and bureaucrats had attitudes even harsher.

Practical problems also barred the way. The Cheyennes and Arapahoes were being asked to farm in a context far different from gardening along the Missouri. Their tradition of women tilling communal fields while men hunted and fought would not mesh easily with white agrarian culture, and whether they were willing to cultivate European-style is questionable. Most important was a simple environmental barrier. High plains farming and ranching were possible only with ensured access to a few essentials, notably water. Even with everything else going for them—trusting agents, plenty of support, their own willing enthusiasm—Indians still would have to possess certain vital habitats that held those resources. Survival as farmers, that is, depended on control of the same kinds of places they needed as pastoral hunters.

And those places were exactly the ones they were losing. In 1856, when the Platte River agent recommended converting Indians to farming, he added that they must be settled where farming would work. In the South Platte basin, for instance, he suggested the Cache la Poudre valley. William Bent made the same point about the Arkansas River tribes and recommended land along Fountain Creek and the Purgatoire River. Those, of course, were the first areas taken by white farmers and ranchers—the Janis brothers on the Cache la Poudre and Autobees, Prowers, and others in the Arkansas valley. In this sense whether the nomads were considering the great conversion was beside the point. Even if they were, they were losing what they needed for the change.

The remaining option, the pursuit of the original dream, was not much more viable. The ranching and farming frontiers ate steadily at the edges of what land was left for hunting, gathering, and raiding. Nomadic life depended absolutely on freedom to cover great distances in reach of scattered resources. As that range of movement was constricted, the Indians' difficulties mounted.

Even the weather turned against them. In the early 1860s droughts reduced still more of their remaining pastures. In other years the horsemen had learned which areas could best support them while waiting for the rains to return. For the Cheyennes, Arapahoes, and Lakotas, one such area was on the upper reaches of several South Platte tributaries. Bijou, Beaver, and Kiowa Creeks flowed over porous, gravelly soil as they approached the river, so in dry years they often sank entirely out of sight. Near their mouths they appeared arid and dead. Upsteam, however, the creek beds ran with life-giving water. In 1856 Francis Bryan found these streams empty at the South Platte, but twenty-five miles toward their heads he described beautiful streams between lush banks, some thick with timber.[62]

Now, when the nomads turned there for a haven from hard times, they found one more door closed. With the onset of drought in 1863, John Iliff quickly seized this vital terrain—up Kiowa Creek from Fremont's Orchard and on the upper reaches of the fan of streams draining to the South Platte—and relied on it while other hopeful ranchers were failing. It became the early core of his empire. The strategy not only froze out ranching competitors; by the same principle it made Indian occupation hopeless. As similar grabs occurred all over the country, the Indians were pressed closer to full calamity. They had spent the past few generations facing the law of the minimum, learning how and where to make the most out of the least. They now saw survival's ground taken and held by men who could call on whatever power they needed to keep it.

ONLY IN THE HEARTLAND, home of the Dog Soldiers, was it still possible to live the dream of the Called Out People, and even there the pull was against them. The gust of goldseekers that blew through the middle country calmed to a breeze after 1859, but few people would have argued that the valleys and pastures would remain for long beyond the invaders' reach. Francis Bryan had predicted a few years earlier that the Republican and Solomon basins would soon attract settlers; a few years later a pamphlet praised the central valleys as "one of the most fertile agricultural districts known to man, surrounded with all the precious metals and minerals, and . . . in a climate best calculated to promote and expand the mind."[63]

On one point, at least, the visions of whites and Indians were in accord: they were mutually intolerable. "At no distant day," the Smoky Hill surveyors predicted, "where now roam the wild Indian and the buffalo, will be heard the sound of the churchbell, and the busy hum of civilization."[64] With their own inflection, the nomads agreed that wherever they were, there could be no cattle or sodbusters. Time and events, however, favored one dream over the other. More than a decade before the gold rush, the Southern Cheyenne Old Bark had seen it coming. His people had ruled the central plains, he said, but now he watched as "our ground [is] diminished to a small circle."[65] That circle tightened quickly after 1858, much like a noose. As the nomads watched the steady abatement of everything they needed to animate the vision of who they were, their last hopes of independence shrank with it.

History Through Nomads' Eyes. Winter counts, visual depictions of memorable events of different years, suggest the Native American perspective during these crucial years. Clockwise: In a symbol borrowed from whites, Lakotas show their alliance with the Cheyennes as part of the great peace of 1840; a Kiowa man howls in agony from cholera contracted from white emigrants during the gold rush of 1849; in summer 1855 a terrible drought left Kiowa men sitting much of the time to relieve their famished horses; Kiowas recalled their ritual in summer 1859 as the "timber-clearing sundance," probably because Colorado goldseekers had cut down most of the trees in a favored spot along the Smoky Hill River. (From Garrick Mallery, *Picture-Writing of the American Indians,* and James Mooney, *Calendar History of the Kiowa Indians*)

George Bent and Magpie. The son of William Bent and his prominent Cheyenne wife, Owl Woman, poses with his Arapaho wife. Influential in plains life before the gold rush, mixed-blood men and women were quickly pushed to the edges of society. (Courtesy of the Colorado State Historical Society)

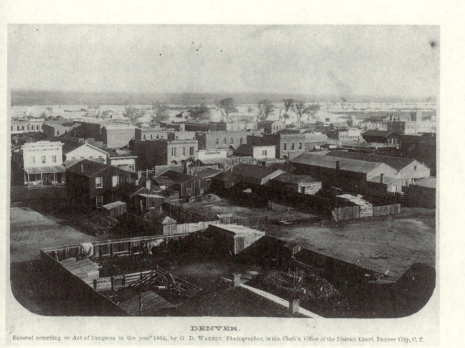

DENVER.

Queen City of the Plains. Denver was well established by 1864, the year of the Camp Weld conference and the Sand Creek massacre. Corrals and manure piles lay behind wide streets with substantial blocks of false-fronted businesses. (Courtesy of the Bancroft Library, University of California, Berkeley)

Camp Weld Conferees. A broad-hatted Ned Wynkoop and bearded Silas Soule pose in front of six Cheyenne and Arapaho leaders who would leave in hopes of a peaceful winter. Black Kettle sits in the center with White Antelope on his far right and Bull Bear to his left. John Simpson Smith stands behind Black Kettle. (Courtesy of the Denver Public Library)

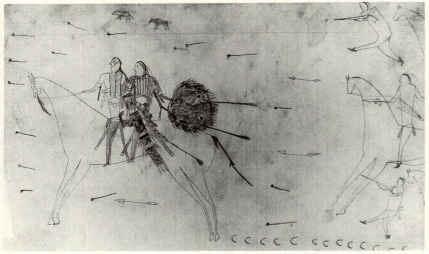

Twilight of Heroism. A ledger book found after the Dog Soldiers' rout at Summit Springs was filled with drawings celebrating feats of bravery among warriors. Bear Man (top), wearing a coyote headdress, sweeps close to the rifle fire of soldiers during the sack of Julesburg in January 1865. Wolf With Plenty of Hair (bottom) wears his Dog Rope as he rescues Tall Bull, who covers the two with his shield. Both men stood their ground and died at Summit Springs. (Courtesy of the Colorado State Historical Society)

11

THE MISERIES OF FAILURE

In July 1868 a party of 108 Kiowas crossed the Arkansas River from the south and approached Fort Lyon. They were led by Satanta (White Bear), well known for his sardonic, skeptical view of whites and his flair for the dramatic. The Kiowas had been camped at what had been the heart of the Arkansas big timbers. The great grove was now gone, and the Kiowas were having a difficult summer. Satanta asked for food, but the fort's commander, Capt. William Penrose, suspected mischief. Penrose sent the supplicants away, accompanied by a guard.

On the way back to camp the Kiowas did something that left Penrose so furious that he seemed to tremble as he wrote. First the men killed several cattle and hogs and carried them away. And then, "although earnestly requested not to do so," Satanta and his people rode their horses deliberately through two large, fine gardens, trampling the corn and other vegetables that grew in neat rows beside the Arkansas.[1]

To Penrose it was a typically thoughtless act by people he considered occasionally dangerous and always irresponsible. In its larger context it seems both a practical move to fill the Kiowas' bellies and a revealing bit of theater.

You may be planting cabbages and running cattle now, Satanta seemed to say, but not long ago these banks had grass, some of it up to a horse's withers, and camps under the shimmer of tall cottonwoods. We'll take some of what you've brought, and we'll let you know what we think of the world's nasty turn.

THE CLASH of visions in mid-America ran parallel to the continent's bloodiest war, and the plains naturally felt reverberations. Just to the south in Indian Territory the Cherokees, Creeks, and others were bitterly divided. Seven thousand unionists, mostly Creeks, fled into southern Kansas early in 1862. In the bitter cold between February and April more than 400 died in camps on the eastern edge of the plains. They "have not rags enough to hide their bodies," an agent wrote; and a surgeon, who had amputated more than 100 frozen limbs, including both feet of an eight-year-old boy, was outraged: "Common humanity demands that more should be done . . . to save them from total destruction." As the refugees dined on rancid bacon condemned at Fort Leavenworth for soap grease, an officer reported more than 1,500 horses starved to death and frozen along the Verdigris River. In the spring they fouled the water and raised an unbearable stench. There were other problems. "Every farmer . . . in this thinly-wooded country [must] husband the little timber which the river bottom affords him," another officer wrote, but Indians from the wooded south "never regard these things, and . . . necessarily commit great damages."[2]

As they unsettled an already disordered country, the exiles played out an accelerated version of the disaster unfolding for thirty years among the plains nomads. Dead horses, cut trees, and famished children: it was a common refrain with familiar causes. Too many expected too much and had too little control over events sweeping over them. A few days to the west of the Creek camps, Cheyennes, Arapahoes, Comanches, and Kiowas tried to survive along the overgrazed, overcut banks of another river. The results were much the same. A doctor sent to examine them in September 1863 found them shot through with diseases and weak with hunger. After waiting for weeks for their yearly food allotments, they were eating green fruit and the rotting flesh of diseased emigrant cattle.[3]

In the midst of the common catastrophes was the army. Its role was typically ambivalent. Soldiers were told to help the starving Creeks; they were to police the starving Cheyennes. Because the military exercised power in its rawest form, it is tempting to think that soldiers were more in control than others. The army, of course, could take resolute action. Under some conditions it could force some people to yield to chosen authority, or it could destroy the material life of some while protecting that of others. Ultimately, however, soldiers acted on the same terms as Indians, townbuilders, freighters, ranchers, and farmers. They too were caught up in the material dynamic of the plains. The army was one more group to learn that a country that offered so much finally hemmed everyone inside the same limits.

The military presence on the central plains was fairly limited in 1858.[4] Fort Kearny was established on the Platte road near Grand Island in 1848, a year before the government purchased Fort Laramie, the prominent trading post on the North Platte. Where the Republican and Smoky Hill Rivers joined to form the Kansas, Fort Riley was built in 1853. In 1850 the army created Fort Atkinson (built of sod and nicknamed Fort Sodom) on the Arkansas near the later site of Fort Dodge. Supplying this post was so difficult and expensive, however, that Atkinson was soon abandoned. Since 1854 there had been no military installation along the Santa Fe road.

The gold rush quickly changed that. In October 1859, a few weeks after Satank's rage at Walnut Creek Station, a military camp was established on Pawnee Fork. Christened Camp Alert and then Fort Larned, it remained an outpost of national power for more than twenty years. Farther up the Arkansas, Fort Wise appeared in 1860. After destroying his famous trading post in 1849, William Bent had built a new one downstream at the big timbers near the mouth of Sand Creek. When the army built a fort nearby and named it for Virginia governor Henry A. Wise, it leased Bent's New Fort for storage. In 1862 the facility was renamed Fort Lyon to honor Nathaniel Lyon, the first Union general to die in the Civil War.

The escalating tension brought a popping of new posts over the next five years. Fort McPherson was built in 1863 on the South Platte just above the Platte forks, and the next year Plum Creek Station appeared on the Platte halfway between Forts McPherson and Kearny. Fort Sedgwick also was established on the South Platte in 1864, about the same time as Fort Collins on the Cache la Poudre, and the following year Fort Morgan appeared on the South Platte between Sedgwick and McPherson. At the great bend of the Arkansas Fort Zarah was constructed in 1864, then Forts Dodge and Aubry the following year, the first near the Cimarron crossing and the second close to the Kansas-Colorado line, roughly equidistant from Forts Dodge and Lyon. In the nomadic heartland Fort Harker was set on the lower reaches of the

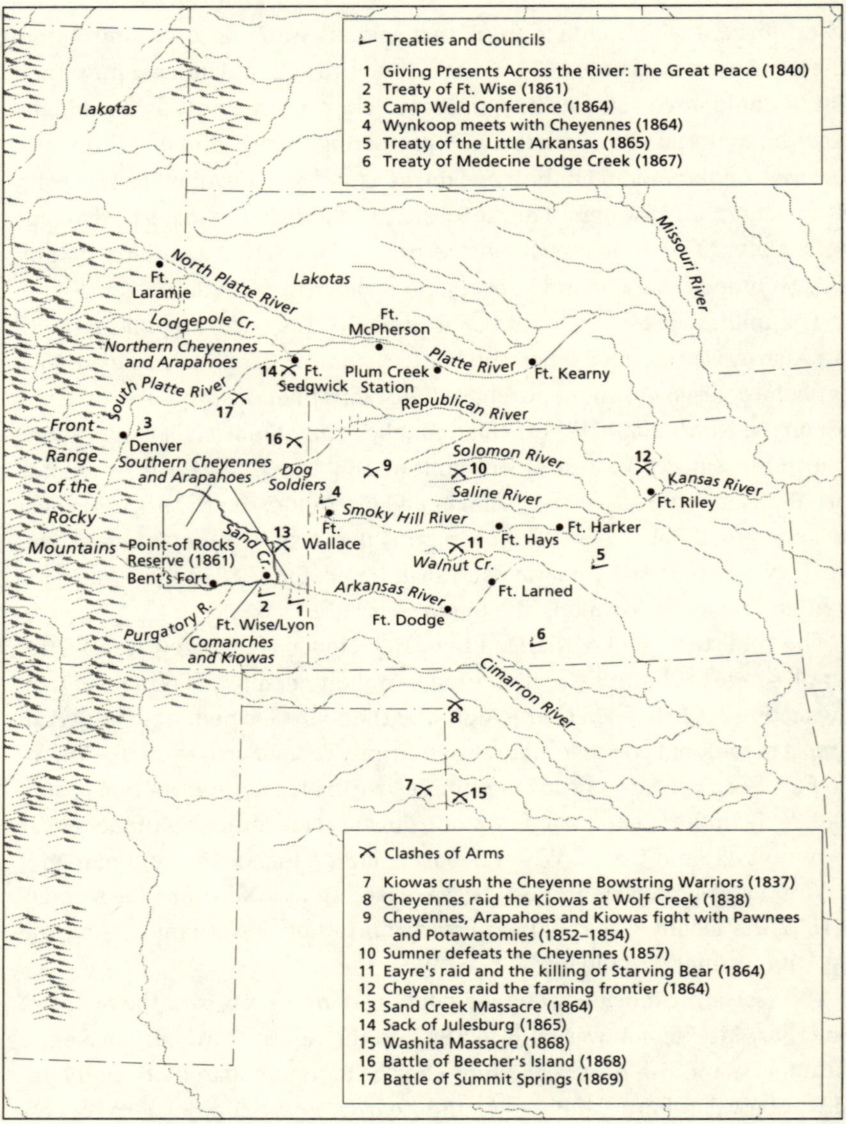
Treaties and Councils
1 Giving Presents Across the River: The Great Peace (1840)
2 Treaty of Ft. Wise (1861)
3 Camp Weld Conference (1864)
4 Wynkoop meets with Cheyennes (1864)
5 Treaty of the Little Arkansas (1865)
6 Treaty of Medecine Lodge Creek (1867)
Lakotas
Missouri River
Ft. Laramie
North Platte River
Lakotas
Lodgepole Cr.
Ft. McPherson
Northern Cheyennes and Arapahoes
Platte River
Ft. Kearny
14
Ft. Sedgwick
Plum Creek Station
South Platte River
17
Republican River
Front Range of the Rocky Mountains
3
Denver
16
Southern Cheyennes and Arapahoes
Dog Soldiers
9
Solomon River
10
12
Kansas River
Ft. Riley
Saline River
4
Smoky Hill River
Ft. Wallace
13
Sand Cr.
Point-of Rocks Reserve (1861)
Ft. Hays
Ft. Harker
11
Walnut Cr.
5
Bent's Fort
Ft. Larned
2
1
Arkansas River
Ft. Dodge
Ft. Wise/Lyon
Purgatory R.
Comanches and Kiowas
6
Cimarron River
8
7
15
Clashes of Arms
7 Kiowas crush the Cheyenne Bowstring Warriors (1837)
8 Cheyennes raid the Kiowas at Wolf Creek (1838)
9 Cheyennes, Arapahoes and Kiowas fight with Pawnees and Potawatomies (1852–1854)
10 Sumner defeats the Cheyennes (1857)
11 Eayre's raid and the killing of Starving Bear (1864)
12 Cheyennes raid the farming frontier (1864)
13 Sand Creek Massacre (1864)
14 Sack of Julesburg (1865)
15 Washita Massacre (1868)
16 Battle of Beecher's Island (1868)
17 Battle of Summit Springs (1869)

The Central Plains at War: 1837–1869

Smoky Hill in 1864, and the following year four forts and military stations were built in the central watershed—Fort Hays (originally Fletcher) near Big Creek's junction with the Smoky Hill, Fort Wallace on that river's south fork just east of the Colorado border, and Downer and Monument Stations, both high up the Saline River.

In the six years after the gold rush fifteen forts appeared where only four had been earlier. They were in country vital to the high plains tribes. The new posts were equally divided among three crucial regions—five on the upper Platte and South Platte, five on the Arkansas between the Purgatoire and the great bend, five on the central watersheds in between. Some (Forts Morgan, Collins, Aubry, and Zarah and Downer and Monument Stations) were short-lived; others would play crucial roles in military struggles for a generation. Their collective message was clear. While millions of soldiers to the east struggled through the nation's greatest military ordeal, the army extended its grip into the last places Native Americans could hope to stand independently.

Usually the forts' locations are explained in terms of potential flashpoints. The army built near trading posts and stations and at spots especially important for emigrants, where Indians and travelers were most likely to come to blows. From that perspective, it is easy to miss a more basic point. Roadside businesses and emigrant camps had not been placed arbitrarily. Merchants, traders, and travelers chose a particular setting because it offered something that other spots did not—precious environmental assets that everyone needed. The soldiers simply followed suit.

Thus Fort McPherson appeared at a shallow ford of the South Platte two miles from a site with the revealing name of Cottonwood Springs; the fort was first called Post of Cottonwood and Fort Cottonwood because of its stand of timber. Fort Wise was established where the famous big timbers had long sheltered overlanders and Indians. Fort Collins sat in the rich valley of the Cache la Poudre, prime grazing country now turning to farms, and Fort Sedgwick near a prominent travelers' stop on the South Platte at the mouth of Lodgepole Creek, so-called for its plentiful pines upstream taken by Indians for their tipis, where Thomas Fitzpatrick had seen twenty miles of Indian camps in 1849. Fort Morgan guarded the spot where the Denver cutoff left the South Platte road and angled over the watersheds of several creeks to the territorial capital. This was close to Elbridge Gerry's store and even closer to the site seized by John Iliff to control the lush courses of Kiowa, Bijou, and Beaver Creeks. Forts Larned and Zarah on the Arkansas were located near the mouths of Pawnee and Walnut Creeks, two streams long cherished by horse nomads, freighters, and travelers for their excellent pastures and rare stands of hardwoods. Fort Wallace was established near the big timbers of the Smoky Hill and the fine grassbeds on Pond Creek.

Forts co-opted sites that plainsmen, Indian and whites, had learned they needed for survival. Erecting a post was an act of both protection and possession. Like everyone who had occupied these spots for centuries, troops were consumers—in their case especially voracious ones—of the vitals around them. Cavalry, who were basically nomads in uniform, put their large herds of horses where Indians had pastured theirs and where freighters had turned loose their oxen. A standard part of the post routine, the bane of a soldier's existence, was the wood-gathering party. Men trudged off to cut wood and haul it back to warm the newest masters of old winter refuges. Soldiers chopped the cottonwoods to heat their barracks, feed their cookstoves, and supply needs that Indians never knew, such as forges in smithies. They added another activity never used by high plains Indians—haying. The mid- and tallgrasses that flourished along the rivers and streams lost most of their nutritive use by the first frosts, unlike the shortgrasses, which cured naturally and remained rich in energy through the winter. Pawnees and other low plains tribes had learned to cut and store the taller grasses during the late summer, capturing their nutrition for their horses to use in the cold time. Now troops did the same along the high plains streams outside their posts, the newest human maneuver to maximize plains energy into usable power.

Other white enterprises quickly struck up a dynamic give-and-take with the posts. Road stores catered to the soldiers' daily needs and vices. Early ranchers found a market for their cattle, farmers for their grains, pumpkins, cabbages, onions, and other produce. Cultivators sold large amounts of oats for the mostly grain-fed cavalry mounts. Locals worked as freighters and herders and contracted to supply hay, cords of wood, and lumber for construction and repairs.

When these military centers were set down, the last pieces of the new order were in place. For centuries, and in some cases millennia, plains peoples had used these sites for their minimal needs. The gold rush almost immediately drew new occupants to the best spots, then others in between. With forts the invading society used its concentrated strength to secure these places. From their protected positions soldiers could then watch over the other new arrivals as they redirected surrounding resources, the grass and trees and water and soil, to new purposes. Ranchers, farmers, and merchants fed the posts and in turn used their pay to expand their reach even further. The various parts of the new system quickened one another; ultimately the meaning of any one was tangled with the rest.

One of the smaller Platte River posts, Plum Creek Station, was a case in point. It was built in 1864 between Forts Kearny and McPherson near the mouths of a few creeks flowing from the south. Trees had been cut mostly from the main basin, but the creek canyons and islands still held cottonwoods and willows. The valley near the post offered better forage than the stretches above and below it. Years earlier an army officer had written near here that his mules were "up to their eyes in grass," a welcome change from the bare days previous.[5] With the rush of 1859, entrepreneurs jumped on these obvious advantages. One of the earliest guidebooks told travelers they could find supplies and mail at Plum Creek, and within a few years several stores had appeared. The longtime trader Barnard Blondeau opened a road ranch there in 1861.[6] It was a sensible location for an army post.

Immediately after establishing the station, its first commander sent patrols up the feeder creeks and found timber and grass, as well as Indian signs. During the first winter he bought 100 tons of hay from locals and commissioned cords of wood and cedar for construction. He hired men to haul offal and to work the weekly supply shuttle to Fort Kearny. In the spring he established a post farm to supply potatoes, cabbages, turnips, and onions during the long winters. The interplay of soldier and citizen was not all to the good. The exasperated commander forbade soldiers from keeping "irregular hours" at road ranches and reminded them not to sell their clothes to passing travelers.

Inevitably, the stress on resources began. New businesses appeared in the neighborhood, including ranches in embryo, merchants who bought thin emigrant cattle to fatten on the grass around the post. A local hay merchant was ordered to stay off the army's "reserved grass . . . [which we] must have." An ancient competition continued for control of the minimum, now with new contestants. Just upstream in 1835, the Arikara Bloody Hand had laid out for Col. Henry Dodge the basic plains dilemma. "I am traveling all over this country, and am cutting the trees of my brothers," he explained; "I don't know whether they are satisfied or not, but we have no land of our own."[7] Thirty years later, a post circular gave its own variation. Troops had recently laid out a parade ground, with exuberant grass and enclosed by transplanted trees "for the purpose not only of beautifying but to add comfort to the soldiers."

Then came trouble. Others, the new Bloody Hands, were drawn to the place while traveling the country. Emigrants were ordered to keep off the grass, and grazing by private horses, mules, or cattle was utterly banned. Offal, garbage, or "deposits of any character" were prohibited. And most emphatic: cutting, chopping, hacking, or otherwise defacing or destroying any tree was forbidden under the strictest penalties. The order ended with an injunction for the latest possessors of this old place: "It is expected that every soldier will regard it his duty to protect the trees."[8]

THE INDIANS also saw their duty. "There is a decided aversion among all the wild tribes of Indians to the establishment of military settlements in their midst," Thomas Fitzpatrick explained in 1853; "they consider that they destroy timber, drive off the game, interrupt their ranges, excite hostile feelings."[9] For years he had recommended more forts, but he also saw the dilemma. On the one hand soldiers should be placed where the Indians were. The South Platte was an obvious start, "partly because that is where Indians seem to congregate and partly because of its agricultural potential and potential for raising stock."[10] But the very reason the Cheyennes were there—its nice stock of scarcities, especially for winter—would arouse them to fierce resistance if any soldiers showed up. Fitzpatrick also recommended a post at the Arkansas big timbers, but warned, "I fear the Indians will strongly object . . . , as it is a great and favorite wintering ground . . . [with] an abundance of buffalo, antelope, deer and elk; good pasture and fuel are also abundant."[11] Indians would object, of course, precisely because these places could not provide for both them and the soldiers. Locating forts at these tested encampments was like seating a family of ten at a table for two.

By the early 1860s, the South Platte was taken by towns, irrigated fields, cattle pastures, and forts, and the Arkansas at the big timbers by soldiers and cattlemen-farmers like John Prowers. Occupation undercut the nomads' two essential strategies. Not only did they lose protective wintering sites, but they were also losing their ability to maneuver. Indians moved over the plains using restorative resting places for their horses and themselves. Soldiers at Plum Creek, for instance, found numerous Indian trails in their first forays into the wooded canyons to the south and a camp of 150 persons, who scattered at the soldiers' approach.[12] Those creeks were travel corridors as well as sanctuaries. Ascending them, then crossing an easy divide, horsemen could follow other wooded streams to the Republican at a point not far down from that river's big timbers. Close by, another prominent trail followed a creek northward to its head, crossed a highland punctuated by water holes, and struck the South Platte at the mouth of Lodgepole Creek—the site of Julesburg and, after 1864, Fort Sedgwick.

In this travel network whites were rapidly taking the best contact points. Every sanctuary along the Platte and most along the Arkansas were gone by 1864. These grabs once again heightened the significance to the Indians of the nomadic heartland, but there, too, the army was looking. "Here might be made a camp for several companies of cavalry for some weeks, as wood, grass, and water are all convenient," Francis Bryan had written from the upper Republican. Farther downstream, after praising the valley as a prime route for a road and white settlement, he added, "I suppose it would . . . be necessary to overawe [the Indians] by posts. . . . Fortunately . . . , many favorable points for the location of posts may be found, and the fertility of the soil would very soon attract settlers."[13] It was only a matter of time before white and Indian interests came head to head in this, the zone of most stubborn resistance.

It was difficult to see a resolution to the crisis, although seasoned hands offered advice. More than a decade earlier Fitzpatrick had written that the government should choose "either an army or an annuity. Either an inducement must be offered to [the Indians] greater than the gains of plunder, or a force must be at hand able to restrain and check their depredations. Any compromise between the two systems will be only productive of mischief, and liable to all the miseries of failure."[14] The choices were simple, he said: Pay off the Indians or sit on them.

But the government did neither. Since first promised in the Treaties of Fort Laramie (1851) and Fort Atkinson (1853), annuities had always been late, and once in hand they never came close to meeting the Indians' needs. If the upper Arkansas annuities for 1858 had been divided equally among all recipients, for instance, each person would have received about three pounds of flour, a pound of rice, and about three ounces of hardtack—an amount roughly equal to a freighter's ration for two days.[15] Agents pleaded for more as relations frayed over the next years. Albert Gallatin Boone, Daniel Boone's grandson who replaced his friend William Bent at the Arkansas agency in 1860, asked for everything from bay-state shawls to goggles and umbrellas, but his main concern was simple subsistence.[16] Annuities remained paltry, however, and months later his charges still were in wretched straits. The next year Boone's successor wrote that more food was needed to placate a new wave of Comanches, hungry and angry, being pushed northward out of Texas to the Arkansas.

Government force was as inadequate as government payments. Truly policing the Indians would take a much larger commitment. Mounted troops would have to move over a huge area under a variety of conditions, coping with the same challenges faced by the nomads. The army, that is, would have to provide the resources—the fuel and feed and protection from an array of difficulties—that the Indians themselves found in such short supply. As other whites transformed the plains to fit a new set of purposes, the military would have to pay to duplicate for itself something like the life that the horse Indians had first envisioned. That was a bill the government would not cover.

Instead, it took a cheaper option. It seized certain sites with resources needed to survive on the plains and to move within them. That occupation, of course, denied those sites' virtues to others, which meant that at some point Indians would have to submit and live out some variation of the whites' mental portrait of the region. For the immediate future, however, they were free to resist. That left the army temporarily on the defensive. Soldiers sat on their valuable real estate and waited to repond to hostile, but ultimately futile, acts.

So the government took neither course that might have prevented outright warfare. Because annuities were not a comfort but a tease, Indians inclined toward peace would most likely lean the other way. The military then would be expected to head off any assault, but it did not have the resources to meet that challenge, either, only the power to deny the Indians long-term access to vital needs. The army did not have the strength to control the Indians, only enough to make their chosen life ultimately impossible.

Government policy led to "all the miseries of failure," as Fitzpatrick had predicted ten years earlier. "It will beget confidence, without providing safety; it will neither create fear, nor satisfy avarice," he had continued, "and, adding nothing to the protection of trade and emigration, will add everything to the responsibilities of the government."[17]

THE SORDID IMPLICATIONS were played out during the next few years. Historians have written in careful detail about these years, a story of rising anxiety that flashed occasionally into violence. The events are so dramatic, and often so appalling, that they deflect attention from the larger context. Cheyennes, Arapahoes, Lakotas, Comanches, and Kiowas were not muscled onto reservations because soldiers defeated and sometimes butchered them. They ended up there because they lost command of the resources they needed to live as they wished. The violent clashes between 1864 and 1869 were simply the most vivid expressions of a fait accompli. They were exclamation points at the end of declarations of the new order.

The government's two inadequate means of dealing with the Indians corresponded roughly with the tribes' two basic arguments for dealing with whites. Trying to buy friendship with allotments and presents appealed to factions who favored trade and peace. The use of force meshed with the outlook of the militants, who called for disengagement with whites and saw a fight for their turf as the natural outcome of events. Whites and Indians ironically pursued similar policies, even as they moved toward war, and the government confirmed entrenched attitudes among two broad tribal factions. Despite their differences, however, the Indians' two routes carried them toward the same disaster.

The peace factions called immediately for a new treaty to compensate for land lost and to protect what they still had. "If you can possibly do anything for them, I would be glad," Bent wrote of the bands at his agency. As for farming, "they are anxious to get at it [and] if you will only give them a start they will go ahead."[18] The government desperately wanted clear title to at least the South Platte valley before the official birth of Colorado Territory. The result was the Treaty of Fort Wise, negotiated in 1860 by Alfred B. Greenwood, commissioner of Indian Affairs, and returned in revised form in February 1861 by Bent's successor, Albert Boone.

In the Treaty of Fort Laramie, Cheyennes and Arapahoes had agreed to rough tribal boundaries that included much of the high plains from the Front Range to western Kansas. Now those groups appeared to acknowledge white possession of most of that country in exchange for annuities for fifteen years and a reservation that included part of the Arkansas's upper watershed and land between the Arkansas and Sand Creek to the north. The government promised to protect them, provide stock and equipment, plow and fence the fields, and build a sawmill, mechanic shops, and dwellings. Artisans and interpreters would show the way to a new life.[19]

On closer look, however, agreements blurred away. The terms were signed by Black Kettle, White Antelope, Little Raven, and Left Hand, the Southern Cheyenne and Arapaho leaders closely connected to the whites. The parley included no Northern Cheyennes and Arapahoes. These bands dominated the South Platte valley and continued to claim this country, the gateway to the gold fields and the center of white occupation. The commissioner of Indian Affairs soon admitted it was still theirs.[20] Neither were militants from the Smoky Hill and Republican at the signing. They refused to give up a single mile of streambed or an acre of pasture and immediately repudiated the treaty. Meanwhile, the new territorial government was established and began operations. In effect federal officials simultaneousy recognized occupation rights of both whites and Native Americans. "It would puzzle a Philadelphia lawyer to tell whether the Utes, Arapahoes, or Uncle Sam owns the ground on which the improvements of Colorado are made," a Colorado editor commented.[21] At most, then, *some* of the more peacefully inclined bands of *part* of the Cheyennes and Arapahoes (and no Comanches or Kiowas) agreed to open *some* of the central plains to white settlement—although no one was sure which part. Whatever was surrendered, furthermore, was contingent on white authorities meeting a considerable commitment.

It was a jurisdictional ball of snakes, a situation perfectly primed for misunderstanding. Within this charged atmosphere the two tribal factions pushed ahead. The cooperative minority tried to step into a new life on the reservation with its headquarters at Point of Rocks, just upstream from Bent's original fort. This experiment depended absolutely on two factors. Agents would have to stand between the Indians and the whites who looked lovingly at the farm and ranch lands along the river. And because reservation land had been hunted almost bare of bison for years, the bands would need ample supplies. The government would have to meet rigorously its promise of food, material, and training.

The first requisite was undermined from the start, since Prowers and others already were ranching and farming on some of the best of the floodplain, especially the superb Purgatoire valley. What land was left eventually might have fed the reservation, but the issue was quickly moot. The lack of week-to-week support crippled the great change almost from the start. The promised food and equipment was slow to arrive. When Boone called Black Kettle and others to Fort Lyon (formerly Fort Wise) to sign the amended treaty in November 1861, he had to tell them that the old annuities, months overdue, were still missing. When food arrived it was appallingly bad. "The most intelligent Indians . . . ask 'Why their Great Father does not send them such goods as the whites use!'" Boone wrote.[22] The situation did not improve under the treaty. Over the next three years Boone's successor, Samuel Colley, repeatedly called for more support and responsibility in delivering it.

Some farming was begun, but by fall 1864 only between 250 and 400 acres had been planted in corn. The terms of the treaty help to put this outcome in perspective. The Fort Wise agreement was an early experiment in allotment; land eventually was to be surveyed, divided, and given out to tribal members. Each man, woman, and child was to receive forty acres with which to fashion lives as sturdy yeomen. In effect the government was setting this portion of land—forty acres per person—as the minimal stake of survival for a new life. Officials certainly would have agreed that only part of each allotment would be planted at any time; perhaps ten acres per person would provide enough to get by. The cornfields of 1864, then, can be set against this standard. By the government's own terms, reservation farms would have fed between twenty-five and forty persons of the hundreds committed to the reservation. After three years the experiment fell hopelessly short for those who had agreed to it, much less for the nomadic bands the government said should live there too.

Living close to the trails, the reservation bands were also chewed by contact diseases. Families were devastated by influenza, pneumonia, bronchitis, catarrhal fever, dysentery, gonorrhea, and syphilis, a doctor reported. An unidentified malady also was raging; it brought high fever and grotesque swelling and often killed its victims within days. In 1864 inoculations came too late to stop smallpox from striking hard at the reservation, and downstream a ravaged camp of twenty-five lodges, too sick to move, was living on diseased carrion left by emigrants.

Ten years earlier Thomas Fitzpatrick had warned that reservations ("limited ranges") would be hopelessly unworkable. At the time he wrote, 1853, tribes could not support themselves on the land they had. Unless massive aid was provided, confinement in smaller areas would only make matters much worse; they would have even less chance to hunt, and farming at first would be infeasible, since the bands "have not now the most distant idea" of the skills needed. Besides, he added, reservations would become "hospital wards" of cholera, smallpox, and other diseases.[23] Life at Point of Rocks between 1861 and 1864 confirmed his doubts.

To survive within this grim situation, reservation bands developed an annual pattern. It caused a lot of misunderstanding and mischief. In spring and summer some left the agency to hunt bison to the east. Farming gave them virtually nothing; annuities were sparse and late; the reservation was virtually devoid of bison and other large game. Visiting the remaining hunting grounds was one of the few options open to them, and Black Kettle and other signatories in fact claimed that such hunting rights were part of the deal, at least until they had fully learned the skills of farming and ranching. As the years passed more and more families took to the field in summer, often camping with the militants on the Smoky Hill, Republican, and Solomon Rivers. In fall they drifted back to Point of Rocks for the winter.

To Cheyennes and Arapahoes this cycle, a variation of one they had lived by for decades, was part of the transition to a new life, a necessary adaptation to the barren reservation and the government's shortcomings. To white agents and officers, it seemed a manipulative device. Indians, they said, fed at the government trough during the cold months and lived as they wished when the weather warmed. And as tensions mounted and hunters headed for the camps of the militants, officials saw their leaving as a defection to the enemy.

There was indeed a decided and understandable drift of support to the militants. The reservation experiment was limping along at the edge of failure, and officials were casting about for at least a symbolic effort to keep the support of the peace faction. In spring 1863 Agent Colley and John Simpson Smith took a delegation of Cheyennes, Arapahoes, Comanches, Kiowas, and Plains Apaches back East to the seats of government.[24] The purpose, as usual, was to encourage friendly relations while strutting the stuff of power. The delegates were indeed impressed. Besides touring Washington, D.C., they visited New York City and attended the exhibitions of Phineas T. Barnum (and in turn were displayed by Barnum to a gawking public). They marveled at the crowded streets and the size of public buildings and were entertained by 1,500 schoolchildren doing calisthenics. It is virtually certain that they were the only plains Indians of their generation to see a hippopotamus.

The high point of the tour, and the most serious business, was an audience with Pres. Abraham Lincoln. Spokesman for the delegation was the Southern Cheyenne Starving Bear, long an advocate of accommodation. He assured Lincoln that his people wanted only peace, but he worried that many of the whites who recently had come into his country did not return the feeling. He promised he would do all he could to avoid trouble. Finally he asked that he and the others be sent home as soon as possible to protect their families. After a short discourse, dramatically using a large globe to make his points, Lincoln told the delegates the reasons that whites were so numerous and powerful. "Pale-faced people," he said, were farmers rather than hunters, and (the Civil War notwithstanding) "were not, as a race, so much disposed to fight and kill one another as our red brethren." He pledged friendship, urged his visitors to take up agriculture, and said his people would "constantly endeavor" to keep the peace. Any whites who behaved badly did so against his wishes, he concluded, but added, smiling at Starving Bear, that "it is not always possible for any father to have his children do precisely as he wishes them to do."

Back at Point of Rocks the assurances must have been harder to embrace. The annuities were as late as always and support as thin. Officers at Fort Lyon, Lincoln's "children," showed little sympathy. "The Indians are all very destitute this season," one wrote in September 1863, five months after the trip to Washington. The drought had left them hungrier than ever, and with winter coming they would soon be in desperate straits: "The government will be compelled to subsist them to a great extent, or allow them to starve to death, which would probably be much the easier way of disposing of them."[25]

These conditions naturally boosted the militants' credibility. They were less exposed to disease. Using familiar methods to hunt the surviving herds, they fared much better than the bands trying to force the great transition, lacking what they needed. Above all the Dog Soldiers lived out more authentically the free-roaming dream of the Called Out People. As the situation deteriorated, more and more restive younger warriors chose that way of life. Most Comanches and Kiowas, pressed from the south into the Arkansas valley and increasingly sullen and leery of accommodations with whites, also identified more with nomads of the heartland.

In stance and style, militant leaders acted out the nomadic virtues and their resistance to accommodation. As tensions rose during the summer of 1863, they reluctantly agreed to confer with Governor John Evans in late September but then never showed up. When Elbridge Gerry was sent to bring them, they listed several reasons why they would not come: many of them were ill, they would not interrupt their hunt in its last weeks, they were angry at the recent shooting of a Cheyenne by an Osage guard at Fort Larned. They also rejected utterly the Treaty of Fort Wise, railing against it and vowing to keep to their hunting ways as long as they lived. It was just the sort of pose that attracted younger discontented warriors.[26]

The militants nonetheless had their own problems. They could not escape disease entirely. They held off from the September conference partly because diphtheria and whooping cough recently had taken thirty-five of their children. The steady growth of white settlement denied them sanctuary along the Front Range, and the preemption of resources elsewhere gradually choked off what they had to have. Droughts in 1861 and 1863 hit the middle country especially hard. The rivers of their chosen country rose on the plains, not in the mountains, and so were terribly vulnerable to dry years. The Smoky Hill went mostly to sand and the others dropped dramatically. The typical response had been to head for the Arkansas, Platte, and South Platte, which brought snow-melt and rain from the Rockies, but those streams were hopelessly crowded. Other dependable sources, like the lovely Bijou and Kiowa Creeks, had been taken by Iliff and others for their cattle. The trend was unmistakable. Events after 1859 relentlessly constricted the twin requirements of nomadic life—freedom to roam and asylum from the storm.

Meanwhile the Dog Soldiers still battled other tribes to control resources being lost to the whites. They fought with Utes in the mountains and Paw-nees, Otos, Potawatomies, Sac, and Fox to the east. The warfare added to the Cheyennes' valorous traditions. Ice, who had sought unsuccessfully to die a few years earlier, led a brave winter foray into the mountains against the Utes and a raid on the Wolf People (Pawnees) at the Platte forks. War-riors accumulated coups and prestige. Their leading men, among them Tall Bull, Big Wolf, Two Crows, Bull Bear, and White Horse, appealed especially to younger members of other bands, and they camped often with the more militant Lakotas, such as Spotted Tail, Pawnee Killer, Bad Wound, and Whistler. Although mortality rates can only be guessed, they surely were at least as high as the appalling ones noted a few years earlier. The warrior cult flourished more than ever. The four Dog Ropes were worn proudly, boastful hopes of defiant death.

For whites, too, these years were the most militarily intense of their his-tory. The Civil War colored their responses to Indians and to events gener-ally. Annuities, never a high national priority, were slower than ever. As in every war, ambitious men saw chances to advance by fighting any available enemies. Most obviously, the Civil War raised the anxiety level immeasur-ably. Settlers wondered whether Confederates would ally with angry Chey-ennes and others in a move for Colorado's gold. Southern agents in fact did make overtures to native militants, although nothing firm ever developed, and a Confederate invasion of the region was turned back in March 1862 at Glorieta Pass in northern New Mexico. Any threat from Indians, real or imagined, still carried the meaner possibility of rebel yells and the mayhem of border fighting.

As troubles deepened, the two factions—nomads of the middle country and the reservation bands—did have one common response. They took things from whites. For fifteen years plains peoples had been stealing horses, cattle, and sheep from overlanders who were consuming the nomads' necessities along the rivers. Frustrated bands in the middle country continued the prac-tice with townspeople and ranchers who were occupying hunting and grazing ranges that even the government agreed had not been secured by treaty. As reservation conditions worsened the agents grew increasingly agitated. "The policy of the government is one of humanity," Samuel Colley wrote. Why then, he asked, did he have nothing to give his hungry families? He added that famished Indians rarely observe the niceties of private property. Soon afterward the territorial governor reported that desperate and destitute Cheyennes and Arapahoes were "commiting depredations . . . and annoying the travel along the public thoroughfairs [sic]."[27] Some gravitated to Forts Lyon and Larned, but the soldiers there seemed nearly as hungry as the Indians, and a special agent in spring 1864 reported widespread cheating by Indian traders and sutlers as well as dissipation of an "astonishing extent." Every day Larned's commander set out to get drunk, "abuse the leading men of the Tribes & make prostitutes of their women."[28]

A grim situation was getting worse. The only solution, agent Colley wrote the governor, was to "place [the Indians] above actual want. Remove from them the necessity of theft—we cannot successfully preach peace and patience to a starving savage."[29] No help came, however, and neither did the western posts get the mounted power to intimidate the restive warriors. The situation drifted closer to confrontation.

The state of affairs in spring 1864 seemed perfectly designed for conflict. Two cultures with a history of discord lived close together in country both sides considered essential. A well-meaning treaty brought confusion and embitterment. Cheyennes and Arapahoes who were inclined toward peace saw every promise bent or broken; those more hostile were increasingly defiant and desperate. Whites, although inherently more powerful, knew they were vulnerable to skilled and mobile warriors, and their own civil conflict left them edgy about dark conspiracies. As tensions built and the Indians' food supplies shrank, hungry thefts provided occasions for confrontation. And inexorably the white invaders appropriated the essentials that Indian peoples needed to live out their vision of who they were.

A YEAR OF BLOODSHED began on April 12, 1864, when troops exchanged fire with several Dog Soldiers accused of stealing four mules. Four Cheyennes were hurt. The army reported four of their men injured, two of whom later died. According to the Cheyennes, Bull Telling Tales killed an officer with an arrow to the heart, cut off his head, and took his watch and jacket as trophies.

Like virtually all soldiers in Colorado, these were from a volunteer regiment called up as the Civil War got under way. As most regular army troops were sent east to fight, these volunteers were federalized as the First and Second Colorado and put in place of the regulars. They were mostly locals with a personal stake in keeping matters under control, and there were more of them than there had been regular army troops. They proved in general to be good at their jobs, and after turning back a Confederate thrust at Glorieta Pass in New Mexico in 1862, the Second was sent to Kansas City to help stop an anticipated attack there. Most of the First was assigned to Fort Lyon, with some left in Denver. It was some of the latter who clashed with the Dog Soldiers on April 12.

This first incident had two things in common with every violent episode of the next several months. Each significant clash occurred near a site that held scarce resources, and in each bloody encounter, no one could agree on which side was responsible. The first fight came at Fremont's Orchard, the strategic junction of Kiowa Creek and the South Platte taken by John Iliff for his ranch the year before. The Cheyennes claimed they had found the mules running loose and asked only a present for returning them.[30] True or not, some Cheyennes clearly had been taking some stock in this area, which had been one of their important ranges, especially during the horse-fattening weeks of spring. The clash occurred at a pivotal time of year, as the bands and their animals recovered from the winter and looked toward the summer's hunts and rituals. The reservation Cheyennes and Arapahoes had spent the winter at Point of Rocks and downstream near Fort Larned. When word arrived of the trouble at Fremont's Orchard, and of several incidents that followed near the South Platte, they grew nervous. In early May they set off for the middle country to camp close to the Dog Soldiers and to harvest bison on the summer range. For the next few months the two factions, militants and accommodationists, were scrambled together. As it turned out, events offered a proving ground for their different approaches.

The first test came almost immediately. Following the fight at Fremont's Orchard, Lt. George Eayre lashed into the central plains heartland on another search for Indians accused of stealing cattle. Eayre led about fifty men armed with two howitzers to the upper Republican, not far from the grassy, game-rich country Francis Bryan had called the Cheyennes' "very home." As he approached Crow Chief's and Raccoon's villages, their residents fled. He confiscated some supplies and burned the rest—robes, food, and weapons—along with the camps. Resupplied in Denver, Eayre's men next marched to the Smoky Hill in early May. On the sixteenth they approached a camp well down the river, across the Kansas line (and out of Eayre's jurisdiction), not far north of Fort Larned. These Cheyennes stood their ground. As Eayre drew near, one of the two strategies was tested in one of the most revealing moments of this bloody time.[31]

It was partly a story of two brothers. Eayre had found the camp of some of the peaceful Arkansas River bands who had recently started north for the middle country. Among them was Starving Bear, head of the delegation to Abraham Lincoln the previous year. Lincoln had asked the Indians to be patient with his nation's miners and soldiers, for no father, he said, can always make his children behave. Starving Bear now told his people to be careful not to alarm Eayre's approaching troops, who had drawn into a battle line. Wearing a peace medal given him by the president, he then rode slowly toward the cavalry with another man, Star, to parley and to declare his friendship. At twenty yards the soldiers opened fire, then rode up and fired again at the fallen figures. The enraged Cheyennes fought back as the troops fired grapeshot from their two howitzers. Eayre later said the Indians began the fight and lost twenty-five warriors and three chiefs. The Cheyennes claimed that they routed the cavalry, who quickly bolted and saved their scalps only because Black Kettle rode frantically among his people, shouting for them to cease their fire.[32]

Starving Bear's brother, Bull Bear, was in camp a short distance to the north. He was among the most respected Dog Soldiers. Bull Bear's differences from his brother lay not in an outright hostility toward whites. Like most Dog Soldiers, he understood the whites' superiority in numbers and preferred not to war with them. He differed, rather, in his dedication to the original lifeways of the Called Out People and to the warrior traditions. He rejected any steps toward reservation life. He deeply distrusted whites and their word and held a strengthening belief that, like it or not, a war to the death with the whites was inevitable. The news of his brother's death, and the image of his body riddled with bullets while wearing a peace medal, cruelly confirmed those notions. Bull Bear spent the next five years following their implications.

Many others found Starving Bear's death an irrefutable argument to cast their lots with the militants. Both tribal factions faced a dim future, but the Dog Soldiers had a more immediate appeal, especially to younger warriors. The troubles of the reservation bands—abject hunger, rampant disease, humiliating subjection—came on faster and were far more apparent. At least the Dog Soldiers were independent for the moment. And if death waited on everyone, there were better ways to find it than Starving Bear's. Eayre's campaign, which was meant to pacify the Cheyennes, instead added to the numbers of those ready to fight.

Soon afterward Gov. John Evans, Gilpin's successor, wrote Washington that white Coloradans were virtually beseiged. His alarm might seem a bit hysterical, given that the cavalry had just moved against several Indian positions, destroyed camps, and seized supplies, but white Colorado was not as secure as it seemed. Most troops were being withdrawn to the East in fear of a Confederate thrust into Kansas, and Evans was worried, especially since Cheyennes had reacted to Starving Bear's death with a flurry of attacks on the road between Forts Riley and Larned, on the Platte west of Fort Kearny, and as far east as the Blue River. More than thirty persons were killed and six women and children taken. Raiders even threatened the Walnut Creek compound on the Arkansas.[33]

The raids, and Evans's reaction, were one more play on an old theme—power as a mix of location and movement. In 1864 whites were sitting firmly on islands of assets. Holding those spots was a major advantage, but only if they were also able to move. Mobility in their case meant the freedom to shuttle safely back and forth along the lifelines of the roads, supplying their towns and posts and knitting together the country with their society beyond. That movement, however, was vulnerable to another kind, the Indians' ability to shift unhindered over open space. The Cheyennes' free-ranging movement, the inspiration and blessing of the life on horseback, was the essence of their own portrait of the plains. Whites could not stop it entirely and so were subject to its considerable power—its threat of random assault, its disruption, and its ability to keep an enemy off balance and fearful. Thus Evans's alarm. Horsemen could come out of the plains and slash at the roads, kill freighters and stage drivers, burn the stations: stop the flow. If they cut those lifelines, the umbilicals feeding the infant settlements, the governor warned, "it will be destruction and death to Colorado."[34]

Evans's next move followed logically from his dilemma. He issued two extraordinary proclamations. The first was precipitated by the hideous murder and mutilation of a ranch manager, Ward Hungate, his wife, and their two young daughters. According to later testimony, the killers were four Northern Arapahoes with a grudge against the ranch owner, but Evans wrote of a general assault ("Indian hostilities on our settlements [have] commenced"), and the public, after seeing the four scalped corpses displayed in a large box on a Denver street, was frenzied and furious. Evans responded on June 27 with a proclamation calling on all friendly Indians to quit the company of those at war and report to designated military posts, "places of safety" where they would be fed and protected.[35]

On August 10 he issued a second proclamation, this one to Colorado's white citizenry. He began with what everyone knew, that few Indians had responded to his first order. He authorized whites to seek out and kill on sight all hostile Indians, defined as anyone who had not come in for protection. The public could take or destroy all property of the hostiles, and men were given permission to organize as militia, with the promise of future pay. "The conflict is upon us," he concluded, "and all good citizens are called upon to do their duty for the defense of their homes and families."[36]

Consciously or not, Evans was trying to maximize his minimal power. Whites would hold their positions—Denver and all significant towns, military posts, and densely settled outlying areas. There they could control any Indians who came in without squandering the army with far-ranging movement. Then a much larger force, the civilian population, would be unleashed to seek out Indians not answering the first maneuver. Thousands of armed men might cover enough ground to kill nomads and, just as important, to destroy reserves of goods the Indians needed to live where they wished.

The problem was that the same conditions that inspired the strategy worked against it. Where, after all, were the Indians told to go? Army posts, the "places of safety," had been built to protect islands of resources that were highly valuable and very limited; Indians were furious precisely because the army sat in places that could support the soldiers and nobody else. Yet Indians were assured that if they gathered at those sites there would be enough food, forage, and protection for them and for white troops. Not surprisingly, they were dubious.

Fort Lyon and Point of Rocks were two of the sites where Indians were told to report. Cheyennes and Arapahoes could not expect much sympathy there; Maj. Scott Anthony, second in command, had been the officer who had written the previous autumn that the best way to dispose of Indians might be to starve them to death. He had little food to feed the Indians that winter, he had added, and saw as the only answer sending the Cheyennes out into the cold on a desperate hunt for game. His own situation had not been much better. Cheyennes called Anthony "Red Eye," referring to a chronic inflammation from scurvy.[37]

Why, if the government could not feed the Indians when hunting was at its worst, should they come in now, in summer, when they had some chance at bison among the herds of the heartland? And if the highest officers were both scurvy-ridden and dismissive of their suffering, why should the Cheyennes believe that they would find even minimal support and understanding for their dilemmas? Evans, in short, was asking the bands to reenter willingly what they knew were starvation cages.

The governor's second maneuver, trying to unleash the populace, ignored that the nomads chosen way of life was at its best during these summer weeks. Cheyennes, Arapahoes, and Lakotas might be losing vital locations, but they remained masters of mobile warfare. Horseback warriors blew over the land like smoke. As equestrian hunters and warriors they rivaled the best in history. A hunter could ride at a full run among a herd of terrified, skittering bison, guiding his horse with his knees through thick dust as he fired arrows from his shortbow, sometimes ten per minute, to drop the huge animals. Warriors fought with the ferocity of absolute commitment and with skills practiced from childhood. Evans was telling farmers, barbers, cobblers, and barkeeps to leave their protecting enclaves and sally forth against the likes of Tall Bull and White Horse, Crazy Head, Two Children, and Touching Cloud, men who had fought Pawnees, Utes, and Osages for years and who knew the trails and wallows of the high plains like a clockmaker knew the insides of a watch. The governor might as well have put a spectator at a bull fight into the ring.

The controversial proclamations, in short, were meant somehow to reach beyond the confines of the situation. Yet they only restated the limits and made them more obvious. Evans could proclaim five or ten times a day for weeks, but the basic dilemmas of whites and Native Americans would not change. The popular response suggested as much. As the summer waned, both groups remained where common sense told them to stay. Warriors did not come in; merchants and tinsmiths did not go out.

Whites held back in part because Evans finally had been authorized to recruit a formal militia, a command of "hundred-day men" to meet the crisis. After his first proclamation warriors struck at some stores on the South Platte and killed a few men along the road. In late July Satanta pulled off a typically theatrical ruse at Fort Larned. His Kiowas offered to amuse the soldiers by having their women perform a dance. As the audience goggled, Satanta's men ran off with the post's horse herd, and when the soldiers turned to pursue, the women ran the other way. Soon afterward Kiowas attacked a

Mexican wagon train and a settler's house.[38] Moreover, a Confederate gang, more thieves than combatants, raised sand on the Arkansas and in the mountains around Fairplay during July. Evans's shrill alarms became a squeal. Goaded by rebels, all "wild tribes" of the plains were in near concert and about to launch the greatest Indian war in history, he predicted. From Texas to Canada the West would be a sheet of flame, he wrote, and Colorado would be isolated and wiped out unless something was done immediately.[39]

The day after his second proclamation Evans received permission to activate militia from Denver and its vicinity. They became the Colorado Third Volunteer Regiment. Unlike the First and Second, the Third was created solely to fight Indians in the present crisis, and its lifespan was to be strictly limited—100 days. It differed from the others in a more fundamental way. The First and Second were generally well led, well disciplined and by now fairly experienced. The Third was composed of untrained locals and included a sizable portion of gutter-scrapings. With the Second stationed in eastern Kansas, the First and Third were under the command of Col. John M. Chivington, a major at the battle of Glorieta Pass who was put in charge of the military district of Colorado on its creation in 1862.

Reports from Colorado were confused by varied perceptions and the ambitious jockeying common to wartime. Chivington, a Methodist minister who had organized Denver's first Sunday school, had prayed to be sent east, perhaps even to the Potomac, but his considerable ambitions were focused mostly on a career in Colorado politics.[40] He was physically impressive, well over six feet and with a thick neck and massive chest suited for puffing, and was well known locally. Events in late August played to anyone hoping to make a name in battle. Raiders took cattle from Gerry's ranch on the Platte, and two men and a boy reportedly were killed south of Denver. In Evans's reports these became "extensive Indian depradations with murder of families." He wrote that "it is impossible to exaggerate our danger" and called again for massive support. Earlier he estimated 10,000 troops were needed to guard the roads and suppress the hostiles.[41]

Evans warned of a united savage front against the settlements, but in fact allegiances among the Cheyennes and Arapahoes were more fragmented and confused than ever. Reservation bands and Dog Soldiers were camping in the heartland. Some leaders, most prominently White Antelope, Black Kettle, and Neva, refrained entirely from fighting and continued to counsel peace, but violence on both sides, especially the killing of Starving Bear, drew many younger men over to the militants, some to fight in temporary retaliation, others in unbending resistance. Lakotas came more often and invited Cheyennes to raid, although all leaders said the offers were turned down.

The situation seemed hopeless. The level of violence and distrust was rising sharply in a confrontation that neither side had the strength to resolve. The army had never come close to breaking its enemy's resistance. Indeed, its actions pushed many Indians to hostility and shook the trust of the peace chiefs. The roads were still vulnerable, and yet white leaders showed no interest in negotiation. Rather, both the military and the citizenry were under standing orders to shoot any Indian who approached within rifle range.

Amazingly, a small Cheyenne delegation did appear with an overture for peace. On September 4 Ochinee (or One-Eye) approached Fort Lyon with his wife and a younger man, Min-im-mie. Expecting to be shot down, he carried a letter he hoped would be found on his body. Instead he was taken to the fort's commander, Edward Wynkoop. Ochinee gave Wynkoop the letter, dictated by Black Kettle, and reported that his people were hungry, fearful of raids, and having increasing difficulty protecting and providing for their families. Some Cheyennes had always wanted peace, he said, and at his God's bidding he was now inviting Wynkoop to parley.[42]

Wynkoop, one of Denver's earliest movers, the man who made the dramatic, foot-freezing dash to Kansas in winter 1858 to protect the Larimer factions's interest, had joined the army early in the Civil War, fought at Glorieta Pass, and taken command at Fort Lyon the previous May.[43] By his own later description he "belonged to the exterminators" and believed Indians were universally treacherous, with "nothing but instincts of a wild beast." As barriers to civilization they "had no rights that we were bound to respect." The courage of Ochinee and the other two Cheyennes left Wynkoop "bewildered" and feeling that he was "in the presence of superior beings." He agreed to a conference. A tense meeting at the big timbers of the Smoky Hill showed the Cheyenne leaders furiously divided, but in the end Wynkoop was given children captured during the previous weeks. He in turn promised to try to organize an immediate conference of white and Indian leaders.[44]

Governor Evans agreed, but with great reluctance. Black Kettle's and Ochinee's overture, the remarkable parley, and Wynkoop's call for a conference fouled the governor's strategy. He had managed to create the Third Colorado, but the clock was ticking on the "hundred-day men," and any move toward peace could only confuse their chances to fight. Evans's position was simple: set loose the Third (and the populace) to kill any Indians outside the posts. Conciliatory Native American leaders muddled what the governor claimed was a clear–cut situation by putting the messy, complicated facts openly on the table.

Evans, on the other hand, could hardly turn down an offer to talk about peace. A meeting at Denver's Camp Weld on September 28 included the governor, several prominent Denverites, Chivington, Wynkoop, and two other officers. For the Cheyennes and Arapahoes, the redoubtable Bull Bear was there, but otherwise the representatives were familiar advocates of peace— Black Kettle, White Antelope, Neva, and three other Arapahoes, all relatives of Left Hand. John Simpson Smith interpreted.[45]

The conference was a display of the confusions and garbled communication that had plagued diplomacy from the start. Cheyenne and Arapaho spokesmen said that most of the violent episodes had arisen from misunderstandings or had been carried out by other tribes. The factions denied they were allied with hostile Lakotas, and in fact they said they would serve as scouts and warriors with the whites against Lakotas, Kiowas, Comanches, and Plains Apaches. They professed a desire for peace. Evans, however, after issuing sweeping orders to Indians and whites during the summer, said he was no longer in charge. Because the two peoples were at war, native leaders would have to make their peace with the military. Chivington then spoke for the only time. His was the conference's final statement: "My rule of fighting white men or Indians is, to fight them until they lay down their arms and submit to military authority. You are nearer Major Wynkoop than any one else, and you can go to him when you get ready to do that."[46]

The Camp Weld Conference ended with hugs and photographs, but an outcome that seemed clear at the time once more contained deadly ambiguities. A long list of questions was unaddressed—the specific process of submission, the protection and support bands could expect, the status of Cheyennes and Arapahoes unrepresented at the conference, and the definition of "hostile" and "friendly" among camps that included some Indians who had fought during the summer. The lingering impression, however, was that Cheyennes and Arapahoes who reported to Fort Lyon would be welcomed and safe, at least to discuss terms with the military. After further discussions between Wynkoop and the peace chiefs, bands began to drift toward Fort Lyon.

Events then were brought to their sticking point by the oldest crisis-maker of the plains—the weather. By October the Cheyennes and Arapahoes were moving with the next turn in the annual cycle they had followed since coming to the plains. Six months earlier summer had drawn the bands together to hunt in the middle country. Over the next six months winter split them up again in search of shelter, food, fuel, and water. The groups moving toward Fort Lyon did so partly from this environmental need. They gravitated toward what was left of traditional sanctuaries on the Arkansas, looking also for help at the reservation and the fort that stood where their old shelter had been.

Circumstances, however, gave that well-worn pattern a new meaning and raised a raft of new questions. Many whites argued that Indians talked peace and drifted toward the posts only because weather had halted their raiding until spring. They had a point. Everyone's options always narrowed from November to April. When moving on the highlands became dangerous, fighting virtually stopped, along with many other activities. But everyone, hostile or not, moved by the same annual rhythm. As the summer congregations fragmented, the natural impulse of white authorities was to sort out the pieces. The question became whether the groups approaching Fort Lyon were belligerent or friendly.

Answers were slippery. Bands and camps were tied together basically by family, not by politics or by attitudes as shifting as current behavior toward whites. The exceptions were the Dog Soldiers, whose roots as a voluntary military society made their membership more of a political choice. They were not an issue, however, since everyone agreed on their resistance to whites, and since they and their militant sympathizers remained on the Smoky Hill, well away from the posts.

The Cheyenne and Arapaho bands that moved toward Fort Lyon were not so easily pegged. They were collections of persons who were loosely related but were fairly mixed and jumbled otherwise. Certainly they included men who had taken part in summer raids. Historically, however, the Arkansas River bands had been friendly, not from a political stance but because, as webs of families, they had traded and intermarried extensively with whites. Their leading men—Black Kettle, Ochinee, White Antelope, Yellow Wolf, Left Hand, and Little Raven—were well-known peace chiefs who had stayed out of the summer fighting. They were the least hostile of the bands, but anyone watching them file into Fort Lyon could have found blood on some hands had he looked for it.

The summer's events, and the five years before them, left many Indians and whites furious and all of them confused. The horse nomads faced desperate conditions. They had no credible solutions, and the government's botched policies left them resentful and humiliated. On all sides were victims of awful violations. Innocents had died, and common decencies had been dishonored. The parley at Camp Weld solved nothing but gave the misleading impression of calmer times ahead.

And then, just when the situation was in greatest disarray, suspicion was sharpest, and tempers at hair-trigger, the nights shortened and cooled. The season pushed the bands back along old migratory grooves toward familiar haunts. Some of those sites were now held by armed men expecting the worst, and elsewhere whites who wanted to kill Indians knew where to look. In November 1864, as hard winter approached, the plains' oldest imperative—that everything ultimately conforms to the land's harshest conditions—brought this broad unease sharply into focus in the most infamous event in the region's modern story.

ABOUT 650 ARAPAHOES under Little Raven and Left Hand arrived at Fort Lyon in mid-October. Black Kettle's people were on the way. Wynkoop issued the Arapahoes emergency rations, and they eagerly bartered for more food with bison robes taken the previous summer. Early in November, however, Wynkoop was removed, apparently a victim of complaints that he had lost control and was coddling Indians. Major Scott Anthony replaced him. Anthony was less sympathetic, to say the least, but within days he began to adopt basically the same approach. He first demanded the Arapahoes give up all arms and any stock taken from whites, then found that the surrendered guns were few and poor and their horses slat-ribbed and exhausted. In fact, he reported, the Arapahoes "could make but a feeble fight if they desired war."[47] He issued a few rations and ordered them to remain as prisoners close to the post. Anthony predicted that Black Kettle's Cheyennes would refuse to give up arms and stock and would wheel around for the Smoky Hill, but once again a meeting changed his mind: "I am satisfied that all the Arapahoes and Cheyennes who have visited this post desire peace."[48]

The problems remained, however: how to distinguish between "hostiles" and "friendlies," and how to control the second while striking the first. Muddling every question were two perennial dilemmas. First, Anthony needed to accommodate two groups of people in a place with barely enough resources for one. Specifically, he wanted Indians kept close so he could watch them, but that brought an obligation he could not meet—feeding them and their horses. Eleven months earlier, as second in command, he thought the best answer was sending the camps off to find their own food. Now, although the situation was far touchier, he could think of only the same answer. The little extra food was being given to the first arrivals, Little Raven's Arapahoes, who were being fed as prisoners. Consequently, "I shall not permit [the Cheyennes] to come in, for the reason that if I do so I shall have to subsist them upon a prisoner's ration." Instead he sent them back to Sand Creek, where they had some chance, albeit slim, for finding game.[49] That, of course, meant he could not be sure what they were up to, but he had no option. Soon, in fact, he also decided to send the Arapahoes, who "are perfectly harmless while here," away from the post, "where they can kill game to subsist upon."[50] Most drifted down the Arkansas, but several lodges associated with Left Hand joined the camp on Sand Creek.

The other dilemma was the equally persistent choice between controlling a few vital sites and moving freely over great areas. Anthony could easily defeat the warriors who had come to the fort, he said, but that would stir up those still running free, and they could just as easily disrupt travel and communication along the roads and hit outlying ranches. He could command the crucial environs around the fort but not the giant circumference where Indians had the initiative: "We are not strong enough to follow them and fight them upon their own ground."[51]

His answer was to stall, mainly by fuzzing what he told the peaceful Cheyennes and Arapahoes close by. Black Kettle and others repeatedly called for terms, but Anthony put them off. "I have been trying to let the Indians . . . think that I have no desire for trouble with them, but that I could not agree upon a permanent peace until authorized by you," he wrote his commander. His aim was "keeping matters quiet for the present, and until troops enough are sent out to enforce any demand we choose to make." Anthony hoped, that is, for an infusion of military power that would allow him to master both sides of the dilemma—holding his present position and the power to rout the bands that had come in while also patrolling the roads and locating and destroying recalcitrant camps. Once the twin keys to power, sites and mobility, were in the military's hands, all Indians, peaceful and hostile, would have to accept "any demand" presented to them.

Until then, Anthony had to keep the Indians he could control close by and peaceful and yet (juggling the first dilemma) independent of the post's scanty provisions. So when Black Kettle asked to bring his people into Fort Lyon, Anthony declined but told them that "they might camp on Sound [Sand] Creek," twenty-five miles or so to the northeast. He had no authority to conclude a permanent peace, he said, but he would consult with his superiors.

In the meantime, he wrote his commander, "I told them . . . that no war would be waged against them until your pleasure was heard."[52]

Later debates centered on whether Black Kettle's camp on Sand Creek was "hostile" and whether it had been assured of the army's protection. By the most formal terms, various answers were feasible, but by common sense there was little room for argument. Anthony and virtually everyone else in the area identified the camp as friendly and recognized that the militants were congregated north on the Smoky Hill. The lodges certainly held some men who had raided during the summer, but by that measure every Indian camp in the region was hostile. On the spectrum between belligerent and friendly, the camp on Sand Creek clearly was far toward the peaceful end. As for the second question, no one gave Black Kettle a formal promise of protection, but Anthony "told them . . . that no war would be waged against them" while his commanders were being consulted, not about whether to fight but about how to proceed with the peace. The particulars suggested Black Kettle had no reason to expect trouble. His people camped by Anthony's order where they could easily be found. On November 27 the longtime trader John Simpson Smith arrived with his son, Jack, to trade. He came with one of the Fort Lyon agent's teamsters and an army private, David Loudermilk—hardly a sign of declared hostilities.[53] Anthony gave the Cheyennes no reason to expect anything but a long, dull, hungry winter.

Anthony, on the other hand, may have been planning a later attack, for by November he was gaining a crucial advantage. As with so much else, the reason had to do with weather and horses. From late spring to midfall, the army was at a critical disadvantage in the field. Large, powerful cavalry mounts were well suited for carrying a trooper with a full pack and fighting gear, but their energy needs were enormous—at least fourteen pounds of hay or grass and twelve pounds of grain every day. That demand could be supplied only with trains of large and ponderous wagons that slowed the march of an attack column. Cut loose from the wagons and fed only on native grass, horses quickly lost weight and stamina. In a few days they were stumbling. Saddles fit poorly and began to shift even when well cinched, and soon the animals suffered running sores that were easily infected. The smaller Indian horses, by contrast, carried far lighter loads and were conditioned to rapid, far-ranging forays. Most important, they had been grass-fed since birth. During summer their fuel grew all around them. This of course was the key to their great remaining advantage—mobility. Cavalry might be lucky and find and destroy villages during the summer, but they rarely could catch the mounted warriors. When Indians fled their positions or withdrew after an attack on a white station, ranch, or outpost, they would break off gradually into smaller groups, leave myriads of dwindling trails, and easily outdistance pursuers.

But winter turned the tables. Grass, the fuel of movement, offered less nourishment as dropping temperatures required more energy. The threat of storms confined people and animals to isolated spots with limited resources, many of them now closed by white occupation. Horses weakened steadily and many died. By the time the weather eased surviving animals were saw-spined and hammer-headed, spindly shadows of their summertime selves. For most of the winter they could scarcely move themselves, much less carry their masters in a chase over the plains.

Cavalry mounts, of course, had to live under the same terms, and in fact needed even more to keep them going, but horse soldiers had a huge advantage. Besides controlling some of the best refuges, they could call on outside reserves of feed to propel their columns where they wished. Wagons of corn and oats, a hindrance in summer, became in winter an invaluable source of power, a weapon Indians could not match. Nomads were confined and immobile during the season of the minimum, when Cold Maker forced them to survive with the country's least. Whites, however, commanded the essentials to move as they wished. And when they did move, the Indians had nowhere to run.

Everyone understood this pattern, and white authorities showed every intention of exploiting it. "The time when you can make war best is in the summer time; the time when I can make war best is in the winter," Governor Evans had told Cheyenne and Arapaho leaders at the Camp Weld conference. "You so far have had the advantage," he admitted, but it was late September as the men spoke, and with every week the screw was turning. Evans drove home his point: "My time is coming."[54]

Then, on November 14, John Chivington suddenly ordered the Third Regiment of the Volunteer Cavalry out of Denver and into the field. Although their 100-day life was about to end, they had done nearly nothing after a first flurry of organization, despite continuing troubles on the plains during September and October. An army unit had routed a camp along Pawnee Fork, losing two men but killing nine, with the rest fleeing toward the Smoky Hill. In the only action by the Colorado Third, forty volunteers attacked a small camp at a spring near the Platte and killed everyone in it—six men, two women, and a boy. They reported a white woman's scalp and freighters' bills of lading in the two lodges. On November 13 Indians (either Cheyennes or

Pawnees) killed a teamster on Ash Creek near Fort Larned.[55] No threats came anywhere near the settlements along the Rockies, but Chivington kept his men in Denver—until, that is, Brig. Gen. Patrick Conner arrived from his command in Utah to look into protecting the overland mail along the Platte. Conner concluded that a campaign with a few troops against Indians spread over such an area would only stir things up, but Chivington, finding Conner's visit an irritating invasion of turf, ordered his men into the field. Stung by their nickname, "the bloodless Third," they eagerly responded.[56]

Chivington, however, did not march against the Smoky Hill camps universally recognized as the core of resistance. Instead he headed to one of the centers of white control, Fort Lyon, where he knew Indians could be found seeking winter shelter and support. When the volunteers arrived at the post on November 28, Anthony apparently made a dramatic pirouette of policy. Now that there were enough troops, he told Chivington, he supported chastising Indians throughout the region, including those he had told "that no war would be waged against them."

Immediately the decision was questioned by several prominent whites. Two stunned subordinates, Capt. Silas Soule and Lt. Joseph Cramer, pressed Anthony. Soule was especially shocked. An Englishman and earlier an ardent Free-Soiler who had been involved in a plot to save John Brown from hanging after Harper's Ferry, Soule went to Anthony and reminded him of the pledges to Black Kettle. Anthony answered that he was mainly concerned with camps on the Smoky Hill, although Black Kettle's would obviously get the first blow. He was only after men at Sand Creek who had engaged in summer raids, and Chivington had sworn that no others would be killed. Anthony "told me that I would not compromise myself by going out," Soule added, "as I was opposed to going."[57] Others focused on Chivington. A delegation of officers, local civilians, and the Indian agent, Colley, tried to dissuade him, but their questions only sent him into a pacing rage.

At 8 P.M. on November 28, Chivington led 700 troops out of Fort Lyon. Four hundred fifty were members of the Third Volunteer Cavalry, the rest from the First. Four mountain howitzers accompanied the cavalry. Also with the column were wagons filled with hay and corn issued at Fort Lyon for the well-fed horses saddled and ready for action. On the calm, cloudless night, cold but not bitter, the command moved northeastward toward Sand Creek in columns of fours.[58]

"Damn any man who is in sympathy with an Indian!" Chivington supposedly told those who tried to pull him away from attack. "And just who are the Indians?" some of the men at Fort Lyon might have wondered. Black Kettle's village was one way of life trying to live its way into another, which made it especially messy on two counts. Its people had acted out a range of answers to a maddening crisis and had met enormously difficult times with a full spread of human emotion. That allowed outsiders to find in the village such a garble of meanings, from a camp of innocent onlookers to a nest of gore-hungry hostiles. In a second way the camp was a jumble—in its open embrace of ethnic messiness. The Cheyennes, to be sure, recognized their own distinct identity, and they realized they were confronting people who saw themselves as both starkly different and superior. The Cheyennes, however, had cultivated a creative blurriness between themselves and the white culture now riding down on them. More than just tolerated, some mix and ethnic clutter had been crucial to living with a larger world. The good life had relied on some cultural interbleed. Anyone walking from lodge to lodge—or touring the surrounding region, for that matter—could not have missed the results.

Chivington himself had drafted as a guide Robert Bent, another son from the eminent lineages of William Bent and Owl Woman. Two of Robert's brothers, Charlie and George, waited at Sand Creek. Also in camp was George's and Charlie's close friend, Ed Guerrier. In September he and George Bent had written the letter of reconciliation dictated by Black Kettle and delivered to Ned Wynkoop by Ochinee, who was also in camp, having recently returned from visiting his daughter, Amache, and her husband John Prowers at their ranch on the Purgatoire. (Chivington ordered Prowers and four of his cowboys arrested and confined to prevent them from warning the village.) The Arapaho Niwot was there with his sister, Ma-Hom, John Poisal's widow, and her daughter Mary, visiting from the ranch where she lived with her husband, Ben Keith. In another lodge was John Simpson Smith. Besides his Cheyenne wife, Zarepta, and his older son, Jack, he shared his space with the Cheyenne wife of a Fort Lyon sutler, Charlie Windsor. Also in his lodge was Smith and Zarepta's youngest child, a four-year-old boy named as another hopeful bridge between cultures: William Gilpin Smith.[59]

The connections snaked out from this camp as interwoven lines of blood and fictive kinships, economic alliances, loyalties, and affections among Native American and white families who lived and moved over 50,000 square miles of the central plains. This cross-fertilization was the healthy growth of the Tsistsistas who had leaned farthest toward trading and working with whites. It was central to the social and emotional world of the central plains at the moment gold was discovered.

It was also anathema to the new ways. For six years goldseekers, town-builders, freighters, ranchers, and farmers had laid down their own social and moral order, broadly conceived. People were sorted, with some solidly above others. Lines had to be firm. Smeared boundaries were a sign of corruption, not health. The rich ethnic muddle was still there, of course. It survived openly where power recognized it. At Robert Moore's ranch up the Arkansas, Mary Bent Moore, daughter of William and Owl Woman, perhaps was practicing her fine piano skills as Chivington led his men out of Fort Lyon. Downstream at Walnut Creek Station, Making Out Road and her daughter, Cheyenne White Girl, were most likely helping Charles Rath in his round of work. But at the warm heart of the new order, in Denver and towns along the mountain foot, the old muddiness would not be recognized, much less accepted.

The Colorado Volunteers who rode out of Denver were more than a military force chasing perceived adversaries, and more than enforcers of a new economic regime. They were also cultural shock troops. The Sand Creek camp, with its ethnic sloppiness and its tangle of links that bound an older social order, was an intolerable affront. Chivington's command rode out to set things straight, and on their own terms.

THE SITE of Black Kettle's camp remains uncertain. It lay some-where along the old trail connecting the big timbers of the Smoky Hill to the timbers, or rather where the timbers had been, on the Arkansas, now the site of Fort Lyon. This path had been used by the horse nomads from their earliest occupation and probably was traveled by natives on foot for centuries before that. Fremont had roughly followed it on his return in 1844 when he crossed from the Arkansas at Bent's Fort to the upper Smoky Hill. After William Bent built his second fort at the timbers, his hunters had shuttled along the trail on meat-gathering forays. Black Kettle's band naturally turned up this road when Anthony sent them away to fend for themselves. About forty miles to the northeast they set up camp on Sand Creek somewhere near the trail's crossing.

By the irreducible demands of a winter camp, they chose a spot offering hard fuel, pasture, water, and protecting landforms. More than 120 lodges stood in a sharp bend of the creek's wide, level streambed. There were low bluffs to break the wind; the water flowed after a rain and otherwise stood in clear pools. Clusters of willows grew among cottonwoods that stood tall and leafless along the sandy bottom. One horse herd was pastured on a flat immediately east of the camp, another on a broad shelf above the bluffs. Black Kettle had followed the seasonal rule and put his people down in one of those rare sanctuaries for the cold months ahead. The main failing of this spot—the lack of food in badly overhunted country—was unavoidable, given his decision to stay close to Fort Lyon.

The first alarm at dawn on November 29, then, was a cry of disbelieving hope—a woman's excited call that a large herd of bison were rumbling toward the camp. Others saw quickly that the hammering came from mounted soldiers advancing in formation. Chivington's troops, after traveling briskly all night, were approaching from the south, with some maneuvering into position and others waiting for the word to attack. John Smith and David Louderback, the soldier Anthony had sent with Smith, hurried out, waving a coat and a white handkerchief on a stick, but gunfire drove them back. The teamster with Smith tied a bison hide to a lodge pole and waved it vigorously; bullets sent him, too, running for shelter.[60]

Downstream Chivington shouted to "remember the murdered women and children on the Platte" and sent his men in. George Bent rushed from his lodge to see cavalry coming up the creekbed at a fast trot. The camp was in chaos:

> men, women, and children rushing out of the lodges partly dressed; women and children screaming at the sight of troops; men running back into the lodges for their arms, other men, already armed, or with lassos and bridles in their hands, running for the herds to attempt to get some of the ponies before the troops could reach the animals and drive them off. I looked toward the chief's lodge and saw that Black Kettle had a large American flag tied to the end of a long lodgepole and was standing in front of his lodge, holding the pole, with a flag fluttering in the grey light of the winter dawn. I heard him call to the people not to be afraid, that the soldiers would not hurt them; then the troops opened fire from two sides of the camp.[61]

White Antelope first ran down the center of the shallow creek, waving frantically at the advancing horsemen, then stood with arms crossed over his chest. The cavalry shot him and rode past.

The cannons lobbed shells from the south while two groups of mounted soldiers moved quickly to separate the camp from the horse herds, then turned to open fire on the camp. The warriors knew their situation was impossible once they were cut off from their mounts. Caught by surprise, badly outnumbered and hopelessly underarmed, panicked by the bursts of shell and grapeshot, the men briefly formed a broken skirmish line before breaking and running for cover. A few found horses and galloped off toward the Smoky Hill villages, and small groups slipped through the smoke and made a dash across the plains. Of the rest, those not killed or crippled among the lodges fled upstream, the only direction free of soldiers. Many hastily dug holes in the dry sand where the high bank was broken by ravines; Chivington later argued these were previously prepared rifle pits that proved the Indians understood they were at war. The refugees crowded this last asylum.

Silas Soule kept his men from firing a shot—Chivington wrote indignantly that the captain "thanked God he had killed no Indians"—but watched others direct a withering fire into the pits. John Smith "saw altogether some seventy dead bodies there; the greater portion women and children."[62] George Bent shared a pit he helped dig with two young girls and their parents. The father "jumped out of the hole and ran towards the Troops that were coming upon us and as he came back into the hole he told me and his wife that he was killed. The Troops were coming near us when myself and two others, Spotted Horse and Bear Shield, jumped out of the hole. Balance of [those who stayed] were all killed, and the two girls taken away." Black Kettle ran back through the rifle fire toward the camp to look for his wife, Ar-no-ho-wah (Woman To Be Here After). He found her near their lodge, and although she had been shot several times he was able to pull her back to shelter.[63]

Ochinee, Knock Knee, War Bonnet, Yellow Shield, and Two Thighs were killed in the camp or the pits. So was Yellow Wolf, the central figure in shifting the southern bands to the Arkansas more than thirty years earlier. Niwot, terribly wounded, escaped but died a few days later. Charlie Bent surrendered and was protected by some New Mexicans. John Smith and others in his lodge were spared in the battle, but the next day his son, Jack, was murdered. Ma-hom and Mary Poisal survived. Although Chivington and others would claim up to 500 Indian dead, the total was around 150. Nine volunteers and soldiers were killed and four more died before the first of the year; how many were killed by hostile or friendly fire was unclear.[64]

The pandemonium was finally over by midafternoon. Volunteers and soldiers picked over the village, took what they wanted, and the next day burned the lodges. Some cut fingers from the dead to take the rings. The extent of other mutilations, as with so much about the battle, became a matter of debate. Some men, almost entirely members of the Third, testified that few or no bodies were violated. Several cavalrymen and civilians told of scalping, body parts hacked away, including women's genitals, even corpses pulled from shallow graves the next day to be further butchered. Chivington testified that he saw no mutilations, no dead children, and only two dead women. One, he said, had hanged herself.[65]

By nightfall survivors straggled northeastward toward the Smoky Hill villages. Those better off covered the injured with grass to give them some warmth. Few slept. Some warriors slipped back toward the village to look for any left alive—there were several alarms that night of attacking savages—while others stood guard as the wounded and grieving moaned and wailed. Before sunrise, stiff and sore, they were on the move. Soon they were met by groups from the Smoky Hill who brought horses, robes, and meat and escorted them to camp.

Chivington first said he would move to the Smoky Hill "to look for more fighting," but instead he returned to the Arkansas in search of Little Raven's Arapahoes, the band that had come in before Black Kettle and been kept on prisoners' rations.[66] Those camps had scattered after hearing of Sand Creek, however, and on December 7 the command started home. Three days before Christmas the volunteers marched into Denver and were greeted by the huzzahs and toasts of happy crowds who filled the streetsides and thronged the saloons. William Byers's *Rocky Mountain News* judged that the campaign would have few rivals among all "the brilliant feats of arms in Indian warfare."[67]

The next day Anthony wrote his brother from Fort Lyon in a blind rage.[68] He had greeted Chivington with great enthusiasm. Here was a rare coincidence of military strength, supplies, and environmental circumstance. Indians, friendly and hostile, were not roaming but in winter camp. Seven hundred fighting men with artillery and ample firearms could find those camps and inflict terrible losses, perhaps even break for good the nomads' resistance. The troops had horses and, more important, wagons to carry fodder, the fuel of winter mobility. Chivington commanded both keys to power—essential sites and the ability to move freely and aggressively.

But he had squandered his opportunity. "He has whipped the only peaceable Indians in the country, (which I wanted him to do if he would go further)," Anthony wrote, but "after having got almost within sight of other Indians, turned back with the largest & best outfitted command that ever went against Indians in the locality, while everything was favorable." Chivington's claims of deep snow and tired horses were lies, he continued, "I say that no command can come from the states with as good stock; the weather was . . . delightful for this time of the year; the season just the right one for an Indian campaign." Yet Chivington had turned away.

And for what? "I am inclined to think the Colonel dared not risk a longer trip into the hostile Indian country for fear he could not get promoted before reports in detail were published," Anthony decided. Politics, the most shadowy and unstable means of control, had seduced Chivington from an attempt at real power. Riding out of Fort Lyon on the starry night of November 28, Anthony implied, Chivington saw the plains at an instant of unique possibility, but he missed the point, and so he missed his chance. Grabbing at one kind of power, he had thrown away another, the kind that had ruled the country for 12,000 years.

As ANTHONY PREDICTED, Cheyennes and Arapahoes responded with an unmatched fury. Within days they were raiding on the Platte near Plum Creek Station, and after the first of the year they hit again and again at ranches and stores along the route. In the last week of January at least seven road ranches were burned and more than 1,500 cattle stolen, and a little later all buildings at the major stopping place of Julesburg were destroyed. At least thirty soldiers, freighters, travelers, and settlers died in the assaults.[69]

Politically the raids resulted in an utterly predictable shift from accommodationists to the militants. The turning tide was clear in the first hours after Sand Creek. "It was awful when we got to the village," George Bent remembered of his arrival on the Smoky Hill: "The whole camp was in an uproar of crying and weeping, as it was customary for [the] whole village to mourn." Warriors "were a little angry at Black K[ettle] at 1st, but soon got over that." Instead they immediately realigned for revenge. At the Camp Weld Conference Cheyenne and Arapaho leaders had firmly denied being in league with hostile Lakotas, particularly Spotted Tail. Now they joined the Lakota leader on the Republican and soon were striking toward the Platte, "as there were more ranches there, it was nearest and [there was the] most travel on that road."[70] The attacks were even more extraordinary because they came in winter, when movement was hardest, raids were riskiest, and horses the most vulnerable. The campaign showed the warrior horsemen at their most dedicated and furious.

Ironically, the winter assault marked the limit of their threat. In far calmer times Evans had predicted that warriors might annihilate white Colorado. The full brunt, however, revealed fewer than fifty killed, property losses of several thousand dollars, and a few weeks' disruption of commerce and travel.

Merchants who avoided attack found the whole disturbance a boon. One reportedly made $25,000 that year, most of it during the war and a good bit from selling soldiers whiskey at fifty cents a jigger.[71] Within a year virtually everything lost had been rebuilt and business was as brisk as ever. The predicted death blow turned out to be a black eye.

If the disaster at Sand Creek proved to many people the bankruptcy of the peace and trade strategy, the fierce offensive of 1864–1865 showed just as clearly the hopelessness of the militants' position. With some freedom to move and raid they could obstruct and harass and inflict some suffering, but they could not win back what was lost or reverse the trends of the day. The free-roaming culture of the Called Out People was doomed.

Still, for four years the details were spun out. Eleven months after Sand Creek white officials appeared to grapple with some of the issues at hand. The Treaty of the Little Arkansas began with an elaborate apology. After extensive investigations the army and Congress concluded that the attack had been a deplorable act against a peaceful village. Because Chivington had resigned his commission in January, he was beyond the army's reach, but the government officially condemned the "gross and wanton outrages" surrounding Sand Creek, granted a section of land each to mixed-blood relations of Cheyennes and Arapahoes and a quarter section to any tribal member who lost a family member in the massacre. Reparations were promised for property destroyed. Cheyenne and Arapaho signatories agreed to accept a reservation in Indian Territory and part of southern Kansas. Thirty years of annuities were provided, and all sides, as usual, pledged to keep the peace. A similar treaty was signed with Kiowas, Comanches, and Plains Apaches.[72]

Once again, however, the people whose consent was needed most, the Dog Soldiers, took no part. The elaborate apologies would probably have meant little anyway, for the year since Sand Creek had brought two infuriating developments. In summer 1865 the Butterfield Overland Despatch opened stage and mail service up the Smoky Hill valley along the old central route, the "cannibal road" of 1859 that a few individuals had always tried to boost. In June 1865 the staging kingpin David Butterfield sent a new survey party, which submitted a typically glowing report. The Smoky Hill was "the garden spot and hunting ground of America," surrounded by "the richest pasture in the world." Far up its course the river might float a large steamboat, and higher up was ample pasture and plenty of water and trees, especially at the big timbers, the famous stand of cottonwoods that "used to be a celebrated camping ground for Indians." The final stretch, in the general region of the old "starvation trail," was also described as an easy passage. And the Indians? "We saw no signs," the surveyor reported. The country was apparently abandoned, the author speculated, and if not he was sure the government fully intended to protect the route. To that end he included several suggestions for fortifications.[73]

Within four months the army had established two major posts in the previously inviolate middle country. Fort Hays (first called Fort Fletcher) was built on the Smoky Hill roughly halfway between its head and its junction with the Kansas River. Fort Wallace (initially Camp Pond Creek) was close to the Colorado border more than 100 miles upstream. Fort Wallace was especially galling to the Indians. It sat in the middle of prime hunting terrain only twenty miles from the thick stand of cottonwoods, the grove that had given the Smoky Hill its Cheyenne name, the Bunch of Timber. The survey report to the contrary, the nomads spent their winters there, tanned their robes in summer, and laid out their dead in the great trees' welcoming arms. The army's threat was immediate. Contractors building Fort Wallace "cut down the fine old trees and entirely destroyed the grove," the veteran mountain man Richens (Uncle Dick) Wootton recalled. Arapahoes and Cheyennes then "declared that for every tree the white men had cut down they would kill a white man"; he added, "and I reckon they did it."[74]

The Dog Soldiers' response to the dual challenge of the forts and the Butterfield stages was relatively restrained—thefts of stock and a few raids on stations, which were built at prime spots for forage and water. Tension mounted, however, from the same dilemmas of power. Soldiers at Fort Wallace could do only what others had done elsewhere—control one important place and try to do their best to protect lines of travel. Troops were in the field much of the time, escorting stages and occasionally searching out Indian camps, but it was difficult to say who was pursuing and who was pursued. By winter 1866–1867, with rumors of war in the air, a crisis was building much like the one that had lead to Sand Creek.

In April 1867 Gen. William Sherman, newly appointed commander of the Military Division of the Missouri, ordered his field commander, Maj. Gen. Winfield Scott Hancock, to the Arkansas valley with 1,400 men to assert control over Indians thought to be close to full-scale assaults. Camped at Fort Larned were a large number of Cheyennes and Lakotas, a mix (again in a repeat of earlier confusions) of bands leaning toward both accommodation and raiding. When Hancock moved his camp close to the Indians, they abandoned their village and fled in the night, fearing another Sand Creek, and when they again attacked stage stations on the Smoky Hill, Hancock ordered their village destroyed. Nearly 300 lodges were burned, and everything in them, including more than 800 bison robes, was seized.

With that the Dog Soldiers blistered the roads and outposts in eastern Colorado and then along the Smoky Hill. At one point warriors were firing "torpedo arrows" with percussion caps on the arrowheads.[75] Losses were heavy among civilians and soldiers, and at one point Fort Wallace was virtually beseiged. Making matters worse was a major outbreak of Asiatic cholera among the troops. One officer was encouraged: "I do hope that the Indians will get the Cholera! One of our Delawares died of it—so it appears that Indians are not exempt." His wish may have been answered. In a large abandoned camp along the Republican, he wrote his wife a short time later, "we found some Indian graves in the trees and on platforms of poles—the dead were mostly children—very little fellows most of them!"[76]

Hancock's War did not pacify the area, but it did add to the pressure for another try at coming to terms, especially after a government-appointed Peace Commission also called for new efforts at treaty-making. The result was a huge gathering and major treaty on Medicine Lodge Creek, between the Arkansas and Cimarron Rivers. The new terms provided for permanent removal of Cheyennes, Arapahoes, Comanches, Kiowas, and Kiowa-Apaches to a reservation in western Indian Territory. The tribes were allowed to hunt south of the Arkansas, but the terms pushed them hard toward the "civilized" life of farmers and stockraisers. Children would be educated in traditional schoolhouses; women would be issued flannel skirts and men given pantaloons, hats, and homemade socks. After considerable pressure, several militants—Tall Bull, Bull Bear, Satanta, Satank, and others—made their marks on the treaties, although reluctantly. Bull Bear, perhaps recalling his brother's death, jabbed the quill pen entirely through the paper.[77]

The aftermath was as confused as ever. Some signers followed the terms, more or less. Black Kettle's followers moved where they were told, although they ranged north in summer in search of food. In August 1868 an officer at Fort Hays wrote his cousin that Little Raven's and Black Kettle's bands stopped at the post on their way to fight Pawnees. "We have come on a long 'journey,'" Black Kettle told the commander. "The waters are dried up and Buffalo are scarce [and] we heard that you fed Indians who came to your post. . . . You have a fine village and pleasant Post. We are glad."[78] Others, however, said they had been coerced at the Medicine Lodge council and had misunderstood the terms. Younger militants continued defiance—but they still expected annuities.

Most Dog Soldiers stayed in their beloved middle country, which by now was feeling pressure on two new fronts. The farming frontier was seeping in from the east, into the lower and middle valleys of the Saline, Solomon, and Republican. Farmers posed the ultimate threat to any vestige of independent nomadic life. And with sodbusters came another challenge just as great. Nine years earlier, when Russell and Jones had run their first stages through that country, orators had filled the air with visions of iron horses galloping close behind. They were slow to snort, but the Kansas Division of the Union Pacific Railroad began building along the central route after the Civil War, and by 1868 it was beyond Fort Harker and pressing westward.[79] When completed to Denver, the band of rails fulfilled the conquering vision of uniting the mountains with the borderland.

That summer saw yet another season of raids and counterraids. Dog Soldiers and others harassed and delayed the railroad construction as best they could, but they could not stop it. There were bloody incidents among the homesteads. The army retaliated with forays and an intriguing experiment—a collection of seasoned civilian scouts organized as a fighting unit. In August 1868 this group, under Maj. George Forsyth and Lt. Fred Beecher, was surprised along the Arickaree Fork of the Republican. They fled to an island and made a stand behind breastworks and the horses they shot. In a remarkable seige they held off their attackers until help came a week later, by the end eating prickly pear, coyotes, and soup from putrid horsemeat. The Cheyennes lost several men at what was called the Battle of Beecher's Island, including their prominent warrior Roman Nose, but the white heroics could not hide the obvious: the Dog Soldiers still held the initiative in their homeland.

On the first anniversary of the Treaty of Medicine Lodge Creek central and western Kansas was again at war after young Cheyennes and Arapahoes, generally restless and specifically irritated by the agent's refusal to issue firearms, raged through the Solomon and Saline valleys, destroying homesteads, killing fifteen men, and raping five women. In official circles the tide had shifted again toward confrontation. The troubles of 1868 added to the support of Peace Commission members who called for a tougher stance. One of them, Sherman, had never had much patience with plains tribes or much hope for mutual possession of the country. "At best we can give [Indians] a chance . . . to so prepare things that our own people may progress in their legitimate routes," he wrote a fellow officer and commission member who favored a search for accommodation. A month later he added, "A few [Indians] may be rescued from destruction but they will not as a whole work the soil, and must be simple paupers or work." As continued fighting strengthened his political position, Sherman turned away from further talk of compromise. "I cannot represent two opposing views, for a man of action must have positive plans," he wrote: "Now this must come to a violent end."[80]

That last blunt opinion carried a certain logic. Whites and Native Americans were trying to live out irreconcilable images of what the plains were to be, which was like trying to pour sand into a bucket full of water without losing any of either. Confrontation was inevitable. As Sand Creek had shown, however, commanders looking for "a violent end" might seek it against those Indians who were not their true opponents. In early winter 1868 Gen. Philip Sheridan commanded a pacification campaign that ended with this same lesson. Rather than moving into the heartland of resistance, the campaign bore down on the area south of Fort Lyon. There a column commanded by Lt. Col. George A. Custer followed a trail through the snow to attack Black Kettle's Cheyenne village on the Washita River in the western part of Indian Territory, an area set aside for reservation bands. A portion of Custer's attackers was isolated and wiped out, but the Cheyennes lost more than 100 persons, including Black Kettle and his wife, Woman To Be Here After.[81]

The familiar cycle followed its path. Furious Dog Soldiers struck back in spring 1869. Warriors attacked Kansas Pacific crews and battered the farmsteads that grew like breadmold farther down the central valleys and on the Big Sandy in Nebraska. They ravaged a recent German settlement, killing thirteen and carrying away two women as captives. Residents and the governor of Nebraska pled for help, and on the first day of June Gen. Christopher Augur, commander of the Department of the Platte, answered with the obvious: the only way to secure the settlements was "to drive the Indians entirely out of the Republican country. This is what I hope to do this summer."[82]

A week later Maj. Eugene Carr and the Fifth Cavalry left Fort McPherson to carry out Augur's pledge. Carr brought with him another innovation—like the company of civilian scouts at Beecher's Island—a battalion of Pawnees, perennial enemies of the Cheyennes, that had recently been formed into their own unit under the command of Maj. Frank North. At a pivotal moment this experiment turned out to be crucial. Chief of scouts was William F. Cody,

already something of a local celebrity for his good looks, gregarious personality, and his prodigious killing of buffaloes to feed railroad construction crews.
The expedition was a large one. Carr brought fifty-four supply wagons, as
well as his two greyhounds. Cody brought his own wagonful of groceries to
sell to soldiers on the side.[83]

Over the next few weeks Carr worked his way southeast to the Republican River and beyond it to the Solomon, but his men had only brief contact
with their quarry, once when some Dog Soldiers tried to steal the mules. He
turned back northwest to the Republican and ascended it through the valley
Francis Bryan had described so exuberantly thirteen years earlier. They
passed the Republican's big timbers, which Carr called the "Thickwood," and
moved up the Arikaree Fork, past the battle remains at Beecher's Island from
the year before and the site where hunters had butchered more than 300
Bison antiquus 10,000 years earlier. Still there were no Cheyennes.[84]

Past the Frenchman's Fork (or North Fork), however, Carr's men began
to find abandoned camps and had a brief brush with some warriors, but
still they had little reason to think their enemies were close. That changed
late on July 8. It was nearly midnight when several Dog Soldiers galloped
into the cavalry's remuda, yelling and reining their mounts in close circles
and trying to stampede the herd. Then they raced directly through the Pawnees' camp, firing and screaming taunts, before fleeing out the other end
and away. Both sides found chances for more tales of courage. In the turmoil a Pawnee, Mad Bull, was killed by friendly fire (and posthumously
awarded the Medal of Honor) as he faced the raiders and tried to rally his
men. A Dog Soldier, Yellow Nose, fell and broke his arm in the run out of
camp. He managed to hide in a shallow ravine, literally at his pursuers'
feet, before crawling away to a streambed and walking two days back to his
camp.[85]

Without knowing it Carr had camped a short distance from a large number of both Dog Soldiers and Lakotas. Their acknowledged leader was Tall
Bull, a near-legendary warrior and perhaps the most eminent surviving Dog
Soldier. The audacious midnight raid apparently was meant to gain some
horses as well as to engage in a bit of nervy beard-pulling before retreating
with a typical maneuver. Tall Bull told the camps to disperse in three directions. The groups would gradually split and split again, leaving the branching
of trails that always frustrated pursuers. Tall Bull struck westward toward
the South Platte with most of his warriors. Moving easily on quick horses

well fed by summer grasses, the Cheyennes had every reason to think this strategy would leave their pursuers as confused and exhausted as it had in the past.

This time, however, the Pawnees with Carr predicted Tall Bull's maneuver and guessed correctly where he was heading. Carr believed them, and rather than dividing his command he led it in a direct line toward the area where the Pawnees had thought the warrior camp would be found. The move was as audacious as the Dog Soldiers' nighttime attack, and it worked. With good advice, intuition, and luck, Carr overcame the horse nomads' traditional summertime advantage.

Tall Bull and his people crossed the creekless highlands of wallows and buffalo grass, familiar earlier campgrounds of Querechos and many before them, and descended to the South Platte on July 10. He probed the river for the best crossing. Some of his men crossed the South Platte immediately, but Tall Bull was especially concerned about the exhausted women, children, and elderly and wanted more time to find an easier ford. Confident that the whites were far behind, he put his people in camp nearby at some springs at the base of White Butte, intending to cross the river the next day. Some horses were tied next to their owners' tipis but most were pastured well away from camp—the ultimate sign of confidence that the camp was safe.

It was a mistake. Led by the Pawnees Carr guided his command directly to the South Platte. Crossing and recrossing Frenchman's Fork, the Fifth Cavalry covered more than sixty miles in two days, and although tired from the rapid march in searing heat, they pressed ahead to take advantage of the luck they hoped they had. Late in the afternoon of July 10 they camped about twenty miles south of the Dog Soldiers. They were up and on the move by 5:00 A.M. the next day. After moving for hours through heavy sand, Carr was discouraged—"I began to think the whole thing was a humbug"—but in midafternoon the main Cheyenne encampment was spotted. Carr brought his men as close as possible, formed them into two ranks of parallel columns, then ordered his bugler to sound the charge.[86]

During the cavalry's rapid move Tall Bull had been in no hurry to cross the river and continue his own march. His men lounged in and around their lodges for several hours as the cool morning of July 11 gave way to a hazy and humid day. About 3:00 P.M., eleven years and five days after William Green Russell's discovery of gold upstream on Dry Creek, Carr's troops and their Pawnee allies swept into the Dog Soldiers' camp. Tall Bull and a friend heard the call that people were coming, but he dismissed the notion until the shooting started. Running out of his lodge, he saw immediately that the situation was desperate.

The attackers had charged from one full mile away, and the smaller, better-conditioned horses of the Pawnees carried them into the camp first, with the heavy cavalry mounts not far behind. Cheyenne warriors who could grab their horses bolted for protection, but many were unable to get to the herd and so were left afoot in camp. With the women and children, many began a headlong flight toward the river. Several mounted Dog Soldiers, particularly Two Crows, Pile of Bones, Lone Bear, and Plenty of Bull Meat, fought hard to shield the women and children trying to escape, but the Pawnees, elated at the rare occasion of having the upper hand against relentless enemies, killed and scalped many of them. Carr's troops also pursued the fleeing Cheyennes through the brutal heat and thick dust. Some refugees escaped, but only because the cavalry mounts gave out more than four miles from the battle site. Of the thirteen horses lost in Carr's command, only one was killed by Indians. The rest dropped and died of exhaustion.

Meanwhile troops were quickly tearing through the village. They found the two women captives, one dead and the other shot. In the sudden attack the Dog Soldiers' main herd was isolated and captured. Carr's men eventually rounded up 274 horses and 144 mules—a devastating loss to the retreating Cheyennes. In the camp they also found hundreds of saddles and fifty-six rifles, powder, lead and percussion caps, sabres, war shields, lances, and knives. There were nearly 10,000 pounds of bison meat and nearly 700 robes as well as moccasins, kettles, hammers, shovels, 100 pounds of tobacco, and $1,500 in gold and bank notes. Some of this was taken. The rest was piled and burned in a huge mound with the eighty-four lodges. In all ways the battle was a rout and a calamity, the effective end of the Dog Soldiers as a force of resistance.[87]

When Tall Bull realized his fatal error, he reportedly called out, "All of you who are on foot and cannot get away, follow me!" He helped one wife and a daughter escape on a horse, then led his other two wives into a nearby ravine, a temporary refuge that was soon an inescapable trap. Many others followed him to find shelter there, including the elderly chief Powder Face, his wife, his son Black Moon, and several younger warriors.

One of the bravest was Wolf With Plenty of Hair. He had been honored with a Dog Rope, and now, as the soldiers and Pawnees tightened their circle around the ravine, he drove the red peg into the ground and stood ready to fight. His body, riddled but still tethered, was found after the firing finally stopped. Tall Bull put his wives as far back in the ravine as he could. He then returned to the gully's mouth, where his followers were firing from the protection of natural stone walls. He was leading his horse. Positioning the animal between him and his enemies, he pulled his knife and drove the blade deep behind the pony's foreleg. As it buckled and quivered into death, Tall Bull waited behind his horse, in his own chosen place to die.[88]

12

EPILOGUE: STORIES IN THE TEETH

OF LIFE

Nellie Buchanan and her husband were determined to homestead on the frontier, and in the mid-1870s western Kansas was an obvious choice. With a wagon, twenty-four chickens, and six cows they headed west from Atchison toward the Rockies. Two days past the last settlement they came across a sod house. The owner advised them to turn around, but they persisted. For two more days they saw no one and found only one structure, an empty hut where they took shelter for a night. For yet another two days there was no sign of human presence. Then, about noon the next day, they saw an unnatural bump on the horizon. As they drew near, they realized it was a covered farm wagon. On its sheeted side was a welcoming sign in large, bold letters: "RESTURANT."[1]

Spelling aside, this wagon eatery explained clearly the course of events after 1858. It is also a reminder that the nomadic tribes were up against much more than soldiers and an unsympathetic government. With the discovery of gold the plains and mountains became another place, not yet in fact but, more important, in the minds of people with the power to act. The country from the Missouri River to the Rockies was rethought as the vital core of a rising empire. True, it lacked almost completely any farms and white communities, but in the heads of people with money and will, the plains were already a place of nascent fields and seeded towns. Restaurants were ordained.

Within a decade of the gold rush the plains nomads had lost the power to pursue the life they envisioned. That did not end the story, however, for the good reason that the story never ends. Just as the horse nomads had been caught in dilemmas embedded in their own vision, so the new visionaries confronted the contradictions in their dream of the plains as an extravagant gardenland bound to mountains of gold. As the white masters set new changes in motion, they inherited the ancient job of living with a demanding country. They soon discovered that power has meaning only within limits.

BLACK KETTLE STANDS under a U.S. flag beside his tipi, staring in disbelief at the charging troops, as White Antelope waits in the middle of Sand Creek, arms folded across his chest.

Tall Bull holds his bloody knife behind his dying horse as Wolf with Plenty of Hair watches nearby, staked on his sacred leash.

The two images are strikingly alike, but the paths that led to them were starkly different. Called to greatness, the Tsistsistas first confronted the limits of the story they composed for themselves, then they faced the power of others summoned by their own imagined land. Some Cheyennes looked for a way to reconcile their vision with that of the new invaders. Others persisted in the great dream and withdrew to where they could still imagine it whole. Both courses led to the same place: standing in a last refuge, waiting to be ridden down.

The wounded, demoralized survivors of Summit Springs fled to Lakota camps on the Frenchman's Fork of the Republican. Some stayed with Northern Cheyenne and Dakota and kept fighting. Many eventually moved south to the Cheyenne and Arapaho reservation where survivors from Black Kettle's people and others were living.[2] In victory's final step white society took mythic control of the story. Within months of Summit Springs William Cody, as Buffalo Bill, first appeared in a dime novel, and more than thirty-five years later a twisted enactment of the battle remained the centerpiece of Cody's wild west show, popular testimony of heroism and progress triumphant.

The Tsistsistas persevered, however, sustained by loyalty to Maheo and to Sweet Medicine's vision. On the reservation they maintained their resilience in the face of the humiliating stresses they had first known at Fort Lyon and Point of Rocks—fudged assurances, corruption, being forgotten.[3] Old fractures continued, especially a division rooted in the split between the Indians who had leaned toward or against accommodation.[4] But their adaptive genius survived. A century later tribal gatherings still drew into a sacred circle every year in high summer. Bands and warrior societies arranged themselves in careful and revealing order, performed renewing sacraments, and kept the story alive.

The central plains meanwhile were swept clear of other Native Americans, who were often caught in the same dismal circumstances. In 1867 a village of Wichitas, perhaps distant descendants of the villagers Coronado had met more than 300 years earlier, contracted cholera from the soldiers escorting them to a reservation on the Washita River. More than 100 died. Survivors headed south in winter but were caught in a storm-driven prairie fire that burned to death eighty-five of their horses. They began to walk the rest of the way, but cholera then reemerged. So many died at one camp that the bodies had to be left beside what came to be called Skeleton Creek. The remnant that straggled into the village on the Washita brought the contagion to those already there. Many died in their lodges, which were then burned.[5]

By 1870 whites were virtually uncontested on the central plains. Transformations continued along the corridors of the Platte and Arkansas. Freight trains rolled on until rail lines were completed, whereupon the number of oxen plummeted and the flow of goods rose sharply. The various connected enterprises fed off each other, with a few men squeezing fortunes out of each exchange. John Burke, the German who began with a store at Cottonwood Springs, dug the area's first ditch, raised oats and vegetables, and sold hay to the army at Fort McPherson. With the help of a tram railway over a divide to Cut Canyon, the nearest source of trees, he supplied fuel to locals and soldiers, poles for the telegraph, and railroad ties to Union Pacific crews. By one account, 30,000 cords sometimes were ricked up at his main wood camp, with profits well over 100 percent. Burke found yet another way to milk his excellent location. He built bridges near Fort McPherson and charged forty-five cents per hundredweight for everything carried across. In June 1872, while helping ferry goods after a bridge was washed out, he fell overboard and was drowned. His fat probate file revealed a mercantile empire, from warehouses and cattle herds to old overcoats and women's hair combs.[6]

The last resources on the two great rivers passed to the new lords—or were used up entirely. Ranching boomed along the Platte, especially as the Union Pacific provided easy transport back East, and along the Arkansas after the Atchison, Topeka and Santa Fe built up the valley in the early 1870s. Although facilities at first were primitive—the first ranch headquarters on the Arkansas were dug into riverbanks and drovers lived in wagons—the cattle increased prodigiously. Within a few years of the first herds driven north out of Texas and pastured along the road where oxen from freight trains had grazed for fifty years, most of the land along the Arkansas was taken up from Dodge to beyond the Colorado line.[7] Earlier cattlemen extended their control, exploiting each historical twist and point of law that offered an opening.

As always, the story was morally messy, as demonstrated by the valley's leading rancher. The Treaty of the Little Arkansas had awarded a section of land to each of several mixed-blood Cheyennes and Arapahoes with relatives at Sand Creek. Local tradition said that the grantees "selected choice river bottom acres, but being nomads, they soon were anxious to trade their lands for money and be on the move again." Enter John Prowers, whose own children were recipients. Prowers quickly bought up the "blood land" at a bargain, and was criticized, but defenders argued he "was only an alert frontiersman."[8] Whether helping his Cheyenne kinsmen or milking them, Prowers tightened his grip on the valley. By then his books show that he was bringing in regular "wood trains" and "lumber trains" from the mountains to feed local demand.[9] They were necessary. In 1871 surveyors set their stakes and transits along the Arkansas bottoms where the big timbers had dominated the land—and its history—for generations. In their notes they mentioned ranches, hay fields, and, again and again, "land gently rolling. Soil 1st rate. No timber."[10]

Roads showed the ultimate sign of total white control: they became fun. By the late 1860s wealthy sportsmen, including European royalty, were playing the hearty nimrod where Indians were making their last stands as subsistence hunters. A visit by the Russian Grand Duke Alexis in 1872 was only the most famous of many outings.[11] The *Leavenworth Daily Conservative* in 1866 reported "Lords, Dukes, Barons, Squires, or whatever they may be called" in the buffalo country. One was Friedrich von Holstein, a supercilious young Prussian diplomat who later served under Bismarck and played a role in the Dreyfus affair. Like many visitors he considered border residents a "race of swindlers and horse-thieves," but the sublime life of plains hunting left him with "the Wallenstein-like feeling that 'here a man is still worth something.'"[12]

"I do not think I was ever in a more perfect hunting-ground than this was in those days," a sportsman recalled of the Republican valley in the mid-1860s, adding some after-the-fact bravado: "The danger from Indians [gave] it that dash of excitement which is always needed to make any life really perfect." With the advent of railroads a much larger crowd came into play. Excursions, such as the group of scientists who rode through western Kansas to hunt bison, could gawk at what had been the lifeblood of plains tribes: "'Oh, my, what monsters!' 'What beards!' 'What horns!' 'Beats a steeple-chase!' . . . 'Sure, they're going home from a divil's wake!'"[13] Once the rails were open to common folk, the whole region and its purposes—farming, ranching, and emerging tourism—were knit together cleanly and tightly. Newlywed homesteaders Gus and Mary Magdalene Brulport went by wagon and train from Rush County, Kansas, to the Front Range. They visited the Garden of the Gods and Manitou Springs, sighed at the scenery ("It was grand"), and bathed in hot springs. On the way out they stopped in Dodge City, where they saw a cattle herd cross the Arkansas, attended the opera, watched Cheyennes perform a "war dance," and listened to a lecture, "Morality."[14]

In 1870 a sickly Canadian, P. G. Scott, came to eastern Colorado in search of a job and improved health. His journal described a country remade, its power fully grasped by a people who had seen it as alien terrain only a dozen years earlier. He began with a ride on the Kansas Pacific to the new town of Kit Carson, along the Smoky Hill road not far from the Blue brothers' cannibalistic route of 1859. He passed near where the Sand Creek wounded took shelter in camps full of wailing and rage and where Dog Soldiers had killed construction workers only two years before. Now passengers blazed away at bison from the car windows; thousands of carcasses lay among the new sod houses and dugouts. Kit Carson was a sprawl of tents, spindly houses, and saloons, "like 100 gipsy encampments."

Scott took work as a freighter with an ox train that followed a variation of the old road from the Smoky Hill to the Arkansas—a trail used by plainsmen for centuries, including Black Kettle's people when they camped at Sand Creek. Other freighters crowded the trail; at one stop more than 100 oxen grazed by a creek. Some details of the trip were more exotic than he wished—a colleague who passed time picking lice from his shirt, the "small, thin, dark, dirty, ragged" Mexicans, the cook who flavored everything with red peppers and turned from cow chips to biscuit dough without a brush of his hands—but it was more an excursion than a launch into the unknown. By the time they reached the Arkansas he was on familiar turf. There were flocks of sheep and ranches selling fresh meat, green corn, and melons, and at the Purgatoire wheatfields growing thick beside the river. Except for the yawning sky and the soft roll of the land, there was little to distinguish this West from the country he had left.[15]

William Green Russell took $20,000 out of Russell's Gulch and went home to Georgia. He later came back to Colorado, farmed along the Huerfano River, and finally moved among the Cherokees in Indian Territory. He died there of malaria in 1877. His brother Levi eventually emigrated to Texas, where he lived a modestly prosperous life as a physician, despite being horsewhipped for what the locals considered eccentric religious views.

After Julia Holmes became the first white woman to climb Pike's Peak, she lived in Santa Fe, where her husband served as territorial secretary and she as a correspondent for a New York newspaper. They moved to Washington, D.C., in 1863. There she bore four children, worked for the Bureau of Education, divorced, and worked tirelessly for women's rights.

Molly and Byron Sanford lived all their lives in Denver. He worked for forty years at the U.S. Mint and helped choose the site of the state university in Boulder; she was remembered as her family's "balance wheel." They died within three months of one another at ages eighty-eight and seventy-six. Ellen Hunt, after nursing her sick infants up the Arkansas Trail in 1859 and then being "nearly worked to death" as a herculean pie-baker in early Denver, died there at the age of forty-four. Before that, however, she became Colorado's first lady when her husband, Alexander Cameron Hunt, was appointed territorial governor.

Until his death in 1894 William Gilpin remained in the city he predicted would become the center of global civilization. He became a railroad promoter and argued passionately for a rail connection between Europe and America. As he saw it, the hemispheres could easily be linked by a bridge over the Bering Strait.

William Denver McGaa, Denver City's firstborn, became a successful cattleman at the Dakota reservation at Pine Ridge, South Dakota. Before dying in 1925, Denver Bill sired eleven children by two wives. His second wife, Mary Pourier (who went by Lovie, a nickname from her father, the mountain man and Denver log-hauler Baptiste [Big Bat] Pourier) was a matron in the Pine Ridge school and hospital. She was still there in 1984, her hundredth year.

By 1869 DENVER'S 4,000 or 5,000 residents could feel increasingly confident about their future. As the Dog Soldiers made their last stand, crews steadily laid tracks through the warriors' heartland. Another line was building north from Denver to the Union Pacific at Cheyenne, along the ancient path that perhaps felt some of America's first footfalls. The following summer the Kansas Pacific and Denver Pacific Railroads were completed within two months of each other. The city then was linked by a great loop both to Kansas City and to the nation's transcontinental railroad. Denver's dream of ascendance seemed more real than ever.

Rail connections drastically reduced shipping costs and energetically boosted the mining industry. Mineral output had bottomed out in 1868 at an anemic $2.2 million. For the next decade it showed a gradual revival, helped along by more efficient smelting techniques, new discoveries, lower transport costs, and infusions of capital. As the mountain economy recovered and farming increased along the Front Range, Denver's position as the region's economic pivot really began to pay off. Its population had stagnated for much of the 1860s, but between 1870 and 1880 it increased nearly eight times over, to 35,629.

Buoyed by growth along and in the mountains, fed by rail connections, the plains between the Platte and the Arkansas were soon filling with new settlement. The sequences were much like those along the big rivers. The first arrivals in Norton County, Kansas, were buffalo hunters, some of them former railroad construction workers. A few were stereotypical eccentrics— Morgan Hansen was known as Longhaired Jesus and Daniel McLaren boasted that "when his hat was on his head, his whole family was under shelter"— but others were college graduates and budding businessmen who stayed to ranch and farm.[16] The Swedish immigrant Caroline Jonasson's husband left his freighting job and took up a homestead, "a good farm," he wrote her, with "black soil on sand bottom [and] . . . a brook straight through."[17]

Men bounced among the enterprises suddenly taking hold. After growing up a farm boy in far eastern Kansas, J. W. McConnell made hunting and haying trips to the Republican valley around 1860 and after the Civil War tried hunting, trapping, and finally stockraising, always tending westward, finally to Osborne and Rooks Counties. Bad luck dogged him. A prairie fire burned his hay, and most of his cattle were stolen or died in a hard winter. He bought a sawmill and cut and planed all the nearby cottonwoods, but grasshoppers drove out local farmers, and "we couldn't sell a board." He finally turned to farming and prospered.[18]

Buffalo hunters, bullwhackers, army veterans, failed merchants, and above all farmers looking for a little more came into the country by the hundreds, then thousands, as the east-to-west Anglo-American frontier took full control. The wave that had begun on the Atlantic and washed over the mountains and through trans-Appalachia finished its roll. Some families had swum with it all the way. Unwed but pregnant, Matilda Jane Brown left Missouri to homestead in Decatur County. She came with her seventy-three-year-old father, Isaac, who had come to Missouri through Ohio after his birth in 1800 near the Boone family on North Carolina's Yadkin River.[19]

A traditional marker for the frontier's arrival was the organization of the first primitive county governments. Between 1870 and 1880, sixteen new counties were formed in western Kansas and several more along the upper Platte valley in Nebraska. The rise in population was spectacular, especially after 1875 (see Table 12.1).[20] In western Kansas 4 million acres were claimed—more land than was in Massachusetts—and more than 1 million acres, an area larger than Connecticut, were plowed and developed.

By simply riding around in such rapid change it was possible to see history telescoped. After an evening's revel and brawl, Levi Davis and four friends set out from Fort Kearny to hunt bison on the Republican River in 1874. For weeks they saw only some friendly Lakotas as they hunted and lived in a cave they dug in the riverbank. When less amicable Indians

Table 12.1. Population of Selected Kansas Counties, 1870–1880

County	1870	1875	1880
Smith	66	3,876	13,883
Norton	—	899	6,998
Osborne	33	3,467	12,517
Rooks	—	567	8,112
Barton	2	99	10,318
Rush	—	451	5,490

appeared, they moved out quickly but over several days met only a man standing by a new well, waiting to sell buckets of water for a quarter each. Suddenly the hunters came across a large celebration marking the founding of two Nebraska counties. As they sold smoked bison hindquarters for eight dollars each, they watched the entertainment—horse races, a new sheriff, judge, and constable giving speeches, and Lakotas dancing for pay under an arbor of pine boughs.[21]

The change was so fast that it was easy to overlook the new order's intricate connections to the past. Counties were not imposed; they were ushered in. Once the gold rush changed the country's meaning, white men on the scene quickly shifted their goals, others soon arrived to activate a new purpose, and together they established the formal claim of political institutions. The aptly named Frontier County, Nebraska, was founded in 1872 just north of the festivities where Davis and his friends later sold their bison meat. Formal organization took place in the tipi of Hank Crawford, a trader and former trapper with a Lakota wife. The main mover was John Bratt, an Englishman who had first emigrated to Chicago, where he began a business but lost everything in a shipwreck. He came to Nebraska to work as a freighter and later turned to ranching after marrying the daughter of the prominent road merchant John Burke. Bratt and Crawford were on the first board of commissioners of Frontier County. The first treasurer was a second rancher, Levi Carter, and the first judge Sam Watts, a trader among the Lakotas who worked out of Charles McDonald's road ranch. Another McDonald employee was the first county clerk.[22]

The recent and the older folded neatly into the new. In rapid overlapping steps an economy took hold and turned resources to its own needs, and humans were sorted according to new values, with fresh arrivals quickly moving to the top. When needed, the old trading elite took some role, usually brief—Crawford disappeared from the record within a few years—and Native Americans came no closer to prestige and power than Crawford's wife, cooking for treasurers and county clerks who squatted in her lodge.

The velocity and breadth of change gave a wonderful momentum to the emerging story of the new masters. A living myth—of a superior people finding their true home in a rising nation's exuberant heartland—took hold. Every people who had ever lived there—Clovis hunters, bison-killing wasp gatherers, ninth-century gardeners, timberline elk-stalkers, moundbuilders, and horseborne warriors—must have seen the country as obviously meant for them and their ways. But these last changes were so astonishingly quick, their results so seemingly sure, that they deluded people more than ever. The illusion of inevitability and control was nearly irresistible.

Through it all ran a rhetoric of destiny. "This is a good stock raising country . . . good [also] for wheat oats barley wry millet buckwheat potatoes turnips sweet po[tatoes] pumpkins melons vines," a settler wrote from the south fork of the Solomon River, near the place where Dog Soldiers had scattered from the sabre-drawn charge of Sumner's cavalry. And you had better come on, he added, for the "nice prairie claims . . . are going like hot cakes."[23] In 1867 Denver created a Board of Trade to publicize the region's flourishing farms and ranches and the city's boom (which hadn't happened yet). The board soon let loose a broad stream of boasts.[24] Ranch promotion in western Kansas and eastern Colorado accelerated after the Indian threat was snuffed. Land beyond the Missouri was "one immense pasture ground, . . . boundless, endless, gateless, and all of it furnishing winter grazing," one book claimed. The main Platte valley was "one of the finest grazing valleys in the world" and the 12 million acres along the South Platte "is perhaps the best watered and most desirable locality for all purposes—fruit, farming, or stock raising, in America."[25] Glowing endorsements were included from cattleking John Wesley Iliff, freighting legend Alexander Majors, and former Indian trader Seth Ward.

Like most tracts, this one linked the rising inland empire with America's ascent to greatness. What had been a place to get across now was an essential part of one national vision. An industrial America needed plenty of food for well-fed laborers, and the cheaper the groceries, the sharper the nation's competitive edge. Fertile fields and bumper crops would help propel the Republic toward its proper place. The blessing of pastureland was even more important. No people in history, the writer observed, had ever found greatness without eating animals. In the ageless contest of fang and claw, carnivores ruled, "vegetable food alone degenerating people to the condition of the Macaroni Eaters of Italy."[26]

John Wesley Iliff built on his holdings until his death in 1878. He died wealthy and respected by other prominent ranchers; one called him "the squarest man who ever rode over these plains." His estate helped found the Iliff School of Theology in Denver.

From his initial investment of $234, John Wesley Prowers eventually owned more than forty miles along the Arkansas River. When he died in 1884 at forty-six, he was Colorado's first millionaire stockman.

Geminien "Jim" Beauvais advised the government on Indian issues after he turned his road ranch over to his son. He accompanied the famous Lakota chief Red Cloud to Washington in 1870 and took part in an unsuccessful attempt to purchase the Black Hills from the Lakotas in 1875. He died three years later in St. Louis.

Nicholas and Joseph Janis found a modest prosperity in ranching and farming along the Cache la Poudre and North Platte. Both eventually sold out and spent their last years on the Pine Ridge reservation.

Elbridge Gerry lived his remaining life on his ranch in Weld County. His name was enshrined in local folklore during the troubles in 1865 when he made a dramatic Paul Revere–style ride to warn neighbors of impending attacks. He was buried on his land beside his Lakota wives.

EVEN AS THE WHITE INVADERS were smothering the vision of the plains Indians, they were beginning to confront the errors of their own. The warnings were clear from the start. In the summer of the gold rush a vicious drought set in, and in some places virtually no rain fell between June 1859 and February 1861. The more thickly settled counties close to the Missouri suffered, but the worst effects were to the west among new emigrants on the edge of the plains. Fields in some areas yielded fewer than three bushels of corn an acre. Farther west cavalry reported Walnut and Cow Creeks and the Smoky Hill perfectly dry and the highland forage wispy at best; they often walked to save their weakened, wobbly horses.[27] As one rainless month followed another, farmers deserted the land. Many headed east, many for the goldfields, some onto the plains, like Frank Stahl, who left his farm for wolf-hunting near the great bend of the Arkansas.[28]

Relief efforts centered in Atchison, where the destitute were given navy beans, corn, dried apples, and salt pork, but there and elsewhere supplies eventually ran low. By the end of the drought some townships had as little as eleven cents per family for all relief. Those who tried to stick it out often ended up stuck, with no food, no money, and at the end of the fall, no clothes or supplies to make a dash for it. An especially frigid, blizzard-blown winter made conditions much worse. As far away as Connecticut towns were plastered with broadsides calling for help:

Forty thousand people are on the verge of Starvation.

Families well supplied in the Fall are now destitute.

Families have died from Starvation while the husband and father have gone to Atchison for food.

A temporary Hospital in Atchison for frozen Teamsters.

Who among us has lost a meal?[29]

Boosters were undeterred. "An erroneous impression has gone forth, that Kansas is subject to drought," the state's Bureau of Immigration noted a few years later. The unpleasantries had been exaggerated ("nobody suffered for want of food") and in any case were an aberration: "The oldest inhabitants universally agree that the drought of 1860 was the only one of any consequence that ever visited Kansas." Settlers could proceed with confidence to claim the yeoman's paradise along the Smoky Hill and Solomon. Useful myths persisted. As late as 1867 a promotional book still had the Smoky Hill rising at the base of Pikes Peak and flowing generously all the way across eastern Colorado and western Kansas.[30] Emigrants responded, despite a couple of dry spells later in the decade. The farming frontier rolled into central Kansas while ranchers settled into the western counties and in eastern Colorado.

A new pastoralism was taking over the land, not nomads with vast horse herds but farmers and ranchers with milch and beef cattle, oxen, mules, sheep, and horses. The ratio of domestic grazers to persons on much of the high plains was as high or higher than when the Cheyennes were at their zenith. The census of 1880 showed the ratio of cattle to people in Meade County, Kansas, to be 22 to 1, in Hamilton County, 60 to 1, in Cheyenne County, 262 to 1. Farmers hoped to apply their craft in regions that had not been cultivated since the wetter times of the ninth to the thirteenth centuries. Even bolder, they plowed and planted the higher land away from the river floodplains, something never tried before. They were sustained by new technologies and, like other settlers from the first days of the gold rush, by deep wells of capital and massive support from the outside. When a homesteader's sister asked whether she could send him anything special, he thought she could: "a yoke of cattle, a wagon, a cow, a well, an orchard full of fruit, a good house & barn, a crib full of corn, 6 big hogs, and a house full of Furniture. put em in bbl & send by express C.O.D."[31] The joke was only a slight inflation of the supplies that outside families in fact provided.

But ultimately, of course, the new occupants would be as confined as everyone who had called the plains home, and eventually they faced the same dilemmas. In the late 1860s Elizabeth Custer found an abandoned ranch in eastern Colorado. Its owner left a crude sign that with minor rewording could have spoken for thousands of whites and Native Americans knocked to their knees during hard times: "Toughed it out here two years. Result: Stock on hand, five towheads and seven yaller dogs. Two hundred and fifty feet down to water. Fifty miles to wood and grass. Hell all around. God bless our home."[32]

Capital, specialized techniques, and equipment produced by an industrializing America could go a long way in establishing the new order and expanding the land's output. Those advantages strengthened the settlers' bargaining position as they negotiated with their environment. But they were only testing limits, not transcending them, and finally they would go too far. When they violated the law of the minimum, they were convicted and fined.

The price, in fact, would be terrifically high, because the vision of these newest plainsmen was so expansive. This would be one of the planet's great gardens, boosters promised, and home to millions of cattle fed on God's hay. Most important, settlers lived by a capitalist, market-oriented dream. Their goal was not that of every earlier inhabitant—to produce enough for themselves, plus some to trade for what they could not provide—but to convert everything they could into something to export and sell for a profit. That goal, pursued with the help of money and technology, led to violations far greater than any in the previous millennia.

Drought in 1872 devastated the cattle business that was barely in its infancy in western Kansas, but as the farming frontier forced the Texas cattle trails westward the lesson was ignored. In the ten years after 1874 the number of Kansas cattle nearly tripled and their value increased nearly five times. The usual tunes were sung. "The question of profit . . . would seem unnecessary to raise, for there is no question about it," a pamphlet on Kansas cattle breeding claimed. "No business has ever been developed that can show the same uniformity of success, none that has fewer risks." Several locals, many with no experience, testified of boundless promise, pleasant society, and a robust climate. A Rush County stock farmer from Illinois gave the ultimate accolade: "A bad place for doctors and lawyers."[33]

Two years after this publication, the region was struck by one of the worst droughts of the era, and the next year the entire plains suffered through the legendary "big blow," a combination of summer drought and a ferocious winter in 1886–1887 that killed tens of thousands of cattle and drove scores of ranchers to bankruptcy. Three years before those boasts, in fact, a vicious dry spell in northwestern Kansas had left most families on relief. "I don't know hardly what to do. . . . It seems like I can hardly stand it to stay here . . . and

I don't know how I could go back there," a Decatur County homesteader wrote
his family in 1880. "I cant see how we are going to get through the winter
with nothing to go on. . . . I must quit for the present for this is all the paper
we have got now."[34]

The pattern was repeated over and over, in the calamitous droughts of
the 1890s, the Dust Bowl of the 1930s, and the great withering of the 1950s.
No people ever pressed the land so far. None inflicted deeper wounds by
failing truly to look at the place and to listen to its past. Whites, however,
were hardly the first to imagine their way into trouble. In countless variations of trial, success, and failure, dozens of cultures had dreamed their way
into this landscape of desire, where the country's greatest power has always
been the fertility of hope.

*John Simpson Smith followed his Cheyenne in-laws to their reservation and
died there in 1871. His entire estate of $609.96 was sent as educational fund
to his son by his Cheyenne wife Zarepta, William Gilpin Smith, who was
living with a Quaker family in Lawrence, Kansas. Although Smith had asked
that "Willie" never live among Indians, his son later moved to the Pine Ridge
reservation and apparently died there.*

*After Thomas Fitzpatrick's death, Maggie Poisal "Chivvy-say" Fitzpatrick
remarried and worked as an interpreter. During negotiations at Medicine
Lodge Creek the British journalist Henry Morton Stanley, who later presumed
to find Dr. David Livingstone in Africa, was impressed by this "intelligent
and rather refined" woman dressed in a crimson petticoat, black cloak, and
a "small coquettish" hat with an ostrich feather. Several years later she froze
to death after falling off her horse while drunk.*

*Charlie and George Bent both fought with the Cheyennes and Lakotas after
Sand Creek. Charlie became one of the most feared raiders of the time and
was probably the inspiration for the terrifying mixed-blood renegade, Blue
Duck, in Larry McMurtry's 1985 novel* Lonesome Dove. *His father William
disowned him. He died from a combination of battle wounds and malaria in
1868. George took part in several raids but removed to the reservation with
his Arapaho wife after Summit Springs. Before dying of pneumonia in 1918
he exchanged dozens of letters with early scholars of Native American life
and became the most valued informant on Cheyenne history and lifeways.*

*Satanta and Satank both were arrested in 1871 by the army for killings
in a raid they led on a government wagon train. When soldiers were taking*

*them back to Texas for trial, Satank began singing his death song, then burst
his manacles, stabbed a guard, and grabbed a rifle before being shot to death.
Satanta was convicted but pardoned in 1873. Accused of more raiding, he
was rearrested and placed in the Texas state penitentiary. In 1878 he became the inspiration for the departure of Lonesome Dove's Blue Duck when
he committed suicide by leaping headfirst through a second-story window.*

*Having fought and survived at Beecher's Island, Summit Springs, and
many smaller engagements after Sand Creek, Bull Bear took his family and
followers to the reservation, and although he fought during the south plains
war of 1874–1875, he eventually followed his brother Starving Bear's path
to accommodation. He was the first Cheyenne to enroll a child in a white
reservation school. A son later attended the Carlisle Indian School in Pennsylvania, took up the printer's trade, and changed his name to Richard Davis.*

*Ned Wynkoop retained the admiration of the Cheyennes for his furious
denunciations of John Chivington. He served for two years as civilian
Indian agent at Fort Larned but became increasingly disillusioned with
government policies. "I will be damned if I don't desert my country [and]
foreswear Christianity and become a hehometan if this state of affairs con-
tinues," he wrote a friend when he heard a rumor (incorrect) that Satanta
and Little Raven had been killed. In later years, however, he held a variety
of federal posts, including warden of the New Mexico penitentiary. He died
in 1891 of Bright's disease.*

*In the investigations of Sand Creek, Silas Soule delivered withering tes-
timony against John Chivington. Soon afterward he was appointed provost
marshal in Denver. In April 1865, less than five months after the massacre,
he was assassinated by a veteran of one of the Colorado volunteer regiments.
His killer was arrested but escaped and fled to California.*

*Ten months after William Gilpin's death, John M. Chivington died in Den-
ver of cancer. He had dabbled in business in Nebraska, California, and Ohio
before returning to Colorado in 1883 to work as a journalist, always arguing
vehemently that he had saved an innocent citizenry from sure destruction. In
time he tried again to use his military career as a step to politics. He finally
succeeded in election to his only public office: Arapaho County coroner.*

THE CONTEST between Indians and whites is usually described
as a power struggle. It was, but the struggle had many more shadings than it
seemed. The two cultures fought over power in its rawest, most common

meanings—physical domination, the command of formal authority, the strength to say who could live where and how people had to behave. That outward control, however, was only a part of a much broader definition. In its more basic expression, power is a fundamental relationship between all creatures and their worlds.

We are surrounded by energy. It pours down on our heads and sits waiting in all organic matter, in tree bark, centipedes, cattle, bull snakes, and grass. Each life-form is constantly converting a tiny part of that abundance into an ability to do something. This is power's larger meaning. It is the translation of energy into act. It accounts for all true animation and allows every human event: a sacred dance, paddling a boat, burning a village, sipping tea. But every organism can take its energy in only a few forms. Leopards have no use for cabbage; camels don't eat sausages; gardenias please people but can't feed them. Once it gets power, furthermore, each living thing applies it in only a few of many available ways. The uses are limited by the creature's awareness of possibilities, and for most animals the prospects they see are narrow. These twin limits—available energy and awareness—set the confines of power.

People have one inestimable edge over everything else. Other animals increase their awareness through accidental trial and error and the excruciatingly slow mechanism of genetic mutation and evolution. People, however, imagine. They create in their heads alternate means of finding energy and using power. Only humans can look at the world and see what's not there yet, and that gives them an enormous manipulative advantage. It stretches their influence far beyond the competition. But this advantage can take people only so far. Despite their ability, human minds can conceive of only so many options, never the full range. Some possibilities always await, undiscovered. And in a painful twist, people's imaginations are forever getting them into serious trouble. They may picture new ways to get and use power, but they fail to imagine the full implications of acting more powerfully upon the world. Like the sorcerer's apprentice, they often find themselves in a fix of their own devising.

The Great Plains and the Front Range provide a fine stage for watching the endless play of power. Energy is extraordinarily abundant in some forms, in others scant and confined. The weather and climate, which can release energy or suck it away, is shockingly erratic from season to season, year to year, and century to century. As an arena of power, the region is among the most unpredictable on earth. And yet something about this country—perhaps the breathtaking openness of the plains and the mountains' dramatic lift—inspires in people a grander sense of possibility than in most other places. It's a heady, dangerous combination.

For thousands of years many peoples worked within those evolving currents of possibility. Each one looked into the country, saw it a particular way, and threaded connections among its pieces to make imagination concrete. It was one of the continent's longest shows, a dance of twelve millennia among renewed invention, changing resources, and shifting climate. Some combinations were more successful and enduring than others, but none stood still. As people dreamed into the land, they often came into conflict, especially when they imagined lives different from one another. Rarely can two cultures chase two unique visions in the same place at the same time.

In the middle of the sixteenth century new people appeared. They did more than bring fresh influence; they joined two hemispheric histories. The sudden merging of different universes, material and imaginative, precipitated changes that were faster and greater than ever in the past. Frontiers, the inwashing of cultures born in Europe, tossed together previously separate biota, technologies, and ideas. The results sometimes were horrifying, but frontiers also set loose more pure creativity than the plains had ever witnessed. The previously unthinkable suddenly could be thought. Indigenous peoples, masters of invention, were the first to sense the potential, and they immediately began to reshape their world. They took what they saw among the newcomers, played with it in their heads, and thought their way into a different future. Above all, the horse inspired a lifting vision of human passion and intelligence married to the strength and grace of a magnificent animal.

Behind this dream was a vast expansion of power made possible by tapping energy that had always been locked beyond reach. Suddenly people could use grass, the most prolific storeplace of the sun's gift, to hunt, move, and fight with a vigor unimaginable before. Native American invaders swept in, seized the possibility, and re-vised the country and themselves. They learned the nuances of an economy that revolved around nomadic pastoralism and bison hunting but reached over the land in filigrees, taking scores of plants and animals, linking water holes, clusters of trees, and streambeds, shuttling goods among distant markets. They earned new stories. They re-membered themselves as people summoned to live and fight in God's donation. It was an astonishing performance of adaptive imagination that easily rivaled any other among the continent's converging frontiers.

They also made mistakes. When people find greater power to reshape their lives, they invariably use it to struggle against the restraints of their surroundings. Their environment pushes back, offering lessons and imposing rules, and when people violate those rules, the environment penalizes them. Sometimes it eats them. Horse nomads pushed harder than most, doing so in country that easily tricked newcomers into overcommitment. Within a couple of generations horseback Indians were suffering the inevitable environmental tit-for-tat. Their new power brought other problems. Military prowess brought appalling losses. Even worse, opportunities and the new environment cracked and pulled at their understanding of themselves. Called to a new and better life, they suffered a social and spiritual splintering. But much worse was just ahead.

The same frontiers that gave the Indians horses and carried them to the plains also brought pioneers who first occupied the Missouri border, then crossed the plains in huge numbers, demolishing some of the same resources the Indians were beginning to deplete. The pioneers' touch was limited, however, because of the way they saw the land. Before 1858, expanding white America looked at the central plains as space to cross on the way to someplace worth inhabiting. The region, Thomas Fitzpatrick wrote in 1853, "now serves only as a disconnecting wilderness between the States of the Pacific and Atlantic slopes."[35]

That changed on July 6, 1858, when a prospecting party panned some modestly lucrative gravel on a small tributary of the South Platte River. Gold, or rather the idea of it, had an unequaled power to transform places. Beyond its marketplace value, gold wielded an ancient cultural weight. Simply by being there it suggested a larger meaning for its surroundings. Golden land was destined for material and cultural progress, and news that the glittering stuff was truly found at Pike's Peak instantly summoned a new vision of the continental center. Green Russell's strike became the pivotal moment in the region's modern history.

The country had resources to give the dream some substance, of course, but for the first critical years, though gold never came close to justifying the enthusiasm, fortunes were shoveled across and onto the plains in a continuing act of financial and cultural faith. The transformation came with mind-twirling speed. Within months an enconomy of transit was growing along the main roads to feed the immediate needs of travelers to and from the ramshackle of towns being hammered together along the Front Range. Freight trains and emigrant stops ushered in other enterprises—ranching and farming to feed the new settlements and finally military posts to confirm and protect the invaders' occupation of these old corridors of power.

All of it grew from a new way of seeing the country. The midcontinent, William Gilpin lectured in 1858, had been "an immense disc of howling wilderness," but gold would reveal its true purpose.[36] The Rockies, the valleys of the Missouri and the Mississippi, and the plains between were all of a piece. The parts of the seamless region would feed each other. Once seen, the connections became real. Plains and valleys and mountains were no longer distance to cross. The American center was now a vital whole unto itself. Beyond that it was united, as place and as vision, to a larger nation that watched itself rising to greatness.

Like every vision, this one had to be sustained by its surroundings. The towns on the mountain face, road ranches, stage stations, dingy stopovers, farms, commercial gardens, hayfields, and cattle ranches—all of them drew their energy from the pool around them. Doing that, of course, denied that same animating force to the horseborne Indians who had taken command of the plains for their own transcendent dream. With a terrible swiftness the changes spun off by the gold rush undercut the nomadic life. Freedom to move across open land meant nothing without a few sanctuaries and reviving enclaves during the hardest turn of the year. By 1864 whites had taken most of those places. They filled them like a foot fills a shoe. They captured the minimum. The plains tribes, already wobbling from their own miscalculations and from other pressures, were pushed quickly to the verge of full-blown disaster.

Whites did not set out, directly at least, to destroy the Indians' life. They were simply following a script that had no Indians in it, except as exotic relics. Cheyennes, Arapahoes, Comanches, Kiowas, and Plains Apaches were pushed aside by the consequences of another dream. Their way of life was implied to death. Once the country was perceived in union with the nation beyond it, the advantages of the invaders were incalculable—a population hundreds of times that of the Indians, gigantic reserves of capital, a technology capable of changing its world with a twitch. Despite their adaptive genius, the plains nomads could not possibly sustain themselves against that force.

Plains Indians were left with two dreadful choices. They could try to accommodate, surrendering their vision, or they could try to resist the irresistible. These awful alternatives coincided with two trends already dividing the tribes, a fracture arising from their own choices and actions. For a decade after the rush those two alternatives played themselves out. Neither result was pretty. White authorities, for their part, never called on enough power to force a quick victory and support a new way of life. They did only enough to make the nomads' vision ultimately unsustainable.

What followed was slow agony—hungry, disease-ridden families along the roads, gradual strangulation of angry bands of hunters and warriors, misunderstanding and paranoia, hopeless heroism and spurned conciliation, mounting deaths of innocents on all sides, and finally the horror of Sand Creek and the debacle at Summit Springs. Chosen paths led to symbolic ends. Black Kettle's people were massacred in a hungry camp he had set, appropriately, halfway between Fort Lyon and the militant villages of the heartland. His search for the middle ground took him to a slaughter pen. The Dog Soldiers' pursuit of independence ended in a dead-end ravine. There Tall Bull took his death behind his bleeding horse, the dying inspiration of an expanding world. Nearby Wolf With Plenty of Hair chose the Dog Rope, the tight final radius of the plains as a warrior's dream.

THIS WAS THE TRUER MEANING of the power struggle of whites and Indians. In the middle of the nineteenth century two cultures acted out two compelling visions in a land that could support only one. The inspired struggle—of both peoples to enliven their dreams, of each to deny the other—was one of the great American stories.

In world history it was the most dramatic collision of two objects that, more than any others, have inspired people to redream their existence. The horse offered spiritual transformation, a union of superior beings, the dream of the centaur: man in flight over the land, in rightful dominion over lesser, leg-bound humanity. Gold was the Great Untarnished, purifier and renewer, God-scat, sunlight crumbled and held in your hand.

For North Americans the story tells of the dynamism unleashed when frontiers rolled into country already tangled in change. The starvation and butchery at the end was part of the horrific consequence of the European intrusion, but when Coronado crossed the Arkansas he also (without having a clue that he was doing it) triggered the greatest explosion of creative energy that country would ever see. Frontiers were messy, and so are their legacies.

For the United States these events played an unrecognized part in nation-making. As the Union was being confirmed in battle to the east, something similar was happening in mid-America from the discovery of gold and its instant impact on millions of minds. The re-vision of plains and mountains was a central moment in a nation imagining itself whole. It also had its bloody confirmation. Chivington's march on Sand Creek came as Sherman was slicing Georgia in half. Investigators were taking testimony on the massacre when they heard of Lee's surrender at Appomattox. Until the "disc of howling wilderness" was rethought as a heartland of promise, Lincoln's nation "so conceived and so dedicated" could not be fully comprehended.

As moral entertainment, the history of Indians and the gold rush, when set in the context of the land's antiquity, should be a caution. The whites who celebrated the final crushing of a rival vision were already suffering from the hubris of their own. Of all peoples over the past 12,000 years, they came to the country with the greatest power to stretch the restraints that hem in everyone. They pulled more than anyone ever had from its reservoir of energy. Seeing only the land's seductive abundance, they extended themselves much further toward its maximum generosity. And when the unbending rules of the minimum were inevitably applied, the result was stunning human and environmental calamities. Looking at the region today, the lessons are clear enough.

It is also hard not to wonder how different those years might have been if all sides had used their prodigious imaginations to picture how varied peoples and dreams might occupy the same place. In their purest forms the visions could not coexist, and it may be that no common ground was possible. We shouldn't waste time wishing frogs had wings. But after all, Indians and whites were masters of change. Their performances were so impressive precisely because they could envision other ways and then muster the will to make them happen. Perhaps their failures should push us to reperceive our own neighborhoods—our modern versions of townsites, stream valleys, and cottonwood groves—into more tolerant shapes. We might find guiding stories that allow a fuller human dignity.

In Wright Morris's novel *Plains Song*, the narrator asks, "Is the past a story we are persuaded to believe, in the teeth of the life we endure in the present?"[37] The question is always open. How we treat our world and each other grows from our vision of how we have come to where we are. Ultimately, of course, the issue is not survival but decency and common sense. Everything passes, the psalmist reminds us. No one escapes. The best we can hope is to learn a little from the speaking dead, to find in our deep past some help in acting wisely in the teeth of life.

Notes

Introduction

1. Thomas Berger, *Little Big Man* (New York: Delta/Seymour Laurence, 1969), 148.
2. Elliott West, *The Way to the West: Essays on the Central Plains* (Albuquerque: University of New Mexico Press, 1995). The essays are expanded versions from the Calvin Horn Lectures on Western History and Culture.
3. For a fascinating exploration of some of the aspects of power, the environment, and human culture in particular people's work, see Richard White, *The Organic Machine: The Remaking of the Columbia River* (New York: Hill and Wang, 1995).

1. Prologue: A Scrap and a Panic

1. The best source on the Cheyenne Expedition and the battle on Solomon's Fork is William Y. Chalfant's excellent *Cheyennes and Horse Soldiers: The 1857 Expedition and the Battle of Solomon's Fork* (Norman: University of Oklahoma Press, 1989). I have drawn on it heavily in the following account.
2. Chalfant, *Cheyennes and Horse Soldiers*, 39–41; Father John Peter Powell, *People of the Sacred Mountain: A History of the Northern Cheyenne Chiefs and Warrior Societies*, 2 vols. (San Francisco: Harper and Row, 1981), 1: 204–5; George E. Hyde, *Life of George Bent, Written from His Letters* (Norman: University of Oklahoma Press, 1968), 101–2.
3. Chalfant, *Cheyennes and Horse Soldiers*, 41–44.
4. Ibid., 139–60. Chalfant also provides a detailed account of the marches of both Sedgwick's and Sumner's columns.
5. George Bird Grinnell, *The Fighting Cheyennes* (Norman: University of Oklahoma Press, 1955), 117–18; Chalfant, *Cheyennes and Horse Soldiers*, 175; Hyde, *Life of George Bent*, 102. According to Robert Miller, Indian agent on the upper Arkansas, Cheyenne warriors had gone before the battle to a lake "in which they had to but dip their hands when the victory over the troops would be an easy one. So the medicine man [*sic*] told them, and they had but to hold up their hands and the balls would roll from the muzzles of the soldiers' guns, harmless, to their feet" (*Report of the Commissioner of Indian Affairs, 1857*, 141).
6. For accounts of the battle, see Chalfant, *Cheyennes and Horse Soldiers*, 181–201; Hyde, *Life of George Bent*, 102–4; Grinnell, *The Fighting Cheyennes*, 119–21; Powell, *People of the Sacred Mountain*, 1: 212–13.

7. Chalfant, *Cheyennes and Horse Soldiers*, 182.

8. George Bent had a wry take on this turn of events. The prophecy, he points out, was that the guns "would fail to go off," and that is in fact what happened (or didn't happen). See Hyde, *Life of George Bent*, 103.

9. Chalfant, *Cheyennes and Horse Soldiers*, 193–208.

10. Ibid., 220–23, 241–54.

11. Powell, *People of the Sacred Mountain*, 1: 213–14.

12. Robert C. Miller to A. Cumming, August 15, 1857, Letters Received, Upper Arkansas Agency, Office of Indian Affairs.

13. On the panic and depression of 1857, see George W. Van Vleck, *The Panic of 1857: An Analytical Study* (New York: Columbia University Press, 1943); James L. Huston, *The Panic of 1857 and the Coming of the Civil War* (Baton Rouge: Louisiana State University Press, 1987); D. Morier Evans, *The History of the Commercial Crisis, 1857–1858 and the Stock Exchange Panic of 1859* (New York: B. Franklin, 1969); Robert Morris, *The Banks of New-York, Their Dealers, the Clearing House, and the Panic of 1857* (New York: D. Appleton and Company, 1858); Robert Sobel, *Panic on Wall Street: A History of America's Financial Disasters* (London: Macmillan Company, 1968), 77–114.

14. Van Vleck, *Panic of 1857*, 63–69; Huston, *Panic of 1857*, 14–18; Sobel, *Panic on Wall Street*, 99–107.

15. Joseph Doneghy to John, October 16, 1857, Chester Franz Papers, Missouri Historical Society.

16. Van Vleck, *Panic of 1857*, 76; *Missouri Republican*, November 14, 1857.

17. Charles W. Marsh, *Recollections, 1837–1910* (Chicago: Farm Implement News Company, 1910), 71.

18. Evans, *History of the Commercial Crisis*, 136–37; James Fergus to father, November 1, 1857, James Fergus Papers, University of Montana Library.

19. *Leavenworth Weekly Journal*, December 18, 1857.

20. W. W. Johns to J. W. Ward, November 18, 1857, Franz Papers.

21. Meriwether Lewis Clark Journal, September 13–October 29, 1857, Missouri Historical Society.

22. (Kansas City, Mo.) *Western Journal of Commerce*, November 21, 1857.

23. *Missouri Republican*, November 13, 14, 1857.

24. Edwin James, *An Account of an Expedition from Pittsburgh to the Rocky Mountains* (Ann Arbor, Mich.: University Microfilms, 1966), 371.

25. Thomas S. Twiss to Secretary of Interior, September 12, 1856, *Report of the Commissioner of Indian Affairs, 1856*, 88.

2. The Old World

1. An alternate scenario of early emigration has gathered growing support in recent years. By this theory, emigrants migrated southward along the Pacific Coast, thus avoiding the harsh climate that would have made passage through the ice-free

corridor difficult. For discussions of these various viewpoints, see, among many other sources, E. C. Pielou, *After the Ice Age: The Return of Life to Glaciated North America* (Chicago: University of Chicago Press, 1991); Brian M. Fagan, *The Great Journey: The Peopling of Ancient America* (New York: Thames and Hudson, 1987); and several essays in *North America and Adjacent Oceans During the Last Deglaciation* (Boulder, Colo.: Geological Society of America, 1987).

2. The most accessible source on the early history of the central plains is Waldo R. Wedel, *Central Plains Prehistory: Holocene Environments and Culture Change in the Republican River Basin* (Lincoln: University of Nebraska Press, 1986). On the climate of the earliest findings, see pp. 39–43.

3. Jack L. Hofman, "Early Hunter-Gatherers of the Central Great Plains: Paleoindian and Mesoindian (Archaic) Cultures," in *Archeology and Paleoecology of the Central Great Plains,* ed. Jack L. Hofman, Arkansas Archeological Research Survey no. 48 (Fayetteville: Arkansas Archeological Survey, 1996), 41–54.

4. Wedel, *Central Plains Prehistory,* 49–61.

5. The leading advocate of the overkill or "blitzkrieg" argument is Paul S. Martin. See his "Pleistocene Overkill," and Paul S. Martin and John E. Guilday, "A Bestiary for Pleistocene Biologists," both in *Pleistocene Extinctions: The Search for a Cause,* ed. Paul S. Martin and Herbert E. Wright, Jr. (New Haven: Yale University Press, 1967), 75–120, 1–62; Paul S. Martin and Richard G. Klein, *Quaternary Extinctions: A Prehistoric Revolution* (Tucson: University of Arizona Press, 1984); and James E. Mosiman, "Simulating Overkill by PaleoIndians," *American Scientist* 63:3 (1975): 304–13.

6. William H. MacLeish, *The Day Before America* (Boston: Houghton Mifflin, 1994), 87–90; Wedel, *Central Plains Prehistory,* 61–71.

7. Dennis J. Stanford, "Preliminary Report of the Excavation of the Jones-Miller Hell Gap Site, Yuma County, Colorado," *Southwestern Lore* 41:4 (1974): 29–36; Wedel, *Central Plains Prehistory,* 64–66.

8. Preston Holder and Joyce Wike, "The Frontier Culture Complex: A Preliminary Report on a Prehistoric Hunters' Camp in Southwestern Nebraska," *American Antiquity* 14:4, part 1 (1949): 260–66; E. Mott Davis and C. B. Scultz, "The Archeological and Paleontological Salvage Program and the Medicine Creek Reservoir, Frontier County, Nebraska," *Science* 115:2985 (1952): 288–90; E. Mott Davis, "Recent Data on Two Paleo-Indian Sites on Medicine Creek, Nebraska," *American Antiquity* 18:4 (1953): 380–86.

9. "Holocene Man in North America: The Ecological Setting and Climatic Background," *Plains Anthropologist* 23:82, part 1 (1978): 273–87.

10. Wesley R. Hurt, "The Altithermal and the Prehistory of the Northern Plains," *Quaternaria* 8 (1966): 101–13; Waldo R. Wedel, "The Prehistoric Plains," in *Ancient Native Americans,* ed. J. D. Jennings (San Francisco: W. H. Freeman and Company, 1978), 201; Bryan Reeves, "The Concept of an Altithermal Cultural Hiatus in Northern Plains Prehistory," *American Anthropologist* 75:5 (1973): 1221–53.

11. Wedel, *Central Plains Prehistory,* 74–75; Larry J. Schmits, "The Coffey Site: Environment and Cultural Adaptation at a Prairie Plains Archaic Site," *Mid-Continental Journal of Archaeology* 3:1 (1978): 69–185.

12. In the following discussion I have drawn on a remarkable body of research by James B. Benedict. See his *Mount Albion Complex: A Study of Prehistoric Man and the Altithermal,* with Byron L. Olson, Research Report no. 1 (Ward, Colo.: Center for Mountain Archeology, 1978); *Arapaho Pass: Glacial Geology and Archeology at the Crest of the Colorado Front Range,* Research Report no. 3 (Ward, Colo.: Center for Mountain Archeology, 1985); "Footprints in the Snow: High-Altitude Cultural Ecology of the Colorado Front Range, U.S.A. ," *Arctic and Alpine Records* 24:1 (1992): 1–16; and *The Game Drives of Rocky Mountain National Park,* Research Report no. 7 (Ward, Colo.: Center for Mountain Archeology, 1996).

13. James B. Benedict, *Old Man Mountain: A Vision Quest Site in the Colorado High Country,* Research Report no. 4 (Ward, Colo.: Center for Mountain Archeology, 1985).

14. For surveys of this period, see Mary J. Adair, "Woodland Complexes in the Central Great Plains," in Hofman, ed. *Archeology and Paleoecology,* 101–22; Wedel, *Central Plains Prehistory,* 81–97; Jack L. Hofman and Robert L. Brooks, "Prehistoric Culture History: Woodland Complexes in the Southern Great Plains," in *From Clovis to Comanchero: Archeological Overview of the Southern Great Plains,* ed. Jack L. Hofman et al., Arkansas Archeological Survey Research Series no. 35 (Fayetteville: Arkansas Archeological Survey, 1989), 61–70; Jeffrey L. Eighmy, "The Central High Plains: A Cultural Historical Summary," in *Plains Indians,* A.D. *500–1500: The Archaeological Past of Historic Groups,* ed. Karl H. Schlesier (Norman: University of Oklahoma Press, 1994), 224–31.

15. Mary J. Adair, *Prehistoric Agriculture in the Central Plains,* University of Kansas Publications in Anthropology 16 (Lawrence: Department of Anthropology, University of Kansas, 1988), 24–36; Wedel, *Central Plains Prehistory,* 81–83; John Ludwickson and John R. Bozell, "The Early Potters: Emerging Technologies," *Nebraska History* 75:1 (Spring 1994): 111–19; Patricia J. O'Brien, "The Central Lowland Plains: An Overview, A.D. 500–1500," in Schlesier, ed., *Plains Indians,* A.D. *500–1500,* 199–212.

16. Floyd Schultz and Albert C. Spaulding, "A Hopewellian Burial Site in the Lower Republican Valley, Kansas," *American Antiquity* 13:4 (1948): 306–13; Wedel, *Central Plains Prehistory,* 89–91.

17. Gayle F. Carlson, "Long-Distance Trade," *Nebraska History* 75:1 (Spring 1994): 98.

18. C. Irwin and H. Irwin, "The Archeology of the Agate Bluff Area, Colorado," *Plains Anthropologist* 8 (1957): 15–38.

19. For surveys, see Brad Logan, "The Protohistoric Period on the Central Plains," in Hofman, ed., *Archeology and Paleoecology,* 123–33; John R. Bozell, "Late Precontact Village Farmers: An Agricultural Revolution," *Nebraska History* 75:1 (Spring 1994): 121–31; Wedel, *Central Plains Prehistory,* 98–133.

20. A few horticultural settlements developed even farther west. In southeastern Colorado a semisedentary village society of farmers developed from about A.D. 1000 to 1225. People of this Sopris phase seem to have been heavily influenced by early Pueblo peoples to the southwest but drew also from Woodland cultures to the east.

See Robert L. Brooks, "Village Farming Societies," in Hofman et al., eds., *From Clovis to Comanchero,* 80.

21. Ibid., 71, 85, 87–88.

22. Wedel, *Central Plains Prehistory,* 106, 229–30.

23. Ibid., 106–11.

24. Patricia J. O'Brien, "Prehistoric Evidence for Pawnee Cosmology," *American Anthropologist* 88:4 (December 1986): 939–46, and "Speculations About Bobwhite Quail and Pawnee Religion," *Plains Anthropologist* 33:122 (November 1988): 489–504.

3. Frontiers and Visions

1. Alfred Barnaby Thomas, *After Coronado: Spanish Exploration Northeast of New Mexico, 1696–1727* (Norman: University of Oklahoma Press, 1935), 5. The renowned archaeologist Waldo R. Wedel has argued most persuasively for the location of Quivira. See his essay, "Coronado and Quiviria" in *Spain and the Plains: Myths and Realities of Spanish Exploration and Settlement on the Great Plains,* ed. Ralph H. Vigil, Frances W. Kaye, and John R. Wunder (Niwot: University Press of Colorado, 1994), 45–66.

2. Herbert Eugene Bolton, *Coronado: Knight of Pueblos and Plains* (Albuquerque: University of New Mexico Press, 1974), 251; William Y. Chalfant, *Cheyennes and Horse Soldiers: The 1857 Expedition and the Battle of Solomon's Fork* (Norman: University of Oklahoma Press, 1989), 261. Bolton, *Coronado,* remains the most accessible source on the famous expedition. For primary accounts of the journey, see George P. Hammond and Edgar F. Good, *Narratives of the Coronado Expedition, 1540–1542* (Albuquerque: University of New Mexico Press, 1960). For examples of the considerable publication on the expedition, see Waldo R. Wedel, "Coronado's Route to Quivira, 1541," *Plains Anthropologist* 15 (August 1970): 161–68; R. M. Wagstaff, "Coronado's Route to Quivira: 'The Greater Weight of the Credible Evidence,'" *West Texas Historical Association Yearbook* 42 (October 1966): 137–66; Chevy Lloyd Strout, "The Coronado Expedition: Following the Geography Described in the Spanish Journals," *Great Plains Journal* 14 (Fall 1974): 2–31; David J. Weber, "Coronado and the Myth of Quivira," *Southwest Review* 70 (Spring 1985): 230–41.

3. Bolton, *Coronado,* 246.

4. Thomas, *After Coronado,* 7–8, 16–22; Elizabeth A. H. John, *Storms Brewed in Other Men's Worlds: The Confrontation of Indians, Spanish, and French in the Southwest, 1540–1795* (Norman: University of Oklahoma Press, 1996), 228–31.

5. Karl H. Schlesier, ed., *Plains Indians, A.D. 500–1500: The Archaeological Past of Historic Groups* (Norman: University of Oklahoma Press, 1994), 346–56; Jack L. Hofman, ed., *Archeology and the Paleoecology of the Central Great Plains* (Fayetteville: Arkansas Archeological Survey, 1996), 126–32, 136–38.

6. Susan C. Vehik, "Wichita Culture History," *Plains Anthropologist* 37:141 (1992): 311–29.

7. Bolton, *Coronado*, 288–92.

8. For a recent thesis on the pattern of these migrations to the plains, see Schlesier, ed., *Plains Indians*, 326–35.

9. Bolton, *Coronado*, 246.

10. Karl H. Schlesier's "Rethinking the Dismal River Aspect and the Plain Athapaskans, A.D. 1692–1768," *Plains Anthropologist* 17:56 (1972): 101–31, also contains the author's ideas on placement and relations among Apachean groups on the plains.

11. Bolton, *Coronado*, 246.

12. The classic discussion of the Indians' use of the high plains by a master of plains archaeology is Waldo R. Wedel, "The High Plains and Their Utilization by the Indian," *American Antiquity* 29:1 (July 1963): 1–16.

13. Walter H. Schoewe, "The Geography of Kansas. Part 2," Kansas Academy of Science, *Transactions* 52:3 (September 1949): 314–22.

14. Bolton, *Coronado*, 246–47.

15. The scholar who has developed this connection most fully is Katherine A. Spielmann. She has combined traditional sources with computer models of use of local resources among the Pueblos, their corn-growing and corn-storage capacities, the potential range of bison hunters, and other factors. See her *Interdependence in the Prehistoric Southwest: An Ecological Analysis of Plains-Pueblo Interaction* (New York: Garland Press, 1991) and "Coercion or Cooperation? Plains-Pueblo Interaction in the Protohistoric Period," in *Farmers, Hunters, and Colonists: Interaction Between the Southwest and the Southern Plains*, ed. Katherine A. Spielmann (Tucson: University of Arizona Press, 1991), 36–50, as well as John D. Speth, "Some Unexplored Aspects of Mutualistic Plains-Pueblo Food Exchange," in Spielmann, ed., *Farmers*, 18–35.

16. Spielmann's and Speth's research and computer analysis show that the storage capacity of the pits in the eastern Pueblos was well above what was needed to feed themselves and to provide an extra buffer. Such an effort and cost of construction suggest a consistent and long-term commitment to trading corn for other products.

17. A considerable debate is in progress over the identity of the middlemen at these entrepots. Traditionally they have been identified as Caddoan with links to the south, but Frank F. Schambach recently has argued that Tunicans of southern and western Arkansas occupied the sites. The exchanges also contain considerable material on the mounds and on trade generally. See Frank F. Schambach, "Some New Interpretations of Spiroan Culture History," in *Archaeology of Eastern North America: Papers in Honor of Stephen Williams*, ed. James B. Stoltman, Archaeological Report no. 25, Mississippi Department of Archives and History, 1993, 187–230, and "Spiroan Entrepots at and Beyond the Western Border of the Trans-Mississippi South," *Caddoan Archeology Newsletter* 4:2 (July 1993): 11–26.

18. On El Cuartelejo, see S. W. Williston and H. T. Martin, "Some Pueblo Ruins in Scott County, Kansas," *Kansas Historical Collections* 6 (1897–1900): 124–30, and John B. Dunbar, "Massacre of the Villazur Expedition by the Pawnees on the Platte

in 1720," *Kansas Historical Collections* 11 (1909–1910): 397–423. Both of these place the pueblo in Scott County, Kansas, but another prominent scholar has argued that the ruins were farther west, in Kiowa County, Colorado: Alfred B. Thomas, "Massacre of the Villasur Expedition at the Forks of the Platte River, August 12, 1720," *Nebraska History* 7 (July and September 1924): 67–81, and Thomas, *After Coronado,* 270–71.

19. Thomas, *After Coronado,* 19; John, *Storms Brewed in Other Men's Worlds,* 228–30.

20. Thomas, *After Coronado,* 33–39.

21. Frank Norall, *Bourgmont, Explorer of the Missouri, 1698–1725* (Lincoln: University of Nebraska Press, 1988), 59–80.

22. Ibid., 81–88.

23. Of the many recent works on diseases, epidemics, and Native Americans, three that deal in part with this region are John C. Ewers, "The Influence of Epidemics on the Indian Populations and Cultures of Texas," *Plains Anthropologist* 18:60 (May 1973): 104–15; Russell Thornton, *American Indian Holocaust and Survival: A Population History Since 1492* (Norman: University of Oklahoma Press, 1987); and Ann F. Ramenofsky, *Vectors of Death: The Archaeology of European Contact* (Albuquerque: University of New Mexico Press, 1987).

24. Peter J. Powell, *Sweet Medicine,* 2 vols. (Norman: University of Oklahoma Press, 1969), 1: 299–300; Margaret Coel, *Chief Left Hand: Southern Arapaho* (Norman: University of Oklahoma Press, 1981), 68.

25. Richard Irving Dodge, *The Plains of the Great West and Their Inhabitants* (New York: G. P. Putnam's Sons, 1877), xxvi–xxvii.

26. Clark Wissler provided one of the earliest and certainly one of the most influential discussions of the impact of the horse on plains peoples: "The Influence of the Horse in the Development of Plains Culture," *American Anthropologist* 16:1 (January–March 1914): 1–25. Among his main arguments was the thesis that horses did not revolutionize plains culture in that "all the essential elements of Plains culture would have gone on, if the horse had been denied them," although those traits were reinvigorated by the introduction of horses and their abilities. The authors of three excellent articles, from which I have drawn deeply in the discussion that follows, challenge Wissler's point and expand on the implications of adapting the horse to this environment: Clyde H. Wilson, "An Inquiry into the Nature of Plains Indian Cultural Development," *American Anthropologist* 65:2 (April 1963): 355–69, James F. Downs, "Comments on Plains Indian Cultural Development," *American Anthropologist* 66:2 (April 1964): 421–22, and Alan J. Osborn, "Ecological Aspects of Equestrian Adaptations in Aboriginal North America," *American Anthropologist* 85:3 (September 1983): 563–91. For other basic works on the horse in plains culture, see Preston Holder, *The Hoe and the Horse on the Plains: A Study of Cultural Development Among the North American Indians* (Lincoln: University of Nebraska Press, 1970); Symmes Oliver, *Ecology and Cultural Continuity as Contribution Factors in the Social Organization of the Plains Indians,* University of California Publications in American Archeology and Ethnology, vol. 48 (Berkeley: University of California,

1962); John C. Ewers, *The Horse in Blackfoot Culture: With Comparative Material from Other Western Tribes,* Bureau of American Ethnology Bulletin no. 159 (Washington, D.C.: Government Printing Office, 1955); Francis Haynes, "The Northward Spread of Horses Among the Plains Indians," *American Anthropologist* 40 (1938): 429–37; and Frank G. Roe, *The Indian and the Horse* (Norman: University of Oklahoma Press, 1955).

27. This argument draws on an "energetics" approach. The most aggressive statement of it is in Leslie White, *The Evolution of Culture: The Development of Civilization to the Fall of Rome* (New York: McGraw-Hill Book Company, 1959), especially chapter 2, "Energy and Tools," pp. 33–57. This argument certainly has its limits, but I have tried to stress its valid applications to the implications of horses in an energy-rich environment.

28. This is the central thesis, beautifully argued, in Downs, "Comments."

29. For a discussion of the horse's adaptation to the plains, see Dan Flores, "Bison Ecology and Bison Diplomacy: The Southern Plains from 1800 to 1850," *Journal of American History* 78:2 (September 1991): 465–85 and Dan Flores, "The Great Contraction: Bison and Indians in Northern Plains Environmental History," in *Legacy: New Perspectives on the Battle of the Little Bighorn,* ed. Charles E. Rankin (Helena: Montana Historical Society Press, 1996), 3–22.

30. N. Scott Momaday, *The Names* (New York: Harper and Row, 1976), 28.

31. Paul Shepard, *The Others: How Animals Made Us Human* (Washington, D.C.: Island Press, 1996), 251–52, 260–61.

32. James B. Benedict, *The Game Drives of Rocky Mountain National Park,* Research Report no. 7 (Ward, Colo.: Center for Mountain Archeology, 1996), 6.

4. The Called Out People

1. Thomas W. Kavanagh, *Comanche Political History: An Ethnohistorical Perspective, 1706–1875* (Lincoln: University of Nebraska Press, 1996), 63–70.

2. Ibid., 126–27, 72.

3. Ibid., 127–28.

4. Ibid., 72, 130; W. Eugene Hollon and Ruth Lapham Butler, eds., *William Bollaert's Texas* (Norman: University of Oklahoma Press, 1956), 375n.

5. Richard White, "The Winning of the West: The Expansion of the Western Sioux in the Eighteenth and Nineteenth Centuries," *Journal of American History* 65: 2 (September 1978): 319–43.

6. Mildred P. Mayhall, *The Kiowas* (Norman: University of Oklahoma Press, 1952), 8–21; George E. Hyde, *Indians of the High Plains: From the Prehistoric Period to the Coming of the Europeans* (Norman: University of Oklahoma Press, 1959), 148–50.

7. On various estimates and comments on population, see Elliott Coues, ed., *The Journal of Jacob Fowler* (Lincoln: University of Nebraska Press, 1970), 65; *Report of the Commissioner of Indian Affairs, 1845;* Thomas Fitzpatrick to Thomas H. Harvey,

September 18, 1847, in *Report of Commissioner of Indian Affairs, 1847*, 243–449; Thomas S. Twiss to Col. Cumming, November 14, 1855, Office of Indian Affairs, Letters Received, Upper Platte Agency, 1855; J. W. Whitfield to Superintendent of Indian Affairs, January 5, 1856, Office of Indian Affairs, Letters Received, Upper Arkansas Agency, 1856; Thomas S. Twiss to Secretary of Interior, *Report of Commissioner of Indian Affairs, 1856*, 96–98; William Bent, Annual Report, in *Report of Commissioner of Indian Affairs, 1859*, 137–39.

8. The standard work is Frank Raymond Secoy, *Changing Military Patterns of the Great Plains Indians*, Monographs of the American Ethnological Society, 21 (Seattle: University of Washington Press, 1953).

9. E. Adamson Hoebel, *The Cheyennes: Indians of the Great Plains* (Fort Worth, Tex.: Harcourt Brace Jovanovich College Publishers, 1978), 3–9; Hyde, *Indians of the High Plains*, 47; John H. Moore, *The Cheyenne Nation: A Social and Demographic History* (Lincoln: University of Nebraska Press, 1987), 129–38.

10. Still the best single source on the role of Cheyennes in this evolving trade is Joseph Jablow, *The Cheyenne in Plains Indian Trade Relations, 1795–1840*, Monographs of the American Ethnological Society, 19 (New York: J. J. Augustin, 1951).

11. Ibid., 10–18.

12. The best discussion, based on the Blackfeet of the northern plains but bringing in other tribes as well, is in John C. Ewers, *The Horse in Blackfoot Culture: With Comparative Material from Other Western Tribes*, Bureau of American Ethnology Bulletin no. 159 (Washington, D.C: Government Printing Office, 1955), 129–47.

13. Jurgen Doring's *Kulturwandel bei den Nordamerikanischen Plainsindianern: Zur Rolle des Pferdes bei den Comanchen und den Cheyenne* (Berlin: Dietrick Reimer, 1984) contains a useful summary over time of estimates of horses per capita among the Cheyennes.

14. John Bradbury, *Travels in the Interior of America in the Years 1809, 1810, and 1811*, vol. 5, in *Early Western Travel, 1748–1846*, ed. Reuben Gold Thwaites (London: Sherwood, Neely and Jones, 1819), 139.

15. Rudolphe C. Petter, *English-Cheyenne Dictionary.* (Kettle Falls, Wash.: Valdo Pe, n.d.), 193.

16. Iron Teeth died in 1928 at the age of about ninety-three. Living until the year of Pres. Herbert Hoover's election, she could recall the great peace of 1840 as well as gardening in the Black Hills. See "Iron Teeth, a Cheyenne Old Woman," in Thomas B. Marquis, *The Cheyennes of Montana* (Algonac, Mich.: Reference Publications, 1978), 53–55.

17. Kelly Kindscher, *Edible Wild Plants of the Prairie* (Lawrence: University Press of Kansas, 1987), 61–62, 81–82, 86, 121, 143–44, 178–79, 185–87.

18. Kelly Kindscher, *Medicinal Wild Plants of the Prairie: An Ethnobotanical Guide* (Lawrence: University Press of Kansas, 1992), 86–88, 115, 138, 143–44, 177, 184–85.

19. Ibid., 77–78; George Bird Grinnell, *The Cheyenne Indians: Their History and Ways of Life*, 2 vols. (Lincoln: University of Nebraska Press, 1972), 2: 166–91.

20. For an interview with contemporary Comanches on the managing of wild rice grass and its uses, see Richard W. Stouffle et al., *Toyavita Piavuhuru Koroin, "Canyon of Mother Earth": Ethnohistory and Native American Religious Concerns in the Fort Carson–Pinon Canyon Maneuver Area* (Denver: U.S. Army and National Park Service, 1984), 198–204.

21. Father John Peter Powell, *People of the Sacred Mountain: A History of the Northern Cheyenne Chiefs and Warrior Societies,* 2 vols. (San Francisco: Harper and Row, 1981), 1: xxxix.

22. Stan Hoig, *The Peace Chiefs of the Cheyennes* (Norman: University of Oklahoma Press, 1980), 16–20.

23. There are many sources for this episode and others of the Cheyenne sacred traditions. See Powell, *People of the Sacred Mountain;* George Bird Grinnell, *By Cheyenne Campfires* (New Haven: Yale University Press, 1962), and Grinnell's *The Cheyenne Indians: Their History and Ways of Life,* 2 vols. (Lincoln: University of Nebraska Press, 1972); George A. Dorsey, *The Cheyenne, Ceremonial Organization,* 2 vols. (Chicago: Field Museum, 1905), vol. 1.

24. A recent reinterpretation of Cheyenne history places this episode much earlier. By this tradition the Cheyennes' ancestors had come onto the northeastern plains from the far north about 500 B.C. Sometime during the next two centuries the *maiyun,* or powerful spirits, instructed them and guided them to their homeland, a region stretching in the four directions from Noaha-vose. The *maiyun* also gave the beautiful Ehyophstah as a wife among the Tsistsistas. The daughter of the thunder and earth spirits, she was transformed into a woman from a female bison, and she brought with her special powers in hunting all animals in the Cheyenne homeland. Centuries later the Cheyennes moved eastward into the woodlands near the Great Lakes, then migrated back to the plains around 1800. By this tradition, then, this recent journey was a return and reclamation of the homeland granted by the *maiyun* more than two millennia earlier. See Karl H. Schlesier, *The Wolves of Heaven: Cheyenne Shamanism, Ceremonies, and Prehistoric Origins* (Norman: University of Oklahoma Press, 1987).

25. For an example of such a map, see Father Peter J. Powell, *The Cheyennes, Maheo's People: A Critical Bibliography* (Bloomington: Indiana University Press, 1980, published for the Newberry Library), xxviii–xxxi.

26. Powell, *People of the Sacred Mountain,* 1: 38–46, 51–66.

27. For various accounts of the peace of 1840, see George Bird Grinnell, *The Fighting Cheyennes* (Norman: University of Oklahoma Press, 1955), 63–69; Donald Berthrong, *The Southern Cheyennes* (Norman: University of Oklahoma Press, 1963), 82–84; Jablow, *The Cheyenne in Plains Indian Trade Relations,* 72–77; James Mooney, *Calendar History of the Kiowa Indians* (1898; rpt., Washington, D. C.: Smithsonian Institution Press, 1979), 275–76; Powell, *People of the Sacred Mountain,* 1: 67–73; George Bent to George Hyde, January 23, 1905, George Bent Papers, Western History Collections, Denver Public Library.

28. The best discussion of the evolution of this pattern and its significance is in John H. Moore, "Cheyenne Political History, 1820–1894," *Ethnohistory* 21:4 (Fall

1974): 329–59. The standard sources on the consequences of horses on Indian military culture and the way the two of them influenced social developments and the quest for rank are Secoy, *Changing Military Patterns of the Great Plains Indians,* and Bernard Mishkin, *Rank and Warfare Among the Plains Indians,* Monographs of the American Ethnological Society, no. 3 (Seattle: University of Washington Press, 1940).

29. Powell, *People of the Sacred Mountain,* 1: 626n.

30. Ibid., 1: 34–37, 116–17, 152–53; Grinnell, *The Fighting Cheyennes,* 13–17, 91–93.

31. Donald Jackson and Mary Lee Spence, *The Expeditions of John Charles Fremont,* vol. 1, *Travels from 1838 to 1844* (Urbana: University of Illinois Press, 1970), 202–3.

32. Edward M. Bruner, "Mandan," in *Perspectives in American Indian Culture Change,* ed. Edward H. Spicer (Chicago: University of Chicago Press, 1961), 201. Adoption, Bruner writes, was "the key mechanism of social structure which enabled members of warring tribes to trade in peace. . . . Plains Indian trade was accomplished by barter between fictitious relatives. From a larger perspective, a vast network of ritual kinship relationships extended throughout the entire Plains." For an interesting approach that uses archaeological methods to argue that these marriages among different groups were used to stabilize trade, see Margaret G. Hanna, "Do You Take This Woman? Economics and Marriage in a Late Prehistoric Band," *Plains Anthropologist* 29:104 (May 1984): 115–29.

33. The classic study is Sylvia Van Kirk, *Many Tender Ties: Women in Fur-trade Society, 1670–1870* (Norman: University of Oklahoma Press, 1983).

34. Edwin James, *An Account of an Expedition from Pittsburgh to the Rocky Mountains,* 2 vols. (Ann Arbor, Mich.: University Microfilms, 1966), 1: 502.

35. Fowler, *Journal,* 61–65.

36. David Lavender, *Bent's Fort* (Lincoln: University of Nebraska Press, 1972), 130–47; Jablow, *The Cheyenne Indians in Plains Indian Trade Relations,* 63–66.

37. The division into northern and southern branches is treated in every history of the Cheyennes. One article in particular places it within the context of continuing stresses within the people: Moore, "Cheyenne Political History, 1820–1894."

38. For a schematic illustration of the spatial demands of keeping horses on the plains, see Moore, *The Cheyenne Nation,* 165–67.

39. Ibid., 178–80.

40. Powell, *People of the Sacred Mountain,* 1: 172–84.

41. For an extended discussion of the significance of homicide within Cheyenne society, using this case and others, including the murder of Walking Coyote by Winnebago after Winnebago stole the same wife, see Karl N. Llewellyn and E. Adamson Hoebel, *The Cheyenne Way: Conflict and Case Law in Primitive Jurisprudence* (Norman: University of Oklahoma Press, 1941), 132–68.

42. Hoebel, *The Cheyennes,* 44.

43. Alice Marriott and Carol K. Rachlin, *Plains Indian Mythology* (New York: Thomas Y. Crowell Company, 1975), 96–97.

44. In addition to sources cited in the following discussion, see the opening chapter of a fine study: James Earl Sherow, "Discord in the 'Valley of Content': Strife over Natural Resources in a Changing Environment on the Arkansas River Valley of the High Plains" (Ph.D. diss., University of Colorado, 1987), 9–35.

45. Richard Irving Dodge, *Our Wild Indians: Thirty-three Years Personal Experience Among the Red Men of the Great West* (Hartford, Conn.: A. D. Worthington and Company, 1883), 501.

46. Richard Irving Dodge, *The Hunting Grounds of the Great West. A Description of the Plains, Game, and Indians of the Great North American Desert* (London: Chatto and Windus, 1877).

47. Fowler, *Journal,* 65; George E. Hyde, *Life of George Bent: Written from His Letters* (Norman: University of Oklahoma Press, 1968), 37; James Bordeaux to Supterintendent of Indian Affairs, *Report of Commissioner of Indian Affairs, 1854,* Louise Barry, *The Beginning of the West: Annals of the Kansas Gateway to the American West* (Topeka: Kansas State Historical Society, 1972), 781, 787; Thomas J. Fitzpatrick to Thomas H. Harvey [?], June 24, 1848, Bureau of Indian Affairs, Letters Received, Upper Platte Agency, 1848.

48. Moore, *The Cheyenne Nation,* 166. Moore provides estimates also for other locations on the plains, with the need for resources and space increasing farther to the north.

49. Powell, *People of the Sacred Mountain,* 1: 93–99; George Bent to George Hyde, January 23, 1905, Bent Papers.

50. Howard Stansbury, *An Expedition to the Valley of the Great Salt Lake of Utah* (Philadelphia: Lippincott, Grambo and Company, 1855), 43–45; Mooney, *Calendar History of the Kiowa Indians,* 289–90; *Report of Commissioner of Indians Affairs, 1849–1850,* 139.

51. For an extended discussion of this important development, see Elliott West, *The Way to the West: Essays on the Central Plains* (Albuquerque: University of New Mexico Press, 1995), 18–19, 27–33.

52. Merlin Paul Lawson, *The Climate of the Great American Desert: Reconstruction of the Climate of Western Interior United States, 1800–1850* (Lincoln: University of Nebraska Press, 1974). A more localized tree-ring study was conducted around North Platte, Nebraska, near the forks of the Platte, an area traversed by the Pacific trails and especially popular as a hunting and camping area for the newly arrived native groups. This study showed an eighteen-year stretch free from drought after the opening of the nineteenth century (1804–1821), followed by eleven dry years (1822–1832), and then, coinciding with the great overland migration and movement of larger numbers of Indians into the area, a quarter century without drought (1833–1857), and after that, at the time of the Colorado gold rush and Indian wars another very dry period, this time nine years (1858–1866). See Harry Weakly, "A Tree Ring Record of Precipitation in Western Nebraska," *Journal of Forestry* 41 (1943): 816–19. Yet another investigation, correlating sunspot occurrence with drought cycles, as indicated through tree-ring analysis, finds conclusive evidence of severe drought from 1859–1861 and suggestions of a major dry spell from 1846–1851

Frederick E. Clements, "Drought Periods and Climatic Cycles," *Ecology* 2:3 (July, 1921): 181–88. See also Edmund Schulman, *Dendroclimatic Changes in Semiarid America* (Tucson: University of Arizona Press, 1956), especially 85–89.

53. The question of the extent, and especially the causes, of the decline of bison population is extraordinarily complicated. For a discussion and suggestion of some of the causes, see West, *The Way to the West,* 51–83.

54. Col. Henry Dodge, *Report of the Secretary of War . . . Journal of the March of a Detachment of Dragoons, Under the Command of Colonel Dodge, During the Summer of 1835,* House Doc. 181, 24th Cong., 1st sess., 16–17.

55. J. W. Abert, *Journal of Lieutenant J. W. Abert from Bent's Fort to St. Louis, in 1845,* Sen. Doc. 438, 29th Cong., 1st sess., 1848.

56. Justus von Liebig, *Die organische Chemie in ihrer Anwendung auf Agricultur und Physiologie* (Braunschweig: F. Vieweg und Sohn, 1840). The first edition in English was *Organic Chemistry and Its Applications to Agriculture and Physiology* London: Taylor and Walton, 1840).

57. D. D. Mitchell to Orlando Brown, in *Annual Report of Commissioner of Indian Affairs, 1849–50,* 132. Mitchell may well have relied on the opinions of his agent on the upper Arkansas, Thomas Fitzpatrick, who made the same point in the same year. The Indians' "complaints are increasing yearly and the grievances of which they complain becoming more sensibly felt. . . . It must be acknowledged that they have full grounds for their complaints, which are as follows. The disturbance and dispersion of game. The cutting down and destroying [of] wood" (Thomas J. Fitzpatrick to D. D. Mitchell, May 29, 1849, Bureau of Indian Affairs, Letters Received, Upper Platte Agency, 1849). On other occasions Fitzpatrick warned that construction of military posts in the region would heighten ill feeling, since the Indians knew full well that such installations would consume great numbers of trees and much game. See Thomas Fitzpatrick to D. D. Mitchell, September 24, 1850, in *Report of Commissioner of Indian Affairs, 1850,* 55, and Thomas Fitzpatrick to A. Cumming, November 19, 1853, in *Report of Commissioner of Indian Affairs, 1853,* 362.

58. "Letter of Thomas S. Twiss, Indian Agent at Deer Creek, U.S. Indian Agency in the Upper Platte," *Annals of Wyoming* 17:2 (July 1945): 148–50.

5. The Gold

1. Hans Biedermann, *Dictionary of Symbolism: Cultural Icons and the Meanings Behind Them,* trans. James Hulbert (New York: Meridian, 1994), 154–55; Nadia Julien, *The Mammoth Dictionary of Symbols: Understanding the Hidden Language of Symbols* (New York: Carroll and Graf, 1996), 182–84; Iona Opie and Moira Tatem, eds., *A Dictionary of Superstitions* (New York: Oxford University Press, 1992), 175.

2. By far the best summary of early gold reports is in Thomas Dean Isern, "The Making of a Gold Rush: Pike's Peak, 1858–1860" (Master's thesis, Oklahoma State University, 1975), 15–30.

3. LeRoy R. Hafen, ed., *Pike's Peak Gold Rush Guidebooks of 1859* (Glendale, Calif.: Arthur H. Clark Company, 1941), 25–26.

4. Hafen, ed., *Pike's Peak Gold Rush Guidebooks,* 26–29.

5. LeRoy R. Hafen, "Cherokee Goldseekers in Colorado, 1849–50," *Colorado Magazine* 15:3 (May 1938): 101–9; Hafen, ed., *Pike's Peak Gold Rush Guidebooks,* 32–43.

6. *Report of the Commissioner of Indian Affairs, 1854,* 94.

7. Isern, "The Making of a Gold Rush," 26–28; Hafen, ed., *Pike's Peak Gold Rush Guidebooks,* 43–47.

8. Hafen, ed., *Pike's Peak Gold Rush Guidebooks,* 48–50, 45–46.

9. On the Russell-Beck expedition, see ibid., 51ff., and Elma Dill Russell Spencer, *Green Russell and Gold* (Austin and London: University of Texas Press, 1966), 42–55. James H. Pierce, a participant, later wrote two accounts: "The First Prospecting of Colorado, Who Did It and What Led to It," *Trail,* 7:5 (October 1914): 5–11, and "With the Green Russell Party," *Trail,* 13:12 (May 1921): 5–14 and 14:1 (June 1921): 5–13.

10. Report of William B. Parsons, from *Lawrence Republican,* October 28, 1858, in Hafen, ed., *Pike's Peak Gold Rush Guidebooks,* 322.

11. For a summary of the formation and trip of the Lawrence party, see Hafen, ed., *Pike's Peak Gold Rush Guide Books,* 59ff. For accounts by and about some of its participants, see Jason T. Younker, "The Early Pioneer, Reminiscences of 1858–59," *Trail* 2:8 (January 1910): 5–12; Frank M. Cobb, "The Lawrence Party of Pike's Peakers (1858) and the Founding of St. Charles (Predecessor of Denver)," *Colorado Magazine* 10:5 (September 1933): 194–97; Eugene Parsons, "John Easter and the Lawrence Party," *Trail* 7:7 (December 1914): 5–10.

12. Younker, "The Early Pioneer," 6.

13. Julia Archibald Holmes, *A Bloomer Girl on Pike's Peak, 1858,* ed. Agnes Wright Spring (Denver: Denver Public Library, 1949), 14.

14. Holmes, *Bloomer Girl,* 17, 24–25.

15. Julia Holmes to mother, August 5, 1858, printed in *Daily Missouri Republican,* October 17, 1858, and quoted in Hafen, ed., *Pike's Peak Gold Rush Guidebooks,* 65n.

16. Holmes, *Bloomer Girl,* 29–30.

17. The comment is noted by William B. Parsons in his report published in the *Lawrence Republican,* October 28, 1858, in Hafen, ed., *Pike's Peak Gold Rush Guidebooks,* 329.

18. His cousin later wrote that Russell, in spite of his "iron nerves," was stunned when a slim majority of the remaining thirty goldhunters voted to return home. Nonetheless, he "stepped out by himself and said: 'Gentlemen, you can all go, but I will stay if two men will stay with me.' From that twelve of us agreed to stay and all the balance went home, or somewhere else" (Pierce, "First Prospecting of Colorado," 7).

19. Dry Creek is in present-day Englewood, Colorado.

20. Pierce, "First Prospecting of Colorado," 8–9.

21. David Lindsey, ed., "The Journal of an 1859 Pike's Peak Gold Seeker," *Kansas Historical Quarterly* 22:4 (Winter 1956): 323–24.

22. Robert H. Bahmer, "The Colorado Gold Rush and California," *Colorado Magazine* 7:6 (November 1930): 222–26.

23. Henry Z. Curtis to Sadie [September 1858], Samuel S. Curtis Letters, Spencer Library, University of Kansas.

24. J. C. Baird, "First Gold Find in the Mountains," *Trail* 14:9 (February 1922): 4.

25. Luke Tierney, *History of the Gold Discoveries on the South Platte River*, in Hafen, ed., *Pike's Peak Gold Rush Guidebooks*, 118–19.

26. Henry Villard, *The Past and Present of the Pike's Peak Gold Regions* (St. Louis: Sutherland and McEvoy, 1860), 11.

27. Jerome C. Smiley, *History of Denver, with Outlines of the Earlier History of the Rocky Mountain Country* (Denver: J. H. Williamson and Company, 1903), 182.

28. For summaries of these early town organizations, see Nolie Mumey, *History of the Early Settlements of Denver with Reproduction of the First City Directory* (Glendale, Calif.: A. H. Clark, 1942).

29. Smiley, *History of Denver*, 198–224.

30. Samuel S. Curtis to Henry, November 2, 1858, copy, Curtis Letters.

31. William H. Larimer, *Reminiscences of General William Larimer and of His Son, William H. H. Larimer, Two Founders of Denver City* (Lancaster, Pa.: Press of the New Era Printing Company, 1918), 39–45.

32. Ibid., 47, 174–75.

33. Ibid., 74–84.

34. Ibid., 87–89.

35. Ibid., 89–94; Smiley, *History of Denver*, 212–21.

36. Edward W. Wynkoop, "Unfinished Colorado History," typescript, 5–10, Colorado State Historical Society; Thomas D. Isern, "The Controversial Career of Edward W. Wynkoop," *Colorado Magazine* 56:1 and 2 (Winter/Spring 1979): 2–3.

37. Spencer, *Green Russell and Gold*, 62–65; Hafen, ed., *Pike's Peak Gold Rush Guidebooks*, 76–78.

6. The Gathering

1. Thomas D. Sanders, reminiscence, 16, Western History Collections, Denver Public Library.

2. *Hannibal [Mo.] Messenger*, October 21, 1858; *New York Times*, September 1, September 28, 1858; Joseph L. Kingsbury, "The Pikes Peak Rush, 1859," *Colorado Magazine* 4:1 (January 1927): 2; James F. Willard, "Spreading the News of the Early Discoveries of Gold in Colorado," *Colorado Magazine* 6:3 (May 1929): 98–104.

3. *Times* (London), September 13, 1858.

4. *Lawrence, Kans. Herald of Freedom*, December 12, 1857.

5. *New York Tribune*, January 29, 1859.

6. E. H. N. Patterson diary, March 25, 1859, in LeRoy R. Hafen, ed., *Overland Routes to the Gold Fields, 1859, from Contemporary Diaries* (Glendale, Calif.: Arthur H. Clark Company, 1942), 75.

7. Thomas J. Farnham, *Travels in the Great Western Prairies, the Anahuac and Rocky Mountains, and in the Oregon Territory,* 2 vols. (London: Richard Bentley, 1843), 1: 107.

8. *New York Times,* September 28, 1858.

9. Calvin W. Gower, "Kansas Territory and the Pike's Peak Gold Rush" (Ph.D. diss., University of Kansas, 1958), 171, 174–75.

10. *Junction City, Kans. Sentinal,* quoted in Gower, "Kansas Territory and the Pike's Peak Gold Rush," 218.

11. Gower, "Kansas Territory and the Pike's Peak Gold Rush," 14.

12. Levi Wilson to N. G. Elliott, October 24, 1858, Newton G. Elliott Collection, Missouri Historical Society.

13. LeRoy R. Hafen, ed., *Colorado Gold Rush: Contemporary Letters and Reports, 1858–1859* (Glendale, Calif.: Arthur H. Clark Company, 1941), 258, 264, 273; Gower, "Kansas Territory and the Pike's Peak Gold Rush," 196, 258; *Hannibal [Mo.] Messenger,* March 10, 17, 1859; *Daily Kansas City Journal of Commerce,* December 17, 1859.

14. [*St. Louis*] *Daily Missouri Democrat,* November 24, 1858.

15. *Hannibal [Mo.] Messenger,* February 9, 1859. For an example of a special edition focusing on the gold fields, see [*Atchison, Kans.*] *Freedom's Champion,* January 1, 1859.

16. Hafen, ed., *Colorado Gold Rush,* 214, 216.

17. Ibid., 94, 129.

18. Samuel S. Curtis to Henry Curtis, November 22, 1858, Curtis Family Letters, Beinecke Library, Yale University; Hafen, ed., *Colorado Gold Rush,* 147, 172.

19. Hafen, ed., *Colorado Gold Rush,* 237–38.

20. Ibid., 199, 249; *Leavenworth [Kans.] Times,* March 5, 1859.

21. *Allen's Guide Book and Map to the Gold Fields of Kansas & Nebraska and Great Salt Lake City* (Washington, D.C.: R. A. Waters, 1859).

22. Dr. J. W. Reed, *Reed's Guide to the Kansas Gold Region. With a Map Embracing the Northern and Southern Routes* (New York: J. H. Colton, 1859), 9.

23. William B. Parsons, *The New Gold Mines of Western Kansas,* in *Pike's Peak Gold Rush Guidebooks of 1859,* ed. LeRoy Hafen (Glendale, Calif.: A. H. Clark, 1941), 187–90.

24. Pratt and Hunt, *Guide to the Gold Mines of Kansas: Containing an Accurate and Reliable Map* (Chicago: Briggs House, 1859), 68, 12, 14 (italics in original).

25. For examples, see Hannibal and St. Joseph Railroad, *New and Short Route Open to the Gold Regions, Pike's Peak and Cherry Creek, and All Parts of Kansas and Nebraska!* (Boston: George C. Rand and Avery, 1859); Cleveland and Toledo Railroad Company, *For Pike's Peak and the Gold Mines, via Cleveland and Toledo Rail Road. A Direct and All Rail Road Line to St. Joseph, Kansas T.,* Broadside, Beinecke Library, Yale University; *Great Western Michigan Central. Traveller's Com-*

panion and Guide Westward (Boston: Fred Rogers, 1860); *Davis' Great Western Business Guide of the Pittsburgh, Fort Wayne and Chicago Railway, and Its Connections* (Philadelphia: F. C. Davis, 1861).

26. Pratt and Hunt, *Guide to the Gold Mines of Kansas.*

27. L. J. Eastin, *Emigrants' Guide to Pike's Peak* (Leavenworth City, K.T., 1859); *Guide to the New Gold Region of Western Kansas and Nebraska* (New York: John W. Oliver, 1859).

28. William B. Parsons, *The New Gold Mines of Western Kansas: Being a Complete Description o the Newly Discovered Gold Mines* (Cincinnati: Geo. S. Blanchard, 1859).

29. Hafen, ed., *Pikes Peak Guide Books,* 227.

30. Pratt and Hunt, *Guide to the Gold Mines of Kansas,* 33–35; *Guide to the New Gold Region,* 17.

31. *Guide to the Kansas Gold Mines at Pike's Peak . . . From Notes of Capt. J. W. Gunnison* (Cincinnati: E. Mendenhall, 1859), 8, 16–18.

32. *Western Journal of Commerce,* March 12, 1859, quoted in Gower, "Kansas Territory and the Pike's Peak Gold Rush," 176.

33. See, for instance, *Hannibal and St. Joseph Railroad. New and Short Route Open to the Gold Regions* (Boston: George C. Rand and Avery, 1859); *Great Western Michigan Central. Traveller's Companion and Guide Westward* (Boston: Fred Rogers, 1860); *Davis' Great Western Business Guide of the Pittsburgh, Fort Wayne and Chicago Railway, and Its Connections* (Philadelphia: F. C. Davis, 1861).

34. "Map of Kansas with Route from Lawrence to the Gold Mines," Spencer Library, University of Kansas.

35. *Traveler's Guide to the New Gold Mines in Kansas and Nebraska* (New York: Polhemus and de Vries, 1859).

36. *Toledo, Wabash and Great Western Railroad Co. Direct Route to Pikes Peak and the Gold Regions* (New York: Robertson, Seibert and Sherman, 1859).

37. John C. Fremont, *A Report of the Exploring Expedition to Oregon and North California, in the Years 1843–44,* 107–8, 289.

38. "Report of Lt. Francis T. Bryan," in *Report of the Secretary of War, 1857,* House Doc. no. 2, Appendix H, 475–77, 35th Cong., 1st sess.

39. Walter B. Sloan, *History and Map of Kansas and Nebraska: Describing Soil, Climate, Rivers, Prairies, Mounds, Forests, Minerals* (Chicago: Robert Fergus, 1855), 3, 19–23, 27, 65.

40. [*Lawrence, Kans.*] *Herald of Freedom,* February 6, May 22, 1858.

41. *Hannibal* [*Mo.*] *Messenger,* September 30, 1858.

42. Augustus Ford Harvey journal, copy of transcript, September 23, 28, October 3, 7, 8, 14, November 7, 1858, Kansas State Historical Society.

43. Gower, "Kansas Territory and the Pike's Peak Gold Rush," 26.

44. [*St. Louis*] *Daily Missouri Democrat,* November 24, 1858.

45. Hafen, ed., *Colorado Gold Rush,* 207, 225, 231.

46. Parker and Huyett, *The Illustrated Miners' Hand-Book and Guide to Pike's Peak* (St. Louis: Parker and Huyett, 1859), 14–16.

47. Hafen, ed., *Pike's Peak Guide Books,* 160, 184, 250, 285.

48. Wilbur Fiske Parker, "'The Glorious Orb of Day Has Rose': A Diary of the Smoky Hill Route to Pike's Peak, 1858," ed. Norman Lavers, *Montana: The Magazine of Western History* 36:2 (Spring 1986): 56–57.

49. Parker and Huyett, *Illustrated Miners' Hand-Book,* 17.

50. Daniel Witter diary, July 1, 1859, Colorado State Historical Society.

51. Charles Hull, "Memories of the Trail," 1, reminiscence, microfilm of original typescript, Missouri Historical Society.

52. Sylvanus Wellman diary, March 5–23, 1859, Colorado State Historical Society.

53. J. A. Locke to George W. Collamore, February 19, 1859, George Collamore Letters, Spencer Library, University of Kansas.

54. Alexander Rooney to Emeline Littlefield, November 22, 1859, April 16, 1860, Rooney-Littlefield Letters, Western History Collections, Denver Public Library; Article of Agreement, March 12, 1859, Darius H. Chapman Papers, Nebraska State Historical Society.

55. *Missouri, Public Works Board, Railroad Report, 1859,* Missouri State Historical Society.

56. J. C. Merrill diary, April 29, 1864, Missouri State Historical Society.

57. Gower, "Kansas Territory and the Pike's Peak Gold Rush," 183.

58. Perry Kline, reminiscence, 6, Colorado State Historical Society; Hiram Alton diary, April 12–28, 1864, Western History Collections, Denver Public Library; E. J. March diary, June 5, 1859, Missouri State Historical Society.

59. Charles Post diary, May 7, 1859, in Hafen, ed., *Overland Routes to the Gold Fields,* 26; John D. Lake journal, September 8, 1860, Western History Collections, Denver Public Library.

60. Hull, "Memories of the Trail," 4.

61. J. S. Baker to Dear Uncle, April 24, 25, 1859, Western Travel Papers, Missouri Historical Society.

62. *Missouri Republican,* March 23, 1859.

63. Merrill diary, April 28, 1864.

64. Augusta H. Block interview, O-14/B62, Oral History Collection, Colorado State Historical Society.

65. A. T. Bartlett diary, April 19, 1860, Missouri Historical Society; Horace Everett to Abiel Leonard, May 16, 1859, Abiel Leonard Papers, Missouri State Historical Society.

66. Gower, "Kansas Territory and the Pike's Peak Gold Rush," 187.

67. Kline reminiscence, 10; Thomas D. Sanders, reminiscence, 25, Western History Collections, Denver Public Library; Julia S. Lambert, "Plain Tales of the Plains," *Trail* 8:8 (January 1916): 4–5; H. M. Judson diary, June 9, 1862, Nebraska State Historical Society.

68. Thomas Wildman to Lucy, April 25, 1859, Augustus and Thomas Wildman Letters, Beinecke Library, Yale University.

69. Anonymous to Harry and Metta, n.d. [1859], Harry Faulkner Papers, Western History Collections, Denver Public Library.

70. Hull, "Memories of the Trail," 4; W. W. Sullivan, "Crossing the Plains in '62," 4–5, Beinecke Library, Yale University; Hafen, ed., *Overland Routes to the Gold Fields*, 91; Rose Bell diary, May 3, 1862, Colorado State Historical Society; V. F. Creel diary, May 25, 1864, Montana State Historical Society.

71. Wellman diary, May 23, 1859; Hafen, ed., *Overland Routes to the Gold Fields*, 72, 78, 81, 84; Anonymous, diary, May 20, 1862, June 1, 1862, Nebraska State Historical Society; Robert Carswell to Mrs. Fraser, April 23, 1864, Montana State Historical Society.

72. Henry Kingman, *The Travels and Adventures of Henry Kingman in Search of Colorado and California Gold* (Delavan, Kans.: Herington Sun Press, 1917), 18.

73. Hafen, ed., *Colorado Gold Rush*, 255, 268.

74. Sam S. Curtis to Henry, November 2, 1858, Curtis Family Letters.

7. The Rush

1. *Missouri Republican*, March 27, 1859, in *Colorado Gold Rush: Contemporary Letters and Reports, 1858–1859,* ed. LeRoy R. Hafen (Glendale, Calif.: Arthur H. Clark Company, 1941), 17.

2. [*Topeka*] *Tribune*, April 7, 1859, quoted in Calvin W. Gower, "Kansas Territory and the Pike's Peak Gold Rush" (Ph.D. diss., University of Kansas, 1958), 53.

3. Walker D. Wyman, "Council Bluffs and the Westward Movement," *Iowa Journal of History* 47:2 (April 1949): 109–10; Joseph L. Kingsbury, "The Pike's Peak Rush, 1859," *Colorado Magazine* 4:1 (January 1927): 2–3; David Lindsey, ed. "The Journal of an 1859 Pike's Peak Gold Seeker," *Kansas Historical Quarterly* 22:4 (Winter 1956): 321–41; Henry Kingman, *The Travels and Adventures of Henry Kingman in Search of Colorado and California Gold* (Delavan, Kans.: Herington Sun Press, 1917), 17–20; Julia S. Lambert, "Plain Tales of the Plains," *Trail* 8:8 (January 1916): 3–4; Albert K. Richardson, *Beyond the Mississippi: From the Great River to the Great Ocean* (Hartford, Conn.: American Publishing Company, 1867), 157.

4. [*Kansas City, Mo.*] *Western Journal of Commerce*, May 25, 1859, in Hafen, ed., *Colorado Gold Rush,* 316; Charles M. Clark, *A Trip to Pike's Peak and Notes by the Way* (Chicago: S. P. Rounds, 1861), 17–18; Bayard Taylor, *Colorado: A Summer Trip* (New York: G. P. Putnam and Son, 1867), 173.

5. Hafen, ed., *Colorado Gold Rush,* 316.

6. The editor was writing a year later, recalling the crowds of 1859. Hafen, ed., *Colorado Gold Rush,* 276–77.

7. Emanuel Downham reminiscence, 3, Missouri State Historical Society; Hafen, ed., *Colorado Gold Rush,* 256; *Missouri Republican,* March 23, 1859.

8. Thomas W. Knox, "To Pike's Peak and Denver," *Knickerbocker* 58:2 (August 1861): 115.

9. Lambert, "Plain Tales of the Plains," 4.

10. Hafen, ed., *Colorado Gold Rush,* 309.

11. Lewis Henry Morgan, *The Indian Journals, 1859–62* (Ann Arbor: University of Michigan Press, 1959), 30.

12. Hafen, ed., *Colorado Gold Rush,* 259, 293, 295; [*Kansas City, Mo.*] *Western Journal of Commerce,* April 3, 1859.

13. *Missouri Republican,* April 21, 1859; E. H. N. Patterson diary, April 23, 1859, in *Overland Routes to the Gold Fields, 1859, from Contemporary Diaries,* ed. LeRoy R. Hafen (Glendale, Calif.: Arthur H. Clark Company, 1942), 100; Richardson, *Beyond the Mississippi,* 157; Thomas Wildman to Lucy, April 25, 1859, Augustus and Thomas Wildman Letters, Beinecke Library, Yale University.

14. *Missouri Republican,* April 21, 1859.

15. Carla Elizabeth Neuhaus, "Transportation to Colorado, 1858–1869" (Master's thesis, University of Colorado, 1928), 32–33.

16. *Missouri Republican,* March 19, 1859; Neuhaus, "Transportation to Colorado," 34–35; Charles Post diary, May 13, 1859, in Hafen, ed., *Overland Routes,* 29.

17. A. Frizzell diary, May 31, 1860, Nebraska State Historical Society; David H. McLaughlin, reminiscence, Nebraska State Historical Society.

18. Neuhaus, "Transportation to Colorado," 35–37; [*Denver*] *Rocky Mountain News,* August 1, 7, 1862, April 2, 1863.

19. Edward S. Ellis, *The Huge Hunter; or, The Steam Man of the Prairies,* Beadle's Half-Dime Library, vol. 11, no. 271 (1868; rpt., New York: Beadle and Adams, 1882).

20. William Lockwood diary, May 20, 1866, in Samuel Finley Blythe diary, typescript, 1866, Nebraska State Historical Society.

21. H. M. Judson diary, June 12, 1861, Nebraska State Historical Society. Judson was on his way to Oregon, but his words describe well the routine of others headed for Colorado during this period.

22. Knox, "To Pike's Peak and Denver," 115.

23. Robert Thoroughman, reminiscence, Special Collections, Montana State University Library.

24. Hafen, ed., *Overland Diaries,* 36.

25. Thomas Sanders, reminiscence, 28, 31, Western History Collections, Denver Public Library; Perry Kline, reminiscence, 44, 46, Colorado State Historical Society; Calvin Clark diary, Western History Collections, Denver Public Library; E. Dunsha Steele, "In the Pike's Peak Gold Rush of 1859: Diary of E. Dunsha Steele," *Colorado Magazine* 29:4 (October 1952): 306.

26. Anonymous diary, June 9, 1862, Nebraska State Historical Society; Anonymous, "Overland Journey to Colorado," journal, May 29, 1863, Western History Collections, Denver Public Library.

27. Lindsey, ed., "Journal of an 1859 Pike's Peak Gold Seeker," 326, 328.

28. Parker and Huyett, *The Illustrated Miners' Hand-Book and Guide to Pike's Peak* (St. Louis: Parker and Huyett, 1859), 19.

29. Walter B. Sloan, *History and Map of Kansas and Nebraksa* (Chicago: Robert Fergus, 1855), 34; Robert W. Baughman, *Kansas in Maps* (Topeka: Kansas State Historical Society, 1961), 54–55.

30. William Henry Harrison Larimer, *Reminiscences of General William Larimer and of His Son William H. H. Larimer, Two of the Founders of Denver City* (Lancaster

Pa.: Press of the New Era, 1918), 266 [*Leavenworth, Kans.*] *Times*, March 5, 1859. D. C. Collier also wrote from the mountains to the [*Lawrence, Kans.*] *Herald of Freedom* that several parties had made the trip and found the Indians friendly and the grass, water, fuel, and game abundant (Hafen, ed., *Colorado Gold Rush*, 230).

31. Wilbur Fiske Parker, "'The Glorious Orb of Day Has Rose': A Diary of the Smoky Hill Route to Pike's Peak, 1858," ed. Norman Lavers, *Montana: The Magazine of Western History* 36:2 (Spring 1986): 55–58.

32. Ibid., 58–61.

33. Kline, reminiscence, 61; Hafen, ed., *Overland Routes*, 147, 266–69, 272–73; Wayne C. Lee and Howard C. Raynesford, *Trails of the Smoky Hill: From Coronado to the Cowtowns* (Caldwell, Idaho: Caxton Printers, 1980), 36–37; Margaret Long, *The Smoky Hill Trail* (Denver: Kistler, 1947), 19–21; Gower, "Kansas Territory and the Pike's Peak Gold Rush," 214–20.

34. Lee and Raynesford, *Trails of the Smoky Hill*, 36–37.

35. Harriet Kimbro, ed., "'A Genuine Western Man Never Drinks Tea': Gustavus French Merriam's Letters from Kansas in 1860," *Kansas History* 8:3 (Autumn 1985): 167.

36. G. S. McCain, "A Trip from Atchison, Kansas, to Laurette, Colorado: Diary of G. S. McCain," *Colorado Magazine* 27:2 (April 1950): 97.

37. Rose Bell diary, May 6, 1862, Colorado State Historical Society.

38. LeRoy R. Hafen, ed., "Diary of Mrs. A. C. Hunt, 1859," *Colorado Magazine* 21:5 (September 1944): 162; Lambert, "Plain Tales of the Plains," 2; Post diary, May 13, 1858, in Hafen, ed., *Overland Routes*, 29; Anson Bradbury, reminiscence, Montana State Historical Society.

39. V. F. Creel diary, June 29, 1864, Montana State Historical Society; Sarah Hively journal, April 12, 1863, Western History Collections, Denver Public Library; Patterson diary, May 13, 1859, in Hafen, ed., *Overland Routes*, 128.

40. Julia Archibald Holmes, *A Bloomer Girl on Pike's Peak, 1858,* ed. Agnes Wright Spring (Denver: Denver Public Library, 1949), 15.

41. Lockwood diary, June 18, 1866, quoted in Blythe diary.

42. Post diary, June 6, 1859, in Hafen, ed., *Overland Routes,* 43; Sanders, reminiscence, 27–28; Kline, reminiscence, 61; James Owen journal, July 17, 1860, Newberry Library; Patterson diary, May 14, 1859, in Hafen, ed., *Overland Routes,* 129.

43. Samuel Mallory diary, June 10, 1860, Colorado State Historical Society.

44. Raymond W. Settle, ed., *The March of the Mounted Riflemen: First United States Military Expedition to Travel the Full Length of the Oregon Trail* (Glendale, Calif.: Arthur H. Clark Company, 1940), 306.

45. Knox, "To Pike's Peak and Denver," 115.

46. Mark Twain [Samuel Clemens], *Roughing It* (Hartford, Conn.: American Publishing Company, 1873), 61.

47. Holmes, *Bloomer Girl*, 18–19; Post diary, May 27, 1859, in Hafen, ed., *Overland Routes*, 36–37; Lucy H. Fosdick, "Across the Plains in '61," typescript, Beinecke Library, Yale University; Sanders, reminiscence; Harry Faulkner diary, April 8, 1859, Western History Collections, Denver Public Library.

48. Holmes, *Bloomer Girl,* 27; H. M. Hudson diary, June 17, 1861, Nebraska State Historical Society; A. M. Gass diary, May 18, 1859, in Hafen, ed., *Overland Routes,* 222.

49. Faulkner diary, April 6, 1859.

50. Alfred Barnitz to wife, September 15, 1867, Alfred Barnitz Papers, Beinecke Library, Yale University.

51. McCain, "A Trip from Atchison, Kansas," 98; Charles B. France diary, May 12, 1865, Missouri State Historical Society; J. A. Wilkinson diary, May 30, 1859, Henry E. Huntington Library.

52. Mollie Dorsey Sanford, *Mollie: The Journey of Mollie Dorsey Sanford in Nebraska and Colorado Territories, 1857–1866* (Lincoln: University of Nebraska Press, 1959), 124; Hiram Allton diary, May 5, 1864, Western History Collections, Denver Public Library.

53. Patterson diary, May 10, 1859, in Hafen, ed., *Overland Routes,* 125–26; Lockwood diary, June 10, 1866, quoted in Blythe diary.

54. Herbert O. Brayer, ed., *Pike's Peak . . . or Busted! Frontier Reminiscences of William Hawkins Hedges* (Evanston, Ill.: Branding Iron Press, 1954) 8–9.

55. Francis Crissey Young, *Across the Plains in '65: A Youngster's Journal from "Gotham" to Pike's Peak"* (Denver: Lanning Brothers, 1905), 155–56; Faulkner diary, April 3, 1859; A. T. Bartlett diary, May 8, 1860, Missouri Historical Society.

56. Lambert, "Plain Tales of the Plains," 6–7; Anonymous, "Overland Journey to Colorado," journal, May 25, 1863; Lockwood diary, June 21, 1866, quoted in Blythe diary; J. C. Merrill diary, June 9, 1864, Missouri State Historical Society.

57. Creel diary, May 29, 1864; Hively journal, April 1, May 4, 1863; Robert G. Athearn, ed., "Across the Plains in 1863: The Diary of Peter Winne," *Iowa Journal of History* 49:3 (July 1951): 23; Sanford, *Mollie,* 120.

58. Allton diary, May 31, 1864; Lavinia Honey Porter, *By Ox Team to California: A Narrative Crossing of the Plains in 1860* (Oakland, Calif.: Oakland Enquirer Publishing Company, 1910), 41; Albert D. Richardson, *Beyond the Mississippi: From the Great River to the Great Basin* (Hartford, Conn.: American Publishing Company, 1867).

59. Bell diary, June 5, 1862; Gass diary, May 27, May 29, 1859, in Hafen, ed., *Overland Routes,* 225; Porter, *By Ox Team to California,* 41; Alonzo Boardman to Nancy, June 10, 1863, Alonzo Boardman Letters, Western History Collections, Denver Public Library.

60. Faulkner diary, March 30, 1859.

61. Porter, *By Ox Team to California,* 19, 78.

62. Holmes, *Bloomer Girl,* 5–9, 16, 21–26; William B. Parsons report, published in the *Lawrence Republican,* October 28, 1858, in *Pike's Peak Gold Rush Guide Books of 1859,* ed. LeRoy Hafen (Glendale, Calif.: A. H. Clark, 1942), 325.

63. Porter, *By Ox Team to California,* 46; Emma Shepard Hill, *A Dangerous Crossing and What Happened on the Other Side* (Denver: Press of the Smith-Brooks Company, 1914), 28–29; Judson diary, June 8, 1862; Hafen, ed., *Overland Routes,* 48; Creel diary, June 10, 1864.

64. Young, *Across the Plains,* 108, 184; Bell diary, May 7, 1862; Kline, reminis-ence, 56–57; Hafen, ed., *Colorado Gold Rush,* 306, 325; John S. Wilson diary, May 2, 1859, Beinecke Library, Yale University; Mary Ronan, *Frontier Woman: The Story of Mary Ronan as Told to Margaret Ronan* (Missoula: University of Mon-tana, 1973), 5.

65. James F. Meline, *Two Thousand Miles on Horseback. Santa Fe and Back* (New York: Hurd and Houghton, 1867), 298; Ralph P. Bieber, ed., "Diary of a Journey to the Pike's Peak Gold Mines in 1859," *Mississippi Valley Historical Review* 14:3 (December 1927): 366.

66. Hafen, ed., *Overland Routes,* 149; J. A. Wilkinson journal, May 14, 1859, Newberry Library; Frizzell diary, May 7, 1860; Fosdick, "Across the Plains in '61"; Edwin R. Pease diary, May 4, 1859, in Hafen, ed., *Overland Routes,* 206; Hedges, *Pike's Peak . . . or Busted!* 90–91; Alden Brooks diary, June 6, 1859, Henry E. Hun-ngton Library.

67. Daniel Witter diary, July 3, 1859, Colorado State Historical Society; Eliphalet Crandall diary, April 11, 1859, Nebraska State Historical Society.

68. Anonymous, "Overland Journey to Colorado," journal, May 24–29, June 8, 1863.

69. Hafen, ed., "Diary of Mrs. A. C. Hunt," 170.

70. Sanford, *Mollie,* 119, 127.

71. Anonymous, "Overland Journey to Colorado," journal, May 24, 25, 26, 30, 1863.

72. Sanford, *Mollie,* 119, 120, 124.

73. George Watson to Friend Baldwin, July 27, 1864, letter, Western History Col-lections, Denver Public Library; Mallory diary, June 23, 24, 1860; Sanford, *Mollie,* 30.

74. Daniel Kellogg, "Across the Plains in 1858," *Trail* 5:7 (December 1912): 10–11. The journal entry is for March 23, 1859.

Path of Empire

1. Louise Barry, "The Ranch at Walnut Creek Crossing," *Kansas Historical Quar-terly* 37:2 (Summer 1971): 133–35; *Report of Commissioner of Indian Affairs, 1859,* 305–7.

2. Correspondents gave varying estimates for the population in the camps dur-ing the winter, ranging from as few as 250 to as many as 2,000. Most likely there were fewer than 1,000 persons in the various settlements in the Cherry Creek area. For estimates of population for the months between November 15, 1858, and March 1859, see LeRoy F. Hafen, ed., *Colorado Gold Rush: Contemporary Letters and Reports, 1858–1859* (Glendale, Calif.: Arthur H. Clark Company, 1941), 152, 154, 170, 184, 204, 215, 225, 239, 245.

3. Hafen, ed., *Colorado Gold Rush,* 219.

4. John Hartzell to Augusta, June 1, 1859, letter, Western History Collections, Denver Public Library.

5. Quoted in Leslie Linville, *The Smoky Hill Valley and Butterfield Trail* (Colby, Kans.: LeRoy's Printing, 1874), 34–35.

6. Hafen, ed., *Colorado Gold Rush,* 317–18.

7. Ibid., 325.

8. C. L. Long diary, May 16, 1859, Kansas State Historical Society.

9. Darius H. Chapman diary, May 9–11, Darius H. Chapman Papers, Nebraska State Historical Society. On go-backs, see also David Lindsey, ed., "The Journal of an 1859 Pike's Peak Gold Seeker," *Kansas Historical Quarterly* 22:4 (Winter 1956): 329; Thomas D. Sanders, reminiscence, 32–33, Western History Collections, Denver Public Library; Edwin R. Pease diary, May 11–25, in *Overland Routes to the Gold Fields, 1859, from Contemporary Diaries,* ed. LeRoy R. Hafen (Glendale, Calif.: Arthur H. Clark Company, 1942), 201–13; Charles Hull, "Memories of the Trail," 7, microfilm of original reminiscence, Missouri Historical Society; Anson Bradbury, reminiscence, Montana State Historical Society; Charles Post diary, May 27, 1859, in Hafen, ed., *Overland Routes,* 36.

10. John S. Wilson diary, May 6, 7, 1859, Beinecke Library, Yale University, E. H. N. Patterson, May 9, 1859, in Hafen, ed., *Overland Routes,* 116–17; Alder Brooks, "Grand Trip Across the Plains," manuscript journal, May 23, 1859, Newberry Library, Chicago.

11. Daniel Gantt journal, Nebraska State Historical Society.

12. Darius H. Chapman diary, June 10, 1859.

13. Luke Tierney, *History of the Gold Discoveries on the South Platte River. To Which Is Appended a Guide of the Route, by Smith and Oaks* [sic] (Pacific City, Iowa: Herald Office, 1859).

14. Oakes's version of events is found in "Statement as to Cause (1883)," D. C Oakes Papers, Western History Collections, Denver Public Library.

15. George _____ to cousin, May 20, 1859, mss. 215, Western Americana Collection, Beinecke Library, Yale University.

16. LeRoy R. Hafen, ed., "George A. Jackson's Diary, 1858–1859," *Colorado Magazine* 12:6 (November 1935), 201–14.

17. On Gregory, see Hubert Howe Bancroft, *The Works of Hubert Howe Bancroft,* vol. 25, *History of Nevada, Colorado, and Wyoming, 1540–1888* (San Francisco: History Company, Publishers, 1890), 377.

18. Elma Dill Russell Spencer, *Green Russell and Gold* (Austin: University of Texas Press, 1966), 107–20; Bancroft, *History of Nevada, Colorado and Wyoming,* 379–80.

19. Charles W. Henderson, *Mining in Colorado: A History of Discovery, Development and Production* (Washington, D.C.: Government Printing Office, 1926), 69 Frank Fossett, *Colorado: Historical, Description, and Statistical Work on the Rock Mountain Gold and Silver Region* (Denver: Daily Tribune, 1876), 465.

20. Edward W. Wynkoop, "Unfinished Colorado History," typescript, 9, Edward W. Wynkoop Papers, Colorado State Historical Society.

21. Hafen, ed., *Colorado Gold Rush,* 371.

22. The report can be found in ibid., 376–82.

23. Samuel S. Curtis to Henry Curtis, November 22, 1858, Curtis Family Letters, Beinecke Library, Yale University; Hafen, ed., *Colorado Gold Rush*, 147, 172.

24. Power of Attorney, Joseph E. Berard and Theodore W. Bayaud to Thomas J. Bayaud, November 1859, Thomas J. Bayaud Papers, Western History Collections, Denver Public Library.

25. *Rocky Mountain News,* September 14, 1883; Allen du Pont Breck, *The Episcopal Church in Colorado, 1860–1963* (Denver: Big Mountain Press, 1963), 5, 8.

26. Another paper, the *Cherry Creek Pioneer,* published a single issue the same day, April 23, 1859, but its editor, Jack Merrick, then sold his equipment to Byers and turned to prospecting. Other papers appeared and vanished quickly during the first couple of years, but Byers's *Rocky Mountain News* quickly established its dominance. David Fridtjof Halaas, *Boom Town Newspapers: Journalism on the Rocky Mountain Mining Frontier, 1859–1881* (Albuquerque: University of New Mexico Press, 1981), 3; Stephen J. Leonard and Thomas J. Noel, *Denver: Mining Camp to Metropolis* (Niwot: University Press of Colorado, 1990), 9.

27. Gunther Barth, *Instant Cities: Urbanization and the Rise of San Francisco and Denver* (New York: Oxford University Press, 1975), 185; Hafen, ed., *Overland Routes,* 53–54.

28. Promotional Circular, *Hannibal and St. Joseph Railroad,* 1860, Missouri State Historical Society.

29. Albert Richardson, quoted in promotional circular, *Hannibal and St. Joseph Railroad,* 1860, Missouri State Historical Society.

30. Hafen, ed., *Colorado Gold Rush,* 249.

31. *Denver City and Auraria, the Commercial Emporium of the Pike's Peak Gold Regions, in 1859* (Denver, 1860), facsimile (Glendale, Calif.: Arthur H. Clark, 1942), passim.

32. Elbridge Gerry Papers, account books, Colorado State Historical Society.

33. Lewis H. Garrard, *Wah-to-Yah and the Taos Trail* (Norman: University of Oklahoma Press, 1955), 63–66.

34. Jerome C. Smiley, *History of Denver, with Outlines of the Earlier History of the Rocky Mountain Country* (Denver: J. H. Williamson and Company, 1903), 221. For McGaa's side of the story, see William McGaa, "A Statement Regarding the Formation of the St. Charles and Denver Town Companies," *Colorado Magazine* 22:3 (May 1945): 125–29.

35. Janet Lecompte, "John Poisal," in *The Mountain Men and the Fur Trade of the Far West,* ed. LeRoy R. Hafen, 10 vols. (Glendale, Calif.: Arthur H. Clark Company, 1968), vol. 6; Hafen, ed., *Colorado Gold Rush,* 222.

36. Garrard, *Wah-to-Yah,* 58–59; Lecompte, "John Poisal," 6: 354–57.

37. Lecompte, "John Poisal," 6: 353.

38. Sarah Hively journal, April 15, May 5, 1863, Western History Collections, Denver Public Library.

39. Smiley, *History of Denver,* 222.

40. The name of the town was later changed to Laporte. Frank Hall, *History of the State of Colorado,* 4 vols. (Chicago: Blakely Printing Company, 1889), 4: 181.

41. LeRoy R. Hafen, "Elbridge Gerry, Colorado Pioneer," *Colorado Magazine* 29:2 (April 1952): 137–49; Elbridge Gerry account books, 1858–1860.

42. Geminien Beauvais file, Nebraska State Historical Society.

43. Donald Jackson and Mary Lee Spence, eds., *The Expeditions of John Charles Fremont*, vol. 1, *Travels from 1838 to 1844* (Urbana: University of Illinois Press, 1970), 437.

44. Quoted in Margaret Coel, *Chief Left Hand: Southern Arapaho* (Norman: University of Oklahoma Press, 1981), 65.

45. William Bent to Charles Meeks, Superintendent of Indian Affairs, October 20, 1858, Letters Received, Upper Arkansas Agency, Office of Indian Affairs.

46. William Bent to Superintendent for Indian Affairs, December 17, 1858, Letters Received, Upper Arkansas Agency, Office of Indian Affairs. This letter is reprinted in *Relations with the Indians of the Plains, 1857–1861,* ed. Leroy R. Hafen and Ann W. Hafen (Glendale, Calif.: Arthur H. Clark Company, 1959), 173–74.

47. For a summary of the one source, a manuscript in the Colorado State Historical Society, see Coel, *Chief Left Hand,* 43–53.

48. Hafen, ed., *Colorado Gold Rush,* 202, 219, 364.

49. Ibid., 341.

50. Ibid., 219.

51. Stan Hoig, *The Peace Chiefs of the Cheyennes* (Norman: University of Oklahoma Press, 1980), 27–37, 104–6.

52. There are various accounts of this famous incident: Father John Peter Powell, *People of the Sacred Mountain: A History of the Northern Cheyenne Chiefs and Warrior Society,* 2 vols. (San Francisco: Harper and Row, 1981), 1: 38–41; George B. Grinnell, *The Fighting Cheyennes,* (Norman: University of Oklahoma Press, 1955), 45–48; George E. Hyde, *Life of George Bent, Written from His Letters* (Norman: University of Oklahoma Press, 1968), 72–73. White Thunder was George Bent's grandfather and father of Owl Woman, wife of William Bent.

53. Hyde, *Life of George Bent,* 338–39; Powell, *People of the Sacred Mountain,* 1: 249.

54. "Sand Creek Massacre," *Report of the Secretary of War,* Sen. Exec. Doc. 26, 39th Cong., 2d sess., 1867, 103–4.

55. John H. Moore has written most vigorously on these changes in the Cheyennes. In the course of this change, he also argues, Dog Soldiers resorted to gang rape, or "putting a woman on the prairie," to coerce their sisters into marrying warriors they wanted to recruit. Other scholars have disagreed with the last contention, though applauding Moore's close attention to changes in the Dog Soldiers' social structure. See John H. Moore, *The Cheyenne Nation: A Social and Demographic History* (Lincoln: University of Nebraska Press, 1987), 197–204, 253–66, and his "Cheyenne Political History, 1820–1894," *Ethnohistory* 21:4 (Fall 1974): 329–59, and "Evolution and Historical Reductionism," *Plains Anthropologist* 26:94, part 1 (November 1981): 261–69. For opposing views, see E. Adamson Hoebel, "On Cheyenne Sociopolitical Organization," *Plains Anthropologist* 25:88, part 1 (May 1980): 161–69, and Lawrence A. Conrad, "Comment: An Early Eighteenth Century Reference to

'Putting a Woman on the Prairies' Among the Central Algonquians and Its Implications for Moore's Explanation of the Practice Among the Cheyenne," *Plains Anthropologist* 28:100 (May 1983): 141–42.

56. "Sand Creek Massacre," 104.

57. Thomas S. Twiss to Secretary of Interior, August 20, 1855, *Report of Commissioner of Indian Affairs, 1855,* 78; Thomas S. Twiss to Secretary of Interior, September 22, 1856, in *Report of Commissioner of Indian Affairs, 1856,* 98.

58. "Proceedings of a Treaty Council," Thomas S. Twiss, September 18, 1859, Office of Indian Affairs, Letters Received, Upper Arkansas Agency.

59. *Report of Commissioner of Indians Affairs, 1859,* 505–7.

9. On the Road to a Flourishing Mountain State

1. Fawn M. Brodie, *The Devil Drives: A Life of Sir Richard Burton* (New York: W. W. Norton and Company, 1967), 179. For other biographies, see Byron Farwell, *Burton: A Biography of Sir Richard Francis Burton* (London: Longmans, 1963), Thomas Wright, *The Life of Sir Richard Burton,* 2 vols. (New York: B. Franklin, 1968), and F. J. McLynn, *Burton: Snow upon the Desert* (London: John Murray, 1990).

2. Sir Richard Burton, *The Look of the West, 1860: Across the Plains to California* (Lincoln: University of Nebraska Press, n.d.), 9, 27, 29, 36, 38, 45. This is a reprint of Burton's *The City of the Saints and Across the Rocky Mountains to California* (London: Longman, Green, Longman and Roberts, 1862).

3. Burton, *Look of the West,* 22, 27, 56–57.

4. Ibid., 12, 23, 37, 61, 65.

5. Harry Faulkner diary, April 20, 1859, Western History Collections, Denver Public Library.

6. Letter, Andrew Drips to Bill, November 24, 1858, Andrew Drips Papers, Missouri State Historical Society. The books of the sutler at Fort Laramie also show some sales, such as gold pans and other such equipment, clearly aimed for the Rockies. Fort Laramie Sutler's Books, 1858–1859, Western History Collection, Denver Public Library.

7. David Lindsey, ed., "The Journal of an 1859 Pike's Peak Gold Seeker," *Kansas Historical Quarterly* 22:4 (Winter 1956): 328.

8. H. M. Judson diary, June 15, 1861, Nebraska State Historical Society; Anonymous, "Overland Journey to Colorado, 1863," Western History Collections, Denver Public Library. The full quote is, "We have yet *failed* to see the untrodden West [my emphasis]," but the context of the passage, with the author writing of road ranches and other businesses all along the road, makes it clear that he meant the opposite.

9. E. M. Stahl diary, passim, Western History Collections, Denver Public Library.

10. Henry Gratiot diary, May 11, 1859, Missouri Historical Society; Louise Barry, "The Ranch at Walnut Creek Crossing," *Kansas Historical Quarterly* 37:2 (Summer 1971): 140–43; Ida Ellen Rath, *The Rath Trail* (Wichita: McCormick-Armstrong Company, 1961), 10–20.

11. On Charles McDonald, see *Nebraska History and Record of Pioneer Days* 1:7 (November 1918); 1. On Burke, see *Nebraska City News,* July 8, 1910.

12. Perry Kline, reminiscence, Colorado State Historical Society.

13. Lavinia Honey Porter, *By Ox Team to California: A Narrative of Crossing the Plains in 1860* (Oakland, Calif.: Oakland Enquirer Publishing Company, 1910), 29.

14. *History of the Arkansas Valley, Colorado* (Chicago: O. L. Baskin and Company, 1881), 769.

15. Frank M. Stahl, *One Way Ticket to Kansas: The Autobiography of Frank M. Stahl. As Told to Margaret Whittemore* (Lawrence: University of Kansas Press, 1959), 50.

16. See, for instance, Penniston and Miller General Store day books, especially for 1867, Nebraska State Historical Society; ledger books, 1862–1878, Charles McDonald Papers, Nebraska State Historical Society; John Burke day books, 1872–1874, John Bratt Papers, Nebraska State Historical Society; Barnard Silvair Blondeau account books, 1858–1867, Nebraska State Historical Society.

17. W. T. E. to James M. Pelot, May 23, 1860, James M. Pelot file, Kansas State Historical Society.

18. Homer Austin journal, January 1863, Western History Collections, Denver Public Library.

19. Justus L. Cozad, reminiscence, Nebraska State Historical Society.

20. What follows is taken from the most complete account of the first stage service across the central plains: George A. Root and Russell K. Hickman, "Pike's Peak Express Companies," *Kansas Historical Quarterly* 13:3, 4 (August and November 1944): 163–95, 211–42.

21. The arrangement also showed just how anxious Missouri valley towns were to be the eastern terminus of such a system. In 1860, when the company was reorganized as the Central Overland California and Pikes Peak Express Company, prominent citizens of St. Joseph offered a remarkable package to make sure they kept this economic plum. Besides pledging the completion of the Hannibal and St. Joseph Railroad within a year, they gave the express company seventy-five lots in St. Joseph, eighteen lots in Ellwood, Kansas, a quarter-section of land, and $1,000 in real estate in another area as well as a house and an office in St. Joseph for employees. See contract, Central Overland and Pike's Peak Express Company, March 2, 1860, Missouri State Historical Society.

22. Although traffic on the Santa Fe Trail did not increase as much as on the Platte, it rose considerably. The number of wagons already was rising at the time of the gold rush, from 549 in 1851 to 1,827 in 1858. Traffic then lunged upward to supply the gold camps. By mid-June of 1860, with half the season still ahead, an observer on Walnut Creek had already counted 1,400 wagons with more than 3,500 tons of freight. Two years later 3,000 wagons carried more than 10,000 tons of goods over the trail, although even these figures may have missed a considerable part of the supplies that went to the Front Range. See Barry, "The Ranch at Walnut Creek Crossing," 137–38, and Walker Wyman, "Freighting: A Big Business on the Santa Fe Trail," *Kansas Historical Quarterly* 1:1 (November 1931): 20–25.

23. As part of this boom, competition quickened for the claim of the closest jumping-off place. Once the Hannibal and St. Joseph Railroad had built a spur to Atchison, town fathers boasted that they now were sixteen miles nearer to Colorado than their archrival, St. Joseph. Calvin W. Gower, "Kansas Territory and the Pike's Peak Gold Rush" (Ph.D. diss., University of Kansas, 1958), 207–9, 249–50.

24. Henry Pickering Walker, *The Wagonmasters: High Plains Freighting from the Earliest Days of the Santa Fe Trail to 1880* (Norman: University of Oklahoma Press, 1966), 194–95.

25. Charles L. Kenner, *A History of New Mexican–Plains Indian Relations* (Norman: University of Oklahoma Press, 1969), 85–86.

26. Stewart Van Vliet to Maj. Gen. T. S. Jesup, July 23, 1850, copy, Fort Laramie Correspondence, 1849–1874, Fort Laramie National Monument Library. Earlier Van Vliet had written of the difficulties in gardening on the windy, semiarid plains and said that a man from the Arkansas valley had settled nearby and was about to open his own farm.

27. John M. Kingsbury to James J. Webb, August 1, 1858, September 25, 1858, October 17, 1858, James Josiah Webb Papers, Missouri Historical Society. For a recent compilation of these two men's correspondence and an excellent commentary on their business and on Santa Fe of the 1850s, see Jane Lenz Elder and David J. Weber, eds., *Trading in Santa Fe: John M. Kingsbury's Correspondence with James Josiah Webb, 1853–1861* (Dallas: Southern Methodist University Press/DeGolyer Library, 1996).

28. John M. Kingsbury to James J. Webb, February 6, 1859, James Kingsbury Papers, DeGolyer Library, Southern Methodist University; James J. Webb to John M. Kingsbury, September 2, 1858, October 25, 1858, March 19, 1859, Webb Papers.

29. John M. Kingsbury to James J. Webb, July 30, 1859, Kingsbury Papers; John M. Kingsbury to James Josiah Webb, May 12, 1860, June 9, 1860, Webb Papers.

30. John M. Kingsbury to James J. Webb, May 6, 1860, Webb Papers.

31. A. T. Bartlett diary, April 30, May 2, May 11, 1860, Missouri Historical Society.

32. William Fulton, "Freighting and Staging in Early Days," and D. P. Rolfe, "Overland Freighting from Nebraska City," in *Proceedings and Collections of the Nebraska State Historical Society*, series 2, 5 (1902): 262 and 286; Walker, *Wagonmasters,* 187–89.

33. H. T. Clarke, "Freighting—Denver and Black Hills," in *Proceedings and Collections of the Nebraska State Historical Society*, series 2, 5 (1902): 302; Percival G. Lowe, *Five Years a Dragoon ('49 to '54) and Other Adventures on the Great Plains* (Kansas City, Mo.: Franklin Hudson Publishing Company, 1906), 359–60.

34. Walker, *Wagonmasters,* 181–82, 196.

35. Ibid., 185–86.

36. *Empire Magazine (Denver Post)*, February 10, 1974, 26–27.

37. Solomon Edwards diary, 1864, typescript, passim, Missouri State Historical Society.

38. William Hawkins Hedges, *Pike's Peak . . . or Busted! Frontier Reminiscences of William Hawkins Hedges,* ed. Herbert O. Brayer (Evanston, Ill.: Branding Iron Press, 1954), 13–14.

39. Rolfe, "Overland Freighting from Nebraska City," 281–82.

40. Ibid., 287.

41. Equipment list, folder 50, Moses U. Payne Papers, Missouri State Historical Society.

42. Rolfe, "Overland Freighting from Nebraska City," 282–83; Alexander Majors, *Seventy Years on the Frontier: Alexander Majors' Memoirs of a Lifetime on the Border* (Minneapolis: Ross and Haines, 1965), 202–5.

43. G. S. McCain, "A Trip from Atchison, Kansas, to Laurette, Colorado: Diary of G. S. McCain," September 10–October 15, 1864 [?], *Colorado Magazine* 27:2 (April 1950): 95–98.

44. Wagon-masters Regulations and Account Book, 1866, Jerome Dauchy Papers, Nebraska State Historical Society.

45. Ibid.

46. McCain, "A Trip from Atchison, Kansas," 98.

47. Edwards diary, June–October, 1864.

48. McCain, "A Trip from Atchison, Kansas," 98–100.

49. Rolfe, "Overland Freighting from Nebraska City," 286; Clifford Clinton Hill, "Wagon Roads in Colorado, 1858–1876" (Master's thesis, University of Colorado, 1949), 21–25; Leroy R. Hafen and Zachary Gussow, *Arapaho-Cheyenne Indians* [reports and findings of U.S. Indian Claims Commission] (New York: Garland Publishing, 1974), 4.

50. Authorities occasionally claimed that Colorado turned out as much as $37 million between 1859 and 1866, but the most reliable figures set the amount at around $25.5 million, with the annual production rising from about $.25 million in 1859 to about $5 million in 1864, then slacking off. The most reliable figures are in Charles W. Henderson, *Mining in Colorado: A History of Discovery, Development and Production* (Washington, D.C.: Government Printing Office, 1926), 69, and in Henderson's chapter, "Mining in Colorado," in *History of Colorado*, ed. James H. Baker, 5 vols. (Denver: Linderman Company, 1927), 2: 525–72. See also Ovando J. Hollister, *The Mines of Colorado* (Springfield, Mass.: Samuel Bowles and Company, 1867), 434–35; Frank Fossett, *Colorado: Historical, Description and Statistical Work on the Rocky Mountain Gold and Silver Region* (Denver: Daily Tribune, 1876), 465; and Hafen and Gussow, *Arapaho-Cheyenne Indians*, 261.

51. Thomas Fitzpatrick to A. Cumming, November 19, 1853, *Report of Commissioner of Indian Affairs, 1853*, 366.

52. J. W. Abert, *Journal of Lieutenant J. W. Abert from Bent's Fort to St. Louis, in 1845*, Sen. Doc. 438, 9, U.S. Senate, 29th Cong., 1st sess.

53. Susan Shelby Magoffin, *Down the Santa Fe Trail and into Mexico. The Diary of Susan Shelby Magoffin, 1846–1847* (New Haven: Yale University Press, 1926), 57–58; Lt. E. G. Beckwith, *Report of Exploration for a Route for the Pacific Railroad, by Capt. J. W. Gunnison, Topographical Engineers, near the 38th and 39th Parallels of North Latitude, from the Mouth of the Kansas River, MO, to the Sevier Lake, in the Great Basin*, H. Doc. 91, 27–28, 33d Cong., 2d sess., 1855.

54. Col. Henry Dodge, *Report of the Secretary of War . . . Journal of the March of a Detachment of Dragoons, Under the Command of Colonel Dodge, During the Summer of 1835*, H. Doc. 181, 13–14, U.S. Congress, 24th Cong., 1st sess.; Osborne Cross

diary, June 8, 1849, in *The March of the Mounted Riflemen: First United States Military Expedition to Travel the Full Length of the Oregon Trail*, ed. Raymond W. Settle (Glendale, Calif.: Arthur H. Clark Company, 1940), 71; Lydia Milner Waters, "Account of a Trip Across the Plains in 1855," *Quarterly of the Society of California Pioneers* 6:2 (June 1929): 64.

55. The ecology of grasses, root systems, and the effects of overgrazing is more complex than this very brief commentary can show. For a slightly more detailed discussion, with citations of some of the more useful works in a large literature, see Elliott West, *The Way to the West: Essays on the Central Plains* (Albuquerque: University of New Mexico Press, 1995), 34–36.

56. Settle, ed., *March of the Mounted Riflemen*, 298; Waters, "Account of a Trip Across the Plains in 1855," 64; Leo M. Kaiser and Priscilla Knuth, eds., "From Ithaca to Clatsop Plains: Miss Ketcham's Journal of Travel," *Oregon Historical Quarterly* 62:3 (September 1961): 278.

57. Hamilton Gardner, ed., "March of the 2nd Dragoons: Report of Lieutenant Colonel Philip St. George Cooke on the March of the 2nd Dragoons from Fort Leavenworth to Fort Bridger in 1857," *Annals of Wyoming* 27:1 (April 1955): 49–57.

58. Lindsey, ed., "The Journal of an 1859 Pike's Peak Gold Seeker," 331; Charles Post diary, June 12, 1859, in *Overland Routes to the Gold Fields, 1859, from Contemporary Diaries*, ed. LeRoy R. Hafen (Glendale, Calif.: Arthur H. Clark Company, 1942), 44–45; Ralph P. Bieber, ed., "Diary of a Journey to the Pike's Peak Gold Mines in 1859," *Mississippi Valley Historical Review* 14:3 (December 1927): 365; LeRoy R. Hafen, ed., "Diary of Mrs. A. C. Hunt, 1859," *Colorado Magazine* 21:5 (September 1944): 161–70.

59. "Diary of E. H. N. Patterson," in Hafen, ed., *Overland Routes to the Gold Fields*, 129–30; Burton, *Look of the West*, 66.

60. Daniel Kellogg, "Across the Plains in 1858," *Trail* 5:7 (December 1912): 11.

61. James Mooney, *Calendar History of the Kiowa Indians* (Washington, D.C.: Smithsonian Institution Press, 1979), 306.

62. See, for instance, J. Robert Brown, "Journal of a Trip Across the Plains of the U.S. from Mo. to Cal," May 17, May 21, June 8, 1856, photocopy of manuscript journal, Newberry Library, Chicago.

63. Alexander Majors to Charles McDonald, October 28, 1863; S. Poteet to Charles McDonald, April 1, 1864, correspondence file, series 1, folder 1; voucher file, series 3, folder 1; ledger and cash book, 1862–1864, series 4, ledger 1, Charles McDonald Papers, Nebraska State Historical Society.

64. Lowe, *Five Years a Dragoon*, 360–61; Silas L. Hopper, "Diary Kept by Silas L. Hopper, Blandinsville, Ill., April 20, 1863," *Annals of Wyoming* 3:2 (October 1925): 119.

10. The People of the Centre

1. Gilpin's speech was reprinted as part of *Guide to the Kansas City Gold Mines at Pike's Peak . . . from Notes of Capt. J. W. Gunnison* (Cincinnati: E. Mendenhall, 1859).

2. The comment on Gilpin's style is from Hubert Howe Bancroft, *The Works of Hubert Howe Bancroft*, vol. 25, *History of Nevada, Colorado, and Wyoming, 1540–1888* (San Francisco: History Company, Publishers, 1890), 414n.

3. John M. Kingsbury to James Josiah Webb, December 2, 1860, James Josiah Webb Papers, Missouri Historical Society.

4. Henry Pickering Walker, *The Wagonmasters: High Plains Freighting from the Earliest Days of the Santa Fe Trail to 1880* (Norman: University of Oklahoma Press, 1966), 180.

5. A series of articles in the *Rocky Mountain News* offers a lot-by-lot description of Denver in early 1860: *Rocky Mountain News*, February 1, February 8, February 22, 1860.

6. Albert D. Richardson, *Beyond the Mississippi: From Beyond the Great River to the Great Ocean* (Hartford, Conn.: American Publishing Company, 1867), 177–78.

7. LeRoy R. Hafen, ed., "Diary of Mrs. A. C. Hunt, 1859," *Colorado Magazine* 21:5 (September 1944): 169–70.

8. William McGaa and Family file, Clipping Files, Biography, Western History Collections, Denver Public Library.

9. Percival G. Lowe, "P. G. Lowe's Journal of the Sumner Wagon Train," in *Relations with the Indians of the Plains, 1857–1861*, ed. LeRoy R. Hafen and Anne W. Hafen (Glendale, Calif.: Arthur H. Clark Company, 1959), 72.

10. Parker and Huyett, *The Illustrated Miners' Hand-Book and Guide to Pike's Peak, with a New and Reliable Map, Showing All the Routes* (St. Louis: Parker and Huyett, 1859), 16; *Hannibal and St. Joseph Railroad. New and Short Route Open to the Gold Regions, Pike's Peak and Cherry Creek, and All Parts of Kansas and Nebraska!* (Boston: George C. Rand and Avery, 1859); [St. Louis] *Daily Missouri Democrat*, November 24, 1858.

11. Alvin T. Steinel, *History of Agriculture in Colorado* (Fort Collins, Colo.: State Agricultural College, 1926), 108–9.

12. Agnes Wright Spring, "'A Genius for Handling Cattle': John W. Iliff," in *When Grass Was King: Contributions to the Western Range Cattle Industry*, ed. Maurice Frink (Boulder: University of Colorado Press, 1956), 345–47; [Denver] *Rocky Mountain News*, April 23, August 20, 1859; Marjorie A. Benham, "Henderson's Island," paper in author's possession.

13. Elbridge Gerry account books, November 10, 1860, Gerry Papers, Colorado State Historical Society; Charles McDonald ledger and cash books, July 1862–January 1863, Charles McDonald Papers, Nebraska State Historical Society; William K. Sloan, "Autobiography of William K. Sloan, Western Pioneer," *Annals of Wyoming* 4:1 (July 1926): 264; John Bratt, *Trails of Yesterday* (Lincoln: University Publishing Company, 1921), 61.

14. Spring, "John W. Iliff," 350.

15. C. B. France diary, May 2, 1865, C. B. France Papers, Missouri State Historical Society.

16. Steinel, *History of Agriculture in Colorado*, 122.

17. Parker and Huyett, *Illustrated Miner's Guide*, 16.

18. Walker, *Wagonmasters*, 195–96; Niel M. Clark, "When the Turkeys Walked," *American Heritage* 15 (December 1963): 92.

19. Steinel, *History of Agriculture in Colorado*, 108–11, 122; John Lawrence McKinley, *The Influence of the Platte River upon the History of the Valley* (Minneapolis: Burgess Publishing Company, 1938), 75–76.

20. Eugene Munn, "Reminiscences of My Life—From Boyhood," typescript, Nebraska State Historical Society; Percival G. Lowe, *Five Years a Dragoon: ('49 to '54) and Other Adventures on the Great Plains* (Kansas City, Mo.: Franklin Hudson Publishing Company, 1906), 355.

21. Spring, "John W. Iliff," 337–43.

22. W. Baillie Grohman, "Cattle Ranches in the Far West," *Fortnightly Review* 28 (1880): 451.

23. Spring, "John W. Iliff," 345–55.

24. Janet Lecompte, *Pueblo, Hardscrabble, Greenhorn: Society on the High Plains, 1832–1856* (Norman: University of Oklahoma Press, 1978), 186–88; Joseph Orlando Van Hook, "Settlement and Economic Development of the Arkansas Valley from Pueblo to the Colorado-Kansas Line, 1860–1900" (Ph.D. diss., University of Colorado, 1933), 146–47.

25. Judge R. M. Moore file, FF 392, Charles W. Hurd Collection, Colorado State Historical Society; *History of the Arkansas Valley, Colorado* (Chicago: O. L. Baskin and Company, 1881), 874–75; Janet Lecompte, "John Poisal," in *The Mountain Men and the Fur Trade of the Far West*, ed. LeRoy R. Hafen, 10 vols. (Glendale, Calif.: Arthur H. Clark Company, 1968), 6: 354–55; Cragin Notebooks, 2, 62, Western History Collections, Denver Public Library.

26. Mary Prowers Hudnall, "Early History of Bent County," *Colorado Magazine* 22:6 (November 1945): 233–35.

27. Baillie Grohman, "Cattle Ranches of the Far West," 452.

28. *History of the Arkansas Valley*, 882–83; Julia S. Lambert, "John W. Prowers," *Trail* 9:3 (August 1916): 12–20; John W. Prowers file, FF 397, Hurd Collection; John Wesley Prowers account book, 1869–1870, John Wesley Prowers Collection, Colorado State Historical Society.

29. George _____ to Rhoda, July 10, 1871, Western History Collection, Denver Public Library; Baillie Grohman, "Cattle Ranches in the Far West," 450.

30. McKinley, *The Influence of the Platte River*, 58; Registration of Brands, Weld County, Colorado, Records, Western History Collections, Denver Public Library; *Resources of Colorado, by the Board of Trade of Denver City, Colorado* (Brooklyn, 1868), 12.

31. *Guide and Map of the Recently Discovered Gold Regions in Western Kansas*, Wm. Hartley and Company (1858), 3–5.

32. W. B. S. and J. H. Combs, *Emigrant's Guide to the South Platte and Pike's Peak Gold Mines* (Terre Haute: R. H. Simpson and Company, 1859), 5, 11–12; *Illustrated Miners' Hand-Book and Guide to Pike's Peak*, 16–17.

33. *Daily Kansas City Journal of Commerce*, December 15, 1859.

34. Quoted in Steinel, *History of Agriculture in Colorado*, 53.

35. Ibid., 180–82, 186–87.

36. Jerome C. Smiley, *History of Denver, with Outlines of the Earlier History of the Rocky Mountain Country* (Denver: J. H. Williamson and Company, 1903), 794.

37. Steinel, *History of Agriculture in Colorado*, 32; *History of the Arkansas Valley*, 765–66.

38. Lowe, *Five Years a Dragoon*, 388–90.

39. Van Hook, "Settlement and Economic Development of the Arkansas Valley," 251; C. W. Hurd, *Boggsville: Cradle of the Colorado Cattle Industry* (Boggsville, Colo.: Boggsville Committee, 1950), 5, 10–11.

40. Steinel, *History of Agriculture in Colorado*, 50–51; S. Douglas Cornell, *Report on the Condition and Prospects of Gold Mining in Colorado* (Buffalo, N.Y.: Leavitt's Press, 1863), 22; *Resources of Colorado*, 12; McKinley, *Influence of the Platte River*, 75–76. The changes were felt along the Arkansas River into the mountains as well. The established businessman John M. Francisco oriented his stores in Canyon City toward the strikes at California Gulch (later Leadville) at the Arkansas headwaters, invested in land in Pueblo where the river left the mountains, and dabbled in absentee farming downstream. A. C. Thomas to John M. Francisco, July 21, 1860, June 7, 1861, John M. Francisco Papers, Colorado State Historical Society.

41. Calvin W. Gower, "Kansas Territory and the Pike's Peak Gold Rush" (Ph.D. diss., University of Kansas, 1958), 265–66.

42. Heinrich Egge diary, translation and transcription, 1857–1860, passim, Nebraska State Historical Society; the quoted entries are from April 1 and April 10, 1858, and the general entry for October 1860.

43. "Report of Lt. Francis T. Bryan," *Report of Secretary of War 1857*, House Doc. 2, App. H, 35th Cong., 1st sess., 474.

44. Ibid, 472–74.

45. *Annual Report of Commissioner of Indian Affairs, 1854*; Father John Peter Powell, *People of the Sacred Mountain: A History of the Northern Cheyenne Chiefs and Warrior Societies*, 2 vols. (San Francisco: Harper and Row, 1981), 1: 173–74; George Bent to George Hyde, January 7, 1905, George Bent Papers, Western History Collections, Denver Public Library.

46. J. W. Whitfield to Superintendent of Indian Affairs, August 15, 1855, Letters Received, Upper Arkansas Agency, Office of Indian Affairs; J. W. Whitfield to Superintendent of Indian Affairs, January 5, 1856, Letters Received, Upper Arkansas Agency, Office of Indian Affairs.

47. According to the U.S. census, the percentage of males between twenty and thirty-nine years old declined from roughly 52 percent in 1860 to 49.6 percent in 1870. Most of that decline certainly came from the deaths of men in the Civil War. Assuming even a vigorous rebound of male population between 1865 and 1870, wartime losses would have had to have been at least three times greater to shrink the number of fighting-age men to a ratio of two to three of women of the same age.

48. *Annual Report of Commissioner of Indians Affairs, 1859*, 137–39.

49. Quoted in Gower, "Kansas Territory and the Pike's Peak Gold Rush," 227.

50. *Report and Map of the Superintendent and Engineer of the Smoky Hill Expedition, Together with the Table of Distances* (Leavenworth: Leavenworth Times, 1861), 2, 19, and passim.

51. Louise Barry, "The Ranch at Walnut Creek Crossing," *Kansas Historical Quarterly* 37:2 (Summer 1971): 130–33; Morris F. Taylor, "The Mail Station and the Military at Camp on Pawnee Fork, 1859–1860," *Kansas Historical Quarterly* 36:1 (Spring 1970): 27–33.

52. Wilbur Fiske Parker, "'The Glorious Orb of Day Has Rose': A Diary of the Smoky Hill Route to Pike's Peak, 1858," ed. Norman Lavers, *Montana: The Magazine of Western History* 36:2 (Spring 1986): 58.

53. Lavinia Honey Porter, *By Ox Team to California: A Narrative of Crossing the Plains in 1860* (Oakland: Oakland Enquirer Publishing Company, 1910), 27–28; "Diary of E. H. N. Patterson," in *Overland Routes to the Gold Fields, 1859, from Contemporary Diaries,* ed. LeRoy R. Hafen (Glendale, Calif.: Arthur H. Clark Company, 1942), 145.

54. Daniel Kellogg, "Across the Plains in 1858," *Trail* 5:7 (December 1912): 6–7.

55. Thomas J. Fitzpatrick to D. D. Mitchell, May 29, 1849, Letters Received, Upper Arkansas Agency, Bureau of Indian Affairs.

56. Porter, *By Ox Team to California,* 27–28; Perry Kline, reminiscence, collection no. 363, Colorado State Historical Society, 37–39, 41; "Diary of E. H. N. Patterson," 145.

57. Parker, "'The Glorious Orb of Day Has Rose,'" 58; W. B. S. and J. H. Combs, *Emigrant's Guide to the South Platte and Pike's Peak Gold Mines,* 16.

58. Cash book and ledgers, 1862–1863, McDonald Papers.

59. Thomas S. Twiss to Secretary of Interior, September 22, 1856, *Report of Commissioner of Indian Affairs, 1856,* 96–98; D. D. Mitchell to Orlando Brown, *Report of Commissioner of Indian Affairs, 1849–50,* 134.

60. Thomas Fitzpatrick to Thomas H. Harvey, September 18, 1847, in *Report of Commissioner of Indian Affairs, 1847,* 242; John Galvin, ed., *Western America in 1846–1847: The Original Travel Diary of Lieutenant J. W. Abert, Who Mapped New Mexico for the United States Army* (San Francisco: John Howell, 1966), 18–19.

61. Thomas Fitzpatrick to Thomas H. Harven, September 18, 1847, in *Report of Commissioner of Indian Affairs, 1847,* 243.

62. "Report of Lt. Francis T. Bryan," 468–69.

63. W. H. Stevens, *Field Notes, Crossing the Prairies and Plains from Atchison, Kansas, to Denver, Through the Mineral Region of Colorado Territory* (Philadelphia: J. B. Chandler, 1865), 6.

64. *Report and Map, Smoky Hill Expedition,* 9.

65. J. W. Abert, *Journal of Lieutenant J. W. Abert from Bent's Fort to St. Louis, in 1845,* S. Doc. 438, 29th Cong., 1st sess.

11. The Miseries of Failure

1. William H. Penrose to Assistant Adjutant, July 10, 1868, Fort Lyon Papers, Colorado State Historical Society. George Custer wrote that except for Satanta's "restless barbarity" and "merciless forays" against the frontier, he was "a remarkable

374 THE CONTESTED PLAINS

man—remarkable for his powers of oratory, his determined warfare against the advance of civilisation, and his opposition to abandoning his accustomed way of life." (*My Life on the Plains* as quoted in Richard Irving Dodge, *The Plains of the Great West and Their Inhabitants* [New York: G. P. Putnam's Sons, 1877], xxvii).

2. *Report of the Secretary of the Interior,* House Doc. no. 1, 37th Cong., 3d sess., (1862), 283, 297, 300–301. During the extreme suffering at the time of the Creeks' arrival on the Verdigris River, they reportedly hanged a woman as a witch. Melissa G. Moore, *The Story of a Kansas Pioneer* (Mt. Vernon, Ohio: Manufacturing Printing Company, 1924), 37.

3. Dr. H. T. Ketchum to William P. Dole, September 30, 1863, Letters Received, Colorado Agency, Bureau of Indian Affairs.

4. For accurate short summaries of the establishment of the forts noted here and others in the West, see Robert W. Frazer, *Forts of the West: Military Forts and Presidios and Posts Commonly Called Forts West of the Mississippi River to 1898* (Norman: University of Oklahoma Press, 1965).

5. Raymond W. Settle, ed., *The March of the Mounted Riflemen: First United States Military Expedition to Travel the Full Length of the Oregon Trail* (Glendale, Calif.: Arthur H. Clark Company, 1940), 68.

6. *A Complete Guide to the Gold Mines in Kansas and Nebraska, with a Description of the Shortest and Only All Railroad Route to Kansas* (Boston: Geo. C. Rand and Avery, 1859); Barnard Silvair Blondeau account books, 1858–1867, Nebraska State Historical Society.

7. Col. Henry Dodge, *Report of the Secretary of War . . . Journal of the March of a Detachment of Dragoons, Under the Command of Colonel Dodge, During the Summer of 1835,* House Doc. 181, 24th Cong, 1st sess., 16–17.

8. Circular 12, May 5, 1865, copy of post orders, Plum Creek File, Nebraska State Historical Society.

9. Thomas Fitzpatrick to A. Cumming, November 19, 1853, *Report of Commissioner of Indians Affairs, 1853,* 362.

10. Thomas J. Fitzpatrick to Thomas H. Harvey, June 24, 1848, Letters Received, Upper Arkansas Agency, Bureau of Indian Affairs.

11. Thomas Fitzpatrick to D. D. Mitchell, September 24, 1850, *Report of Commissioner of Indian Affairs, 1850,* 55.

12. Capt. Thomas J. Majors to Lt. F. A. McDonald, December 12, 1864, Plum Creek file.

13. "Report of Lt. Francis T. Bryan," *Report of the Secretary of War, 1857,* House Doc. 2, App. H, 35th Cong., 1st sess., 475.

14. Thomas Fitzpatrick to A. Cumming, November 19, 1853, *Report of the Commissioner of Indian Affairs, 1853,* 362–63.

15. Robert C. Miller to A. M. Robinson, Superintendent of Indian Affairs, July 21, 1858, Letters Received, Upper Arkansas Agency, Office of Indian Affairs. To arrive at these averages, I have used the population figures from an agent's report in 1855: J. W. Whitfield to Superintendent of Indian Affairs, January 5, 1856, Letters Received, Upper Arkansas Agency, Office of Indian Affairs.

16. Boone's list is included in a letter from William Gilpin to William P. Dole, August 3, 1861, Letters Received, Colorado Superintendency, Office of Indian Affairs.

17. Thomas Fitzpatrick to A. Cumming, November 19, 1853, *Report of the Commissioner of Indian Affairs, 1853,* 362.

18. William Bent to Robinson, Superintendent for Indian Affairs, December 17, 1858, Letters Received, Upper Arkansas Agency, Bureau of Indian Affairs.

19. Charles J. Kappler, *Indian Affairs: Laws and Treaties* (Washington, D.C.: Government Printing Office, 1904), 2: 807–11; Francis Paul Prucha, *American Indian Treaties: The History of a Political Anomaly* (Berkeley: University of California Press, 1994), 269–70. The most extended description of negotiations is in Gary Leland Roberts, "Sand Creek: Tragedy and Symbol" (Ph.D. diss., University of Oklahoma, 1984), 76–108.

20. On several occasions during the years between the Treaty of Fort Wise and the disastrous events of late 1864, officials noted that the treaty left the issue of what land was surrendered (and by whom) hopelessly muddled, and in any case much of the land between the North and South Plattes was unaffected. Attempts to negotiate new arrangements with tribes of the upper Platte were unavailing. See S. E. Browne to William P. Dole, December 29, 1862, John Evans to William P. Dole, April 10, 1863, and John Evans to William P. Dole, November 11, 1863, all in Letters Received, Colorado Superintendency, Office of Indian Affairs. The chief justice of the territorial supreme court wrote that the treaty had been concluded "in utter ignorance," and the commissioner of Indian Affairs, after examining the proceedings, concluded that at the very least all land north of the South Platte still was the Indians'. This last opinion, the territorial delegate observed, placed "more than half of the people of Colorado Territory . . . on unceded lands of Arapahoes and Cheyennes" (Roberts, "Sand Creek: Tragedy and Symbol," 150–52).

21. (*Black Hawk*) *Mining Journal,* quoted in Roberts, "Sand Creek: Tragedy and Symbol," 211.

22. Boone's report is included in William Gilpin to William P. Dole, August 3, 1861, Letters Received, Colorado Superintendency, Office of Indian Affairs.

23. Thomas Fitzpatrick to A. Cumming, November 19, 1853, *Report of Commissioner of Indian Affairs, 1853,* 368–69.

24. On this visit, see *Report of the Commissioner of Indians Affairs, 1863,* 239–57. An excellent account is in Stan Hoig, *The Western Odyssey of John Simpson Smith: Frontiersman, Trapper, Trader and Interpreter* (Glendale, Calif.: Arthur H. Clark Company, 1974), 123–36. For the Cheyenne account, see Father John Peter Powell, *People of the Sacred Mountain: A History of the Northern Cheyenne Chiefs and Warrior Societies,* 2 vols. (San Francisco: Harper and Row, 1981), 243–47.

25. *The War of the Rebellion,* 70 vols. (Washington, D.C.: Government Printing Office, 1880–1901), series 1, vol. 22, part 2, 572.

26. *Report of Commissioner of Indian Affairs, 1863,* 129–30.

27. Samuel Colley to William Gilpin, April 2, 1862, and William G. Evans to William P. Dole, June 24, 1862, Letters Received, Colorado Superintendency, Office of Indian Affairs.

28. Roberts, "Sand Creek: Tragedy and Symbol," 211.

29. Ibid., 210–11; Samuel Colley to William P. Dole, in *Annual Report of Com missioner of Indian Affairs, 1863.*

30. "Sand Creek Massacre," *Report of the Secretary of War,* Sen. Doc. 26, 39th Cong., 2d sess., 1866–1867, 181–82; *War of the Rebellion,* series 1, vol. 34, part 1 880–83. For excellent overviews of the military conflict of this period, see two land mark works by Robert M. Utley: *Frontiersmen in Blue: The United States Army and the Indian, 1848–1865* (New York: Macmillan, 1967) and *Frontier Regulars: The United States Army and the Indian, 1866–1891* (New York: Macmillan, 1973).

31. *War of the Rebellion,* series 1, vol. 34, part 1, 880–82; Roberts, "Sand Creek Tragedy and Symbol," 219–20.

32. Stan Hoig, *The Sand Creek Massacre* (Norman: University of Oklahoma Press 1961), 50–53; *War of Rebellion,* series 1, vol. 34, part 1, 935, part 4, 402–4; Roberts "Sand Creek: Tragedy and Symbol," 237–38.

33. Roberts, "Sand Creek: Tragedy and Symbol," 238; Hoig, *Sand Creek Massa cre,* 93.

34. Hoig, *Sand Creek Massacre,* 57; *War of the Rebellion,* series 1, vol. 34, part 4 97–99.

35. *War of the Rebellion,* series 1, vol. 41, part 1, 963–64.

36. The second proclamation is reprinted in "Massacre of Cheyenne Indians," *Re port on the Conduct of the War,* 38th Cong., 2d sess., 1865, 47.

37. Ibid., 124.

38. Hoig, *Sand Creek Massacre,* 80, 85–86.

39. *War of the Rebellion,* series 1, vol. 41, part 2, 756, 809.

40. In January 1862, when Chivington heard rumors that the Colorado First might find itself "on the *Potomac*!!!" in active service, he was thrilled: "May God Mr. Lincoln, Genl McClellan—Hunter or some one else having competent author ity *Grant Amen, So Mot It Be.*" By the following October, however, he was "inclined to the opinion that the 1st will be mounted and remain on the '*Frontier*' and that I will be in command of 'Colorado' and will get a Brig Gen ship" (J. M. Chivington to S. F. Tappan, January 10, 1862, October 7, 1862, Samuel F. Tappan Papers, Colo rado State Historical Society).

41. Ibid., 68, 70, 131.

42. "Sand Creek Massacre," 122–25, 169.

43. On Wynkoop, see Thomas D. Isern, "The Controversial Career of Edward W Wynkoop," *Colorado Magazine* 56:1 and 2 (Winter/Spring 1979): 1–18.

44. Wynkoop's personal recollection of these events is in his "Unfinished Colo rado History," typescript of original, Edward W. Wynkoop Papers, Colorado State Historical Society.

45. The following summary is taken from the transcripts of the Camp Weld Con ference in "Sand Creek Massacre," 213–17.

46. Ibid., 217.

47. *War of the Rebellion,* series 1, vol. 41, part 1, 912–13.

48. Ibid., 913–14.

49. Ibid., 913.

50. Ibid., 914.

51. Ibid.

52. Ibid.

53. Hoig, *Sand Creek Massacre*, 128.

54. "Sand Creek Massacre," 214.

55. *War of the Rebellion*, series 1, vol. 41, part 3, 696, 798–99.

56. Ibid., 908–10.

57. "Sand Creek Massacre," 25.

58. Hoig, *Sand Creek Massacre*, 143, 145.

59. Merrill J. Mattes, "Seth Ward," in *The Mountain Men and the Fur Trade of the Far West* ed. LeRoy R. Hafen, 10 vols. (Glendale, Calif.: Arthur H. Clark Company, 1966), vol. 3: 371.

60. "Sand Creek Massacre," 135–36. The best short summary of the battle is Hoig, *Sand Creek Massacre*, 145–62. The most complete description again is Roberts, "Sand Creek: Tragedy and Symbol," 411–438.

61. George E. Hyde, *Life of George Bent Written from His Letters* (Norman: University of Oklahoma Press, 1968), 151–52.

62. Hoig, *Sand Creek Massacre*, 152.

63. George Bent to Col. S. F. Tappan, February 23, 1889, Tappan Papers.

64. Anthony reported that he had buried a total of thirteen persons by Christmas Eve. S. J. Anthony to brother, December 23, 1864, copy, box 1, Scott J. Anthony Papers, Colorado State Historical Society.

65. Chivington's statement on the Indian casualties is in "Massacre of the Cheyenne Indians," 102–3. Testimony of others is scattered throughout that document and in "Sand Creek Massacre."

66. Hoig, *Sand Creek Massacre*, 159.

67. [*Denver*] *Rocky Mountain News* editorial, reprinted in "Massacre of Cheyenne Indians," 56.

68. S. J. Anthony to brother, December 23, 1864, box 1, Anthony Papers.

69. For a short but complete summary of these raids, see "A Brief Chronology of Battles and Skirmishes, 1864–65," *Colorado Heritage* (Autumn 1996) 38–41. The classic account from the period is Eugene Fitch Ware, *The Indian War of 1864* (Topeka: Crane, 1900), reprinted several times.

70. George Bent to George Hyde, December 21, 1905, George Bent Letters, Western History Collections, Denver Public Library.

71. C. B. Hadley, "The Plains War in 1865," *Proceedings and Collections of the Nebraska State Historical Society* series 2, 5 (1902): 278.

72. Kappler, *Laws and Treaties*, 2: 887–91.

73. The report, by Lt. Julian R. Fitch of the U.S. Signal Corps, is reprinted in Mrs. Frank C. Montgomery, "Fort Wallace and Its Relation to the Frontier," *Kansas Historical Society Collections* 17 (1926–1928): 190–94. See also Wayne C. Lee and Howard C. Raynesford, *Trails of the Smoky Hill: From Coronado to the Cowtowns* (Caldwell, Idaho: Caxton Printers, 1980), 51–73.

74. Howard Louis Conard, *Uncle Dick Wootton: The Pioneer Frontiersman of the Rocky Mountain Region,* ed. Milo Milton Quaife (Chicago: Lakeside Press; R. R. Donnelly and Sons Company, 1957), 387–88. See also Cragin Notebooks, 28, 2, Western History Collections, Denver Public Library.

75. Albert Barnitz to Jennie, June 29, 1867, Alfred Barnitz to wife, July 1, 1867, Albert Barnitz Papers, Beinecke Library, Yale University.

76. Alfred Barnitz to wife, August 13, 1867, September 3 1867, Barnitz Papers. Because cholera kills essentially from rapid dehydration through dysentery, and because children are far more vulnerable to dehydration than adults, the predominance of young on the funereal platforms may suggest cholera as the cause of death. For a look at Barnitz's fascinating letters, see Robert M. Utley, ed., *Life in Custer's Cavalry: Diaries and Letters of Albert and Jennie Barnitz, 1867–1868* (New Haven: Yale University Press, 1977).

77. Kappler, *Laws and Treaties,* 2: 977–89; Prucha, *American Indian Treaties,* 280–81; Douglas C. Jones, *The Treaty of Medicine Lodge: The Story of the Great Treaty Council as Told by Eyewitnesses* (Norman: University of Oklahoma Press, 1966); Utley, *Frontier Regulars,* 130–33.

78. J. A. Souders to Cousin Cora, August 15, 1858, copy, Kansas State Historical Society.

79. Joseph W. Snell and Robert W. Richmond, "When the Union and Kansas Pacific Built Through Kansas," *Kansas Historical Quarterly* 32 (Summer 1966): 161–86.

80. W. T. Sherman to S. F. Tappan, September 6 and November 21, 1868, Tappan Papers.

81. The standard work is Stan Hoig, *The Battle of Washita: The Sheridan-Custer Indian Campaign of 1867–1869* (Garden City, N.Y.: Doubleday and Company, 1976). See also George Bird Grinnell, *The Fighting Cheyennes* (Norman: University of Oklahoma Press, 1955), 298–309, and Donald Berthrong, *The Southern Cheyennes* (Norman: University of Oklahoma Press, 1963), 326–28.

82. James T. King, "The Republican River Expedition, June–July, 1869, 1, On the March," *Nebraska History* 41 (September 1960): 166–68. The campaign is also covered in King's biography of Carr, *War Eagle: A Life of General Eugene A. Carr* (Lincoln: University of Nebraska Press, 1963).

83. Ibid., 1, 170–74.

84. Ibid., 1, 175–91.

85. Ibid., 1, 191–95.

86. Ibid., 2, 281–84.

87. The most detailed account of the battle itself is in ibid., 2, 285–92.

88. The particulars of Tall Bull's death became a minor controversy, mainly involving the question of who actually killed him. Both William Cody and Frank North claimed the honor, as well as Lt. George Mason. The Dog Soldier leader was killed by a bullet to the head. Apparently he was shot while firing over the ravine's rim. In several accounts of his death, from white and Cheyenne sources, some do not mention the horse. The horse and his killing of it at the mouth of the ravine does appear,

however, in the account closest to the events—the report of Carr, written nine days after the fight. Carr does not say how Tall Bull killed the horse, but George Bird Grinnell, relying on Cheyenne informants, writes of his use of a knife behind the foreleg.

12. Epilogue: Stories in the Teeth of Life

1. Nellie Buchanan interview, 350/4, Civil Works Administration interviews, Kit Carson County, Colorado State Historical Society.

2. Father John Peter Powell, *People of the Sacred Mountain: A History of the Northern Cheyenne Chiefs and Warrior Societies,* 2 vols. (San Francisco: Harper and Row, 1981), 2: 733–35.

3. Donald J. Berthrong, *The Cheyenne and Arapaho Ordeal: Reservation and Agency Life in the Indian Territory, 1875–1907* (Norman: University of Oklahoma Press, 1976).

4. For analyses of the evolution and persistence within Cheyenne society, see the work by John H. Moore: *The Cheyenne Nation: A Social and Demographic History* (Lincoln: University of Nebraska Press, 1987); with Gregory R. Campbell, "An Ethnohistorical Perspective on Cheyenne Demography," *Journal of Family History* 14:1 (1989): 17–42; "The Developmental Cycle of Cheyenne Polygyny," *American Indian Quarterly* 15 (Summer 1991): 311–28; and "Cheyenne Political History, 1820–1894," *Ethnohistory* 21:4 (Fall 1974): 329–59.

5. Ramon Powers and Gene Younger, "Cholera on the Plains: The Epidemic of 1867 in Kansas," *Kansas Historical Quarterly* 37:4 (Winter 1971): 377–78.

6. *Nebraska City News,* July 8, 1910; John Bratt, *Trails of Yesterday* (Lincoln: University Publishing Company, 1921), 146; John Burke estate file, 1872, Lincoln County probate books, Nebraska State Historical Society. Burke's account books show the remarkable range of his enterprises—as employer, merchant, wholesaler, and supplier. Some individual accounts run into the hundreds of dollars. His ledger books are in the papers of his son-in-law: John Bratt Papers, Nebraska State Historical Society.

7. Leola Howard Blanchard, *Conquest of Southwest Kansas: A History and Thrilling Stories of Frontier Life in the State of Kansas* (Wichita: Wichita Eagle Press, 1931), 45–51.

8. Comments on the maneuver are from an article in the [*Pueblo, Colo.*] *Star-Journal,* October 19, 1952, John W. Prowers File, FF 397, Charles W. Hurd Collection, Colorado State Historical Collection.

9. Account book, 1869, John Wesley Prowers Collection, Colorado State Historical Society.

10. Townships, T23S R50W, T23S R51W, T23S R52W, General Land Office Records, Bureau of Land Management, Denver.

11. James Albert Hadley, "A Royal Buffalo Hunt," *Transactions of the Kansas State Historical Society, 1907–1908* (Topeka: State Printing Office, 1908), 564–80.

12. Ralph H. Pickett, "Friedrich von Holstein's Hunting Trips, 1865–1866," *Kansas Historical Quarterly* 32:3 (Autumn 1966): 314–24.

13. Charles Alston Messiter, *Sport and Adventures Among the North American Indians* (London: R. H. Porter, 1890), 133; W. E. Webb, *Buffalo Land: An Authentic Narrative of the Adventures and Misadventures of a Late Scientific and Sporting Party upon the Great Plains of the West* (Cincinnati and Chicago: E. Hannaford and Company, 1872), 124.

14. Mary Magdalene Bower Brulport diary, July 11, August 24–30, 1877, Kansas State Historical Society.

15. P. G. Scott diary, August 19–30, 1870, P. G. Scott Collection, Colorado State Historical Society.

16. Francis Marion Lockard, "Reminiscences," Kansas State Historical Society, 12–13; John H. Nicholson, "A History of Norton County, Kansas" (Master's thesis, Colorado State College of Education [Greeley], 1941), 158–59.

17. Caroline Jonasson to Ola Jonasson, December 5, 1874, typed translation of original in Swedish, Kansas State Historical Society.

18. "Early Kansas Experiences of J. W. McConnell," reprinted from *Rooks County Record*, March 22–April 5, 1912, copy in Kansas State Historical Society.

19. *Decatur County, Kansas* (Lubbock, Texas: Specialty Publishing, 1983), 119–20.

20. Tenth Census, 1880, U.S. Census Office, *Statistics of the Population* (Washington, D.C.: Government Printing Office, 1883), 60–61.

21. "Buffalo Hunt," Levi Davis interview, File WH 11, box 5, Works Progress Administration Papers, Denver Public Library.

22. Ren Allen, "Frontier County Nebraska History," typescript, Nebraska State Historical Society; Bratt, *Trails of Yesterday,* 152–57.

23. Jacob Adams to Robert W. Gray, May 14, 1872, Kansas State Historical Society.

24. For an example of an early pamphlet, see Denver Board of Trade, *Resources of Colorado, by the Board of Trade of Denver City, Colorado* (Brooklyn, 1868).

25. Dr. Hiram Latham, *Trans-Missouri Stock Raising. The Pasture Lands of North America: Winter Grazing* (Omaha: Daily Herald Steam Printing House, 1871), 6, 23.

26. Ibid., 5.

27. Joseph G. Gambone, "Economic Relief in Territorial Kansas, 1860–1861," *Kansas Historical Quarterly* 36:2 (Summer 1970): 149–54; Maj. John Sedgwick to Capt. D. R. Jones, August 11, 1860, and "J. E. B. Stuart's Official Journal," May 21, 1860, both in *Relations with the Indians of the Plains, 1857–1861,* ed. LeRoy R. Hafen and Ann W. Hafen (Glendale, Calif.: Arthur H. Clark Company, 1959), 213, 220–21.

28. Frank M. Stahl, *One-Way Ticket to Kansas: The Autobiography of Frank M. Stahl* (Lawrence: University of Kansas Press, 1959), 49.

29. Gambone, "Economic Relief in Territorial Kansas," 149–74; "The Famine in Kansas. Things to Be Remembered," broadside, New Haven [Conn.] Kansas Relief Committee, February 22, 1861, Beinecke Library, Yale University.

30. Kansas Bureau of Immigration, *The State of Kansas. A Home for Immigrants. Agricultural, Mineral, and Commercial Resources of the State. Great Inducements*

Offered to Persons Desiring Homes in a New Country (Topeka: MacDonald and Baker, 1865), 5–7; Josiah Copley, *Kansas and the Country Beyond, On the Line of the Union Pacific Railway, Eastern Division, From the Missouri to the Pacific Ocean* (Philadelphia: J. B. Lippincott and Company, 1867), 18.

31. Uriah Oblinger to family, October 28, 1872 [1874?], Oblinger Family Papers, Nebraska State Historical Society.

32. Elizabeth Bacon Custer, *Tenting on the Plains, or General Custer in Kansas and Texas* (Norman: University of Oklahoma Press, 1971), 594.

33. *Impartial Testimony as to the Profits of Sheep and Cattle Raising in Southwest Kansas, Together with Official Reports on the Condition and Number of Live Stock in the State, and an Estimate of the Profits and Expenses of a Ranch in the Arkansas Valley of Kansas* (Topeka: Hamilton, Woodruff and Company, 1884), 4, 25–33.

34. E. A. Claar to Earl H. Claar, August 14, 1880, typed copy of letter, Kansas State Historical Society.

35. Thomas Fitzpatrick to A. Cumming, November 19, 1853, *Report of the Commissioner of Indian Affairs, 1853,* 370.

36. *Guide to the Kansas Gold Mines at Pike's Peak . . . from Notes of Capt. J. W. Gunnison* (Cincinnati: E. Mendenhall, 1859), 39.

37. Wright Morris, *Plains Song for Female Voices* (Boston: David R. Godine, 1980), 1.

Bibliography

Government Documents

Abert, J. W. *Journal of Lieutenant J. W. Abert from Bent's Fort to St. Louis, in 1845.* Senate Exec. Doc. 438. 29th Cong., 1st sess. 1848.

Beckwith, Lt. E. G. *Report of Exploration for a Route for the Pacific Railroad, by Capt. J. W. Gunnison, Topographical Engineers, near the 38th and 39th Parallels of North Latitude, from the Mouth of the Kansas River, MO, to the Sevier Lake, in the Great Basin.* House Exec. Doc. 91. 33d Cong., 2d sess. 1855.

Bryan, Lt. Francis. "Report of Lt. Francis T. Bryan." *Report of the Secretary of War, 1857.* House Exec. Doc. 2, Appendix H. 35th Cong., 1st sess. 1857.

Bureau of Land Management. General Land Office Records. Denver, Colorado.

Dodge, Colonel Henry. *Report of the Secretary of War . . . Journal of the March of a Detachment of Dragoons, Under the Command of Colonel Dodge, During the Summer of 1835.* House Ex. Doc. 181. 24th Cong., 1st sess., 1835.

Henderson, Charles W. *Mining in Colorado: A History of Discovery, Development and Production.* Washington, D.C.: Government Printing Office, 1926.

Kappler, Charles J. *Indian Affairs: Laws and Treaties.* Vol. 2. Washington, D.C.: Government Printing Office, 1904.

"Massacre of Cheyenne Indians." *Report on the Conduct of the War.* 38th Cong., 2d sess. 1865.

Office of Indian Affairs. Colorado Agency. Letters Received.

————. Upper Arkansas Agency. Letters Received.

————. Upper Platte Agency. Letters Received.

Report of the Commissioner of Indian Affairs, 1845.

————, *1847.*

————, *1849–50.*

————, *1850.*

————, *1853.*

————, *1854.*

————, *1855.*

————, *1856.*

————, *1857.*

————, *1859.*

————, *1863.*

Report of the Secretary of the Interior. House Exec. Doc. 1. 37th Cong., 3d sess. 1862.

"Sand Creek Massacre." *Report of the Secretary of War.* Senate Exec. Doc. 26. 39th Cong, 2d sess. 1867.

U.S. Census Office. *Statistics of the Population of the United States at the Tenth Census, June 1, 1880.* Washington, D.C.: Government Printing Office, 1883.

The War of the Rebellion: A Compilation of the Official Records of the Union and Confederate Armies. 70 vols. Washington, D.C.: Government Printing Office, 1880–1901.

Warren, Lieut. G. K. *Preliminary Report of Explorations in Nebraska and Dakota, in the Years 1855–'56'57.* Washington, D.C.: Government Printing Office, 1875.

Primary Sources

ARCHIVES

Adams, Jacob. Letter. Kansas State Historical Society.

Allen, Ren. "Frontier County Nebraska History." Typescript. Nebraska State Historical Society.

Allton, Hiram. Diary. Western History Collections. Denver Public Library.

Anonymous. Diary. Nebraska State Historical Society.

Anonymous. "Overland Journey to Colorado." Journal. Western History Collections. Denver Public Library.

Anthony, Scott J. Papers. Colorado State Historical Society.

Armstrong, Hugh. Letter. Missouri Historical Society.

Austin, Homer. Journal. Western History Collections. Denver Public Library.

Baker, J. S. Letter. Western Travel Papers. Missouri Historical Society.

Barnitz, Albert. Papers. Beinecke Library. Yale University.

Bartlett, A. T. Diary. Missouri Historical Society.

Bayaud, Thomas J. Papers. Western History Collections. Denver Public Library.

Beauvais, Geminien. File. Nebraska State Historical Society.

Bell, Rose. Diary. Colorado State Historical Society.

Bemis Family. Papers. Missouri Historical Society.

Bent, George. Papers. Western History Collections. Denver Public Library.

Bent-Hyde. Papers. Western History Collections. University of Colorado Library.

Blondeau, Barnard Silvair. Account books. Nebraska State Historical Society.

Blythe, Samuel Finley. Diary. Typescript. Nebraska State Historical Society.

Boardman, Alonzo. Letters. Western History Collections. Denver Public Library.

Bradbury, Anson. Diary. Montana State Historical Society.

Bratt, John. Papers. Nebraska State Historical Society

Brooks, Alden. Diary. Henry E. Huntington Library, San Marino, California.

Brooks, Alden. "Grand Trip Across the Plains." Journal. Newberry Library. Chicago.

Brown, J. Robert. "Journal of a Trip Across the Plains of the U.S. from Mo. to Cal." Copy of manuscript journal. Newberry Library. Chicago.

Brulport, Mary Magdalene Bower. Diary. Kansas State Historical Society.

Burbridge Family. Papers. Western History Collections. Denver Public Library.

Carswell, Robert. Letter. Montana State Historical Society.

Central Overland California and Pike's Peak Express Company. Contract. Copy. Missouri State Historical Society.

Chapman, Darius H. Papers. Nebraska State Historical Society.

Chase, Wilder. Letters. Colorado State Historical Society.

Civil Works Administration. Interviews. Colorado State Historical Society.

Claar, E. A. Letter. Kansas State Historical Society.

Clark, Calvin. Diary. Western History Collections. Denver Public Library.

Clark, Meriwether Lewis. Journal. Missouri Historical Society.

Collamore, George. Letters. Spencer Library. University of Kansas.

Cozad, Justus L. Reminiscence. Nebraska State Historical Society.

Cragin Notebooks. Western History Collections. Denver Public Library.

Crandall, Eliphalet. Diary. Nebraska State Historical Society.

Creel, V. F. Diary. Montana State Historical Society.

Curtis Family. Letters. Beinecke Library. Yale University.

Curtis, Samuel S. Letters. Spencer Library. University of Kansas.

Dauchy, Jerome. Papers. Nebraska State Historical Society.

Downham, Emanuel Ethelbert. Reminiscence. Copy of typescript. Missouri Historical Society.

Drips, Andrew. Papers. Missouri State Historical Society.

Edwards, Solomon. Diary. 1864. Typescript. Missouri State Historical Society.

Egge, Heinrich. Diary. Translation and transcription. Nebraska State Historical Society.

Elliott, Newton G. Papers. Missouri Historical Society.

Faulkner, Harry. Papers. Western History Collections. Denver Public Library.

Fergus, James. Papers. University of Montana Library.

Fleeder, Martin. Letter. Western History Collections. Denver Public Library.

Fort Laramie. Correspondence File. Fort Laramie National Monument Library. Fort Laramie, Wyoming.

Fort Laramie. Sutler's books. Western History Collections. Denver Public Library.

Fort Lyon. Papers. Colorado State Historical Society.

Fosdick, Lucy H. "Across the Plains in '61." Typescript. Beinecke Library. Yale University.

France, Charles B. Diary. Missouri State Historical Society.

Francisco, John M. Papers. Colorado State Historical Society.

Franz, Chester. Papers. Missouri Historical Society.

Fraser, Duncan. Letters. Montana State Historical Society.

Frizzell, Alexander. Diary. Nebraska State Historical Society.

Gantt, Daniel. Journal. Nebraska State Historical Society.

George ———. Letter [to Rhoda ———]. Western History Collections. Denver Public Library.

Gerry, Elbridge. Papers. Colorado State Historical Society.

Gratiot, Henry. Diary. Journals and Diaries Collections. Missouri Historical Society.

Hartzell, John. Letter. Western History Collections. Denver Public Library.

Harvey, Augustus Ford. Journal. Copy of transcript. Kansas State Historical Society.

Hill, Nathaniel P. Papers. Colorado State Historical Society.

Hively, Sarah. Journal. Western History Collections. Denver Public Library.

Hooper, John T. Letter. Western History Collections. Denver Public Library.

Hudson, H. M. Diary. Nebraska State Historical Society.

Hull, Charles. "Memories of the Trail." Reminiscence. Microfilm of typescript. Missouri Historical Society.

Hurd, Charles W. Collection. Colorado State Historical Society.

Jonasson, Caroline. Letter. Translation. Kansas State Historical Society.

Judson, H. M. Diary. Nebraska State Historical Society.

Kerwin, M. W. Diary. Western History Collections. Denver Public Library.

Kingsbury, James. Papers. DeGolyer Library. Southern Methodist University.

Kline, Perry. Reminiscence. Colorado State Historical Society.

Lake, John D. Journal. Western History Collections. Denver Public Library.

Leonard, Abiel. Papers. Missouri State Historical Society.

Lincoln, Lewis A. Papers. Western History Collections. Denver Public Library.

Lockard, Francis Marion. Reminiscence. Kansas State Historical Society.

Long, C. L. Diary. Kansas State Historical Society.

Lowman, Mary Foster. Letter. Nebraska State Historical Society.

Mallory, Samuel. Diary. Colorado State Historical Society.

"Map of Kansas with Route from Lawrence to the Gold Mines." Spencer Library. University of Kansas.

March, E. J. Diary. Missouri State Historical Society.

McDonald, Charles. Papers. Nebraska State Historical Society.

McGaa, William, and Family. Clipping files, biography. Western History Collections. Denver Public Library.

McLaughlin, David H. Reminiscence. Nebraska State Historical Society.

Merrill, Julius Caesar. Diary. Missouri State Historical Society.

Miller, Paul E. Papers. Colorado State Historical Society.

Munn, Eugene. "Reminiscences of My Life—from Boyhood." Nebraska State Historical Society.

New Haven [Connecticut] Relief Committee. "The Famine in Kansas. Things to Be Remembered." Broadside. Beinecke Library. Yale University.

Oakes, D. C. Papers. Western History Collections. Denver Public Library.

Oblinger Family. Papers. Nebraska State Historical Society.

Owen, James. "Journal of a Route to Pikes Peak." Newberry Library. Chicago.

Payne, Moses U. Papers. Missouri State Historical Society.

Pelot, James M. File. Kansas State Historical Society.

Penniston and Miller. General Store day books. Nebraska State Historical Society.

Plum Creek File. Nebraska State Historical Society.

Prowers, John Wesley. Collection. Colorado State Historical Society.

Reed, Joseph M. Letters. Spencer Library. University of Kansas.

Rooney-Littlefield Family. Letters. Western History Collections. Denver Public Library.

Sanders, Thomas D. Reminiscence. Western History Collections. Denver Public Library.

Scott, P. G. Collection. Colorado State Historical Society.

Seymour, James H. Letter. Western History Collections. Denver Public Library.

Sheriff, Matthew. Diary. Colorado State Historical Society.

Souders, J. A. Letter. Kansas State Historical Society.

Stahl, E. M. Diary. Western History Collections. Denver Public Library.

Stephens, George. Letter. Nebraska State Historical Society.

Sullivan, W. W. "Crossing the Plains in '62." Reminiscence. Beinecke Library. Yale University.

Tappan, Samuel F. Papers. Colorado State Historical Society.

Thoroughman, Robert. Reminiscence. Montana State University Library.

Walker, Alexander Warfield. "Memories of My Life." Reminiscence. Missouri State Historical Society.

Watson, George. Letter. Western History Collections. Denver Public Library.

Webb, James Josiah. Papers. Missouri Historical Society.

Weld County, Colorado. Records. Western History Collections. Denver Public Library.

Wellman, Sylvanus. Diary. Colorado State Historical Society.

Wildman, Augustus, and Thomas Wildman. Letters. Beinecke Library. Yale University.

Wilkinson, J. A. Diary. Henry E. Huntington Library, San Marino, California.

Wilson, John S. Diary. Beinecke Library. Yale University.

Wisely, J. S. Letter. Western History Collections. Denver Public Library.

Witter, Daniel. Diary. Colorado State Historical Society.

Works Progress Administration Papers. Interviews. Western History Collections. Denver Public Library.

Wynkoop, Edward W. "Unfinished Colorado History." Typescript, 5–10. Colorado State Historical Society.

GUIDES TO THE GOLD MINES

The following guides to the Colorado diggings were published in 1858 and 1859—broadsides, maps, pamphlets, and books. I have included some brief annotations when appropriate and have identified the depositories of the rarer items.

Allen's Guide Book and Map to the Gold Fields of Kansas and Nebraska and Great Salt Lake City. Washington, D.C.: R. A. Waters, 1859.

Byers, William N., and Jno. H. Kellom. *A Hand Book to the Gold Fields of Nebraska and Kansas.* Chicago: D. B. Cooke and Company, 1859.

Byram, A. and P. *Great Central Route! By the Way of Nebraska City to Pike's Peak, Oregon and California!* Nebraska City: News Power Press, 1859. Small broadside. Beinecke Library. Yale University.

Cleveland and Toledo Railroad Company. *For Pike's Peak and the Gold Mines, via Cleveland and Toledo Rail Road. A Direct and All Rail Road Line to St. Joseph, Kansas T.* Broadside. Beinecke Library. Yale University.

Combs, W. B. S., and J. H. Combs. *Emigrant's Guide to the South Platte and Pike's Peak Gold Mines.* Terre Haute: R. H. Simpson and Company, 1859. Western History Collections. Denver Public Library.

Complete Guide to the Gold Mines in Kansas and Nebraska, with a Description of the Shortest and Only All Railroad Route to Kansas. Boston: Geo. C. Rand and Avery, 1859. Small pamphlet promoting the Great Western and Michigan Central Railroad. Beinecke Library. Yale University.

Davis' Great Western Business Guide of the Pittsburgh, Fort Wayne and Chicago Railway, and Its Connections. Philadelphia: F. C. Davis, 1861. Includes map published by Chicago, Burlington and Quincy Railroad. Beinecke Library. Yale University.

Eastin, L. J. *Emigrants' Guide to Pike's Peak.* Leavenworth City, K.T.: 1859. In form of a newspaper. Recommends Smoky Hill River route. Western History Collections. Denver Public Library.

Great Western Michigan Central. Traveller's Companion and Guide Westward. Boston: Fred Rogers, 1860. With map showing Platte River route. Beinecke Library. Yale University.

Guide and Map of the Recently Discovered Gold Regions in Western Kansas. Wm. Hartley and Company, 1858. Earliest known guide written by one of the Lawrence party of goldseekers. Brief (eight pages), with map. Western History Collections. Denver Public Library.

Guide to the Kansas Gold Mines at Pike's Peak . . . from Notes of Capt. J. W. Gunnison. Cincinnati: E. Mendenhall, 1859.

Guide to the New Gold Region of Western Kansas and Nebraska. New York: John W. Oliver, 1859.

Gunn, O. B. *New Map and Hand-Book of Kansas and the Gold Mines. Containing Description and Statistics of the Indian Tribes, Settlement, Soil, Productions, Climate, Roads, Rail Roads, Telegraphs, Mail Routes, Land Districts, Legislatures, etc. With Description of All the Routes to the New Gold Mines.* Pittsburgh: W. S. Haven, 1859.

Hannibal and St. Joseph Railroad. New and Short Route Open to the Gold Regions, Pike's Peak and Cherry Creek, and All Parts of Kansas and Nebraska! Boston: George C. Rand and Avery, 1859. Broadside. Apparently meant to accompany *Complete Guide to the Gold Mines in Kansas and Nebraska.* Beinecke Library. Yale University.

Horner, W. B. *The Gold Regions of Kansas and Nebraska. Being a Complete History of the First Year's Mining Operations. Also, Geographical, Climatological, and Statistical Description of the Great Northwest, Showing an Unoccupied Territory of over One Million Square Miles of Rich Country. Being a Complete Guide to the Gold Mines.* Chicago: W. H. Tobey and Company, 1859.

Map and Guide of the Routes to Pike's Peak. St. Louis, 1859. Beinecke Library. Yale University.

Marcy, Randolph B. *The Prairie Traveler. A Hand-Book for Overland Expeditions. With Maps, Illustrations, and Itineraries of the Principal Routes Between the Mississippi and the Pacific.* New York: Harper and Brothers, 1859.

McGowan, D., and George A. Hildt. *Map of the United States West of the Mississippi Showing the Routes to Pike's Peak, Overland Mail Route to California and Pacific Rail Road Surveys.* St. Louis: Leopold Gast and Brothers, 1859. Meant to accompany *Map and Guide of the Routes to Pike's Peak*. Remarkably detailed map. Beinecke Library. Yale University.

"North Platte Route to the Gold Mines." Map, otherwise unidentified, but probably published in connection with the Chicago and Rock Island Railroad and the Mississippi and Missouri Railroad. Western History Collections, Denver Public Library.

Olmstead, S. R. *The Gold Mines of Kansas and Nebraska*. New York: 1859.

Parker and Huyett. *The Illustrated Miners' Hand-Book and Guide to Pike's Peak*. St. Louis: Parker and Huyett, 1859.

Parsons, William B. *The New Gold Mines of Western Kansas: Being a Complete Description of the Newly Discovered Gold Mines*. Cincinnati: Geo. S. Blanchard, 1859.

Peace and Cole. *Complete Guide to the Gold Districts of Kansas and Nebraska Containing Valuable Information with Regard to Routes, Distances. etc*. Chicago: Wm. H. Rand, 1859.

Penton, White and Company. *Pike's Peak Transportation and Express Company*. March, 1859. Broadside. Beinecke Library. Yale University.

Pike's Peak. Great Through Line Between East and West, via Cincinnati and St. Louis by the Ohio and Mississippi Broad Gauge Railroad. N.p., n.d.

Pratt and Hunt. *Guide to the Gold Mines of Kansas: Containing an Accurate and Reliable Map*. Chicago: Briggs House, 1859.

Redpath, James, and Richard J. Hinton. *Hand-Book to Kansas Territory and the Rocky Mountains' Gold Region; Accompanied by Reliable Maps and a Preliminary Treatise on the Preemption Laws of the United States*. New York: J. H. Colton, 1859.

Reed, Dr. J. W. *Reed's Guide to the Kansas Gold Region. With a Map Embracing the Northern and Southern Routes*. New York: J. H. Colton, 1859.

Tierney, Luke. *History of the Gold Discoveries on the South Platte River. To Which Is Appended a Guide of the Route, by Smith and Oaks* [sic]. Pacific City, Iowa: Herald Office, 1859.

Toledo, Wabash and Great Western Railroad Company. Direct Route to Pikes Peak and the Gold Regions. New York: Robertson, Seibert and Sherman, 1859. Beinecke Library. Yale University.

Traveler's Guide to the New Gold Mines in Kansas and Nebraska. New York: Polhemus and de Vries, 1859.

BOOKS AND ARTICLES

Athearn, Robert G., ed. "Across the Plains in 1863: The Diary of Peter Winne." *Iowa Journal of History* 49:3 (July 1951): 221–40.

Baird, J. C. "First Gold Find in the Mountains." *Trail* 14:9 (February 1922): 3–10.

Barney, Libeus. *Early-Day Letters from Auraria (Now Denver)*. Denver: A. J. Ludditt Press, 1860.

Bieber, Ralph P., ed. "Diary of a Journey to the Pike's Peak Gold Mines in 1859." *Mississippi Valley Historical Review* 14:3 (December 1927): 360–78.

Bishop, Mrs. Julia A. "How and Why I Came to Denver." *Trail* 5:2 (July 1912): 21–23.

Blanchard, Leola Howard. *Conquest of Southwest Kansas: A History and Thrilling Stories of Frontier Life in the State of Kansas.* Wichita: Wichita Eagle Press, 1931.

Bradbury, John. *Travels in the Interior of America in the Years 1809, 1810, and 1811.* Vol. 5. Reuben Gold Thwaites, ed., *Early Western Travel, 1748–1846.* London: Sherwood, Neely and Jones, 1819.

Bratt, John. *Trails of Yesterday.* Lincoln: University Publishing Company, 1921.

Brayer, Herbert O., ed. *Pike's Peak . . . or Busted! Frontier Reminiscences of William Hawkins Hedges.* Evanston, Ill.: Branding Iron Press, 1954.

Burton, Sir Richard. *The City of the Saints and Across the Rocky Mountains to California.* London: Longman, Green, Longman and Roberts, 1862.

———. *The Look of the West, 1860: Across the Plains to California.* Lincoln: University of Nebraska Press, n.d.

Clark, Charles M. *A Trip to Pike's Peak and Notes by the Way.* Chicago: S. P. Rounds, 1861.

Clarke, H. T. "Freighting—Denver and Black Hills." *Proceedings and Collections of the Nebraska State Historical Society,* Series 2, 5 (1902): 299–307.

Cobb, Frank M. "The Lawrence Party of Pike's Peakers (1858) and the Founding of St. Charles (Predecessor of Denver)." *Colorado Magazine* 10:5 (September 1933): 194–97.

Conard, Howard Louis. *Uncle Dick Wootton: The Pioneer Frontiersman of the Rocky Mountain Region.* Ed. Milo Milton Quaife. Chicago: Lakeside Press, R. R. Donnelly and Sons Company, 1957.

Copley, Josiah. *Kansas and the Country Beyond, On the Line of the Union Pacific Railway, Eastern Division, From the Missouri to the Pacific Ocean.* Philadelphia: J. B. Lippincott and Company, 1967.

Cornell, S. Douglas. *Report on the Condition and Prospects of Gold Mining in Colorado.* Buffalo, N.Y.: Leavitt's Press, 1863.

Coues, Elliott, ed. *The Journal of Jacob Fowler.* Lincoln: University of Nebraska Press, 1970.

Custer, Elizabeth Bacon. *Tenting on the Plains, or General Custer in Kansas and Texas.* Norman: University of Oklahoma Press, 1971.

Denver Board of Trade. *Resources of Colorado, by the Board of Trade of Denver City, Colorado.* Brooklyn, 1868.

Denver City and Auraria, the Commercial Emporium of the Pike's Peak Gold Regions, in 1859. Glendale, Calif.: Arthur H. Clark, 1942.

Dodge, Richard Irving. *Our Wild Indians: Thirty-three Years Personal Experience Among the Red Men of the Great West.* Hartford, Conn.: A. D. Worthington and Company, 1883.

———. *The Hunting Grounds of the Great West. A Description of the Plains, Game, and Indians of the Great North American Desert.* London: Chatto and Windus, 1877.

———. *The Plains of the Great West and Their Inhabitants.* New York: G. P. Putnam's Sons, 1877.

Elder, Jane Lenz, and David J. Weber, eds. *Trading in Santa Fe: John M. Kingsbury's Correspondence with James Josiah Webb, 1853–1861*. Dallas: Southern Methodist University Press/DeGolyer Library, 1996.

Farnham, Thomas J. *Travels in the Great Western Prairies, the Anahuac and Rocky Mountains, and in the Oregon Territory*. 2 vols. London: Richard Bentley, 1843.

Fremont, John Charles. *A Report of the Exploring Expedition to Oregon and North California, in the Years 1843–44*.

Fulton, William. "Freighting and Staging in Early Days." *Proceedings and Collections of the Nebraska State Historical Society*. Series 2, 5 (1902): 261–64.

Galvin, John, ed. *Western America in 1846–1847: The Original Travel Diary of Lieutenant J. W. Abert, Who Mapped New Mexico for the United States Army*. San Francisco: John Howell, 1966.

Gardner, Hamilton, ed. "March of the 2nd Dragoons: Report of Lieutenant Colonel Philip St. George Cooke on the March of the 2nd Dragoons from Fort Leavenworth to Fort Bridger in 1857." *Annals of Wyoming* 27:1 (April 1955): 43–60.

Garrard, Lewis H. *Wah-to-Yah and the Taos Trail*. Norman: University of Oklahoma Press, 1955.

Greeley, Horace. *An Overland Journey from New York to San Francisco in the Summer of 1859*. New York: C. M. Saxton, Barker and Company, 1860.

Grohman, W. Baillie. "Cattle Ranches in the Far West." *Fortnightly Review* 28 (1880), 438–57.

H. Fotheringham and Company's Elwood Directory. St. Joseph, Mo.: F. M. Posegate, 1860.

Hadley, C. B. "The Plains War in 1865." *Proceedings and Collections of the Nebraska State Historical Society*, Series 2, 5 (1902): 273–78.

Hafen, LeRoy R., ed. *Colorado Gold Rush: Contemporary Letters and Reports, 1858–1859*. Glendale, Calif.: Arthur H. Clark Company, 1941.

———, ed. "Diary of Mrs. A. C. Hunt, 1859." *Colorado Magazine* 21:5 (September 1944): 161–70.

———, ed. "George A. Jackson's Diary, 1858–1859." *Colorado Magazine* 12:6 (November 1935), 201–14.

———, ed. *Overland Routes to the Gold Fields, 1859, from Contemporary Diaries*. Glendale, Calif.: Arthur H. Clark Company, 1942.

———, ed. *Pike's Peak Gold Rush Guidebooks of 1859*. Glendale, Calif.: Arthur H. Clark Company, 1941.

Hafen, LeRoy R., and Ann W. Hafen, eds. *Relations with the Indians of the Plains, 1857–1861*. Glendale, Calif.: Arthur H. Clark Company, 1959.

Hedges, William Hawkins. *Pike's Peak . . . or Busted! Frontier Reminiscences of William Hawkins Hedges*. Ed. Herbert O. Brayer. Evanston, Ill.: Branding Iron Press, 1954.

Hill, Emma Shepard. *A Dangerous Crossing and What Happened on the Other Side*. Denver: Press of the Smith-Brooks Company, 1914.

Hollon, W. Eugene, and Ruth Lapham Butler, eds. *William Bollaert's Texas*. Norman: University of Oklahoma Press, 1956.

Holmes, Julia Archibald. *A Bloomer Girl on Pike's Peak, 1858.* Ed. Agnes Wright Spring. Denver: Denver Public Library, 1949.

Hopper, Silas L. "Diary Kept by Silas L. Hopper, Blandinsville, Illinois, April 20, 1863." *Annals of Wyoming* 3:2 (October 1925): 117–26.

Howbert, Irving. *Memories of a Lifetime in the Pike's Peak Region.* New York: G. P. Putnam's Sons, 1925.

Hudnall, Mary Prowers. "Early History of Bent County." *Colorado Magazine* 22:6 (November 1945): 233–47.

Hyde, George E. *Life of George Bent, Written from His Letters.* Norman: University of Oklahoma Press, 1968.

Impartial Testimony as to the Profits of Sheep and Cattle Raising in Southwest Kansas, Together with Official Reports on the Condition and Number of Live Stock in the State, and an Estimate of the Profits and Expenses of a Ranch in the Arkansas Valley of Kansas. Topeka: Hamilton, Woodruff and Company, 1884.

Jackson, Donald, and Mary Lee Spence, eds. *The Expeditions of John Charles Fremont.* Vol. 1. *Travels from 1838 to 1844.* Urbana: University of Illinois Press, 1970.

James, Edwin. *An Account of an Expedition from Pittsburgh to the Rocky Mountains.* 2 vols. Ann Arbor, Mich.: University Microfilms, 1966.

Kaiser, Leo M., and Priscilla Knuth, eds.. "From Ithaca to Clatsop Plains: Miss Ketcham's Journal of Travel." *Oregon Historical Quarterly* 62:3,4 (September and December 1961): 237–87, 337–402.

Kansas Bureau of Immigration. *The State of Kansas. A Home for Immigrants. Agricultural, Mineral, and Commercial Resources of the State. Great Inducements Offered to Persons Desiring Homes in a New Country.* Topeka: MacDonald and Baker, 1865.

Kellogg, Daniel. "Across the Plains in 1858." *Trail* 5:7 (December 1912): 5–12.

Kidd, William H. *Glittering Gold; or, Pencillings About Pike's Peak.* St. Louis: Missouri Democrat, 1860.

Kimbro, Harriet, ed. "'A Genuine Western Man Never Drinks Tea': Gustavus French Merriam's Letters from Kansas in 1860." *Kansas History* 8:3 (Autumn 1985): 162–75.

Kingman, Henry. *The Travels and Adventures of Henry Kingman in Search of Colorado and California Gold.* Delavan, Kans.: Herington Sun Press, 1917.

Knox, Thomas W. "To Pike's Peak and Denver." *Knickerbocker* 58:2 (August 1861): 115–28.

Lambert, Julia S. "John W. Prowers." *Trail* 9:3 (August 1916): 12–20.

———. "Plain Tales of the Plains." *Trail* 8:8 (January 1916): 1–8, 8–9 (February 1916): 5–12, 8:10 (March 1916): 5–13, and 8:11 (April 1916): 5–11.

Larimer, William H. *Reminiscences of General William Larimer and of His Son, William H. H. Larimer, Two Founders of Denver City.* Lancaster, Pa.: Press of the New Era Printing Company, 1918.

Latham, Dr. Hiram. *Trans-Missouri Stock Raising. The Pasture Lands of North America: Winter Grazing.* Omaha: Daily Herald Steam Printing House, 1871.

Lavers, Norman, ed. "'The Glorious Orb of Day Has Rose': A Diary of the Smoky Hill Route to Pike's Peak, 1858." *Montana: The Magazine of Western History* 36:2 (Spring 1986): 150–61.

"Letter of Thomas S. Twiss, Indian Agent at Deer Creek, U.S. Indian Agency on the Upper Platte." *Annals of Wyoming* 17:2 (July 1945): 148–52.

Lewis, Edward J. "Diary of a Pike's Peak Gold Seeker in 1860." *Colorado Magazine* 14:6 (November 1937): 201–19, and 15:1 (January 1938): 20–33.

Lindsey, David, ed. "The Journal of an 1859 Pike's Peak Gold Seeker." *Kansas Historical Quarterly* 22:4 (Winter 1956): 321–41.

Linville, Leslie. *The Smoky Hill Valley and Butterfield Trail*. Colby, Kans.: LeRoy's Printing, 1874.

Linville, Leslie, and Bertha Linville. *Up the Smoky Hill Trail in 1867 in an Ox Drawn Wagon Train*. Osborne, Kans.: Osborne Publishing Company, 1983.

Lowe, Percival G. *Five Years a Dragoon ('49 to '54) and Other Adventures on the Great Plains*. Kansas City, Mo.: Franklin Hudson Publishing Company, 1906.

Lubers, H. L. "William Bent's Family and the Indians of the Plains." *Colorado Magazine* 13:1 (January 1936): 19–22.

Lyon, Herman Robert. "Freighting in the 60s." *Proceedings and Collections of the Nebraska State Historical Society*. Series 2, vol. 5 (1902): 265–72.

Magoffin, Susan Shelby. *Down the Santa Fe Trail and into Mexico. The Diary of Susan Shelby Magoffin, 1846–1847*. New Haven: Yale University Press, 1926.

Majors, Alexander. *Seventy Years on the Frontier: Alexander Majors' Memoirs of a Lifetime on the Border*. Minneapolis: Ross and Haines, 1965.

Marsh, Charles W. *Recollections, 1837–1910*. Chicago: Farm Implement News Company, 1910.

Maurice O'Conner. *Rambles in the Rocky Mountains*. London: Smith, Elder, 1864.

McCain, G. S. "A Trip from Atchison, Kansas, to Laurette, Colorado: Diary of G. S. McCain. " *Colorado Magazine* 27:2 (April 1950): 95–102.

McGaa, William. "A Statement Regarding the Formation of the St. Charles and Denver Town Companies." *Colorado Magazine* 22:3 (May 1945): 125–29.

Meline, James F. *Two Thousand Miles on Horseback. Santa Fe and Back*. New York: Hurd and Houghton, 1867.

Messiter, Charles Alston. *Sport and Adventures Among the North-American Indians*. London: R. H. Porter, 1890.

Missouri. Public Works Board. *Railroad Report, 1859*. Missouri State Historical Society.

Moore, Melissa G. *The Story of a Kansas Pioneer*. Mt. Vernon, Ohio: Manufacturing Printing Company, 1924.

Morgan, Lewis Henry. *The Indian Journals, 1859–62*. Ann Arbor: University of Michigan Press, 1959.

Mumey, Nolie. *History of the Early Settlements of Denver with Reproduction of the First City Directory*. Glendale, Calif.: A. H. Clark, 1942.

Peabody, Frances Clelland. "Across the Plains DeLuxe in 1865." *Colorado Magazine* 18:2 (March 1941): 71–76.

Pierce, James H. "With the Green Russell Party." *Trail* 13:12 (May 1921): 5–14, and 14:1 (June 1921): 5–13.

———. "The First Prospecting of Colorado, Who Did It and What Led to It." *Trail* 7:5 (October 1914): 5–11.

Porter, Lavinia Honey. *By Ox Team to California: A Narrative Crossing of the Plains in 1860*. Oakland, Calif.: Oakland Enquirer Publishing Company, 1910.

Report and Map of the Superintendent and Engineer of the Smoky Hill Expedition, Together with the Table of Distances. Leavenworth, Kans.: Leavenworth Times, 1861.

Richardson, Albert K. *Beyond the Mississippi: From the Great River to the Great Ocean*. Hartford, Conn.: American Publishing Company, 1867.

Riley, Paul D., ed. "A Winter on the Plains, 1870–1871—The Memoirs of Lawson Cooke," *Kansas Historical Quarterly* 37:1 (Spring 1971): 33–40.

Rockwell, William S., et al. *Colorado: Its Mineral and Agricultural Resources*. N.p., [1865?].

Rolfe, D. P. "Overland Freighting from Nebraska City." *Proceedings and Collections of the Nebraska State Historical Society*. Series 2, 5 (1902): 279–93.

Ronan, Mary. *Frontier Woman: The Story of Mary Ronan as Told to Margaret Ronan*. Missoula: University of Montana, 1973.

Sanford, Mollie Dorsey. *Mollie: The Journey of Mollie Dorsey Sanford in Nebraska and Colorado Territories, 1857–1866*. Lincoln: University of Nebraska Press, 1959.

Settle, Raymond W., ed. *The March of the Mounted Riflemen: First United States Military Expedition to Travel the Full Length of the Oregon Trail*. Glendale, Calif.: Arthur H. Clark Company, 1940.

Sloan, Walter B. *History and Map of Kansas and Nebraska: Describing Soil, Climate, Rivers, Prairies, Mounds, Forests, Minerals*. Chicago: Robert Fergus, 1855.

Sloan, William K. "Autobiography of William K. Sloan, Western Pioneer." *Annals of Wyoming* 4:1 (July 1926): 235–64.

Sopris, W. R. "My Grandmother, Mrs. Marcellin St. Vrain." *Colorado Magazine* 22:1 (March 1945): 63–68.

Stahl, Frank M. *One Way Ticket to Kansas: The Autobiography of Frank M. Stahl As Told to Margaret Whittemore*. Lawrence: University of Kansas Press, 1959.

Stansbury, Howard. *An Expedition to the Valley of the Great Salt Lake of Utah*. Philadelphia: Lippincott, Grambo and Company, 1855.

Steele, E. Dunsha. "In the Pike's Peak Gold Rush of 1859: Diary of E. Dunsha Steele." *Colorado Magazine* 29:4 (October 1952): 299–309.

Stevens, W. H. *Field Notes, Crossing the Prairies and Plains from Atchison, Kansas, to Denver, Through the Mineral Region of Colorado Territory*. Philadelphia: J. B. Chandler, 1865.

Stobie, Charles Stewart. "Crossing the Plains in Colorado in 1865." *Colorado Magazine* 10:6 (November 1933): 201–12.

Taylor, Bayard. *Colorado: A Summer Trip*. New York: G. P. Putnam and Son, 1867.

Twain, Mark [Samuel Clemens]. *Roughing It*. Hartford, Conn.: American Publishing Company, 1873.

Utley, Robert M., ed. *Life in Custer's Cavalry: Diaries and Letters of Albert and Jennie Barnitz, 1867–1868.* New Haven: Yale University Press, 1977.

Villard, Henry. *The Past and Present of the Pike's Peak Gold Regions.* St. Louis: Sutherland and McEvoy, 1860.

Waters, Lydia Milner. "Account of a Trip Across the Plains in 1855." *Quarterly of the Society of California Pioneers* 6:2 (June 1929): 59–79.

Webb, W. E. *Buffalo Land: An Authentic Narrative of the Adventures and Misadventures of a Late Scientific and Sporting Party upon the Great Plains of the West.* Cincinnati and Chicago: E. Hannaford and Company, 1872.

Wheatley, Mary L. "Reminiscences of the Early Sixties." *Trail* 3:8 (January 1911): 5–11.

Wheeler, Col. Homer W. *Buffalo Days: Forty Years in the Old West: The Personal Narrative of a Cattleman, Indian Fighter and Army Officer.* Indianapolis: Bobbs-Merrill, 1923.

Witter, Mrs. Daniel. "A Pioneer Woman's Story Written for Her Children." *Trail* 18:3 (August 1925): 3–10.

Younker, Jason T. "The Early Pioneer, Reminiscences of 1858–59." *Trail* 2:8 (January 1910): 5–12.

Young, Francis Crissey. *Across the Plains in '65: A Youngster's Journal from "Gotham" to "Pike's Peak".* Denver: Lanning Brothers, 1905.

Secondary Sources

BOOKS

Adair, Mary J. *Prehistoric Agriculture in the Central Plains.* University of Kansas Publications in Anthropology no. 16. Lawrence: Department of Anthropology, University of Kansas, 1988.

Baker, James H., ed. 5 vols. *History of Colorado.* Denver: Linderman Company, 1927.

Bamforth, Douglas B. *Ecology and Human Organization on the Great Plains: Interdisciplinary Contributions to Archaeology.* New York: Plenum Press, 1988.

Bancroft, Hubert Howe. *The Works of Hubert Howe Bancroft.* Vol. 25. *History of Nevada, Colorado, and Wyoming, 1540–1888.* San Francisco: History Company, Publishers, 1890.

Barry, Louise. *The Beginning of the West: Annals of the Kansas Gateway to the American West.* Topeka: Kansas State Historical Society, 1972.

Barth, Gunther. *Instant Cities: Urbanization and the Rise of San Francisco and Denver.* New York: Oxford University Press, 1975.

Baughman, Robert W. *Kansas in Maps.* Topeka: Kansas State Historical Society, 1961.

Benedict, James B. *Arapaho Pass: Glacial Geology and Archeology at the Crest of the Colorado Front Range.* Research Report no. 3. Ward, Colo.: Center for Mountain Archeology, 1985.

———. *The Game Drives of Rocky Mountain National Park.* Research Report no. 7. Ward, Colo.: Center for Mountain Archeology, 1996.

———. *Old Man Mountain: A Vision Quest Site in the Colorado High Country.* Research Report no. 4. Ward, Colo.: Center for Mountain Archeology, 1985.

Benedict, James B., with Byron Olson. *The Mount Albion Complex: A Study of Prehistoric Man and the Altithermal.* Research Report no. 1. Ward, Colo.: Center for Mountain Archeology, 1978.

Berthrong, Donald J. *The Cheyenne and Arapaho Ordeal: Reservation and Agency Life in the Indian Territory, 1875–1907.* Norman: University of Oklahoma Press, 1976.

———. *The Southern Cheyennes.* Norman: University of Oklahoma Press, 1963.

Biedermann, Hans. *Dictionary of Symbolism: Cultural Icons and the Meanings Behind Them.* Trans. James Hulbert. New York: Meridian, 1994.

Bolton, Herbert Eugene. *Coronado: Knight of Pueblos and Plains.* Albuquerque: University of New Mexico Press, 1974.

Breck, Allen du Pont. *The Episcopal Church in Colorado, 1860–1963.* Denver: Big Mountain Press, 1963.

Brodie, Fawn M. *The Devil Drives: A Life of Sir Richard Burton.* New York: W. W. Norton and Company, 1967.

Chalfant, William Y. *Cheyennes and Horse Soldiers: The 1857 Expedition and the Battle of Solomon's Fork.* Norman: University of Oklahoma Press, 1989.

Clements, F. E., and R. W. Chayney. *Environment and Life in the Great Plains.* Washington, D.C.: Carnegie Institution, 1936.

Coel, Margaret. *Chief Left Hand: Southern Arapaho.* Norman: University of Oklahoma Press, 1981.

Collins, Scott L., and Linda L. Wallace, eds. *Fire in the North American Tallgrass Prairies.* Norman: University of Oklahoma Press, 1990.

Decatur County, Kansas. Lubbock, Tex.: Specialty Publishing, 1983.

Doring, Jurgen. *Kulturwandel bei den Nordamerikanischen Plainsindianern: Zur Rolle des Pferdes bei den Comanchen und den Cheyenne.* Berlin: Dietrick Reimer, 1984.

Dorsey, George A. *The Cheyenne. Ceremonial Organization.* 2 vols. Chicago: Field Museum, 1905.

Eberstadt, Charles. *On Colorado Guidebooks of '59.* New York: New York Public Library, 1943.

Eggan, Fred, ed. *Social Anthropology of North American Tribes.* Chicago: University of Chicago Press, 1955.

Evans, D. Morier. *The History of the Commercial Crisis, 1857–1858 and the Stock Exchange Panic of 1859.* New York: B. Franklin, 1969.

Ewers, John C. *The Horse in Blackfoot Culture: With Comparative Material from Other Western Tribes.* Bureau of American Ethnology, Bulletin no. 159. Washington, D.C.: Government Printing Office, 1955.

Fagan, Brian M. *The Great Journey: The Peopling of Ancient America.* New York: Thames and Hudson, 1987.

Farwell, Byron. *Burton: A Biography of Sir Richard Francis Burton.* London: Longmans, 1963.

Fossett, Frank. *Colorado: Historical, Description, and Statistical Work on the Rocky Mountain Gold and Silver Region.* Denver: Daily Tribune, 1876.

Frazer, Robert W. *Forts of the West: Military Forts and Presidios and Posts Commonly Called Forts West of the Mississippi River to 1898*. Norman: University of Oklahoma Press, 1965.

Frink, Maurice. *When Grass Was King: Contributions to the Western Range Cattle Industry*. Boulder: University of Colorado Press, 1956.

Grinnell, George Bird. *By Cheyenne Campfires*. New Haven: Yale University Press, 1962.

———. *The Cheyenne Indians: Their History and Ways of Life*. 2 vols. Lincoln: University of Nebraska Press, 1972.

———. *The Fighting Cheyennes*. Norman: University of Oklahoma Press, 1955.

Hafen, LeRoy R., ed. *The Mountain Men and the Fur Trade of the Far West*. 10 vols. Glendale, Calif.: Arthur H. Clark Company, 1965–.

Hafen, Leroy R., and Zachary Gussow. *Arapaho-Cheyenne Indians* [reports and findings of U.S. Indian Claims Commission]. New York: Garland Publishing, 1974.

Halaas, David Fridtjof. *Boom Town Newspapers: Journalism on the Rocky Mountain Mining Frontier, 1859–1881*. Albuquerque: University of New Mexico Press, 1981.

Hall, Frank. *History of the State of Colorado*. 4 vols. Chicago: Blakely Printing Company, 1889.

History of the Arkansas Valley, Colorado. Chicago: O. L. Baskin and Company, 1881.

Hoebel, E. Adamson. *The Cheyennes: Indians of the Great Plains*. Fort Worth: Harcourt Brace Jovanovich, 1978.

Hofman, Jack L., ed. *Archeology and Paleoecology of the Central Great Plains*. Arkansas Archeological Research Survey no. 48. Fayetteville: Arkansas Archeological Survey, 1996.

——— et al., eds. *From Clovis to Comanchero: Archeological Overview of the Southern Great Plains*. Arkansas Archeological Survey Research Series no. 35. Fayetteville: Arkansas Archeological Survey, 1989.

Hoig, Stan. *The Battle of Washita: The Sheridan-Custer Indian Campaign of 1867–1869*. Garden City, N.Y.: Doubleday and Company, 1976.

———. *The Peace Chiefs of the Cheyennes*. Norman: University of Oklahoma Press, 1980.

———. *The Sand Creek Massacre*. Norman: University of Oklahoma Press, 1961.

———. *The Western Odyssey of John Simpson Smith: Frontiersman, Trapper, Trader and Interpreter*. Glendale, Calif.: Arthur H. Clark Company, 1974.

Holder, Preston. *The Hoe and the Horse on the Plains: A Study of Cultural Development Among the North American Indians*. Lincoln: University of Nebraska Press, 1970.

Hollister, Ovando J. *The Mines of Colorado*. Springfield, Mass.: Samuel Bowles and Company, 1867.

Hurd, C. W. *Boggsville: Cradle of the Colorado Cattle Industry*. Boggsville, Colo.: Boggsville Committee, 1950.

Huston, James L. *The Panic of 1857 and the Coming of the Civil War*. Baton Rouge: Louisiana State University Press, 1987.

Hyde, George E. *Indians of the High Plains: From the Prehistoric Period to the Coming of the Europeans*. Norman: University of Oklahoma Press, 1959.

Jablow, Joseph. *The Cheyenne in Plains Indian Trade Relations, 1795–1840*. Monographs of the American Ethnological Society, 19. New York: J. J. Augustin, 1951.

Jennings, J. D., ed. *Ancient Native Americans*. San Francisco: W. H. Freeman and Company, 1978.

John, Elizabeth A. H. *Storms Brewed in Other Men's Worlds: The Confrontation of Indians, Spanish, and French in the Southwest, 1540–1795*. Norman: University of Oklahoma Press, 1996.

Jones, Douglas C. *The Treaty of Medicine Lodge: The Story of the Great Treaty Council as Told by Eyewitnesses*. Norman: University of Oklahoma Press, 1966.

Julien, Nadia. *The Mammoth Dictionary of Symbols: Understanding the Hidden Language of Symbols*. New York: Carroll and Graf, 1996.

Kavanagh, Thomas W. *Comanche Political History: An Ethnohistorical Perspective, 1706–1875*. Lincoln: University of Nebraska Press, 1996.

Kenner, Charles L. *A History of New Mexican–Plains Indian Relations*. Norman: University of Oklahoma Press, 1969.

Kindscher, Kelly. *Edible Wild Plants of the Prairie*. Lawrence: University Press of Kansas, 1987.

———. *Medicinal Wild Plants of the Prairie: An Ethnobotanical Guide*. Lawrence: University Press of Kansas, 1992.

King, James T. *War Eagle: A Life of General Eugene A. Carr*. Lincoln: University of Nebraska Press, 1963.

Lavender, David. *Bent's Fort*. Lincoln: University of Nebraska Press, 1972.

Lawson, Merlin Paul. *The Climate of the Great American Desert: Reconstruction of the Climate of Western Interior United States, 1800–1850*. Lincoln: University of Nebraska Press, 1974.

Lecompte, Janet. *Pueblo, Hardscrabble, Greenhorn: Society on the High Plains, 1832–1856*. Norman: University of Oklahoma Press, 1978.

Lee, Wayne C., and Howard C. Raynesford. *Trails of the Smoky Hill: From Coronado to the Cowtowns*. Caldwell, Idaho: Caxton Printers, 1980.

Leonard, Stephen J., and Thomas J. Noel. *Denver: Mining Camp to Metropolis*. Niwot: University Press of Colorado, 1990.

Liebig, Justus von. *Die organische Chemie in ihrer Anwendung auf Agricultur und Physiologie*. Braunsweig: F. Viewig und Sohn, 1840.

———. *Organic Chemistry and Its Applications to Agriculture and Physiology*. London: Taylor and Walton, 1840.

Llewellyn, Karl N., and E. Adamson Hoebel. *The Cheyenne Way: Conflict and Case Law in Primitive Jurisprudence*. Norman: University of Oklahoma Press, 1941.

Long, Margaret. *The Smoky Hill Trail*. Denver: Kistler, 1947.

MacLeish, William H. *The Day Before America*. Boston: Houghton Mifflin, 1994.

Mallery, Garrick. *Picture-Writing of the American Indians*. 2 vols. New York: Dover Publications, 1972.

Marquis, Thomas B. *The Cheyennes of Montana*. Algonac, Mich.: Reference Publications, 1978.

Marriott, Alice, and Carol K. Rachlin. *Plains Indian Mythology*. New York: Thomas Y. Crowell Company, 1975.

Martin, Paul S., and Richard G. Klein. *Quaternary Extinctions: A Prehistoric Revolution*. Tucson: University of Arizona Press, 1984.

Martin, Paul S., and Herbert E. Wright, Jr., eds. *Pleistocene Extinctions: The Search for a Cause*. New Haven: Yale University Press, 1967.

Mayhall, Mildred P. *The Kiowas*. Norman: University of Oklahoma Press, 1952.

McClung, Quantrille D. *Carson-Bent-Boggs Genealogy*. Denver: Denver Public Library, 1962. Supplement published in 1973.

McKinley, John Lawrence. *The Influence of the Platte River upon the History of the Valley*. Minneapolis: Burgess Publishing Company, 1938.

McLynn, F. J. *Burton: Snow upon the Desert*. London: John Murray, 1990.

Mishkin, Bernard. *Rank and Warfare Among the Plains Indians*. American Ethnological Monograph no. 3. Seattle: University of Washington Press, 1940.

Momaday, N. Scott. *The Names*. New York: Harper and Row, 1976.

Monahan, Doris. *Destination: Denver City: The South Platte Trail*. Athens: Swallow Press/Ohio University Press, 1985.

Mooney, James. *Calendar History of the Kiowa Indians*. Washington, D.C.: Smithsonian Institution Press, 1979.

Moore, John H. *The Cheyenne Nation: A Social and Demographic History*. Lincoln: University of Nebraska Press, 1987.

Morris, Robert. *The Banks of New-York, Their Dealers, the Clearing House, and the Panic of 1857*. New York: D. Appleton and Company, 1858.

Morris, Wright. *Plains Song for Female Voices*. Boston: David R. Godine, 1980.

Norall, Frank. *Bourgmont, Explorer of the Missouri, 1698–1725*. Lincoln: University of Nebraska Press, 1988.

O'Brien, Patricia J. *Archaeology in Kansas*. Lawrence: University of Kansas Museum of Natural History, 1984.

Oliver, Symmes. *Ecology and Cultural Continuity as Contribution Factors in the Social Organization of the Plains Indians*. University of California Publications in American Archeology and Ethnology, vol. 48. Berkeley: University of California, 1962.

Opie, Iona, and Moira Tatem, eds. *A Dictionary of Superstitions*. New York: Oxford University Press, 1992.

Petter, Rudolphe C. *English-Cheyenne Dictionary*. Kettle Falls, Wash.: Valdo Pe, n.d.

Pielou, E. D. *After the Ice Age: The Return of Life to Glaciated North America*. Chicago: University of Chicago Press, 1991.

Powell, Father John Peter. *People of the Sacred Mountain: A History of the Northern Cheyenne Chiefs and Warrior Societies*. 2 vols. San Francisco: Harper and Row, 1981.

———. *The Cheyennes, Maheo's People: A Critical Bibliography*. Bloomington: Indiana University Press, 1980.

———. *Sweet Medicine*. 2 vols. Norman: University of Oklahoma Press, 1969.

Prucha, Francis Paul. *American Indian Treaties: The History of a Political Anomaly*. Berkeley: University of California Press, 1994.

Ramenofsky, Ann F. *Vectors of Death: The Archaeology of European Contact.* Albuquerque: University of New Mexico Press, 1987.

Rath, Ida Ellen. *The Rath Trail.* Wichita, Kans.: McCormick-Armstrong, Company, 1961.

Renaud, E. B. *Archaeological Survey of Eastern Colorado.* Reports 1–3. Denver: University of Denver, 1931–1933.

———. *Archaeology of the High Western Plains: Seventeen Years of Archaeological Research.* Denver: Department of Anthropology, University of Denver, 1947.

Richardson, Jane. *Law and Status Among the Kiowa Indians.* Monographs of the American Ethnological Society, no. 1. New York: J. J. Augustin, 1940.

Roe, Frank G. *The Indian and the Horse.* Norman: University of Oklahoma Press, 1955.

Ruddiman, W. F., and H. E. Wright, eds. *North America and Adjacent Oceans During the Last Deglaciation.* Boulder, Colo.: Geological Society of America, 1987.

Schlesier, Karl H. *The Wolves of Heaven: Cheyenne Shamanism, Ceremonies, and Prehistoric Origins.* Norman: University of Oklahoma Press, 1987.

———, ed. *Plains Indians, A.D. 500–1500: The Archaeological Past of Historic Groups.* Norman: University of Oklahoma Press, 1994.

Schulman, Edmund. *Dendroclimatic Changes in Semiarid America.* Tucson: University of Arizona Press, 1956.

Secoy, Frank Raymond. *Changing Military Patterns of the Great Plains Indians.* American Ethnological Society Monograph 21. Seattle: University of Washington Press, 1953.

Shelford, Victor E. *The Ecology of North America.* Urbana: University of Illinois Press, 1978.

Shepard, Paul. *The Others: How Animals Made Us Human.* Washington, D.C.: Island Press, 1996.

Smiley, Jerome C. *History of Denver, with Outlines of the Earlier History of the Rocky Mountain Country.* Denver: J. H. Williamson and Company, 1903.

Sobel, Robert. *Panic on Wall Street: A History of America's Financial Disasters.* London: Macmillan Company, 1968.

Spencer, Elma Dill Russell. *Green Russell and Gold.* Austin: University of Texas Press, 1966.

Spicer, Edward H., ed. *Perspectives in American Indian Culture Change.* Chicago: University of Chicago Press, 1961.

Spielmann, Katherine A. *Interdependence in the Prehistoric Southwest: An Ecological Analysis of Plains-Pueblo Interaction.* New York: Garland Press, 1991.

———, ed. *Farmers, Hunters, and Colonists: Interaction Between the Southwest and the Southern Plains.* Tucson: University of Arizona Press, 1991.

Steinel, Alvin T. *History of Agriculture in Colorado.* Fort Collins, Colo.: State Agricultural College, 1926.

Stoltman, James B., ed. *Archaeology of Eastern North America: Papers in Honor of Stephen Williams.* Archaeological Report no. 25, Mississippi Department of Archives and History, 1993.

Stouffle, Richard W. et al. *Toyavita Piavuhuru Koroin, "Canyon of Mother Earth":*

Ethnohistory and Native American Religious Concerns in the Fort Carson–Pinon Canyon Maneuver Area. Denver: U.S. Army and National Park Service, 1984.

Thomas, Alfred Barnaby. *After Coronado: Spanish Exploration Northeast of New Mexico, 1696–1727.* Norman: University of Oklahoma Press, 1935.

Thornton, Russell. *American Indian Holocaust and Survival: A Population History Since 1492.* Norman: University of Oklahoma Press, 1987.

Utley, Robert M. *Frontier Regulars: The United States Army and the Indian, 1866–1891.* New York: Macmillan, 1973.

———. *Frontiersmen in Blue: The United States Army and the Indian, 1848–1865.* New York: Macmillan, 1967.

Van Kirk, Sylvia. *Many Tender Ties: Women in Fur-trade Society, 1670–1870.* Norman: University of Oklahoma Press, 1983.

Van Vleck, George W. *The Panic of 1857: An Analytical Study.* New York: Columbia University Press, 1943.

Verano, John W., and Douglas H. Ubelaker, eds. *Disease and Demography in the Americas.* Washington, D.C.: Smithsonian Institution Press, 1992.

Walker, Henry Pickering. *The Wagonmasters: High Plains Freighting from the Earliest Days of the Santa Fe Trail to 1880.* Norman: University of Oklahoma Press, 1966.

Ware, Eugene Fitch. *The Indian War of 1864.* Topeka: Crane, 1900.

Weaver, J. E. *North American Prairie.* Lincoln: Johnsen Publishing Company, 1954.

Weaver, J. E., and F. W. Albertson. *Grasslands of the Great Plains.* Lincoln: Johnsen Publishing Company, 1956.

Wedel, Waldo R. *Central Plains Prehistory: Holocene Environments and Culture Change in the Republican River Basin.* Lincoln: University of Nebraska Press, 1986.

———. *Prehistoric Man on the Great Plains.* Norman: University of Oklahoma Press, 1961.

West, Elliott. *The Way to the West: Essays on the Central Plains.* Albuquerque: University of New Mexico Press, 1995.

White, Leslie. *The Evolution of Culture: The Development of Civilization to the Fall of Rome.* New York: McGraw-Hill Book Company, 1959.

Wright, Thomas. *The Life of Sir Richard Burton.* 2 vols. New York: B. Franklin, 1968.

ARTICLES

Axelrod, D. I. "Rise of the Grassland Biome, Central North America." *Botanical Review* 51 (1985): 163–202.

Bahmer, Robert H. "The Colorado Gold Rush and California." *Colorado Magazine* 7:6 (November 1930): 222–29.

Barry, Louise. "The Ranch at Walnut Creek Crossing." *Kansas Historical Quarterly* 37:2 (Summer 1971): 121–47.

Bartlett, Richard A. "Reception of the Pike's Peak Fever in the Chicago Press and Tribune." *Colorado Magazine* 25:1 (January 948): 30–34.

Benedict, James B. "Footprints in the Snow: High-Altitude Cultural Ecology of the Colorado Front Range, U.S.A.." *Arctic and Alpine Records* 24:1 (1992): 1–16.

Bozell, John R. "Late Precontact Village Farmers: An Agricultural Revolution." *Nebraska History* 75:1 (Spring 1994): 121–31.

"Brief Chronology of Battles and Skirmishes, 1864–65." *Colorado Heritage* (Autumn 1996): 38–41.

Carlson, Gayle F. "Long-Distance Trade." *Nebraska History* 75:1 (Spring 1994): 98.

Carpenter, J. Richard. "The Grassland Biome." *Ecological Monographs* 10 (1940): 617–84.

Clark, Niel M. "When the Turkeys Walked." *American Heritage* 15 (December 1963): 92.

Clements, Frederick E. "Drought Periods and Climatic Cycles." *Ecology* 2:3 (July 1921): 181–88.

Conrad, Lawrence A. "Comment: An Early Eighteenth Century Reference to 'Putting a Woman on the Prairies' Among the Central Algonquians and Its Implications for Moore's Explanation of the Practice Among the Cheyenne." *Plains Anthropologist* 28:100 (May 1983): 141–42.

Creel, Darrell. "Bison Hides in Late Prehistoric Exchange in the Southern Plains." *American Antiquity* 56:1 (1991): 40–49.

Creel, Darrell, Robert F. Scott IV, and Michael B. Collins. "A Faunal Record from West Central Texas and Its Bearing on Late Holocene Bison Population Changes in the Southern Plains." *Plains Anthropologist* 35:127 (February 1990): 55–69.

Davis, E. Mott. "Recent Data on Two Paleo-Indian Sites on Medicine Creek, Nebraska." *American Antiquity* 18:4 (1953): 380–86.

Davis, E. Mott, and C. B. Scultz. "The Archeological and Paleontological Salvage Program and the Medicine Creek Reservoir, Frontier County, Nebraska." *Science* 115:2985 (1952): 288–90.

Dillehay, Tom D. "Late Quaternary Bison Population Changes on the Southern Plains." *Plains Anthropologist* 19:65 (August 1974): 180–96.

Downs, James F. "Comments on Plains Indian Cultural Development." *American Anthropologist* 66:2 (April 1964): 421–22.

Dunbar, John B. "Massacre of the Villazur Expedition by the Pawnees on the Platte in 1720." *Kansas Historical Collections* 11 (1909–1910): 397–423.

Ewers, John C. "The Influence of Epidemics on the Indian Populations and Cultures of Texas." *Plains Anthropologist* 18:60 (May 1973): 104–15.

Flores, Dan. "Bison Ecology and Bison Diplomacy: The Southern Plains from 1800 to 1850." *Journal of American History* 78:2 (September 1991): 465–85.

Fryxell, John M., John Greever, and A. R. E. Sinclair. "Why Are Migratory Ungulates So Abundant?" *American Naturalist* 131:6 (June 1988): 781–98.

Gambone, Joseph G. "Economic Relief in Territorial Kansas, 1860–1861." *Kansas Historical Quarterly* 36:2 (Summer 1970): 149–74.

Goodykoontz, Colin B. "The People of Colorado." *Colorado Magazine* 23:5 (September 1946): 240–55.

Hadley, James Albert. "A Royal Buffalo Hunt." *Transactions of the Kansas State Historical Society, 1907–1908*. Topeka: State Printing Office, 1908, 564–80.

Hafen, LeRoy R. "Cherokee Goldseekers in Colorado, 1849–50." *Colorado Magazine* 15:3 (May 1938): 101–9.

———. "Early Mail Service to Colorado, 1858–60." *Colorado Magazine* 2:1 (1925): 23–32.

———. "Elbridge Gerry, Colorado Pioneer." *Colorado Magazine* 29:2 (April 1952): 137–49.

———. "Thomas Fitzpatrick and the First Indian Agency in Colorado." *Colorado Magazine* 6:2 (March 1939): 53–62.

———, ed. "The Voorhees Diary of the Lawrence Party's Trip to Pike's Peak, 1858." *Colorado Magazine* 12:2 (March 1935): 41–54.

Hanna, Margaret G. "Do You Take This Woman? Economics and Marriage in a Late Prehistoric Band." *Plains Anthropologist* 29:104 (May 1984): 115–29.

Haynes, Francis. "The Northward Spread of Horses Among the Plains Indians." *American Anthropologist* 40 (1938): 429–37.

Hoebel, E. Adamson. "On Cheyenne Sociopolitical Organization." *Plains Anthropologist* 25:88, part 1 (May 1980): 161–69.

Holder, Preston, and Joyce Wike. "The Frontier Culture Complex: A Preliminary Report on a Prehistoric Hunters' Camp in Southwestern Nebraska." *American Antiquity* 14:4, part 1 (1949): 260–66.

"Holocene Man in North America: The Ecological Setting and Climatic Background." *Plains Anthropologist* 23:82, part 1 (1978): 273–87.

Hurt, Wesley R. "The Altithermal and the Prehistory of the Northern Plains." *Quaternaria* 8 (1966): 101–13.

Irwin, C., and H. Irwin. "The Archeology of the Agate Bluff Area, Colorado." *Plains Anthropologist* 8 (1957): 15–38.

Isern, Thomas D. "The Controversial Career of Edward W. Wynkoop." *Colorado Magazine* 56:1 and 2 (Winter/Spring 1979): 1–18.

Jacobsen, R. Brooke, and Jeffrey L. Eighmy. "A Mathematical Theory of Horse Adoption on the North American Plains." *Plains Anthropologist* 25:90 (November 1980): 333–41.

King, James T. "The Republican River Expedition, June–July, 1869, I, On the March," and "The Republican River Expedition, June–July, 1869, II, The Battle of Summit Springs," *Nebraska History* 41 (September and December 1960): 165–99, 281–97.

Kingsbury, Joseph L. "The Pikes Peak Rush, 1859." *Colorado Magazine* 4:1 (January 1927): 1–6.

Ludwickson, John, and John R. Bozell. "The Early Potters: Emerging Technologies." *Nebraska History* 75:1 (Spring 1994): 111–19.

Mock, S. D. "Effects of the 'Boom' Decade, 1870–1880, upon Colorado Population." *Colorado Magazine* 11:1 (January 1934): 27–34.

Montgomery, Mrs. Frank C. "Fort Wallace and Its Relation to the Frontier." *Kansas Historical Society Collections* 17 (1926–1928): 189–283.

Moore, John H. "Cheyenne Political History, 1820–1894." *Ethnohistory* 21:4 (Fall 1974): 329–59.

————. "Evolution and Historical Reductionism." *Plains Anthropologist* 26:94, part 1 (November 1981): 261–69.

————. "The Developmental Cycle of Cheyenne Polygyny." *American Indian Quarterly* 15 (Summer 1991): 311–28.

Moore, John H., and Gregory R. Campbell. "An Ethnohistorical Perspective on Cheyenne Demography." *Journal of Family History* 14:1 (1989): 17–42.

Mosiman, James E. "Simulating Overkill by PaleoIndians." *American Scientist* 63:3 (1975): 304–13.

O'Brien, Patricia J. "Prehistoric Evidence for Pawnee Cosmology." *American Anthropologist* 88:4 (December 1986): 939–46.

————. "Speculations About Bobwhite Quail and Pawnee Religion." *Plains Anthropologist* 33:122 (November 1988): 489–504.

Osborn, Alan J. "Ecological Aspects of Equestrian Adaptations in Aboriginal North America." *American Anthropologist* 85:3 (September 1983): 563–91.

Parker, Mrs. C. F. "Old Julesburg and Fort Sedgwick." *Colorado Magazine* 7:4 (August 1930): 139–46.

Parsons, Eugene. "John Easter and the Lawrence Party." *Trail* 7:7 (December 1914): 5–10.

Pickett, Ralph H. "Friedrich von Holstein's Hunting Trips, 1865–1866." *Kansas Historical Quarterly* 32:3 (Autumn 1966): 314–24.

Powers, Ramon, and Gene Younger. "Cholera on the Plains: The Epidemic of 1867 in Kansas." *Kansas Historical Quarterly* 37:4 (Winter 1971): 351–93.

Reeves, Bryan. "The Concept of an Altithermal Cultural Hiatus in Northern Plains Prehistory." *American Anthropologist* 75:5 (1973): 1221–53.

"R. J. Pierce and Jacob T. Masterson, Members of the Famous Russell Prospecting Party of 1858." *Colorado Magazine* 27:2 (April 1950): 102–7.

Root, George A., and Russell K. Hickman. "Pike's Peak Express Companies." *Kansas Historical Quarterly* 13:3, 4 (August and November 1944): 163–95, 211–42.

Schambach, Frank A. "Spiroan Entrepots at and Beyond the Western Border of the Trans-Mississippi South." *Caddoan Archeology Newsletter* 4:2 (July 1993): 11–26.

Schlesier, Karl H. "Rethinking the Dismal River Aspect and the Plains Athapaskans, A.D. 1692–1768." *Plains Anthropologist* 17:56 (1972): 101–31.

Schmits, Larry J. "The Coffey Site: Environment and Cultural Adaptation at a Prairie Plains Archaic Site." *Mid-Continental Journal of Archaeology* 3:1 (1978): 69–185.

Schoewe, Walter H. "The Geography of Kansas. Part 2," Kansas Academy of Science, *Transactions* 52:3 (September 1949): 314–22.

Schultz, Floyd, and Albert C. Spaulding. "A Hopewellian Burial Site in the Lower Republican Valley, Kansas." *American Antiquity* 13:4 (1948): 306–13.

Shields, Lillian B. "Relations with the Cheyennes and Arapahoes in Colorado to 1861." *Colorado Magazine* 4:4 (August 1927): 145–54.

Snell, Joseph W., and Robert W. Richmond. "When the Union and Kansas Pacific Built Through Kansas." *Kansas Historical Quarterly* 32 (Summer 1966): 161–86.

Spring, Agnes Wright. "Food Facts of 1859." *Colorado Magazine* 22:3 (May 1945): 113–16.

Stanford, Dennis J. "Preliminary Report of the Excavation of the Jones-Miller Hell Gap Site, Yuma County, Colorado." *Southwestern Lore* 41:4 (1974): 29–36.

Taylor, Morris F. "The Mail Station and the Military at Camp on Pawnee Fork, 1859–1860." *Kansas Historical Quarterly* 36:1 (Spring 1970): 27–39.

Thomas, Alfred B. "Massacre of the Villasur Expedition at the Forks of the Platte River, August 12, 1720." *Nebraska History* 7 (July and September 1924): 67–81.

Vehik, Susan C. "Late Prehistoric Plains Trade and Economic Specialization." *Plains Anthropologist* 35:128 (May 1990): 125–45.

———. "Wichita Culture History." *Plains Anthropologist* 37:141 (1992): 311–29.

Weakly, Harry. "A Tree Ring Record of Precipitation in Western Nebraska." *Journal of Forestry* 41 (1943): 816–19.

Wedel, Waldo R. "The High Plains and Their Utilization by the Indian." *American Antiquity* 29:1 (July 1963): 1–16.

———. "Some Problems and Prospects in Kansas Prehistory." *Kansas Historical Quarterly* 7 (May 1938): 115–32.

———. "Toward a History of Plains Archeology." *Great Plains Quarterly* 1 (Winter 1981): 16–38.

White, Richard. "The Winning of the West: The Expansion of the Western Sioux in the Eighteenth and Nineteenth Centuries." *Journal of American History* 65:2 (September 1978): 319–43.

Willard, James F. "Spreading the News of the Early Discoveries of Gold in Colorado." *Colorado Magazine* 6:3 (May 1929): 98–104.

Williston, S. W., and H. T. Martin. "Some Pueblo Ruins in Scott County, Kansas." *Kansas Historical Collections* 6 (1897–1900): 124–30.

Wilson, Clyde H. "An Inquiry into the Nature of Plains Indian Cultural Development." *American Anthropologist* 65:2 (April 1963): 355–69.

Wissler, Clark. "The Influence of the Horse in the Development of Plains Culture." *American Anthropologist* 16:1 (January–March 1914): 1–25.

Wyman, Walker D. "Council Bluffs and the Westward Movement." *Iowa Journal of History* 47:2 (April 1949): 99–118.

———. "Freighting: A Big Business on the Santa Fe Trail." *Kansas Historical Quarterly* 1:1 (November 1931): 17–27.

Newspapers

[*Atchison, Kans.*] *Freedom's Champion.*
[*Columbia*] *Weekly Missouri Statesman.*
[*Denver*] *Rocky Mountain News.*
Hannibal [*Mo.*] *Messenger.*
[*Kansas City, Mo.*] *Western Journal of Commerce.*
[*Lawrence, Kans.*] *Herald of Freedom.*

[Leavenworth, Kans.] Times.
Leavenworth Weekly Journal.
Missouri Republican.
Nebraska City News.
New York Times.
New York Tribune.
[St. Louis] Daily Missouri Democrat.
Times (London).

Theses and Dissertations

Gisinger, Anne. "A Spatial Analysis of Regional Human Adaptation Patterns Using Continental-Scale Data." Master's thesis, University of Arkansas, 1996.

Gower, Calvin W. "Kansas Territory and the Pike's Peak Gold Rush." Ph.D. diss., University of Kansas, 1958.

Grosser, Roger Douglas. "Late Archaic Subsistence Patterns from the Central Great Plains." Ph.D. diss., University of Kansas, 1977.

Hill, Clifford Clinton. "Wagon Roads in Colorado, 1858–1876." Master's thesis, University of Colorado, 1949.

Isern, Thomas Dean. "The Making of a Gold Rush: Pike's Peak, 1858–1860." Master's thesis, Oklahoma State University, 1975.

Neuhaus, Carla Elizabeth. "Transportation to Colorado, 1858–1869." Master's thesis, University of Colorado, 1928.

Nicholson, John H. "A History of Norton County, Kansas." Master's thesis, Colorado State College of Education (Greeley), 1941.

Roberts, Gary Leland. "Sand Creek: Tragedy and Symbol." Ph.D. diss., University of Oklahoma, 1984.

Sherow, James Earl. "Discord in the 'Valley of Content': Strife over Natural Resources in a Changing Environment on the Arkansas River Valley of the High Plains." Ph.D. diss., University of Colorado, 1987.

Van Hook, Joseph Orlando. "Settlement and Economic Development of the Arkansas Valley from Pueblo to the Colorado-Kansas Line, 1860–1900." Ph.D. diss., University of Colorado, 1933.

Index